DATE DUE

NO 2 '00			
NO 22 '00			
DE 13 '0			
FE 7 '02			
MY 2 6 '06			

Second Edition

Humanitarian Intervention:

An Inquiry into Law and Morality

Fernando R. Tesón

Transnational Publishers, Inc.
Irvington-on-Hudson, New York

Library of Congress Cataloging-in-Publication Data

Tesón, Fernando R., 1950-
    Humanitarian intervention : an inquiry into law and morality /
Fernando R. Tesón.—2nd ed.
        p.   cm.
    Includes bibliographical references and indexes.
    ISBN 0-941320-80-4
    1. Intervention (International law) 2. Human rights. 3. Law and
    ethics. I. Title.
JX4481.T32   1996
341.4.81—dc20   96-22200
                                                              CIP

TABLE OF CONTENTS

FOREWORD

There's a special reward in teaching that cannot be compared to any other career or profession that I know of, and that happens when a graduate student seeks you out to take your courses and to write a dissertation under your direction. Fernando Tesón came as a doctoral candidate to Northwestern Law School in 1982 to see if there was anything I could teach him about international law and ended up giving more than he received. The book you are holding in your hand is the dissertation he produced, revised for publication. I could not be more proud of any book.

Before coming to Northwestern, Professor Tesón served for four years in the Argentine Foreign Service as a career diplomat. He was also Associate Professor of International Law at the University of Buenos Aires. He brings to his book a practical knowledge of International diplomacy and law that noticeably contributes to its breadth of vision. The result is a book that may have a substantial impact not only upon international legal scholarship but also upon the way nations view the permissible limits of their foreign policy.

Up to now, students of international law who have addressed humanitarian intervention have adopted a noticeably narrow approach to their subject. Some writers have preferred to look at single case studies, but in doing so found it hard to articulate broad-based rules of law that would transcend the case under investigation. Others have looked at the more traditional topic of intervening abroad to protect one's own nationals.[1] Perhaps the reason that no one up to now has attempted a comprehensive study of humanitarian intervention is that the very topic presents a frontal challenge to the theory and underlying philosophy of

---

[1] Reference to these works may be found in Professor Tesón's bibliography, which is among the most comprehensive available on the topic of humanitarian intervention in international law.

international law. The theory is challenged because any state-based system (which the term "international" seems to suggest) would hardly countenance a rule allowing for one nation to "meddle" in another's internal affairs.

Yet humanitarian intervention is preeminently a case of meddling, of minding another nation's business. That is something we do only when it is morally required. But when interference is morally required, then we must interfere. If we were to witness an adult hitting a child so severely as to endanger the child's life, we have no choice but to interfere, even if the assault is occurring in the adult's own house. Of course, we first try persuasion, but the adult may ignore anything we say. Next we might try to call for the police or for help, but time may be too short for that. Finally, we interfere physically if we are able, stopping him. We are not deterred even if the adult says, "it's my child, it's my home, and this is my business," because he has no right to jeopardize the life of a child.

Humanitarian intervention among nations is morally justified for similar reasons. Nation A has no moral right to stand by while Nation B proceeds to imprison, torture, and slay a large number of a minority group within its population. Although the victims may be citizens of Nation B, nationality from a moral standpoint is even less relevant than parenthood is in the previously given example. Nation A must intervene, forcibly or otherwise, in order to prevent or mitigate the criminal acts.

The moral proposition I have just suggested has always been true. Basic moral imperatives do not change over time or space. Yet the idea of humanitarian intervention in international law is a quite recent phenomenon. Surely, then, law has not fully caught up with morality. States in the past have been able to get away with the idea that what they do to their own nationals within their own territory is no other nation's business. And so it was in the early 1930s that Stalin presided over the genocide of some ten million Russian farmers (who did not quite fit into his vision of agrarian reform), and the world took very little note. The general popular reaction was, "regrettable, but it's not my concern." Times are changing; the Nuremberg trials were a watershed in the development of a popular attitude that genocide conducted by a government even within its own territory is a heinous crime under international law. But times have not changed fast enough. As I write these words, the gentle Ba'hai people in Iran are being slaughtered. The world outside Iran is doing nothing about it. Although the Iran-Iraq war has acted as a smoke screen for the genocide being practiced within Iran, the main reason for nonintervention by other nations is the lingering power of the international law concept that a nation's boundaries are sacrosanct. Professor Tesón's book will help achieve a reorientation of priorities, putting basic human rights above any absolute notion of border impermeability.

But Professor Tesón has not merely taken on the conceptually simple task of criticizing existing international law from the standpoint of morality. To do that would be to adopt legal positivism, which insists on a fundamental difference between law and morality. Positivists are perfectly willing to adopt morality as a critique of the law, so long as the two domains are kept separate. Ordinary language reinforces the distinction between things that are "moral" and things that are "legal" (and there is historically an affinity between positivist philosophy and ordinary-language philosophy). Hence a positivist would find no difficulty in describing the moral imperatives of humanitarian intervention and the shortcomings of present international law, and concluding that hopefully the law will be revised to become closer to morality.

Professor Tesón does not take the positivist approach, and herein lies the intellectual challenge of his enterprise as well as its critical importance.

Professor Tesón's argument is a demonstration of morality informing the law. Morality is not something apart from the law; rather, moral imperatives and legal imperatives continually intersect each other over time because they are a function of the same human aspirations: to live in peace in a world society. Law floats upon a sea of morality, and even though the legal vessel is distinct from the water in which it is immersed, one could not begin to explain the shape or purpose of the vessel without making any reference to water.

We must be careful not to say that moral and legal imperatives are identical. Clearly, customary international law at any given time may depart from morality. Moreover, we should be careful not to be the victims of wishful thinking in describing what the current norms of customary international law really are. If, for example, we are convinced that there ought to be an international rule allowing humanitarian intervention to prevent a nation from violating the fundamental human rights of its own citizens, that is certainly not the same thing as saying that there exists such an international rule.

Professor Tesón examines in this book whether such an international rule exists. But to determine whether such a rule exists necessarily requires us, as part of our legal methodology, to look at the moral imperatives that may be reflected in state practice over time which inform the content of the rule. In effect this requires the researcher to do something which is not easy; to describe the morality latent in legal rules without contaminating that description by the researcher's personal convictions of what those moral rules ought to be. Yet the difficulty does not end with just this separation, because the researcher, as a human being, necessarily swims in the moral sea. His or her own convictions may be part of the data. Personal convictions cannot simply be jettisoned without possibly skewing the results too much in the non-moral direction. The task clearly calls for dispassionate discernment—one of the most difficult challenges of good legal scholarship.

When we take seriously the morality that informs the law, we begin to find that even the rules that appear to run in opposition to moral imperatives may once have been morally based. We should not hastily conclude, for example, that humanitarian intervention is a "moral" rule whereas nonintervention is simply an amoral rule of fiat. For nonintervention itself is grounded in a historical conviction (which may be in error but nevertheless is real) that the transboundary use of force is evil in itself. In the Pact of Paris of 1928, Germany, the United States, Great Britain and many other signatory nations somewhat sanctimoniously renounced war "as an instrument of national policy in their relations with one another." Liberal-minded people may believe, with the signatories of the Pact of Paris, that "wars never solve anything" and must be stopped at all costs. Yet one of those costs may be too high a price to pay; allowing a government to violate the fundamental human rights of its own citizens.

Hence we see that what is at issue is not a moral rule (humanitarian intervention) against an amoral rule (nonintervention), but rather than clash of two rules that both have a claim to moral support. This helps us to ask two questions: the moral one (which rule ought to supersede the other?) and the legal question (which rule reflects the practice of states in the international community?). The legal rule, which itself contains a moral component reflecting the purpose that animates state practice, may turn out to be not "nonintervention at all costs" but something like "nonintervention unless the costs are too high." But how do we measure "too high?" And what, after all, are "costs"? Are they to be determined as a matter of morality? Or law? Or the morality within law?

I hope these questions help as an orientation to the book. Professor Tesón's work of course speaks for itself. His frequent summaries of argument throughout the book render unnecessary any attempt to recapitulate its content here.

The reader should be careful not to misconstrue Professor Tesón's purpose because of the way he organizes his book. He deals first with the moral dimension, and then with the more "legalistic" considerations arising out of state practice. He could have done it the other way round. Or he could have mixed morality and law throughout—but that, I think, would have led to a great deal of redundancy. The ideal organization would be to present the moral and legal dimensions at the same time. That might require two parallel books, one printed and one on audiocassettes. The reader could then read and listen at the same time. Naturally this "technology" is beyond human ability at the present time, and I mention it only to illustrate the importance of the task presented to the reader: to read each part of the book in light of the other. A book is a linear technology, while the subject of Professor Tesón's book has a two-part message that is dimensional.

His book will have a life of its own, extending into the distant future. As for its author, I can only wish that Professor Tesón will have future students who may provide him the kind of reward that he provided me.

Anthony D'Amato

Chicago, 1987

PREFACE TO THE SECOND EDITION

Much has happened since this book was first published in 1988. In the Post-Cold-War world, state practice and scholarly and popular opinion have moved away dramatically from the statist paradigm that was, among other things, the target of that first edition. The doctrine of humanitarian intervention was as valid then as it is now, but it now enjoys (unlike then) a respectable status. People are gradually realizing that unrestricted sovereignty is incompatible with the respect of human rights. In the first edition I tried to emphasize that point as a matter of both law and ethics. I don't believe the moral argument has changed: if a philosophical argument is correct, then it is correct forever. For that reason, I have left the first part of the book almost untouched, although I have developed the ideas contained therein in my subsequent writings. The law, on the other hand, has changed in the direction recommended by the book. The interpretation offered here, that the United Nations Charter allows the right of humanitarian intervention in appropriate cases is, I believe, more clearly supported in 1996 by state practice and textual authority than it was in 1988. The most important development in this regard is the recent practice of humanitarian intervention authorized by the United Nations Security Council. This aspect of humanitarian intervention was omitted in the first edition, in great part because Security Council action to protect human rights seemed to me utopian at the time. Happily, I was wrong, and collective intervention is now addressed in a new chapter. There are a few other changes, the most important of which is a general discussion of the concepts of intervention and domestic jurisdiction at the beginning of Chapter Seven.

As always, I am grateful to my institution, Arizona State University College of Law, for its generous support.

Fernando R. Tesón
Tempe, Arizona, April 1996

PREFACE

The idea for this book first occurred to me in the late 1970s, during the somber years of the military dictatorship in my native Argentina. An inexperienced diplomat and international law instructor, I watched in astonishment as the Junta time and again invoked the principle of nonintervention as a shield against external demands for compliance with human rights. The traumatic experience of seeing many, including some dearest friends, "disappear," suffer, and die at the hands of the dictators convinced me at that time that there was something wrong with the notion of the moral and legal enclosure of states. My reading in 1978 of John Rawl's masterpiece, *A Theory of Justice*, and of Karl Popper's inspired defense of liberal democracy, *The Open Society and its Enemies*, made me think about the plausibility of a global moral-political theory that would combine international law with a liberal conception of human rights. Shortly thereafter, the Tanzanian invasion in Uganda and the French intervention in Central Africa confirmed for me the intuitive appeal of the doctrine of humanitarian intervention. Anthony D'Amato suggested the topic to me in 1982. It was in 1983, while I was starting the research for the book, that I understood the relevance for my thesis of Ronald Dworkin's jurisprudence. The Grenada intervention that same year, and the decision of the International Court of Justice in the *Nicaragua* case in 1986 provided two additional pieces for the puzzle.

This book contains a unified thesis. Yet it is really two books. It attempts to blend two disciplines into one coherent whole. It is a book about international law and about moral philosophy. As a result, not only are many of the substantive arguments novel for lawyers or philosophers, as the case may be, but also the rather disparate argumentative techniques of each of those disciplines co-exist in the text. A reading of the whole text is recommended. Nevertheless, for those exclusively interested in philosophy, it is possible to read chapters 1 to 6, and perhaps also Chapter 8 (where the cases are analyzed). Readers exclusively interested in international law may want to read Chapter 1, then Chapter 6 (which summarizes the normative theory); and then chapters 7, 8 and 9.

The book is an outgrowth of my S.J.D. dissertation presented at Northwestern University School of Law. Very little of it has been published before. Part of the section on relativism in Chapter 2 was adapted from my article "International Human Rights and Cultural Relativism," 25 *Virginia Journal of International Law* 869 (1985), Part of Chapter 9 on the *Nicaragua* case was published as "Le Peuple, C'Est Moi: The World Court and Human Rights," 81 *American Journal of International Law* 173 (1987).

I am indebted to many persons who encouraged and helped me throughout this project and my career. I should first mention my teachers in Argentina. I received my legal and philosophical education in the University of Buenos Aires, under very difficult political conditions, from first-rate scholars, later colleagues. Robert Vernengo, Eugenio Bulygin, Carlos Alchourrón, and Carlos Nino are only a few of them; my intellectual indebtedness to them is enormous. The exchange of ideas, both personal and, over the years, by correspondence, with Guido Pincione from the University of Buenos Aires, has been most influential in the evolution of my thinking. Through constant re-examination and probing of my beliefs, he exercised a decisive influence which definitely inclined my moral-political thought toward the liberal-liberation mold. Raúl Vinuesa introduced me to international law and, with characteristic generosity, gave me the opportunity to teach the course at the University of Buenos Aires. My former colleague in the Argentine diplomatic service and friend Pedro Villagra Delgado tried to inject (not with much success, I am afraid) occasional doses of political realism. I learned much from my teachers in the University of Brussels, most particularly Jean Salmon and Eric David. They taught me the importance of the rigor in research methods in international law and provided me for the first time with a totally free academic environment in that charming European city.

The project started at Northwestern University School of Law in 1982–1983, under a James N. Raymond Fellowship. I very much enjoyed the two years spent at that superb institution. Anthony A. D'Amato, my thesis supervisor, initiated me to the fascinating world of Northern American scholarships. I am most indebted to him both in intellectual matters and for his continuous support and friendship throughout these years.

Arizona State University College of Law provided the ideal working environment for the completion of the book. The project was supported by a Faculty-Grant-In-Aid for the 1984–85 academic year and by two Edward Cleary summer grants. I am grateful to Dean Paul Bender of the College of Law for having relieved me from much of my teaching responsibilities during the spring of 1987. Many thanks should go to the staff and students of Arizona State. Marcelle Chase, the International Law Librarian, provided indispensable support for the project. Paula Gambill and Dottie Swanson did a wonderful job in typing and preparing the final manuscript. I wish to thank also my research assistants, Rosemarie Christofolo, Sandra Salazar and Michael Ryan, for their competent help.

Several colleagues read parts of the manuscripts. I am indebted to Anthony D'Amato, Thomas Pogge, Guido Pincione, David Kaye, and Dennis Kariala for their insightful comments. Most powerful has been the intellectual influence of Jeffrie Murphy here in Arizona. He read the first part of the book and I owe much to his comments, and to his writings generally. My long and stimulating talks with David Kader were a source of inspiration throughout. All of these persons helped improve the text and saved me from critical mistakes. Needless to say, I alone am responsible for those that remain.

This book was written at a time of great controversy over the proper limits of the use of force, especially by democratic nations. Current events in Central America and elsewhere highlight the difficult moral dilemmas that liberalism must face in foreign relations. The argument in this book ultimately rests on a deep conviction about the universality and moral primacy of human rights. That belief, I am somewhat reluctant to say, attempts to be both an act of faith and a tribute to reason.

I could not have completed this project (nor any other) without the love and unfailing support of my sons Fernando and Marcelo (although they do not realize it yet), my mother Marta and my brother Daniel. Finally, no words can express the contribution to whatever I may have accomplished, through the years and across the continents, of my wife Maria Teresa. To her I dedicate this book.

Tempe, Arizona, April 1987

PART ONE

A PHILOSOPHICAL DEFENSE OF HUMANITARIAN INTERVENTION

CHAPTER 1

INTERNATIONAL LAW, HUMANITARIAN INTERVENTION, AND MORAL THEORY

---

1. INTRODUCTION

This book is about one particular instance of use of force—humanitarian intervention. My hope is that the analysis of humanitarian intervention will illuminate the contours of the permissibility of international violence generally. One of the aims of this effort is to show that, if war can be justified at all, it can be so only by appealing to a unified and coherent theory of international law. It is now almost commonplace to say that international legal discourse suffers from a congenital tension between the concern for human rights and the notion of state sovereignty—two of the pillars of international law. A most pressing challenge of our times is to solve that tension. Nowhere is the tension between principles more dramatic than where governments abuse their power and mistreat persons to such an extent that our normal intuitive moral reaction is to come to the rescue of the victims. This intuition, however, clashes with what has been called the moral reality of war: War is hell; it kills; that is all it does. Peace is, and should be, a major purpose of the organized international system. Both principles—that states should refrain from using force and that individuals are entitled to fundamental human rights—thus occupy today a major place among our considered legal and moral judgments. This is attested to, on one hand, by the growing worldwide awareness of human rights violations, and on the other by the continued assertion of the fundamental place

3

that the prohibition of the use of force and the rule of nonintervention have in international relations.

The problem of the lawfulness of humanitarian intervention, and, more generally, the issue of the relationship between human rights and state sovereignty, have been the subjects of intense debate, both in the legal[1] and philosophical[2] literature. The debate has underscored the need for a fresh reformulation of our conceptions of the nature of international law, the use of force and human rights, at both the legal and moral levels. The dilemma is indeed one with which it is difficult to come to terms. May states unilaterally intervene by force in order to put an end to serious human rights violations? Or should states instead absolutely abide by the prohibition of the use of force embodied in article 2(4) of the United Nations Charter, and thus refrain from forcibly intervening in such cases? The first horn of the dilemma opens the door for unpredictable and serious undermining of world order. The second horn of the dilemma entails the seemingly morally intolerable proposition that the international community, in the name of the nonintervention rule, is impotent to combat massacres, acts of genocide, mass murder and widespread torture. The attempt to find a solution to this dilemma raises a number of fundamental questions about international

---

[1] *See*, inter alia, N. Ronzitti, *Rescuing Nationals Abroad and Intervention on Grounds of Humanity* (1985); Brownlie, "Humanitarian Intervention," in *Law and Civil War in the Modern World* 219 (J. N. Moore ed. 1974); and Lillich, "Humanitarian Intervention: A Reply to Ian Brownlie and a Plea for Constructive Alternatives," id., at 229. The debate has been recently revived by the Grenada and Nicaragua interventions. See Reisman, "Coercion and Self-determination: Construing Charter Article 2(4)," 78 *A.J.I.L.* 642 (1984) (hereinafter "Coercion"); and the reply by Schachter, "The Legality of Pro-Democratic Invasion," 78 *A.J.I.L.* 645 (1984) (hereinafter "Invasion"). See Bibliography, *infra*.

[2] The main philosophical works on just war generally, and humanitarian intervention in particular, are M. Walzer, *Just and Unjust Wars* (1977) (hereinafter *Wars*); C. Beitz, *Political Theory and International Relations* (1979); and M. Frost, *Towards a Normative Theory of International Relations* (1986). Articles include Luban, "Just War and Human Rights," 9 *Phil. & Pub. Aff.* 160 (1979–80) (hereinafter "Just War"); Doppelt, "Walzer's Theory of International Relations," 8 *Phil. & Pub. Aff.* 3 (1978–79); Walzer, "The Moral Standing of States: A Reply to Four Critics," 9 *Phil. & Pub. Aff.* 209 (1978–79); (hereinafter "Moral Standing"). The debate continued with Luban, "The Romance of the Nation-State," 9 *Phil. & Pub. Aff.* 392 (1980) (hereinafter "Romance"); Doppelt, "Statism Without Foundations," 9 *Phil. & Pub. Aff.* 398 (1980) (hereinafter "Statism"); Beitz, "Nonintervention and Communal Integrity," 9 *Phil. & Pub. Aff.* 354 (1979–80); and Montaldi, "Toward a Human Rights Based Account of the Just War," 11 *Social Theory and Practice* 123 (1985).

law and morality. Those questions are intertwined with issues concerning the legal and moral standing of states and governments. The normative force of the principle of state sovereignty is thus put to a difficult test in those instances where it clashes with our firm belief that individuals are entitled to claim fundamental human rights as moral barriers against the state.

I argue that forcible action to stop serious human rights deprivations is permitted by international law, properly construed. I will try to show that the *best* interpretation of relevant treaty materials and state practice is that humanitarian intervention is consistent with the present international legal order. I define humanitarian intervention as the *proportionate transboundary help, including forcible help, provided by governments to individuals in another state who are being denied basic human rights and who themselves would be rationally willing to revolt against their oppressive government.* My argument is conceptually articulated in several steps. I first address methodological issues. In the rest of this chapter I suggest a methodology of international legal interpretation in which political philosophy plays a crucial role. I will then attempt (Chapters 2 and 6) to devise a moral theory of international law by critiquing the prevailing noninterventionist paradigm. The argument is aimed at showing why, contrary to prevailing views, a recognition of the right of humanitarian intervention is mandated by an appropriate normative theory of international relations. I will then examine in detail the legal concept of humanitarian intervention (Chapter 7); post-1945 state practice (Chapter 8); recent U.N. practice on collective humanitarian intervention (Chapter 9); and the *Nicaragua* decision by the International Court of Justice (Chapter 10). My purpose is to suggest, once all the pieces are put together, that the *best* interpretation of the available materials commands the conclusion that states possess a right to intervene to help victims of serious human rights deprivations.

A word of caution: My inquiry will be circumscribed to one type of humanitarian intervention—the forcible transboundary action undertaken for the purpose of protecting the rights of individuals against violations by their own governments. The second type of humanitarian intervention is the one undertaken by a state (or a group of states) to protect its (their) own nationals, whose rights are being violated by the target government—the "rescue mission." It has been doubted whether this second kind of intervention is truly humanitarian, because it can arguably be conceived of as an outgrowth of either self-defense principles or the law of diplomatic protection of nationals.[3] However, because the law of human rights has a universal reach, that is, it extends equally to nationals and aliens, there is no reason in principle why the protection of nationals of the intervening state should be, by definition, less humanitarian than the action undertaken to protect nationals of the target state.[4] However, I do not discuss here the issues generated by the interaction of principles of self-defense and protection of human rights in the case of protection of nationals.[5]

II. THE NEED FOR A PHILOSOPHY OF INTERNATIONAL LAW

The present effort differs significantly from standard legal scholarship in that it attempts to incorporate political philosophy as an integral part of international legal discourse. Oddly enough, the debate on human rights and intervention has taken place so far in two unjustifiably divorced settings: the lawyers' and the philosophers'. Yet there is no doubt that the principles of international law involved in the debate on humanitarian intervention have a fundamental moral dimension. There is therefore no immediately apparent reason why moral analysis should be absent from the debate.[6] But I attempt to go further. Following Ronald Dworkin, I will suggest that moral philosophy is necessarily part of the

---

[3] See, e.g., Jhabvala, "Unilateral Humanitarian Intervention and International Law," 21 Indian J. Int'l L. 208, 210–12 (1981).

[4] See generally R. Lillich, The Human Rights of Aliens in Contemporary International Law 1984.

[5] See generally Ronzitti, supra n. 1; and Schweisfurth, "Operations to Rescue Nationals in Third States Involving the Use of Force in Relation to the Protection of Human Rights," 23 German Y.B. Int'l L. 162 (1980).

[6] A similar complaint has been made recently by Levitin, "The Law of Force and the Force of Law: Grenada, the Falklands, and Humanitarian Intervention," 27 Harv. Int'l L.J. 621, 651 (1986) (international law must be made congruent with its moral basis). Cf. Franck & Rodley, who, although strongly opposing the right of humanitarian intervention, have recognized that the decision to intervene to protect human rights belongs in the realm of moral choice. Franck & Rodley, "After Bangladesh: The Law of Humanitarian Intervention by Military Force," 67 A.J.I.L. 275, 304 (1973). This statement obviously presupposes a sharp separation between law and morals, a problematic theoretical assumption.

articulation of legal propositions.[7] Moral philosophy is now routinely part of the debates in other areas of the law; for example, in the controversy over the justification of substantive judicial review in constitutional cases.[8] International law writing, however, remains well behind the times. It appears to be immersed in a theoretical framework informed by a mixture of "realism" and old-fashioned positivism that unjustifiably excludes independent moral analysis. Almost no moral arguments are put forward for or against humanitarian intervention by the participants in the legal debate. This seems to focus exclusively on the issue of whether state practice or the U.N. Charter permits or forbids humanitarian intervention.[9]

There is one obvious preliminary objection to this methodology: Why is moral philosophy relevant here? If the legal conclusion is sound, why do we need to look for additional reasons, or for reasons of a different kind? Are not states supposed to obey international law anyway? The response to these questions requires some elaboration.

Over the last ten years there has been a revival of the debate about the moral justification of humanitarian intervention in philosophical[10] and legal[11] scholarship. The philosopher Michael Walzer, for example, has rejected as "morally false" the claim that waging war on behalf of human rights is justified.[12] Professor Oscar Schachter has argued that a re-interpretation of article 2(4) of the United Nations Charter which would allow for humanitarian intervention "should not be law."[13] Professor Roger Clark has asserted, along the same lines, that "the argument that intervention is justifiable on humanitarian grounds is simply not on . . . because . . . it is bad policy."[14]

---

[7] See R. Dworkin, *Taking Rights Seriously* 81–90 (1978) (hereinafter *Rights*). *See also* id., Law's Empire 97–98 (1986).

[8] *See,* e.g., Dworkin, *Rights, supra* n. 7, Chapter 5.

[9] This is clear in two recent works on humanitarian intervention: Ronzitti, *supra* n. 1; and Verwey, "Humanitarian Intervention under International Law," 33 *Netherlands Int'l L. Rev.* 357 (1985). The only exception, the New Haven approach, is discussed *infra,* this chapter, text, accompanying nn. 52–61.

[10] *See* references *supra* n. 2 and the Bibliography.

[11] *See* references *supra* n. 1 and the Bibliography.

[12] Walzer, "Moral Standing," *supra* n. 2, at 212.

[13] Schachter, "Invasion," *supra* n. 1, at 650. This editorial comment was in response to Reisman, "Coercion," *supra* n. 1.

[14] Clark, "Humanitarian Intervention: Help to Your Friends and State Practice." 13 *Am. U. J. Int'l L.* 211 (1983).

Unfortunately, the legal debate has not been very illuminating. By and large, legal commentators have failed to uncover the moral underpinnings of the international legal order and their bearing on the problem of humanitarian intervention. International lawyers have confined themselves to arguing within narrow theories of law-finding and legal interpretation. Their writings emphasize textual analysis, intent and behavior and official statements by governments, in the most arid tradition of positivism. As a result, the controversy has been articulated as one between two competing principles of *positive* international law—the principle that states should refrain from the use of force[15] and the principle that individuals are entitled to fundamental human rights.[16] Yet each of the legal scholars dealing with the topic has failed to address the fundamental issues of the moral justification of humanitarian intervention or, as the case may be, of a broad rule of nonintervention. One critic of the doctrine of humanitarian intervention correctly contends that those who favor military intervention on behalf of human rights have failed "to present a philosophical analysis that would be based either on deontological grounds or on a consequentialist utilitarian approach."[17] An influential article written in the aftermath of the Indian intervention in Bangladesh also underscored the ethical dimension of the problem, but as something separate from what is thought of as pure legal analysis. In this view, the sense of superior necessity embodied in humanitarian intervention "belongs in the realm not of law but of moral choice."[18] These writers go much farther than just claiming that international law forbids intervention on grounds of humanity. They make the stronger claim that humanitarian intervention is wrong as a matter of morality or policy.[19] An elucidation of the moral aspects of humanitarian intervention, therefore, can no longer be avoided.

Unlike legal scholars, philosophers have recently undertaken an inquiry into the moral principles that underlie the relations among nations.[20] The debate that ensued the publication of Michael Walzer's *Just*

---

[15] Art. 2(4), U.N. Charter.

[16] Art. 1(3) and 55, U.N. Charter.

[17] Schachter, "Invasion," *supra* n. 1, at 647. He does not, however, offer any philosophical analysis in support of his absolute rule of nonintervention.

[18] Franck & Rodley, *supra* n. 6, at 30.

[19] *See* also Donnelly, "Human Rights, Humanitarian Intervention and American Foreign Policy. Law, Morality and Politics," 37 *J. Int'l Aff.* 311 (1984), at 322.

[20] *See* works cited *supra* n. 2.

and Unjust Wars focused, somewhat unexpectedly, on the moral status of states with special reference to humanitarian intervention.[21] By concentrating on Walzer and his critics, I shall analyze the plausibility of noninterventionism from the standpoint of political theory. The thrust of my analysis is that the meaning and scope of the prohibition of article 2(4) and the best meaning of subsequent state practice can only be determined in the light of an appropriate moral theory of international law and relations. From a conventional view of separation of law and morals, my task could be conceived of as a challenge to *both* the legal proposition that the right of humanitarian intervention is not the law and the moral proposition that it "should not be the law."

Yet those two propositions cannot be easily separated. There is a necessary link between international law and moral and political philosophy. Finding a response to the question of whether it is morally right for nations to intervene on behalf of human rights requires an inquiry into the ethical foundations of the international legal system. Such inquiry, I shall assume, is directly relevant to legal discourse. Indeed, this unity between international law and moral philosophy is consistent with the Grotian tradition of international legal scholarship. In contrast to positivism, the Grotian tradition regards international law as an offspring of some system of universal morality.[22] There is a crucial difference, however, between classical natural law theory as articulated by Aquinas, Grotius and others and the kind of analysis offered by modern political philosophers. A persistent difficulty with classical natural law writers, whether religious or rationalist, has been their tendency to dogmatism, their emphasis on self-evident principles which admitted no critical challenge. This essay adopts instead three methodological assumptions suggested by modern "rights" philosophers.[23] First, ethical

---

[21] *See* references *supra* n. 2. Most of these articles, as well as excerpts from Walzer's Wars, *supra* n. 2, are collected in a volume entitled *International Ethics* (C. Beitz, M. Cohen, T. Scanlon & A. J. Simmons eds. 1985).

[22] *See generally* Lauterpacht, "The Grotian Tradition in International Law," 1946 *British Y.B. Int'l L.* 46. See *also* D'Amato, "What Does Tel-Oren Tell Lawyers? Judge Bork's Concept of the Law of Nations is Seriously Mistaken," 79 *A.J.I.L.* 92, 101–105 (1985) (arguing that positivism changed the prior cosmopolitan nature of international law, and that today's emphasis on human rights has restored that cosmopolitanism).

Grotius certainly advocated humanitarian intervention, at least for egregious cases of tyranny. See *infra*, Chapter 3. *See also* C. S. Edwards, *Hugo Grotius, The Miracle of Holland* 134–138 (1981).

[23] I am relying primarily on political philosophers of the last two decades, notably J. Rawls, *A Theory of Justice (1971) (hereinafter Theory)*, and R. Dworkin, *Rights, supra*

inquiry is aimed at finding moral principles to which all rational agents would give allegiance.[24] Second, we cannot be completely sure that a particular moral principle or intuition[25] which we have on reflection accepted is correct, and so we must be ready to revise the principle or intuition in case of disharmony.[26] Third, moral reasoning is a necessary ingredient of legal reasoning.[27] To be sure, there is nothing new in these proposals. Indeed, they have been frequently made by philosophers of law in connection with domestic legal systems, although they are far from being uncontroversial.[28] It is here submitted that if those assumptions are accepted, they hold for international legal reasoning as well. If Professor Ronald Dworkin is right in his jurisprudential assertion that legal and moral propositions are necessarily intertwined (at least in "hard" cases), this must also hold for international law. Similarly, if any moral theory, and especially a theory of rights, is correct (or plausible), then it is *universally* correct (or plausible).[29] I therefore part company with Rawls and Dworkin in that these writers seem to confine their theories ("justice as fairness" and "rights thesis") to Western, or, rather, Anglo-American realities.[30] There is no philosophical reason to confine

---

n. 7; id.; *Law's Empire, supra* n. 7. For a comprehensive bibliography on Rawls, *see* Wellbank, Snook & Mason, "John Rawls and His Critics." *An Annotated Bibliography* (1982). As my argument will make clear, however, I disagree with Rawls's theory of *international law. See infra*, Chapter 3.

[24] In his more recent article, Rawls has warned that his theory does not address the issue of moral objectivity. *See* Rawls, "Justice as Fairness: Political not Metaphysical," 14 *Phil. & Pub. Aff.* 223 (1985) (hereinafter "Political not Metaphysical"). But his "reflective equilibrium" suggestion is a good example of moral methodology in which we try to reach moral principles to which rational agents would agree. I assume here that we do not need an infallible moral method to start speaking about what rights people should have. On relativism, see *infra*, Chapter 2.

[25] I use the word "intuition" in a harmless sense, to mean a settled moral conviction of any level of generality. The collected intuitions operate as provisional fixed points to organize the underlying moral ideas and principles in a coherent structure. *See* Rawls, "Political not Metaphysical," *supra* n. 24, at 228–29.

[26] This is the very essence of Rawls's "reflective equilibrium." *See* Rawls, *Theory, supra* n. 23, at 48–51.

[27] *See* R. Dworkin, *Rights, supra* n. 7, at 46, and *infra* Chapter 2.

[28] For critiques to Rawls, *see* the collection of essays in *Reading Rawls* (N. Daniels ed. 1975). For critiques to Dworkin see the essays in *Ronald Dworkin and Contemporary Jurisprudence* (M. Cohen ed. 1984).

[29] *See infra*, Chapter 2.

[30] *See* Rawls, "Political not Metaphysical," *supra* n. 24, at 225. Dworkin's work has not been concerned with international human rights, but Professor Mervyn Frost, *supra* n. 2, has recently attempted to furnish a Dworkin theory of international relations.

political morality to constitutional justice. The continuing debate on the morality of governments' international conduct and the impressive rise of human rights concerns have underscored both dimensions (theory of rights and relation between law and morality) as particularly important for any philosophy of international law. Any ethical theory of international law necessitates both a conceptual theory of the relationship between law and ethics in international relations, and a normative theory of rights to explain the notions of state sovereignty and states' rights and their interrelationship with human rights.[31]

III. CUSTOM AND MORAL THEORY

This unity between law and ethics operates most strongly in the field of international law. A major methodological dilemma faced by international legal scholars is that of deciding why particular instances of state practice ought to be regarded as configurating a new customary rule rather than as violating old international law.[32] More specifically, international courts and scholars must decide whether precedents of what seem to be instances of humanitarian intervention, taken together, have carved out an exception to article 2(4) of the United Nations Charter, or should instead be regarded as violations of that principle.

I suggest that a proposition of the form "N is an international legal customary rule" requires a reliance on a value judgment which in turn can only be understood within the framework of a broader moral-political theory. When a court or an impartial observer (such as a scholar) is surveying history in order to find patterns of international conduct, the search is not unprejudiced, in the sense of being free of a preexisting set of beliefs. Rather, the selection of instances of state practice, of those pieces of past history that count as custom, is informed by a theoretical framework within which ethical considerations play an important role.

---

[31] Thus I join Professor Frost, who convincingly suggests that international theory should benefit from Dworkin's suggestion that hard cases can only be resolved by an appeal to a background theory, i.e., a theory of political philosophy. See Frost, *supra* n. 2, chapters 3 and 4. Unfortunately, the theory he suggests amounts to a bold version of Hegelianism that fails to achieve his purpose of reconciling state sovereignty with human rights. See *infra*, chapters 6 and 7.

[32] See A. D'Amato, *The Concept of Custom in International Law* 13 (1971) (a new rule cannot possibly be required by "preexisting" customary law).

In this sense, finding customary law is not an objective or value-neutral process, nor should it be so. If we are equipped with a moral theory which on reflection seems to us correct, our process of selecting those precedents that shape a customary rule shall be naturally guided by such theory. I suggest that in this important sense, moral philosophy is part of what we think of, rather loosely, as "international law." Accordingly, a primary reason why the cases of humanitarian intervention studied in Chapter 8 of this book count as custom is that the process and the outcome of those cases are justified by a moral theory that, I hope to demonstrate, is preferable to the current noninterventionist alternative.

A discussion of humanitarian intervention is particularly apt to illustrate the philosophical underpinnings of international law. This is so because the legal principles and rules that deal with human rights and the use of military force are not just technical, or morally neutral, precepts. Instead, they speak to some of our most basic moral principles, convictions and intuitions.[33] Those principles and rules are supposed to embody fundamental moral perceptions. On one hand, the legal norms in question are inextricably linked with our notions about the justice or injustice of war. On the other hand, our interpretation of those norms reflects the place we are willing to accord to basic human rights in international relations. The way we think about those issues is also closely linked to, and dependent upon, our notions about the conditions of moral legitimacy of states and governments. Consequently, unless we can make a plausible case for the existence of a *moral* right of nations to wage war in defense of human rights, no "purposive" interpretation of article 2(4) of the United Nations Charter will be convincing or indeed possible. Purposive interpretation is interpretation in the light of values, and so no display of state practice will be sufficient to prove the case for humanitarian intervention unless we can show that such instances are not to be regarded simply as violations of international law,[34] and that can only be done by articulating the values that inform

---

[33] *See* H. L. A. Hart, *The Concept of Law* 222–25 (while many rules of international law are morally "neutral" or technical, some may embody moral principles).

[34] For example, Brownlie suggests that the examples of humanitarian intervention do not qualify as state practice: They are just violations of international law. Brownlie, "Humanitarian Intervention," *supra* n. 1, at 221 ("The truth is that one cannot treat all state conduct as practice.").

the "purpose" of the applicable rule or principle.[35] There are strong philosophical reasons for regarding instances of humanitarian intervention as justified. We need to articulate those reasons through independent philosophical analysis.

The relevance of the view of custom suggested here to the issue of humanitarian intervention may seem at first sight at odds with a recent decision of the International Court of Justice. In the recent *Nicaragua* case, the Court had to deal with the issue whether recent interventions "for the benefits of forces opposed to the government of another State" had undermined the general customary rule prohibiting intervention.[36] The Court asked the question whether

> there might be indications of a practice illustrative of belief in a kind of general right of States to intervene, directly or indirectly, with or without armed force, in support of an internal opposition in another State, whose cause appeared particularly worthy by reason of the political and moral values with which it was identified.[37]

The Court responded in the negative, reasoning that "the significance . . . of cases of State conduct prima facie inconsistent with the principle of non-intervention lies in the nature of the ground offered as justification."[38] And states in general, and the United States in particular, had not asserted that their intervention was *legally* justified. Rather, the Court thought, these were statements of international policy.[39] Consequently, the Court concluded, "no such *general* right of intervention, in support of the opposition within another State, exists in contemporary international law."[40]

These excerpts by the Court may create the impression that precedents of humanitarian intervention do not count as "custom" and that they should be treated instead as violations of international law. To

---

[35] For a full discussion, *see infra*, Chapter 7.

[36] Case of Military and Paramilitary Activities in and Against Nicaragua (Merits), 1986 *I.C.J. Rep.* 14, 108.

[37] Id.

[38] Id. at 108–109.

[39] Id.

[40] Id. at 109 (emphasis added).

begin with, the Court's description of the nature of the reasons offered by governments to justify intervention in the past is inaccurate. (The intervention in Grenada, for example, was justified by the United States on several *legal*, and not just political, grounds.[41]) But more importantly, this dictum stands for the proposition that no *general* right of intervention exists in support of internal opposition of another state. No state has a right to intervene in a civil war just because it sympathizes with the rebels, any more than it has the right to intervene for other reasons, for example, for strategic reasons. But genuine humanitarian interventions are responses to gross violations of international human rights—that is, to flagrant violations of international law. So although the Court is correct that there is no *general* right of intervention, that does not dispose of the issue whether there are *specific* grounds to intervene.[42] Alternatively, if the Court's holding is read as dismissing the relevance of humanitarian intervention for the formation of custom, there still remains the issue of why the Court chose to discount those precedents.[43] The response, I will suggest, is that the facts in that particular case were not persuasive enough for the Court to make the value judgment that the United States' intervention in Nicaragua was, on the whole, morally justified.[44]

To sum up: I suggest that, at least in the areas of use of force and human rights, the determination of "custom" in international law presupposes a value judgment. In this sense, the assertion of a rule or principle of customary law is an *internal* assertion in Hart's sense, rather than an external or descriptive proposition.[45] It is true that we can say, for instance, "N is custom in society X." This is a purely descriptive assertion and does not imply a value judgment. We are not, however, part of society X; our judgment, therefore, is just external. In contrast, the assertion by an international court or a legal scholar that "N is an

---

[41] *See infra,* Chapter 8.

[42] I examine the *Nicaragua* case at length in Chapter 10.

[43] The Court's approach to custom is highly unsatisfactory. *See* Franck, "Some Observations on the ICJ's Procedural and Substantive Innovations," 81 *A.J.I.L.* 116, 118–119 (1987) (criticizing the Court's superficial dismissal of the relevance of state practice contrary to the principle of nonuse of force); and a similar critique by D'Amato, "Trashing Customary Law," id. at 101, 102–03.

[44] *See infra,* Chapter 10.

[45] *See* Hart, *supra* n. 33, at 55–56.

international customary legal rule," is made from an internal perspective. International law concerns us all; whether we like it or not, we are all "subjects" of the international legal system. The very fact that the person making that assertion makes a choice, a selection of precedents, shows the claim-oriented nature of arguments directed to demonstrate the existence of a norm of customary international law.[46]

This value choice, however, is not exercised from nowhere, in a vacuum. International legal discourse is not co-extensive with moral philosophy. Rather, international legal propositions are the children *both* of institutional history (diplomatic history, treaty texts) and political philosophy, in the sense of a background political theory.[47] Thus, state practice (that is, institutional history) is *interpreted* in the ascertainment of international law.[48] State practice thus remains a central touchstone of international legal reasoning. But international lawyers—and international courts—cannot solve the dilemma posed by humanitarian intervention by a purported value-free analysis of state practice and treaty texts. State practice and treaty texts must be interpreted. And that can only be done by confronting the moral problems prescribed by the uneasy relationship between human rights and state sovereignty. It is therefore necessary to articulate and make explicit the moral-political theory that underlies and justifies our international legal notions, as well as our considered judgments of international justice.

IV. AN OUTLINE OF THE MORAL ARGUMENT FOR HUMANITARIAN INTERVENTION

In this book I attempt to meet that challenge. I argue that the assertion of a right of humanitarian intervention is the best philosophical position; consequently, it is also the best interpretation of international legal materials. My main argument is that because the ultimate justification of the existence of states is the protection and enforcement of the natural rights of the citizens, a government that engages in substantial

---

[46] *See* A. D'Amato, *supra* n. 32, at 18–20.

[47] *See* R. Dworkin, *A Matter of Principle* 146–148 (1985).

[48] Here I do not need to differentiate between state practice proper and *opinio juris,* within the meaning of article 36 (1) (a) of the Statute of the International Court of Justice. Both are part of institutional history for the purposes of the point made in the text.

violations of human rights betrays the very purpose for which it exists and so forfeits not only its domestic legitimacy, but its international legitimacy as well. Consequently, I shall argue, foreign armies are morally entitled to help victims of oppression in overthrowing dictators, provided that the intervention is proportionate to the evil which it is designed to suppress. A further requirement is that the intervention be welcomed, actually or ideally, by those citizens whose human rights are being violated. I will further argue that humanitarian intervention is justified not only to remedy egregious cases of human rights violations, such as genocide, enslavement or mass murder, but also to put an end to situations of serious, disrespectful, yet not genocidal, oppression.[49]

Underlying these specific conclusions about humanitarian intervention are more basic theses about the moral foundations of international law and about the interrelationship between rights of states and human rights. I suggest that, from an ethical standpoint, the rights of states under international law are properly derived from individual rights. I therefore reject the notion that states have any autonomous moral standing—that they hold international rights that are independent from the rights of individuals who populate the state. I hope to demonstrate the philosophical force of these proposals through an examination of traditional and modern arguments offered in support of state sovereignty. The purpose of this work, therefore, goes beyond suggesting that humanitarian intervention is sometimes justified. More generally, I suggest some ideas for a normative philosophy of international law.

It is worth noting in passing that I share a common ground with those philosophers, like Walzer, whose work will otherwise be the main target of my critique. That common ground is the assumption that morality matters in international relations. My critique to the noninterventionist model thus proceeds on the assumption, shared also by many defenders of a strong principle of nonintervention based on broad conceptions of state sovereignty, that "realism" and power politics are profoundly wrong, and that therefore there is a fundamental moral

---

[49] The argument developed here is similar to the one suggested by David Luban, "Just War," *supra* n. 2; and Gerald Doppell, "Walzer's Theory," *supra* n. 2. However, I elaborate the thesis in more detail and depart from those authors on important points. While I agree with the general approach taken by Charles Beltz in his important work, *supra* n. 2, I part company with him on substantial issues as well. Mervyn Frost, *supra* n. 2, also attempts to develop a normative theory of international relations, but his substantive proposal differs from mine.

dimension of international politics. States are not in a Hobbesian state of nature. Michael Walzer,[50] Charles Beitz,[51] Marshall Cohen,[52] and Mervyn Frost[53] have convincingly underscored the need for moral discourse in international relations. Governments are constrained by moral principles in their international behavior, just as they are constrained by moral principles in their domestic behavior. While many versions of moral skepticism entail noninterventionism,[54] the controversy between supporters and detractors of the right of humanitarian intervention does not necessarily stem from a metaethical disagreement between moral skeptics and moral objectivists. Rather, it is to a large extent an authentic moral dispute, a dispute about values. For the ones, nation-states hold international rights above and beyond human rights; for the others, the international rights of states are but a derivation of human rights. Both sides are asserting different normative international ethics; both sides therefore believe in the possibility of meaningfully articulating a system of transboundary moral norms. The purpose of this study is to furnish philosophical reasons for preferring a normative theory of international law grounded on human rights. This theory will in turn color our examination of treaty materials and state practice.

V. A NOTE ON THE NEW HAVEN APPROACH TO INTERNATIONAL LAW

The methodological approach adopted here should be contrasted with another school of thought with which it shares some features. I am referring to the collective work of the New Haven school of international law.[55] This influential theory emphasizes the nature of international law as a process of authoritative decision interwoven by the multiple actors in the international arena. The New Haven approach

---

[50] In *Wars, supra* n. 2, at 3–20.

[51] In Beitz, *supra* n. 2, at 11–66.

[52] *See* Cohen, "Moral Skepticism and International Relations," 13 *Phil. & Pub. Aff.* 299 (1984).

[53] Frost *supra* n. 2, Chapters 1 and 2.

[54] *See infra*, Chapter 2.

[55] A representative collection of their writings can be found in M. McDougal & W.M. Reisman, *International Law Essays* (1981).

advocates a "policy-oriented, configurative approach to the study of world constitutive process."[56] That process consists of the five following intellectual tasks:

(1) The clarification of general community goals about constitutive decision;

(2) The description of past trends in decision toward or from the realization of such goals;

(3) Analysis of the conditions that appear to have affected past decision;

(4) The projection of probable future developments in decision, assuming no influence by the observer;

(5) Invention and evaluation of alternatives for the better realization of preferred goals.[57]

The New Haven approach emphasizes the need to have policy goals clarified at the outset of the law-finding process. The approach has been criticized for that reason as being "value-oriented," i.e., as not being neutral enough, and therefore, as not providing an objective basis for the ascertainment of rules and principles of international law.[58] This criticism is unfounded. As noted above, some values are always presupposed in the articulation of legal propositions. Law and morality are indissolubly intertwined, and not only in hard cases. This is not a contingent but a logical truth: When we assert that a certain rule is law, we may be just asserting a fact, or we may be also saying that the agent to whom the rule is addressed has a prima facie duty of obedience (provided the law complies with minimal moral requirements). It is fair to say, however, that most people use the word "law" in the latter sense, as implying a prima facie, or presumptive, duty of obedience. But the proposition asserting a duty of obedience cannot itself be legal: Rather, it is something that we say about the law, a metalegal assertion. In sum, even the most legalistic and value-free approach to the law has to deal

---

[56] McDougal, Lasswell & Reisman, The World Constitutive Process of Authoritative Decision, in *International Law Essays, supra* n. 55, at 191, 200.

[57] Id. at 200–201.

[58] *See*, e.g., F. Boyle, *World Politics and International Law* 61–67 (1985). A similar objection was made by Professor Anthony D'Amato in his remarks at the meeting of the International Law Section of the American Association of Law Schools, New Orleans, Jan. 6, 1986.

with the problem of the duty of obedience, which is itself a moral issue.[59] McDougal and his associates are therefore quite right in assuming that any formulation of the "world process of authoritative decision" (i.e., international law) presupposes a value judgment on the part of the court that is applying, or the observer who is describing, international law.

The New Haven approach, however, is insufficient. Despite its apparent comprehensiveness, it has nowhere furnished a normative philosophy of international law. To be sure, the New Haven writers advocate a fundamental value, human dignity, which is defined as "the inherent and equal value of every human being."[60] Assuming that "human dignity" here is roughly equivalent to "human rights," there are two possible interpretations of this teleological dimension of the New Haven approach, both of them suggested by their writings. The first treats human dignity as a *postulate*. As such, despite their admirable reminder that "the ultimate actor in every interaction is the individual,"[61] nowhere do Professor Myres McDougal and his associates attempt to provide a philosophical analysis which would discard the mystical notions associated with unrestrained state sovereignty in favor of a human rights-oriented approach to international relations. Nevertheless, in this interpretation the New Haven scholars have taken the first important step of recognizing that legal discourse is inseparable from value judgments and that as such it is but a branch of normative philosophy.

At times, however, the New Haven writers create the impression that "human dignity" is to be found in the "expectations" of national policy-makers. This approach is evident, for example, in the above-quoted methodological requirement that in order to formulate international law we must first "clarify" the "community goals." This, of course, is very different from postulating human dignity as a *moral* value in the light of appropriate principles of political morality, regardless of community goals, and then proceeding with the analysis. If the starting point is the "community expectations," then the New Haven approach

---

[59] Here I follow C. Nino, *La Validez del Derecho* 41–68 (1985).

[60] McDougal, Lasswell & Reisman, *supra* n. 55, at 201.

[61] Id.

should be characterized as sociological positivism. From a philosophical perspective, the response to that approach is simply that community goals and expectations may be morally wrong.

A striking example of this disharmony between actual community expectations and the realization of human dignity as a moral value is the legal status of international terrorism. The problem of international terrorism has given scholars and even judges a tough dilemma: On one hand, the "community values" seem to point to the legitimacy of certain forms of terrorism.[62] But as Judge Robb replied to his colleagues in the *Tel-Oren* case, by reaching such a conclusion "we corrupt our own understanding of evil."[63] A view of international law as engrained in minimal notions of human dignity should exclude the legalistic approach of the *Tel-Oren* court and like-minded commentators.[64] Simply put, here the "community expectations"—meaning the expectations of the United Nations majority which presumably tolerates or encourages certain forms of terrorism—are plainly immoral. If the observer's criterion for authoritative decision-making is determined by actual community expectations, then he must adhere to the legitimacy of politically motivated terrorist acts, because his criterion is purely descriptive, not normative: He articulates the guiding values by observing reality, by empirically clarifying the expectations of the multiple actors in the global arena. If the observer's task is instead informed by appropriate principles of political morality, which of course are independent of any community expectations, then he should reject as incompatible with a modicum of human dignity any proposed rule or principle that has the result of legitimizing terrorist practices.

Despite the difficult jargon used, the New Haven approach can be instructive and fruitful as a sociology of international law. The New

---

[62] *See Hanoch-Tel-Oren v. Libyan Arab Republic,* F. Supp. 542 (D.D.C. 1981), *aff'd per curiam,* 726 F.2d 774 (D.C. Cir. 1984), *cert. denied* 53 U.S.L.W. 3612 (1985), at 795–96 (Edwards, H., concurring). While Judge Bork avoided reaching the merits by refusing to grant a "cause of action" to the plaintiffs, he also pointed to international terrorism as an unsettled area of international law. 726 F.2d at 806–808.

[63] 726 F.2d at 823. (Robb, J., concurring). Judge Robb, however, also corrupted his own understanding of evil by shielding the terrorist acts behind the "political question" doctrine. *See id.* at 823–827.

[64] *See,* e.g., Lillich, "Invoking International Human Rights in Domestic Courts," 54 *Cin. L. Rev.* (1985), at n. 161 (customary law as yet contains no general prohibition on terrorism).

Haven theorists have provided us with useful insights into the process of formation of international law and the mechanisms by which international law bears upon national decision-making. Most important, their writings have taught us to look beyond positive international legal materials and think about the policies, purposes and principles that underlie customary or conventional prescriptions. Particularly important has been their emphasis on international law as a process. That approach has prepared the ground for breaking with the positivist thinking that has traditionally dominated the discipline.

Yet this descriptive approach needs to be supplemented by a normative philosophy of international law directed to demonstrate the philosophical preeminence of human rights. The utility of the New Haven approach is conditioned upon a reliance on human dignity as a paramount postulated *moral* value. If their theory is read instead as a call to articulate values by empirically observing and ascertaining the expectations of decision-makers and other international actors, then it is just a sophisticated version of ideological positivism, incompatible with independent moral inquiry.

CHAPTER 2

THE ASSUMPTIONS OF THE NONINTERVENTIONIST MODEL

I. GENERAL CONCEPTS

The moral case for intervention in defense of human rights is best shown by unveiling the philosophical inadequacies of the noninterventionist model. In this and the following three chapters I shall attempt to elucidate and critique the ethical foundations upon which the conventional conception of the international legal system is said to rest. Those foundations, some explicit, some implicit, provide the best known and most powerful arguments against humanitarian intervention. My strategy will be thus to scrutinize the noninterventionist model using humanitarian intervention as a canvas. I will then outline what I consider to be a more defensible system of international ethics.

There are three basic positions regarding humanitarian intervention.[1] Absolute noninterventionism claims that the use of force is only justified as a reaction against aggression (self-defense).[2] Limited interventionism

---

[1] I use the word "intervention" throughout this chapter in the sense of forcible intervention or its equivalent.

See 1 Oppenheim, *International Law* 305 (8th ed. H. Lauterpacht 1955). For other actions I use the word "interference." For a full discussion of the meaning of "intervention" in international law, *see infra*, Chapter 10.

[2] As indicated above, this is the position adopted by most legal scholars. *See* references, *supra* Chapter 1, n. 1, and *infra*, Chapter 7, n. 5. Among the philosophers, *see* Benn & Peters, *Social Principles and the Democratic State* 361–63 (1959) (hereinafter *Social Principles*. Arguably, Rawls endorses this position. For a full discussion, *see* Chapter 3. Noninterventionists, however, usually concede that humanitarian interven-

is the thesis that humanitarian intervention is only acceptable in cases of extreme human rights violations, such as genocide, mass murder or enslavement.[3] Finally, broad interventionism claims that humanitarian intervention is acceptable in cases of serious human rights violations which need not, however, reach genocidal proportions.[4] I shall argue here for a broad interventionist position in the sense just defined. Current state practice and the import of the United Nations Charter will then be examined in the light of that theory.[5]

The philosophical arguments that have been offered against both the limited and broad versions of the right of humanitarian intervention fall into two general categories. Arguments in the first group rely on some notion of *rights* of nation-states which would morally shield them against foreign intervention. Indeed, the notion of rights of states (nations, national communities) is basic to current international legal discourse, and for that reason seems an attractive starting point for a conceptual analysis of the morality of intervention. The idea of states'

---

tion by an internal authority may be justified. But, aside from the fact that such centralized enforcement procedures have never existed nor are likely to exist, they are philosophically irrelevant. We are looking for valid substantive reasons, if any, to intervene. The U.N. may act as immorally as anyone else.

[3] This is the position endorsed by most legal scholars who support humanitarian intervention. *See* references *supra* n. 2 and *infra*, Chapter 7, n. 7. Among the philosophers, its champion is Michael Walzer. *See* his *Just and Unjust Wars* 86–108 (1977) (hereinafter Wars).

[4] Among legal scholars, A. D'Amato, *International Law: Process and Prospect* 225–232 (1987) and Reisman, "Coercion and Self-determination: Construing Article 2(4)," 78 *A.J.I.L.* 642 (1984), defend this view. Among philosophers, Luban, "Just War and Human Rights," 9 *Phil. & Pub. Aff.* 160 (1979–80); and Doppelt, "Walzer's Theory of Morality in International Relations," 8 *Phil. & Pub. Aff.* 3 (1978–79). Of course, there are still more interventionist positions: that states may intervene for strategic reasons, or to install friendly governments, or to increase their territory, etc. I will assume, however, that these types of interventions are morally and legally indefensible.

[5] The attachment of legal scholars to the noninterventionist model is witnessed by the fact that while they debate whether *any* humanitarian intervention is accepted by international law, philosophers debate whether the right of humanitarian intervention should be recognized to remedy serious human rights violations short of genocide, enslavement and mass murder, thus conceding that those egregious cases warrant military intervention. Michael Walzer, for example, espouses a right of humanitarian intervention for egregious cases, while denying it for cases of ordinary oppression. *See* Walzer, *Wars, supra* n. 3, at 89–90, 101–108. Thus, while among philosophers he is the champion of nonintervention and state sovereignty, when measured against legal scholars he is a pro-interventionist. Paradoxically, in his defense of a thesis of limited intervention, Walzer has articulated the moral basis of *noninterventionism* better than anybody else. This is the reason why I here concentrate on his work.

rights is associated with certain theoretical assumptions about the moral standing of governments and about the scope of moral reasoning in international relations. A noninterventionist stance based on states' rights dismissed humanitarian intervention, not necessarily because of its undesirable consequences (for example in terms of human suffering), but as a matter of principle.

Arguments of the second type emphasize instead the undesirable consequences of adopting a rule permitting humanitarian intervention. Utilitarian calculations, it is thought, advise against intervening in virtually all cases. Utilitarian noninterventionism does not rely on a pure principle of national sovereignty as such. It need only make calculations in terms of human happiness or general utility in order to show that opening the door to military interventions will not yield good consequences; and that therefore it is preferable, from a utilitarian standpoint, to forbid virtually all transboundary uses of force.

I shall attempt to show that noninterventionists are wrong at both levels. They are wrong in their philosophical assumptions about the moral value of states and the interrelationship between rights of states and rights of individuals—indeed, about the ethical basis of international law. They are also wrong in most of the utilitarian assumptions on which they reject the propriety of humanitarian intervention for most cases.

II. THE NONINTERVENTIONIST MODEL

The prohibition against all kinds of military intervention, including humanitarian, is a key component of what Michael Walzer has aptly called "the legalist paradigm."[6] It will be convenient for our purposes to reformulate the paradigm into the following three propositions:[7]

---

[6] Wars, *supra* n. 3, at 58 ff.

[7] Walzer's six propositions are as follows:

"1. There exists an international society of independent states. . . .

2. This international society has a law that establishes the rights of its members—above all, the rights of territorial integrity and political sovereignty. . . .

3. Any use of force or imminent threat of force by one state against the political sovereignty or territorial integrity of another constitutes aggression and is a criminal act. . . .

4. Aggression justifies two kinds of violent response: a war of self-defense by

i. The Rule of Noninterference

States must refrain from interfering in the domestic affairs of other states.

There is a *prima facie* duty to refrain from interfering in the internal affairs of other states. Each state must respect the autonomy (sovereignty, self-determination) of its neighbors. The assumption here is that there are two spheres of political action: the government's relationship with the governed and its relations with other governments. Foreign governments have no right to interfere in the domestic sphere of politics. In particular, states may not question other states' legitimacy on humanitarian grounds. In the words of Walzer, "[t]hough states are founded for the sake of life and liberty, they cannot be challenged in the name of life and liberty."[8]

ii. The Representation Theory

For any given state, the government always represents the people in international relations, regardless of its legitimacy of origin or its effective observance of human rights.

This proposition is the twin sister of proposition (i). The representation theory, itself an offspring of classical positivism, conceives the international community as formed by independent states, not by individuals.[9] Consequently, "men and women are protected and their interests represented only by their own government."[10] This is why international law establishes for the most part rights and duties of states, not of individuals. While in the light of appropriate principles of justice citizens may be entitled to revolt against an unjust government, until

---

the victim and a war of law-enforcement by the victim and any other member of international society. . . .

5. Nothing but aggression can justify war. . . .

6. Once the aggressor state has been militarily repulsed, it can also be punished." Id. at 61–62.

[8] Id. at 61.

[9] *See*, e.g., the classic statement in 1 Oppenheim, *International Law* 459–461 (1922) (individuals cannot be subjects of international law, but only its objects).

[10] Walzer, *Wars, supra* n. 3, at 61.

that happens, and while the unjust government exercises effective political control, other states ought to regard it as presumptively legitimate.

iii. The Broad Prohibition of the Use of Military Force

States may wage war only as a response to aggression.

The noninterventionist thrust of the legalist paradigm is nowhere better illustrated than in the quasi-absolute prohibition of the use of force. This "border impermeability"[11] finds its clearest expression in Articles 2(4) and 51 of the U.N. Charter read together, as interpreted by most governments and international legal scholars.[12] A war is just if, and only if, it is in response to an aggressive war. Nothing but aggression justifies war, and so "domestic heresy and injustice are never actionable in the world of states."[13] Foreigners may perhaps sometimes verbally criticize governments for human rights abuses, but they may never act on that disapproval. Following Vitoria, Walzer reminds us that only a wrong inflicted by a state against another justifies the use of armed force by the latter.[14] Because humanitarian intervention is not a use of force in self-defense, it is virtually never justified.

Note that this principle does not presuppose (i) or (ii). We may concede that foreigners have a right to pass judgments about human rights violations, thereby denying proposition (i), or refuse to accept that a tyrant represents its people in international relations, thereby denying (ii); and still reject the propriety of *using force* to put an end

---

[11] The expression belongs to D'Amato, "Nicaragua and International Law: The Academic and the Real," 79 *A.J.I.L.* 657, 659 (1985), now reprinted in A. D'Amato, *International Law: Process and Prospect, supra* n. 4, at 223, 225.

[12] *See generally,* I. Brownlie, *International Law and the Use of Force by States* (1963); Schachter, "The Rights of States to Use Armed Forces," 82 *Mich. L. Rev.* 1620 (1984).

[13] Walzer, *Wars, supra* n. 3, at 61. Similarly, Frost writes:

In spite of the . . . commitment to democratic institutions and human rights . . . , it is settled that there are strict limits to what states may do to bring about the mentioned conditions in a recalcitrant site. I refer here to the rule of non-intervention in the domestic affairs of other states. It precludes military involvement against other states except where such action is in self-defence. . . .

M. Frost, *Toward a Normative Theory of International Relations* 126 (1986).

[14] Walzer, *Wars, supra* n. 3, at 62.

to human rights violations. It is the case, however, that most non-interventionists assert (iii) in conjunction with some form of (i) and (ii). The reason is that anyone who asserts (iii) has to show why the use of force *within a state* (i.e., violence employed by the subjects themselves) to overthrow tyrannical governments (revolution) is sometimes justified (unless one is an extreme pacifist), while the use of *international* force for similar purposes (humanitarian intervention) never is.

The legalist paradigm is thus supported by several intertwined arguments. Its basic thrust is the sacredness of national borders and the primacy of state sovereignty over most other considerations. The rule of nonintervention conveys the idea that states and governments deserve respect, even those that are repressive and do not represent the people. While at first sight this notion may run counter to some of our moral intuitions, we must take it seriously, because it underlies classic and modern international legal thought. Nonintervention is taught in our classrooms, defended in scholarly writings, and proclaimed in national and international fora. It is time to examine critically its philosophical underpinnings. In the rest of this chapter, two preliminary objections to the doctrine of humanitarian intervention need to be examined. First, the contention that self-determination (sovereignty, autonomy) is, in the nature of things, more basic than other human rights. Second, we must examine the popular claim that nation-states are morally enclosed—better known as moral relativism.

III. IS THE RIGHT TO SELF-DETERMINATION MORE BASIC THAN OTHER HUMAN RIGHTS?

In an essay published in 1859, John Stuart Mill argued that self-determination, that is, the situation in which, in a given society, the people themselves resolve their political differences and establish their institutions without foreign interference, is a necessary, although not a sufficient, condition for the enjoyment of freedom by those people.[15] One reason offered by Mill in support of his thesis is that "the only test possessing any real value, of a people's having become fit for popular

---

[15] J. S. Mill, "A Few Words on Non-Intervention," in 3 *Dissertations and Discussions* 153, 171–176 (1867) (hereinafter "Words").

institutions, is that they . . . are willing to brave labour and danger for their liberation."[16] In the prose of Walzer, "self-determination is the more inclusive idea, it describes not only a particular institutional arrangement—or does not."[17] According to this theory, no external force can ever set men and women free; they have to attend the "school" of the political process.[18] Without it, freedom either cannot be attained or it is not true freedom. Walzer summarized this idea in a subsequent article: "Against foreigners, individuals have a right to a state of their own. Against state officials, they have a right to political and civil liberty. Without the first of these rights, the second is meaningless: as individuals need a home, so rights require a location."[19] This notion is apparently embodied in the two United Nations International Covenants on human rights, where the right to self-determination (of peoples) precedes the (individual) rights recognized by the two conventions.[20]

Before discussing this claim any further, it is necessary to clarify in what sense the expression "self-determination" is used here. Following

---

[16] Id. at 173. His second reason, which I discuss below, is that "there can seldom be anything approaching to assurance that intervention, even if successful, would be for the good of the people themselves." Id.

[17] Walzer, *Wars, supra* n. 3, at 87.

[18] Thus, Mill writes:

When a people has had the misfortune to be ruled by a government under which the feelings and the virtues needful for maintaining freedom could not develop themselves, it is during an arduous struggle to become free by their own efforts that these feelings and virtues have the best chance of springing up.

Mill, "Words," *supra* n. 15, at 175.

[19] Walzer, "The Moral Standing of States," 9 *Phil. & Pub. Aff.* 209, 228 (1978–79). The same idea is conveyed by Walzer's reminder that we accord respect and yield room to "the political process itself, with all its messiness and uncertainty, its inevitable compromises and its frequent brutality." Id. at 229. Frost arrives at a similar conclusion in a different way: Following Hegel, he argues that the very notion of individual rights is meaningless outside a state framework. *See* Frost, *Normative Theory, supra* n. 13, at 173–184, especially 174, 180–184.

[20] *See* art. 1, International Covenant on Economic, Social and Cultural Rights, opened for signature, Dec. 19, 1966. Entered into force, Jan. 3, 1976. U.N. G.A. Res. 2200 (XXI), 21 U.N. G.A.O.R., (Supp. No. 16) 49, U.N. Doc. A/6316 (1966), reprinted in *I.L.M.* 360 (1967); and art. 1, International Covenant on Civil and Political Rights, opened for signature, Dec. 19, 1966. Entered into force, Mar. 23, 1967. U.N. G.A. Res. 2200 (XXI), 21 U.N. G.A.O.R., (Supp. No. 16) 52, U.N. Doc. A/6316 (1966), reprinted in *I.L.M.* 368 (1967).

standard international law terminology, it is possible to distinguish between external and internal self-determination.[21] External self-determination is the right of peoples to be free from alien rule, the paradigm of which is colonial domination. Determining the content of external self-determination thus is the same as determining under what conditions a community has a right to form a separate state, as well as the processes by which the community exercises such right. This in turn raises complex issues about the definition of "people" and the claims to territorial integrity by the parent state in case of secession.

I am not concerned here with external self-determination in this sense. I use instead the expression "self-determination" in the nontechnical sense in which Mill uses it; that is, as the right of peoples to establish their own political, economic, and cultural institutions without interference from other states. This concept, sometimes referred to as "internal" self-determination, is the flip side of the nonintervention principle.[22] I am therefore concerned here, not with the issue of whether a group of individuals has a right to create a political association, thus freeing themselves, as a community, from prior alien domination, but with the *kind of political association* they are morally entitled to create. Self-determination in this Millian sense thus refers to the right of peoples to reach social arrangements through a political process free of foreign interference.

However, Walzer (but not Mill[23]) seems to confuse the two meanings of self-determination. It is one thing to say that citizens have a right "to a state of their own" and a very different thing to claim that foreigners may never intervene when such intervention is aimed, not at denying that right, but rather at reforming unfree institutions. Foreign states may intervene to uphold human rights without denying citizens their right

---

[21] *See* M. Pomerance, *Self-Determination in Law and Practice* 130–138 (1982).

[22] Beitz explains this distinction well:

The difference between these two aspects of state autonomy is that nonintervention imposes a negative requirement that other states not interfere, while self-determination imposes a positive requirement that other states (here, specifically, the colonial or dominant power) stop exercising control over entities claiming the right to be allowed independent statehood.

C. Beitz, *Political Theory and International Relations* 93 (1979) (hereinafter *Political Theory*).

[23] *See* his discussion in "Words," *supra* n. 15, at 176–78.

to "a state of their own," that is, their right to *external* self-determination. In fact, I argue below that interventions aimed at depriving citizens of "a state of their own" (wars of conquest or domination) are always unjust wars, and that in no sense may they be called "humanitarian."[24] We may therefore assume that external self-determination is mandated by an appropriate account of international morality.[25] But that assumption is not inconsistent with the claim that internal self-determination need not be accorded similar respect in cases where the result is a tyranny.

Assuming, then, that the principle of internal self-determination or nonintervention is at issue, the Mill-Walzer claim can be understood in two ways: as an empirical assertion or as a normative proposal. As an empirical claim, the argument holds that foreign nonintervention is a *necessary condition* for the enjoyment of human rights. In this view, there is a causal connection between the absence of foreign intervention and individual liberty. In support of this claim it is argued that since individuals have rights as members of political communities, international law, by protecting states, indirectly protects individual rights.[26] A further consequence is that *in fact* people who receive outside help to overthrow tyrants can never conquer the freedom they seek. Mill, for example, suggests that after a humanitarian intervention, "it is only a question in how few years or months that people will be enslaved."[27] In a sense, the argument is appealing because it does not give up the idea of human rights altogether. It only makes the empirical claim that human rights can only be established, enforced and observed as the result of a purely domestic political process. Political processes that do

---

[24] Thus, I reject the suggestion by some writers that accepting humanitarian intervention would validate acts like Hitler's invasion of Czechoslovakia. *See*, e.g., Franck & Rodley, "After Bangladesh: The Law of Humanitarian Intervention by Military Force," 67 *A.J.I.L.* 275, 284 (1973); Brownlie, "Thoughts on Kind-Hearted Gunmen," in *Humanitarian Intervention and the United Nations* 139, 143 (R. Lillich ed. 1973). Hitler's "humanitarian" reasons for invading Czechoslovakia and Mussolini's "civilized" justification for invading Abyssinia do not count. It is not the case that a government's mere words about humanitarian reasons will morally justify the intervention, just as after-the-fact hypocritical rationalization does not justify individual conduct. *See* the discussion *infra*, Chapter 6.

[25] *See* Beitz's appealing contractarian justification of the rejection of colonial rule. Beitz, *Political Theory*, *supra* n. 22, at 98–105.

[26] *See* T. Nardin, *Law, Morality, and the Relations of States* 238 (1983).

[27] Mill, Words, *supra* n. 15, at 174.

not yield free institutions, while regrettable, are preferable to foreign involvement or intervention in that process. The main reason is that in the latter case individuals do not fight for their rights and therefore do not learn the value of freedom. In short, self-determination is causally related to (is a necessary condition of) the enjoyment of individual rights.

Yet as a matter of history this is simply wrong. Many communities have conquered their freedom with outside help—history abounds in examples.[28] Conversely, all too frequently peoples are subjugated and subject to unspeakable suffering as the result of processes of pure self-determination. Take the example of the 1971 takeover in Uganda by Idi Amin.[29] Surely not even Mill or Walzer would say that this was an instance of the Uganda "people" exercising their right to self-determination. The "self" (the Ugandan people) did not "determine" anything. The "self" here is not the real people, but some mystical entity called the "nation" which "determines itself" through the "political process."[30] Suppose the alternatives for a foreign power were then (a) to let the Ugandan "political process" unfold, with the inevitable success of Amin, or (b) to intervene in order to prevent Amin from coming to power and allow free elections in Uganda.[31] Leaving aside for the moment what the correct course of action may be, if Mill and Walzer are claiming that freedom can never result from alternative (b), then this is simply falsified by experience. This is denied by some writers in spite of the empirical evidence. Stanley Hoffman, for example, endorses the Walzer/Mill view:

> [Beitz's view that self-determination is not a necessary condition for freedom] takes into account neither the importance of self-determination as a constitutive principle of international society . . . nor the fact that for most people independence is a precondition for social justice.[32]

---

[28] *See* the modern cases discussed in Chapter 8.

[29] For a thrilling account of Amin's reign, *see* M. Richardson, *After Amin, the Bloody Pearl* (1980).

[30] For a critique of the holistic assumptions of this kind of discourse, *see infra*, Chapters 3 and 4.

[31] Note that I am not yet taking into account the genocide actually committed by Amin against his own people. The issue here is whether self-determination is a condition for freedom, for which I need not presuppose genocide. For a full discussion of the Tanzanian intervention in Uganda, *see infra*, Chapter 8.

[32] S. Hoffman, *Duties Beyond Borders* 65 (1981).

This argument is unconvincing. To say that self-determination is a constitutive principle of international society does no more than restate the principle without justifying it. Further, Professor Hoffman is obviously referring to *external*, and not internal, self-determination. Humanitarian intervention by definition does not deny the people their right to independence.[33] Many persons enjoy human rights as a result of liberating foreign intervention. Consequently, the assertion that without self-determination (that is, with foreign intervention) the rest of human rights are meaningless is contradicted by the facts. Surely the Bengalis liberated by India did not consider the restoration of their human rights as meaningless. Internal self-determination, then, is not a necessary condition for freedom.[34]

The normative aspect of the Mill-Walzer claim is as follows. Even if self-determination is not a necessary condition for freedom, it nevertheless has *philosophical priority* over individual human rights. To sustain this claim, noninterventionists must show that there is something about self-determination that overrides the imperative of respect for individual rights. They must make some claims about the moral standing of governments, about the rights of states and about their relationship with the rights of citizens. Such claims usually focus on the proposition that the essential characteristic of statehood, sovereignty, gives rise to international rights of states which are held over and above the rights of its citizens.[35] In the rest of this chapter I shall examine the relativist objection: that humanitarian intervention is always unjustified because human rights standards do not possess any ascertainable transboundary

---

[33] Professor Hoffman, however, seems to endorse Walzer's justification of humanitarian intervention for extreme cases. Id. at 64.

[34] Of course, Mill and Walzer may be attempting to redefine "freedom" or "human rights" to mean "freedom conquered by the people's own efforts." In that case, their conclusion is just a tautology. For them, it does not matter how truly free in fact a given people are: If they have not attained that freedom by their own efforts they are not "really" free. Readers need not be reminded that we cannot reach any normative conclusions by stipulating definitions.

[35] That Walzer must make such an argument is made clear by his hypothetical example of whether Swedish officials should administer a wondrous chemical to Algerians in order to transform them into liberal democrats à la Swedish. *See* Walzer, "The Moral Standing of States," *supra* n. 19, at 225–226. By eliminating considerations relative to the evils of using military force, Walzer makes clear that there is something about states and governments that makes them worthy of protection regardless of their conformity with the requirements of justice.

meaning. In subsequent chapters I shall examine several nonutilitarian arguments usually offered in support of the sovereignty thesis: that states have a right to autonomy analogous to the individual right to autonomy and that the international representativeness or legitimacy of governments is based on facts other than explicit or implicit consent of the governed and the observance of human rights. I shall then discuss utilitarian arguments offered in support of the noninterventionist thesis.

IV. RELATIVISM AND PLURALISM

A frequent assertion of noninterventionists is that moral discourse, and especially rights discourse, can only possess meaning within concrete socioeconomic realities—within domestic societies.[36] Therefore, the argument runs, liberal criticism of social practices in foreign societies, especially in Third World societies, represents at best misguided attempts to extend the sphere of authority of our liberal-democratic values to social contexts in which by definition those values do not hold. Such an approach, we are assured, amounts to a form of imperialism, moral imperialism.[37] Even worse is to act on that condemnation; that is, forcibly to intervene in defense of human rights, for in that case we would be enforcing our own notions of morality upon foreigners. This is the position commonly known as moral relativism, that is, the ethical theory that denies the existence of transboundary ethical values, and consequently of any universal human rights standard. Of course, if relativism is true, the basis for the claim to intervene on behalf of human rights is removed. Indeed, if relativism is accepted, not only is humanitarian intervention tantamount to aggression, but any act of interference, such as open criticism for human rights abuses, is misplaced as well. The rejection of relativism is thus a necessary step to ground a theory of humanitarian intervention.

In his argument against a broad right of humanitarian intervention, Michael Walzer has defended a sophisticated version of relativism,

---

[36] See, e.g., Tushnet, "An Essay on Rights," 64 Tex. L. Rev. 1363, 1364–65 (1984).

[37] See, e.g., Batailler-Demichel, "Droits de l'homme et droits des peuples dans l'ordre international," in Le droit des peuples a disposer d'eux-mêmes. Mélanges offerts à Charles Chaumom 23, 30–31 (1984).

which he calls "pluralism."[38] In a reply to his critics, Walzer makes a distinction between domestic and international legitimacy. The first kind of legitimacy, he writes, is singular in character, and reflects our democratic values. Citizens of an illegitimate state in this sense have a right to revolt against the dictators. We (the foreigners) can also argue that the government is indeed illegitimate from the standpoint of appropriate principles of justice and does not represent the political community.[39] According to Walzer, then, at the verbal level we need not be relativists.

In contradistinction, international legitimacy is pluralist in character. "Here the judgments we make," writes Walzer, "reflect our recognition of diversity and our respect for communal integrity and for different patterns of cultural and political development."[40] If the citizens do not make use of their right to revolt against the dictators, foreigners cannot act in lieu of them. And so, out of deference to different cultures, foreigners are bound to respect (in the sense of not intervening by force) governments who extensively violate human rights, even where the citizens themselves have a right to revolt against the tyrants.[41] At the level of deeds, therefore, we ought to be relativists. Answering to a critic's charge that this self-determination means nothing more than the "right" to live in a civil society of almost any sort, Walzer replies, in connection with the example of the first failed Nicaraguan revolution, that this means the right to live in a society "of a Nicaraguan sort."[42] Notwithstanding his claims to the contrary, here Walzer leaves little room for extending moral reasoning across national boundaries. His principle of pluralism indicates that there are local moralities (a Nicaraguan morality, a European morality, a Chinese morality) and not a system of moral political principles held valid for all persons regardless of

---

[38] Walzer, "The Moral Standing," *supra* n. 19, at 215–16. Terry Nardin takes a similar view: "International law . . . expresses a concern for individual liberty . . . because it reinforces global pluralism." Nardin, *supra* n. 26, at 238–39.

[39] Walzer, "The Moral Standing of States," *supra* n. 19, at 215–16.

[40] Id.

[41] However, Walzer crucially concedes that that presumption can be ignored in case of massacre, enslavement or massive deportation. *See Wars, supra* n. 3, at 101–108; "The Moral Standing of States," *supra* n. 19, at 217.

[42] Walzer, "The Moral Standing of States," *supra* n. 19, at 220 (responding to Wasserstrom, Book Review, 92 *Harv. L. Rev.* 544 (1978).

geographic circumstances. Again, the logical consequence of this view seems to be that even criticism of human rights abuses would be inappropriate, but Walzer does not go that far. He concedes that we can make such criticisms, but what we cannot do is to *force* our notions of right and wrong on other peoples—their traditions, loyalties, "hidden currents" and feelings are different.[43] Therefore, we must let the political process work, we should not speed it up artificially, apart from moral support for those who fight for freedom. True, the outcome of the process may be a tyranny, but it is "their" tyranny. In short, "the opposition of philosophers is [not] a sufficient grounds for military invasion."[44] This is the main tenet of relativism: Judgments about human rights abuses are no more than opinions of philosophers. And since there are, after all, many contradictory philosophical opinions, we should not base our actions on such beliefs.[45] Walzer's pluralism, therefore, does not differ significantly from outright moral relativism. His claim is that the truth of moral propositions is confined within domestic societies, at least insofar as those propositions function as reasons for action. This is an important, far-reaching, and widespread philosophical claim, the inadequacy of which needs to be shown before proceeding with the analysis.

To analyze the moral status of relativism, several types of the doctrine must be carefully distinguished.[46] First, different societies have different perceptions of right and wrong. This assertion—which may be called "descriptive" relativism—finds support among anthropologists who consider themselves relativists.[47] Descriptive relativism has been challenged, mainly on the grounds that empirical research may be interpreted to show that there is no *basic* ethical disagreement even among the most disparate societies.[48] Be that as it may, the argument here does not depend upon the answer to this question.

---

[43] Walzer, "The Moral Standing of States," *supra* n. 19, at 215.

[44] Id. at 229.

[45] This claim is closely related to the claim, also defended by Walzer and others, that foreigners can never really understand the indigenous political process. I discuss this claim in Chapter 5.

[46] *See* Brandt, "Ethical Relativism", in 3 *Encyclopedia of Philosophy* 75 (P. Edwards ed. 1967).

[47] *See*, e.g., M. Herskovits, *Man and His Works* 61–78 (1949).

[48] *See* Brandt, *supra* n. 46, at 75.

The second type of relativism, metaethical relativism, asserts that it is impossible to discover moral truth. Metaethical relativism may take the form of a thesis about the meaning of moral terms:[49] The relativist can adopt either some version of emotivism[50] or a straight nihilist position.[51] A milder version of metaethical relativism contends that there is no valid *method* for moral reasoning; that is, no method that would have, on moral matters, the same persuasive force as scientific method.[52]

Normative relativism asserts instead that persons, depending on their cultural attachments, ought to do different things and have different rights.[53] This is the version of relativism with which I am concerned here. As a preliminary matter, neither descriptive nor metaethical relativism logically entails normative relativism. Descriptive relativism operates at a different logical level than its normative counterpart. Anthropological or descriptive relativism claims that different cultures in fact have different conceptions of morality. The normative relativist asserts that individuals of different cultures have different rights, and that they *ought* to do or to abstain from doing different things. It is therefore perfectly possible for the descriptive relativist to concede that different societies have different social practices and conflicting views about morality and yet consider some practices or views morally preferable to others.[54]

The relationship between metaethical and normative relativist theories is more complex, but the two theories are still logically distinguishable. The metaethical relativist doubts the possibility of demonstrating the correctness of any particular moral principle. Yet, as a matter of

---

[49] Id. at 75.

[50] For the emotivists, moral propositions are no more than interjections or emotive utterances. *See generally*, A. Ayer, *Language, Truth and Logic* (1946); C. L. Stevenson, *Ethics and Language* (1944).

[51] Nihilism, in this context, claims that moral terms lack any meaning whatsoever.

[52] Brandt, *supra* n. 46, at 76.

[53] *See* E. Westemarck, *supra* n. 6, ch. 5; Benedict, "Anthropology and the Abnormal," 10 *J. Gen. Psych.* 59 (1934). Even "relativism" is too charitable a name for this theory, which may properly be called instead "moral positivism." *See* the brilliant critique in 2 K. Popper, *The Open Society and Its Enemies* 392–96 (1966).

[54] *See* Douglas, "Morality and Culture," 93 *Ethics* 786 (1983). ("Two conversations are running parallel, one the philosophers' about the rational formulation of ethics, one the anthropologists' about the interaction between moral ideas and social institutions. The conversations, as they are set at the present time, will never converge.")

moral decision, he may adhere to some universal moral principles (thus rejecting normative relativism) while denying that any moral principle or system is demonstrably correct. An appealing illustration of the independence of ethics from metaethics is the methodology adopted by John Rawls. "Reflective equilibrium" is Rawls's suggested framework within which it is possible to make moral judgments without encountering the problem of demonstration. He suggests that moral conclusions may be reached by checking one's moral intuition against one's moral principles with the crucial proviso that both be subject to modification.[55] At the very least, Rawls demonstrates that it is unnecessary to have an infallible method of discovering moral truth in order to speak about the rights all people should enjoy. I analyze Rawls's theory in more detail below and in the next chapter.[56]

As a moral theory, normative relativism cannot withstand scrutiny.[57] First, its straightforward formulation reflects a basic incoherence. It affirms at the same time that (a) there are no universal moral principles; (b) one ought to act in accordance with the principles of one's own group, and (c), (b) is a universal moral principle.[58] David Lyons has argued that the typical anthropologists' version of relativism ("an act is right if, and only if, it accords with the norms of the agent's group") does not validate conflicting moral judgments because each group is regarded as a separate moral realm, and so in this sense it is not incoherent.[59] But the incoherence attached to normative relativism springs from the fact that the very assertion of universal relativism is self-contradictory, not from the fact that it validates conflicting substantive moral

---

[55] J. Rawls, *A Theory of Justice* 48 (1971) (hereinafter *Theory*).

[56] *See infra*, text accompanying 91–106. Of course, the acceptance of reflective equilibrium as a plausible description of moral methodology is completely independent from (1) the acceptance of Rawls's contractarian justification for principles of social justice; (2) the acceptance of the principles themselves; or (3) the acceptance of his solution to the priority problem. For a critique of Rawls's view that "undeveloped" societies may fail to observe human rights in certain situations, *see infra*, 91–105 and accompanying text. For a critique of his theory of international law, *see infra*, Chapter 3.

[57] Bernard Williams calls relativism "the anthropologists' heresy, possibly the most absurd view to have been advanced even in moral philosophy." B. Williams, *Morality: An Introduction to Ethics* 20 (1972).

[58] Id. at 20–21; Lyons, "Ethical Relativism and the Problem of Incoherence," 86 *Ethics* 107, 109 (1975–76).

[59] Id. at 109.

judgments. If it is true that no universal moral principles exist, then the relativist engages in self-contradiction by stating the universality of the relativist principle.[60] As Bernard Williams observed, this is a "logically unhappy attachment of a nonrelative morality of toleration or noninterference to a view of morality as relative."[61]

However, this objection over the incoherence of normative relativism is not decisive. Normative relativism can be reformulated to avoid the threat of incoherence as follows: (a) there are no universal moral principles, save one; (b) one ought to act in accordance with the principles of one's own group, and; (c) the only universal moral principle is (b).[62] Yet, if the normative relativist is also a metaethical relativist, he cannot justify why (b) is a universal moral principle. If the relativist has a method of discovering universal moral principles—for example, Rawls's "reflective equilibrium" or the utilitarian principle—then it is difficult to see why the only principle yielded by such method would be (b) above. Thus, this new version of relativism avoids inconsistency, but it is epistemologically weak.

A second problem with normative relativism is that it overlooks an important feature of moral discourse, its *universalizability*.[63] Independently of substantive morals, when we talk about right and wrong or rights and duties, and act accordingly, we are logically committed to "act in accordance with the generic rights of [our] recipients as well as of [our]selves," on pain of self-contradiction.[64] This not only means that

---

[60] This problem resembles the one exhibited by ideologism, the theory that everything is ideology, which for some mysterious reason does not apply to itself. I do not discuss here Gilbert Harman's narrower version of moral relativism because Harman intended for his version to apply only to "inner" judgments, i.e., judgments that someone who had already settled upon a moral code ought or not to have acted in a certain way. His theory does not apply to the judgment that a given institution is unjust, which is most relevant for my purposes. Harman, "Moral Relativism Defended," 84 *Phil. Rev.* 3, 4 (1975). *See* the critique of Harman's theory by Copp, "Harman on Internalism, Relativism and Logical Form," 92 *Ethics* 227 (1981–82).

[61] B. Williams, *supra* n. 57, at 21. *See also* the profound critique of relativism in B. Williams, *Ethics and the Limits of Philosophy*, ch. 9 (1985).

[62] On this point I am indebted to David Kaye.

[63] The requirement of universalizability is usually traced to book IV, I. Kant, *Critique of Practical Reason* § 436 (L. Beck trans. 1949). It has been revived in recent philosophical literature, mainly by A. Gewirth, *Reason and Morality* (1978) and M. Singer, *Generalization in Ethics* (1961).

[64] *See* A. Gewirth, *Human Rights: Essays on Justification and Application* 128–41 (1982).

we cannot make exceptions in our own favor, but also that individuals must be treated as equally entitled to basic rights regardless of contingent factors such as their cultural surroundings. This requirement of universalizability may be thought of as having a logical nature,[65] or alternatively as being a requirement of moral plausibility.[66] If the first approach is correct, the relativist is simply refusing to engage in meaningful moral discourse. Under the second approach, the relativist endorses the highly implausible position that the moral point of view need not be impartial or universal, and that in moral matters we can pass judgments containing proper names, and that consequently we may make exceptions in our own (or in our own group's) favor.[67]

The relativist has two responses to the universalizability argument. First, the relativist may argue that belonging to different communities is a morally relevant circumstance.[68] Universalizability, he would argue, is not violated when individuals are situated in different factual conditions. To say that if A ought to do X in circumstances C, then B also ought to do X in circumstances C, presupposes a similarity of circumstances. If such circumstances vary substantially, that is, if cultural creeds and practices differ, then we would not violate the universalizability requirement by holding that individuals who belong to different cultures ought to have different basic rights. Sometimes relativists articulate this position in the form of an attack on the assertion of the existence of abstract rights, as opposed to the assertion of concrete rights and duties in materially defined social conditions.[69]

---

[65] *See* id. at 89; book IV, I. Kant, *supra* n. 63, §436 ("All maxims have . . . a form, which consists in universality; and in this respect the formula of the moral imperative requires that the maxims be chosen as though they should hold as universal laws of nature"); M. Singer, *supra* n. 63, at 34 ("The generalization principle . . . is involved in or presupposed in every genuine moral judgment, for it is an essential part of . . . distinctively moral terms"); Frankena, "The Concepts of Morality," 63 *J. Phil.* 688, 695–96 (1966). Professor D'Amato makes a convincing linguistic case against relativism, showing that when we ordinarily refer to some conduct as "moral," we usually mean that it is universally valid. Conversely, when we are prepared to be tolerant about some conduct (for example, sexual habits), we regard such conduct as "mores" or "custom," and not as "morality in the stronger sense." D'Amato, "Lon Fuller and Substantive Natural Law," 26 *Am. J. Juris.* 202, 204 (1981).

[66] *See*, e.g., Rawls, *Theory*, *supra* n. 55, at 132 (principles apply to everyone by virtue of their being moral persons).

[67] *See* J. Hospers, *Human Conduct*, 276–77, 285 (1972).

[68] *See* the elementary but excellent discussion in id., at 283–90.

[69] *See* Tushnet, *supra* n. 36, at 1363, 1364–65 ("It does not advance understanding to speak of rights in the abstract. It matters only that some specific right is or is not

This argument is not convincing. The fact that one belongs to a particular social group or community is hardly a *morally* relevant circumstance. The place of birth and cultural environment of an individual are not related to his moral worth or to his entitlement to human rights. An individual's claim to basic rights cannot be ignored by his being born in one society rather than in another, for one deserves neither one's cultural environment nor one's place of birth. There is nothing, for example, in the nature of a Third World woman that makes her less eligible for the enjoyment of human rights (though she might perhaps consensually waive her rights[70]) than a woman in a Western democracy. If the initial conditions are not morally distinguishable, the requirement of universalizability fully applies to statements about individual rights, even where the agents are immersed in different cultural environments.

There is another important fact of moral life that militates against the relativist position. Relativists confuse the circumstances in which one learns moral concepts with the *meaning* of those concepts.[71] A person who learns a moral concept (such as that of "wrong") by applying it in situations peculiar to his culture, is perfectly able to apply that concept to a set of facts he has never encountered before. As Bernard Williams said in his most recent work:

> The fact that people can and must react when they are confronted with another culture, and do so by applying their existing notions—also by reflecting on them—seems to show that the

recognized in some specific social setting. . . . In this way rights become identified with particular cultures and are relativized"). Tushnet's article astonishes in several regards. For example, he states that "[t]he use of rights in contemporary discourse impeded advances by progressive social forces." Id. at 1364. Such criticism, of course, assumes that it is morally desirable for the "progressive social forces" (whatever that means) to dictate conducts and impose ends and conceptions of moral excellence on other individuals (i.e., to those who presumably would be accused of militating in the ranks of the "regressive social forces"). John Rawls artfully responded to this assertion in an often-quoted sentence: "Each person possesses an inviolability founded on justice that even the welfare of society as a whole cannot override." Rawls, *Theory, supra* n. 55, at 3. This is the thrust of the idea of rights in the abstract.

[70] One must be careful not to overstate this exception. Dictators typically assert that they represent the people or that they have their support. Even if a particular dictator enjoys popular support, however, such support does not entitle him to oppress the dissenters who have not consented to his rule. The majoritarian principle is thus useless when assessing human rights violations. *See* the discussion in Rawls, *Theory, supra* n. 55, at 356–62. *See infra*, Chapter 4.

[71] *See* R. Trigg, *Reason and Commitment* 20 (1973).

ethical thought of a given culture can always stretch beyond its boundaries. Even if there is no way in which divergent ethical beliefs can be brought to converge by independent inquiry or rational argument, this fact will not imply relativism. Each outlook may still be making claims it intends to apply to the whole world, not just to that part of it which is his 'own world.'[72]

By claiming that moral judgments only have meaning within particular cultures, the relativist underestimates the ability of the human intellect to confront, in a moral sense, new situations.

The relativist's second objection to universalizability has a logical nature. As noted above, the relativist may contend that (a) his only principle is that culture determines human rights, and (b) (a) is universal.[73] The relativist thus claims that he universalizes a principle after all. But the requirement of universalizability applies to *substantive* moral statements, which (a) is not. The principle that culture determines human rights is a principle of *renvoi*; that is, it refers us to different normative systems in order to determine the rights of individuals. The principle does not establish rules governing the rights of any particular individual. Universalizability requires that *if* we make a statement about the right of X to freedom of thought, we are committed to grant that right to Y under similar, morally relevant, circumstances. Because the relativist principle does not address issues of substantive morality in this respect, it is not susceptible of being universalized in the same way. The violation of universalizability becomes apparent when one translates the relativist principle into substantive moral statements (i.e., X, who lives in culture C1, has the right R; while Y, who lives in culture C2, does not have the right R). In other words, the relativist principle may be regarded as *metamoral*, even where it is asserted as the basis of normative morality.[74]

Third, normative relativism runs counter to the principle that persons have moral worth *qua* persons and must be treated as ends in themselves, not as functions of the ends of others—a non-trivial version of

---

[72] B. Williams, *Ethics and the Limits of Philosophy, supra* n. 61, at 159.

[73] *See supra* text accompanying n. 57–62.

[74] The characterization of relativism as metamoral differs from the assertion of meta-ethical relativism. As indicated above, normative relativism does not need support from metaethical skepticism. But normative relativism is still not strictly a substantive moral theory. It only tells us where to look for the norms that determine individual rights.

the Kantian principle of autonomy.[75] This principle or moral worth forbids the imposition upon individuals of cultural standards that impair human rights. Even if relativists could show that authoritarian practices are somehow required by a community—a claim that in many cases remains to be proven—they would still fail to explain why individuals should surrender their basic rights to the ends of the community. If the "untouchables" in India are discriminated against, it is not enough to say that a tradition, no matter how old and venerable, requires such discrimination. The only defense consistent with the principle of autonomy would be a showing that each pariah has consented to waive his rights. However, because of the mystical and holistic assumptions that often underlie relativism, presumably the relativist would not regard such a test as relevant or necessary.

Finally, there is another way out of normative relativism that does not necessitate postulating the ontological existence of an objective morality. One could subscribe to a theory of "primary goods" along the lines suggested by John Rawls.[76] The idea is that whatever one's system of ends, there are things that everybody would want as necessary means, regardless of what else they want. And liberties would be at the top of the list of primary goods.[77] If this thesis is plausible, then, even though there is no objective Platonic morality, there exists some moral objectivity in an important sense: that related to the satisfaction of rational desires.[78] Whether one accepts the natural rights model in the traditional sense, or the more modest "self-interest" model, is immaterial for the thesis suggested here.

Quite apart from the moral implausibility of normative relativism, it is worth noting the extreme conservatism of the doctrine.[79] Normative

---

[75] *See* Ping-Cheung Lo, "A Critical Reevaluation of the Alleged 'Empty Formalism' of Kantian Ethics," 91 *Ethics* 181, 182 (1980–81).

[76] *See* Rawls, *supra* n. 55, at 92–95.

[77] *See* id. at 93.

[78] Another appealing attempt to show that some moral principles would be accepted by all persons on grounds of rational interest can be found in D. Gauthier, *Morals by Agreement* (1986).

[79] A similar point is made by Amy Gutman in her response to modern critics of liberalism. Gutman, "Communitarian Critics of Liberalism," 41 *Phil. & Pub. Aff.* 308, 309 (1985). As the text demonstrates, anti-liberal theories that emphasize the priority of communal values are necessarily relativist.

relativism tells us that if a particular society has always had authoritarian practices it is morally defensible that it continue to have them. It works as a typical argument of authority: It has always been like this, this is our culture, so we need not undertake any changes.[80] Normative relativism thus conceived amounts to the worst form of moral and legal positivism: It asserts that the rules enacted by the group are necessarily correct as a matter of critical morality.[81]

Admittedly, the force of the critique of relativism articulated here depends on the intuitive acceptance of certain moral premises. The relativist can successfully resist the attack by rejecting metaethical relativism so as to avoid logical incoherence, denying that universalizability is an ingredient of moral judgments, and rejecting the principle of autonomy. But this is a high price to pay. Normative relativism would then be a poor and implausible moral doctrine, and it is doubtful that many relativists, upon careful reflection, would accept the harsh applications. Despite being vindicated as the supposed basis of international law, relativism reveals profound flaws both in its underlying philosophical structure and in its practical consequences.

---

[80] Tushnet asserts that his radical critique of rights "is a Schumpeterian act of creative destruction that may help us to build societies that transcend the failures of capitalism." Tushnet, *supra* n. 36, at 1363. This apocalypsis is later expressed in relativistic terms: "The critique of rights takes a strong relativist position: it insists that rights-talk is meaningful only when placed within a full social and legal context." Id. at 1394. Thus, relativism is to Tushnet a basic assumption of radical politics, an essential underpinning of left-wing scholarship and politics. Yet nothing is farther from the truth. Relativism is tantamount to moral positivism and to "legalism," two of the most reactionary doctrines in the history of ideas. Tushnet himself seems to realize this. He tells us that "to say that some specific right is (or ought to be) recognized in a specific culture is to say that the culture is what it is, ought to recognize what its deepest commitments are, or ought to be transformed into some other culture." Id. at 1365. Thus, for Tushnet the only way of talking about rights is to describe rights as they are recognized by this or that culture. Those are the only *existing* rights. Because he has been precluded from even talking about rights in the abstract, he has lost the best and most effective philosophical tool for criticizing positive law: the idea that individuals have rights independent of contingent cultural standards. Thus, when criticizing a particular culture, a Tushnet-type relativist may not rely on the proposition that individuals are entitled to some other social arrangement or that their rights have been violated.

[81] This indictment only attacks what Professor Carlos Nino has called "ideological positivism," the theory that the norms of a group are necessarily correct as a matter of critical morality. See C. Nino, *Introdución al Análisis del Derecho,* 32–35 (1980). I am not concerned here with the more fertile, although ultimately unsuccessful, concept of "methodological positivism," that is, of the separation between law and morality defended by H. L. A. Hart and others.

V. TWO BY-PRODUCTS OF RELATIVISM: ELITISM AND CONSPIRACY

I will now discuss two doctrines closely associated with relativism. The first asserts that one can appropriately honor human rights in certain societies, usually the most sophisticated ones, but not in others, on account, for example, of the latter's insufficient economic development or their fundamentally different perceptions of social values. This doctrine, which can be called "elitism," necessarily follows from relativism. The second theory states that the law of human rights results from a conspiracy of the West to perpetuate imperialism. The "conspiracy theory," by contrast, does not follow inevitably from, and is not required by, cultural relativism.

During the dark years of the military dictatorship in Argentina, one commonly heard many well-intentioned commentators complain that Argentina, a country that springs from Western tradition, could not be forgiven for not respecting human rights. The corollary of this position seems to be that citizens in countries that do not spring from a Western tradition somehow do not have the same moral entitlements as Westerners and therefore their governments are justified in not complying with the international law of human rights. This elitist theory of human rights holds that human rights are good for the West but not for much of the non-Western world. Surprisingly, the elitist theory of human rights is quite popular in the democratic West, not only in conservative circles but also, and even more often, among liberal and radical groups.[82] The right-wing version of elitism embodies the position, closely associated with colonialism, that backward peoples cannot govern themselves and that democracy only works for superior cultures. The left-wing version, often articulated by Western liberals who stand for civil rights at home but support leftist dictatorships abroad, reflects a belief that we should be tolerant of and respect the cultural identity and political self-determination of Third World countries (although, of course, it is seldom the people who choose to have dictators; more often the dictators decide for them).

---

[82] See, e.g., Pollis, "Liberal, Socialist and Third World Perspectives on Human Rights," in Toward a Human Rights Framework 1, 22–23 (A. Pollis & P. Schwab eds. 1982); Tushnet, supra n. 36, at 1394.

The position of relativist scholars who are human rights advocates eloquently illustrates the difficulties of elitism.[83] Such persons find themselves in an impossible dilemma. On the one hand they are anxious to articulate an international human rights standard, while on the other they wish to respect the autonomy of individual cultures. The result is a vague warning against "ethnocentrism,"[84] and well-intentioned proposals that are deferential to tyrannical governments and insufficiently concerned with human suffering. Because the consequence of either version of elitism is that certain national or ethnic groups are somehow less entitled than others to the enjoyment of human rights, the theory is fundamentally immoral and replete with racist overtones.

Another claim associated with relativism is what Karl Popper might describe as the conspiracy theory of human rights.[85] This theory asserts that human rights are a Machiavellian creation of the West calculated to impair the economic development of the Third World. Starting from the Marxist assumption that civil and political rights are "formal" bourgeois freedoms that serve only the interests of the capitalists,[86] the conspiracy theory holds that human rights serve the same purpose in the international arena. It sees them as instruments of domination because they are indissolubly tied to the right to property, and because in the field of international economic relations, the human rights movement fosters free and unrestricted trade, which seriously hurts the economies of Third World nations. Furthermore, proponents of the conspiracy theory charge that human rights advocacy amounts to moral imperialism.[87] In short, "the effect, if not the design, of such an exclusive political preoccupation [is] to leave the door open to the most ruthless and predatory economic forces in international society."[88]

---

[83] *See,* e.g., Pollis, *supra* n. 82, 22–23.

[84] Id. Another example is E. McWhinney, *United Nations Law Making* 209 (1984) ("eurocentrism").

[85] *See* K. Popper, *supra* n. 53, at 94.

[86] *See,* e.g., Marx, "On the Jewish Question," in *The Marx-Engels Reader* 42 (2d ed. Tucker 1978).

[87] For a contemporary Marxist perspective on human rights, see Weichelt, "On the Historical Nature of Basic and Human Rights" in *Legal Theory-Comparative Law. Studies in Honour of Professor Imre Szabo* 419, 420–21 (1984).

[88] McWhinney, *supra* n. 84, at 211. Cf. Tushnet, *supra* n. 36, at 1398 (the fact of unnecessary human suffering alone is enough to support the critique of "rights" theory).

The conspiracy theory, however, fails to justify the link between the support for human rights and support for particular property rights or trade policies—a fundamental flaw. Human rights claims need not presuppose any position in this regard. Moreover, to claim that civil and political rights must be suppressed as a necessary condition for the improvement of Third World economies grossly distorts the facts. As Louis Henkin put it:

> [H]ow many hungry are fed, how much industry is built, by massacre, torture, and detention, by unfair trials and other injustices, by abuse of minorities, by denials of freedoms of conscience, by suppression of political association and expression?[89]

The contention that the West imposed human rights on the world and that "poor peoples" do not care about freedom is simply a myth. That claim is contradicted by the growing awareness in the Third World of the need for reinforcing the respect for human rights.[90] Further, even if, *gratia argumentandi*, some Western plot created human rights philosophy, that fact alone would not necessarily undermine its moral value. Conspiracy theories (such as vulgar Marxism, "ideologism," and Critical Legal Studies) assert that the true explanation of a phenomenon consists of discovering the groups of people or hidden interests which are interested in the occurrence of the phenomenon and which have plotted to bring it about.[91] While conspiracies do occur, the fact that they rarely succeed ultimately disproves the conspiracy theory. Social life is too complex and the unforeseen consequences of social action

---

[89] L. Henkin, *The Rights of Man Today* 130 (1978).

[90] Cf. the statement by the All Africa Council of Churches/World Council of Churches (1976), cited by Haile, "Human Rights, Stability and Development in Africa: Some Observations on Concept and Reality," 24 *Va. J. Int'l L.* 575, 584 (1984) (describing the system of checks and balances that prevented gross abuses of human and civil rights in traditional African societies); and the statement by the Arab Lawyers' Union at their meeting of December 1983, reprinted in 9 *Human Rights Int'l Rep.* 564 (1984) ("The basis of the legitimacy of any regime or system of government is related to its effective observance of human rights, particularly those set forth in the Universal Declaration.") *See also* Nickel, "Cultural Diversity and Human Rights," in *International Human Rights: Contemporary Issues* 43, 45 (J. Nelson & V. Green eds. 1980) (human rights appeal to many peoples, not just to Westerners).

[91] *See* Popper, *supra* n. 53, at 94.

too many to support conspiracy as the explanation of every social phenomenon.[92] Institutions originally designed for a certain purpose often turn against their creators. The Magna Carta was originally extracted from King John of England by some nobles just for their own benefit, yet it turned into the springboard for the protection of individual rights in the oldest liberal democracy in the world. Similarly, even if the law of human rights was originally conceived, say, as an ideological tool against communism, today human rights have achieved a universal scope and inspire the struggle against all types of oppression. South Africa is another case in point. Perhaps in 1948 the framers of the Universal Declaration on Human Rights did not intend for it to apply to the black majority in South Africa. Perhaps they thought that democracy "among whites" was enough to comply with the Declaration. The international community has subsequently rejected that interpretation, however, and today the law and philosophy of human rights are the main bases for the claims for freedom by the non-white majority in South Africa. In short: The circumstances surrounding the origins of human rights principles are irrelevant to their intrinsic value and cannot detract from their beneficial features.

VI. JOHN RAWLS AND CULTURAL RELATIVISM

The relativist trap is one that is much more difficult to avoid than one would think at first sight. Vivid illustration of this is the evolution of the thought of John Rawls on the matter of whether the principles he proposes, and especially his "equal liberty" principle, hold for all kinds of societies.[93] Needless to say, the answer to this question is crucial to the issue of whether it is possible to provide a contractarian foundation for international human rights. Here I will confine myself to discussing Rawls's recent departure from the cosmopolitan and universalist nature of his original theory of justice. I shall leave his theory of international law and intervention for the next chapter. First, however, it will be useful to give a brief summary of Rawls's celebrated theory of domestic justice.

---

[92] See id. at 95.

[93] Rawls's first principle of justice is roughly equivalent to civil and political human rights. See generally Rawls, Theory, supra n. 55; id., "The Basic Liberties and Their Priority," in 3 The Tanner Lectures on Human Values 1 (1982) (hereinafter Tanner Lectures). See also R. Martin, Rawls and Rights (1985). For recent fully developed views of John Rawls on this matter, see John Rawls, Political Liberalism (1994). The criticism in the text remains valid.

Rawls claims that just principles for domestic societies are those that would be chosen by free, rational parties in a situation of uncertainty—in the "original position."[94] According to Rawls, the parties in the original position would choose the principle of equal liberty (roughly corresponding to civil and political rights) and the principles that social and economic inequalities are only permissible if they work to the advantage of the worst-off group in society—the "difference" principle.[95] These principles result from the parties in the original position applying the *maximin* rule of rational choice, according to which individuals in a situation of uncertainty rationally choose that course of action that contains the minimum of losses should the worst alternative occur.[96] These two principles—equal liberty and difference principle—are ranked in lexical order, so that liberty has priority over social and economic claims.[97] Rawls calls this theory "justice as fairness."

In *A Theory of Justice*, Rawls imposed a significant limitation on the applicability of this theory of justice. That constraint is basically that where economic conditions are harsh, equal liberty, i.e., civil and political human rights, may sometimes be curtailed, but only to the extent necessary to achieve the social conditions that will allow future full enjoyment of those rights. Writes Rawls:

---

[94] Rawls, *Theory, supra* n. 55, at 11–12.

[95] The full statement of the principles of justice that according to Rawls the parties would choose are the following:

First Principle

Each person is to have an equal right to the most extensive total system of equal liberties compatible with a similar system of liberty for all.

Second Principle

Social and economic equalities are to be arranged so that they are both:

(a) to the greatest benefit of the least advantaged, consistent with the just savings principle, and

(b) attached to offices and positions open to all under conditions of fair equality of opportunity.
Id. at 302.

Recently Rawls has somewhat modified the statement of the first principle, substituting "fully adequate scheme" of equal liberties for "most extensive total system of equal liberties." *See* Rawls, *Tanner Lectures, supra,* n. 93, at 5. This amendment is immaterial for our purposes.

[96] Rawls, *Theory, supra* n. 55, at 152 ff.

[97] Id. at 40–45.

> Thus in adopting a serial order [i.e., giving priority to equal liberty over economic well-being] we are in effect making a special assumption, namely, that . . . the conditions of . . . society, whatever they are, admit the effective realization of the equal liberties.[98]

It follows that when that is not the case, i.e., when material conditions, whatever they are, do not admit the effective realization of human rights, these rights can be curtailed or ignored, presumably to effect some redistribution of wealth or increase in the national income, but always with the purpose of achieving the conditions of "moderate scarcity" under which the enjoyment of liberties is possible.[99] This limitation has important consequences for international human rights. Because there are many societies where the material conditions are significantly harsher than in the democratic West, "justice as fairness" apparently would not hold for them, although of course it would be a matter of establishing precisely at which point on the economic scale curtailment of human rights is justified. In Rawls's defense one might say that because it is morally justified to limit human rights *only* to the extent necessary to create the material conditions necessary to their full enjoyment, this limitation does not render his theory hopelessly relativist. Political ideologies and methods of government that deny those rights as a matter of principle, such as fascism, communism, and Moslem fundamentalism, are seemingly never justified. So Rawls's original limitation, while not entirely convincing (why are poor individuals less capable of enjoying freedom?)[100] seems compatible with a contractarian foundation of international human rights. Further, there are some interesting consequences of this view for international relations that I cannot pursue here. If rights are a part of justice, and justice can fully apply only when the circumstances of justice are present, then pro-human rights nations perhaps have an obligation to help raise the economic level of Third World countries for that reason.[101]

However, in his most recent article Rawls explicitly limited his theory of justice to societies that are *already* constitutional democracies,

---

[98] Id. at 151–52.

[99] *See* id. at 126–30.

[100] *See* B. Barry, *The Liberal Theory of Justice* 77 (1973).

[101] On international distributive justice, *see generally* Beitz, *supra* n. 22.

thereby refusing to extend his case for human rights beyond the democratic industrial West, or even perhaps beyond the Anglo-Saxon world.[102] While Rawls cautiously warns us that he does not want to prejudge the larger issue of the validity of justice as fairness for other kinds of societies,[103] it is hard to avoid the conclusion that Rawls has made a crucial concession to relativism and its authoritarian implications. This new version of justice as fairness is much more relativistic than the initial limitation imposed in A Theory of Justice—i.e., that curtailment of human rights is only allowed to pave the way for the effective exercise of liberty. By allowing for the possibility that other—i.e., non-Western—societies may legitimately refuse to value liberty, Rawls seems to have become sensitive to the relativist attacks. The main thrust of those attacks is simply that the "primary goods" that according to Rawls the parties would pursue in the original position,[104] and especially liberty, are not goods that it is rational for all people to pursue no matter what else they want.

There is a decisive objection to the relativist version of justice as fairness. Despite Rawls's disclaimer to avoid prejudging the larger issue of the global validity of justice as fairness, his parochial confinement of social contract theory to Western (or Anglo-Saxon) societies is inconsistent with a crucial pillar of his theory: the assertion of fundamental moral traits of persons. Already Professor D'Amato has pointed out that in several passages of A Theory of Justice Rawls conveyed the impression that his theory concerned mankind in general, because of his emphasis on universal traits of persons.[105] More recently Rawls supplied as grounds for the priority of liberty the possession by persons of two powers of moral personality:

> These two powers are the capacity for a sense of right and justice (the capacity to honor fair terms of cooperation and thus to be reasonable), and the capacity for a conception of the good (and thus to be rational).[106]

---

[102] See Rawls, "Justice as Fairness: Political not Metaphyscial," 14 Phil. & Pub. Aff. 223, 225 (1985) (hereinafter "Political not Metaphysical").

[103] Id. at 225.

[104] See Rawls, Theory, supra n. 55, at 90–95.

[105] See A. D'Amato, Jurisprudence 260–61 (1984).

[106] Rawls, Tanner Lectures, supra n. 93, at 13–18.

Rawls then proceeded to specify further traits of individuals *qua* moral persons, notably self-respect. Self-respect, according to Rawls,

[I]s rooted in our self-confidence as a fully cooperating member of society capable of pursuing a worthwhile conception of the good over a complete life. Thus self-respect presupposes the development and exercise of both moral powers and therefore an effective sense of justice.[107]

Now, to maintain that justice as fairness with its priority of liberty applies only to Western democracies, one has to take the position that persons in non-Western societies do not possess these fundamental moral traits; that persons in such societies are incapable of pursuing "a worthwhile conception of the good" without resorting to violence and intolerance; that they are somehow inept to develop and exercise moral powers; that they are either inherently unreasonable or irrational; in short, one has to defend an elitist theory of human rights. I argued above that such a theory is unacceptable. Again, if Rawls's assumptions about fundamental traits of persons are true, then they are true for all persons. Then Rawls has the burden of demonstrating why it is that although all persons (and not only citizens of Western democracies) possess these traits, justice as fairness and the priority of liberty do not hold for non-Western societies. If the principle of equal liberty derived from social contract theory is sound, then it is, at that basic level, sound for any human society. Variations in political, legal and economic organization do not affect the universal validity of human rights derived from appropriate principles of critical morality.

It may be thought that my critique of Rawls's new relativism is unfair for the following reason.[108] We would not morally worry about intervening in other countries at all unless we valued their citizens as persons and thought of them as worthy of self-respect. So Rawls's noninterventionist position is really evidence that he does value citizens of other nations in this sense. If Rawls really thought that persons in some cultures lacked these traits, then he could argue (as he surely would not want to do) that we can permissibly treat them any way we feel like, including invading them, subjugating them, and even killing them. In

---

[107] Id.

[108] I am indebted to Jeffrie Murphy on this point.

short, Rawls's relativism breeds tolerance, while the caricature that I have suggested would breed just the opposite—aggression and subjugation.

But this objection to my critique stems from a failure to distinguish between two different kinds of rights. Rights against the state, human rights, are the primary rights. Other types of rights, and particularly the right *to* a nation-state, are derivative. One has a duty to respect the foreigners' right to have their own state and government provided that that is what the foreigner wants—that he lives in a state where his rights are respected. If this is the case, it is correct to say that a Rawls-type noninterventionist position is grounded on respect for persons. But where those persons' *individual rights* are violated by their government, a hands-off policy reflects a respect *only* for the *second* type of rights, the derivative right to a state "of your own." But these derivative rights have collapsed once individual or primary rights are thwarted. No right to a "government of your own" exists independently of the moral standing of that government in terms of rights observance. A Rawls-type noninterventionism-relativism fails to respect persons in the sense described. For such a position grants primacy to the mystical sanctity of the state over the individual rights of those very same persons that this "tolerant" position purports to protect.

A theory of justice that serves to explain only what most Westerners think about justice is at best a philosophically uninteresting exercise. Furthermore, this relativist version of justice as fairness fails to explain the whole area of international human rights. Therefore, an extension of contract theory designed to provide an ethical foundation to this important body of international law must be an enterprise well worth undertaking. Methodologically, then, one can simply choose to ignore the limitation and insist on the attempt to globalize justice as fairness, *malgré* the reluctance of its author to do so.[109] For our purposes it is best, therefore, to adhere to the cosmopolitanism of *A Theory of Justice* and disregard Rawls's subsequent retreat to relativism.

---

[109] Two interesting efforts in that sense are Skubik, "Two Models for a Rawlsian Theory of International Law and Justice," 14 *Denv. J. Int'l L. & Pol.* 231 (1986); and Pogge, "Globalizing Justice as Fairness" (unpublished manuscript, 1987).

We do make moral judgments across boundaries. We normally do not regard contingent national borders as somehow being also "moral borders."[110] This empirical truth about ordinary moral language is also philosophically sound. If human rights have any meaning at all, then they have a universal, transboundary meaning.[111] In the words of Luban, human rights "accrue to people no matter what country they live in and regardless of history and traditions."[112] Relativists are wrong, then, in asserting that cultural differences are sufficient grounds for prohibiting humanitarian intervention. No cultural tradition can justify a violation of basic human rights. Our notions about political philosophy are either right or wrong, but they cannot be right "for us" and wrong "for them."

While inadequate when applied to human rights, the idea of pluralism contains an important insight about international relations: We must accord respect to different customs, ways of life and institutional arrangements that *do not* impinge upon basic human rights. Different conceptions of individual excellence should be respected;[113] in particular, economic arrangements of *different* types are consistent with human rights observance. It follows that it would be wrong to interfere in another society on the grounds, say, that it has a centralized or planned economy, where such planning is not at the same time part of a broader governmental practice which violates human rights. I shall return to this important point later.[114]

Of course, the rejection of relativism alone does not establish that humanitarian intervention, or the use of force to protect rights, is morally justified. Even accepting the validity of an international human rights standard, as indeed most lawyers and philosophers do, humanitarian intervention can be opposed on account of the moral justification of the state, or on other ethical constraints upon the use of transboundary force. Those arguments need to be examined.

---

[110] *See generally* C. Beitz, *Political Theory, supra* n. 22, Part One. For a lucid study of the moral significance of national boundaries, *see* Lichtenberg, "National Boundaries and Moral Boundaries: A Cosmopolitan View," in *Boundaries. National Autonomy and Its Limits* 79 (P. G. Brown and H. Shue eds., 1981).

[111] This is true also as a matter of positive international law. *See* my article "International Human Rights and Cultural Relativism," 25 *Va. J. Intl'l L.* 869, 875–884 (1985).

[112] Luban, "The Romance of the Nation-State," 9 *Phil. & Pub. Aff.* 392, 396 (1980).

[113] *See* Rawls, *Tanner Lectures, supra* n. 93, at 17–18.

[114] *See* the discussion of Rawls's theory of international law in Chapter 3.

CHAPTER 3

THE HEGELIAN MYTH

I. HEGEL AND CLASSICAL INTERNATIONAL LAW WRITERS

A classic argument for nonintervention regards the state as holding a right of autonomy, or freedom, analogous to the freedom to which individuals are entitled within civil society. It is reasonable to suppose that we have a moral duty not to interfere with a person's liberty to pursue his or her ends as long as that pursuit does not impair the equal liberty of others.[1] Similarly, it is argued, we have a moral duty not to interfere with a nation-state pursuing its ends through the unfolding of an indigenous process of self-determination. The state is regarded as a moral being, capable of making moral choices, of being autonomous in a moral sense, and consequently capable of having rights *qua* state-rights that are logically independent from the rights of the individuals that populate the state. Just as persons' moral choices deserve respect from others, so state choices deserve respect from foreigners. Foreign intervention is a violation of that autonomy, even when it is undertaken for benign purposes. I shall call this idea "The Hegelian Myth."[2]

Classic international legal scholarship has presented two distinct versions of the Hegelian Myth. The mild version regards the state as a

---

[1] *See* C. Beitz, *Political Theory and International Relations* 76 (1979).

[2] For an extended philosophical criticism of the Hegelian Myth, *see* F. R. Tesón, "The Kantian Theory of International Law," 92 *Colum. L. Rev.* 53 (1992); F. R. Tesón, "International Abductions, Low-Intensity Conflicts and State Sovereignty: A Moral Inquiry," 31 *Colum. J. Transnat'l L.* 551 (1994).

moral entity, but acknowledges some limit to the lawful exercise of sovereignty by recognizing a restricted right of intervention for cases of extreme tyranny. The strong version of the Hegelian Myth recognizes no such limits. The state is seen as a free entity, meaning here by freedom the absolute right of rulers not to be interfered with in their dealings with subjects. The combined force of Hegel's philosophy and nineteenth-century legal positivism weakened the humanitarian component of the notion of sovereignty, and soon the second trend prevailed.

The first group, represented by Grotius and Vattel, postulated the notion of international law as deeply ingrained in the law of nature. Because the law of nature partly specified, albeit in rudimentary form, the rights of individuals and their claims against the state, international law had to be somehow connected with that larger system of thought. And while both Grotius and Vattel believed that the state had some independent right of autonomy, both attempted to establish moral limits to the international legitimacy of governments. Each of them recognized that when governments exceeded those limits they became vulnerable to foreign invasion aimed at rescuing the victims of such excesses.

Hugo Grotius, after stating that the treatment of subjects was a matter submitted only to the judgment of the sovereign, recognized that if a tyrant "should inflict upon his subjects such treatment as no one is warranted in inflicting, the exercise of the right vested in human society is not precluded."[3] There are two elements in this passage. First, certain types of treatments are such that no ruler is warranted in inflicting them. Second, mankind has a right to intervene when rulers cross the humanitarian threshold. For Grotius, humanitarian intervention, as an ingredient of a theory of just war, was an extension of his doctrine of legitimate

---

[3] H. Grotius, *De Jure Belli Ac Pacis* [1646] 584 (Kelsey trans., 1925). Kelsey's translation is slightly more faithful to the Latin original than Whewell's, 2 H. Grotius, *De Iure Belli Ac Pacis* 440 (Whewell's trans., 1825). Whewell translates:

> If a tyrant . . . practices atrocities toward his subjects, which no just man can approve, the right of human social connexion is not cut off in such a case.

Grotius's original text reads:

> [S]i quis Busiris, Phalaris, Thrax Diomedes ea [i.e., injuria] in subditos exerceat, quae aequo nulli probentur, ideo praeclusum eris ius humanae societatis.

"*Ius humanae Societatis*" more properly means "right vested in human society (or humanity)" than the more ambiguous "right of human social connexion." Whewell, id.

resistance against political power.[4] The reasons that justify resistance and humanitarian intervention are identical: the governmental conduct against which subjects may lawfully revolt also gives rise to the right of foreign nations to intervene on behalf of the oppressed subjects. Despite its generality, Grotius's statement is remarkable in a world and at a time of absolute royal authority, when the notion of human rights as we conceive it today, while perhaps already foreseeable, was virtually unknown. Professor Edwards aptly summarized Grotius's thought:

> At this highest stage of his thought on resistance, then, Grotius was reminding rulers that their authority was not absolute. . . . [He] . . . told the monarchs of his day that they were not free to commit crimes and to perpetrate injustice either internally or externally. Tyrannous acts within their own state associations . . . constituted crimes for which these rulers were liable to punishment.[5]

The same concern with balancing the moral personality of the state against the humanitarian limits of sovereignty is present in the important work of Emerich de Vattel. This French scholar defined the state as a political body that became a "moral person having an understanding and a will peculiar to itself, and susceptible at once of obligations and of rights."[6] Thus, "Nations . . . must be regarded as . . . free persons living together in a state of nature."[7] However, like Grotius before him, Vattel accepted the right of humanitarian intervention for extreme cases. After stating that "[n]o foreign state may inquire into the manner in which a sovereign rules," he conceded that

> if a prince, by violating the fundamental laws, gives his subjects a lawful cause for resisting him; if, by his unsupportable tyranny, he brings on a national revolt against him, any foreign power may rightfully give assistance to an oppressed people who asked for its aid.[8]

---

[4] *See* C.S. Edwards, H. Grotius, *The Miracle of Holland* 136 (1981) and references therein.

[5] Id. at 138.

[6] 1 E. de Vattel, *The Law of Nations or the Principles of Natural Law Applied to the Conduct and to the Affairs of Nations and Sovereigns* [1758] 3 (C. Fenwick trans. 1964).

[7] Id.

[8] Id. at vol. 2, Ch. IV, paras. 55–56, p. 131.

While for both Grotius and Vattel the right to humanitarian intervention was restricted to extreme cases of tyranny, so was at that time the right to revolution. Both writers' confinement of humanitarian intervention to egregious cases of oppression can be explained by recalling that in the Ancien Régime the right of *revolution* was subject to a similar limitation. The underlying principle for both is therefore that humanitarian intervention is justified whenever revolution is. The important point here is that there is a parallel between the *domestic* legitimacy of the prince *vis-à-vis* his subjects and the *international* legitimacy of the prince *vis-à-vis* other nations. While today we would perhaps put the intervention-revolution threshold considerably lower, Grotius and Vattel had the merit of underscoring the identity between the humanitarian limits of both domestic and international public conduct. Finally, it is worth noting that both Vattel and Grotius rightfully conceived of humanitarian intervention as assistance to an oppressed people, thus underscoring both the importance of avoiding excessive paternalism and the need to minimize the dangers of war.[9]

Classic international law writers of the second group attempted to develop systematically the notion of the moral autonomy of the state independently from domestic political morality. Like Vattel's, Christian Wolff's argument is premised on the assertion that "nations are to be regarded as individual *free persons* living in a state of nature."[10] Yet unlike Vattel, Wolff thought that a necessary consequence of this freedom was the rejection of humanitarian intervention:

> If the ruler of a state should burden his subjects too heavily or treat them too harshly, the ruler of another state may not resist that by force. . . . For no ruler of a state has a right to interfere in the government of another, nor is this a matter subject to his judgement.[11]

And in his discussion of religious wars, Wolff reminds us that "force is a means not suited to inculcate truth."[12] Thus for Wolff the "freedom"

---

[9] On the requirement of acceptance of humanitarian intervention by the victims of oppression, *see infra* Chapter 6.

[10] 2 C. Wolff, *Ius Gentium Methodo Scientifica Pretractatus* [1749], sec. 2, p. 9 (Drake trans. 1964) (emphasis added).

[11] Id. at sec. 258, p. 132. Wolff concedes, however, that the foreign government may intercede, short of using force, on behalf of the oppressed. Id.

[12] Id. at sec. 259, p. 132.

of the nation in the state of nature entails the proposition that the ruler is absolutely sovereign, and that no foreign state may interfere with his power. The ruler's international legitimacy is thus illimited, which is tantamount to saying that it is not affected by the way he treats his subjects.

But it was Hegel who most famously articulated the notion of the moral personality of the state. In a well-known passage, the German philosopher exclaimed: "The state is the actuality of the ethical idea. It is ethical *mind* . . . knowing and thinking itself. . . . The state is absolutely *rational*. . . . This substantial unity [i.e., the state] is an absolute unmoved end in itself, *in which freedom comes into its supreme right.*"[13] Assuming that some meaning can be gleaned from these quotations, Hegel's idea is that the state is a moral entity, mysteriously capable of thinking and enjoying the supreme right of freedom. "Freedom" as the state's attribute may mean several things in the muddled Hegelian philosophy, but one of its implications is that other states may not intervene in the state's choices. Just as individual freedom can be analyzed as a general prohibition addressed to the rest of individuals of interfering with individual choices, so freedom of the state amounts to a similar prohibition addressed to the rest of nations. Of course, this analysis is not completely faithful to Hegel, who thought that *aggressive war was inevitable among states, and a laudable means of restoring the state's temper and vitality.*[14] Thus Hegel's theory embodies the classic assumptions of the most aggressive forms of nationalism: states may not challenge other states' treatment of their own subjects, but they may wage war to achieve national glory—to further the "national spirit."

While the Hegelian Myth is notorious for having served as the basis of various kinds of totalitarian theories of domestic justice, it was also uncritically accepted by many, although not all, international legal scholars of the nineteenth and twentieth century. Under the influence of reigning positivism, legal scholars by and large disregarded the humanitarian limits of authority set forth by Grotius and Vattel and followed instead the path established by Wolff and Hegel. Thus, in 1895

---

[13] G. F. Hegel, *The Philosophy of Right* [1821] sec. 257–258, p. 155–56 (T.M. Knox trans., 1965) (emphasis added). *See* the devastating critique in 2 K. Popper, *The Open Society and Its Enemies* ch. 12 (1966).

[14] *See* J. N. Findlay, *Hegel: A Re-Examination* 330 (1962); D.A. Zoll, *Reason and Rebellion* 234–235 (1963).

Hall could say that "it is postulated of . . . independent states . . . that they have a moral nature identical with that of individuals, and that with respect to one another they are in the same relation as that in which individuals stand to each other. . . ."[15] And Paul Fauchille, in his discussion of the fundamental rights and duties of states, claimed that "freedom is a primitive and necessary right of states . . . because it is held by them as a necessary consequence of their very existence. . . ."[16] Trying to explain the limitations to that freedom, the French scholar relied on the analogy with the individual: "[J]ust as there is no absolute freedom for the individual, there cannot be absolute sovereignty for the state. . . ."[17]

Prominent positivists such as Oppenheim, however, while strongly underscoring the primacy of the state in international law, recognized that when a state rendered itself guilty of actions that "shocked the conscience of mankind," humanitarian intervention was permissible.[18] It is worth noting that Oppenheim's definition appealed to some moral, not legal, standard. The standard, however, was still too stringent: state sovereignty was considered too basic, and only extreme atrocities would justify intervention. In sum: even for those authors like Oppenheim, who followed Grotius and Vattel, the moral autonomy of the state was the overriding principle that could only be abandoned in rare and extreme cases of oppression.

The holistic premises of nationalism underlie the notion of the moral autonomy of the state. These illusions refuse to die, and Hegelianism in various forms still haunts political and legal philosophy. Emphasis on communal rights and collective goals reveals the mesmerizing appeal of this enduring revolt against freedom and reason. Such emphasis is hardly suprising in the writings of advocates of different forms of nationalism and collectivism. Yet the fact that even prominent liberal philosophers have succumbed to the temptation of grounding international law on some version of the moral autonomy of the state shows that the effort to shake off Hegelianism has been slower in international than in

---

[15] W. E. Hall, *International Law* 18 (4th ed. 1895).

[16] P. Fauchille, 1 *Droit International Public* 427 (1922) (author's translation).

[17] Id. at 429.

[18] 1 Oppenheim, *International Law* 312 (H. Lauterpacht ed. 1955).

constitutional liberal thought. Before undertaking a full critique of the Hegelian Myth, therefore, it is necessary to examine two modern versions of it suggested in the philosophical literature.

II. JOHN RAWLS'S THEORY OF INTERNATIONAL LAW[19]

John Rawls, perhaps the most influential political philosopher of this century, has defended a theory of international law that relies heavily on the analogy between state and individual. In his sketched attempt to suggest the philosophical principles that should underlie the law of nations, Rawls proposes an extension of his well-known contractarian justification of principles of domestic justice.[20] I will only discuss and challenge here Rawls's claim that a contractarian scheme would yield an unqualified rule of nonintervention as a basic principle of international justice, an issue intimately related with the globalization of Rawls's principle of equal liberty as the moral basis of international human rights. I will therefore avoid the difficult issue whether his principle of distributive justice is susceptible of being globalized.[21]

In his discussion of conscientious refusal, Rawls suggests that we can extend the contractarian scheme, initially conceived as a theory of domestic justice, to account for the moral basis of the law of nations.[22] Thus, we may "think of the parties as representatives of different nations who must choose together the fundamental principles to adjudicate conflicting claims among states."[23] These representatives, like the parties in the domestic original position, are deprived of information about "the particular circumstances of their own society, its power and strength in comparison with other nations," and about their own place

---

[19] The analysis in this section applies to the work of John Rawls up until 1988. For an extended commentary on his recent work on international ethics, see F. R. Tesón, "The Rawlsian Theory of International Law," 9 *Ethics & Int'l Aff.* 79 (1995). While Rawls endorses a relatively high degree of tolerance toward nonliberal societies, he also supports humanitarian intervention for grave violations of human rights. See J. Rawls, "The Law of Peoples," 20 *Critical Inquiry* 36, 59, 67 (1993).

[20] J. Rawls, *A Theory of Justice* 378 (1971) (hereinafter *Theory*).

[21] On this issue, see Beitz, *Political Theory, supra* n. 1, at 127–176.

[22] For a sumary of Rawls's theory, see *supra* Chapter 2, text accompanying nn. 91–110.

[23] Rawls, *Theory, supra* n. 18, at 378.

in their society.[24] They know they represent some nation, but they do not know whether it is large or small, rich or poor, free or unfree. And most important, the representative does not know whether *he* will be rich or poor, powerful or weak, talented or untalented in his society.

Rawls believes that from the international original position thus defined the parties would choose "familiar principles."[25] The first of these principles is that of the equality of nations, which according to Rawls "is *analogous to the equal rights of citizens in a constitutional regime.*"[26] For Rawls, a consequence of the equality of nations "is the principle of self-determination, *the right of a people to settle its own affairs without the interference of foreign powers.*"[27] Rawls here attempts a direct transmutation of the notion of equal liberty from constitutional to international justice. Just as in a liberal-democratic society individuals are politically free, so in a just international society nations are sovereign and hold the right of self-determination. This right of self-determination is really a rule of nonintervention. Rawls does not elaborate on this point, but it seems plausible to infer here that the parties in the original position would reject humanitarian intervention as a violation of the right of peoples to settle their "own affairs without the interference of foreign powers." Thus Rawls believes that the same reasons that justify equal liberty for individuals justify sovereignty for states. This view is further confirmed by Rawls's discussion of the morally acceptable concept of national interest. "A nation," writes Rawls, ". . . is not moved by the desire of world power or national glory; nor does it wage war for purposes of economic gain or the acquisition of territory."[28] A just state "will aim above all to maintain and to preserve *its just institutions* and the conditions that make them possible."[29] Thus, states are mainly concerned with upholding their own just institutions. Interference in other societies, even with the purpose of promoting human rights and free institutions, is a violation of the equal rights of nations.

---

[24] Id.

[25] Id.

[26] Id. (emphasis added).

[27] Id. (emphasis added).

[28] Id. at 379.

[29] Id. (emphasis added).

The uncritical acceptance of an unqualified rule of state sovereignty and the apparent rejection of humanitarian intervention are surprising features of a theory of justice so firmly and admirably grounded on human rights. Rawls's moral foundation of international law appears as an uneasy mixture of the liberal tradition of individual rights and the holistic and mystical traditions associated with nationalism—as a surprising blend of Kant and Hegel. In order to critique Rawls's theory of international justice one must address two issues:

(a) Does justice as fairness, and especially the first principle of justice with its priority, hold for all kinds of human societies? I gave an affirmative response to this question by rejecting the relativist version of justice as fairness and its corollary, the elitist theory of human rights.[30]

(b) If (a) is responded to in the affirmative, would the parties in the original position agree upon an absolute rule of nonintervention? This is the issue that must be addressed here.

To begin with, it is not clear why we should assume that the parties in the original position would be representatives and deal with the other groups as separate states.[31] The characterization of the parties as representatives presupposes the contingent truth that the world is divided into states. Yet this is precisely one of the central problems that a normative philosophy of international law must resolve: why we should have states at all. There are two ways in which one could argue within Rawls's theory for the justice of a world divided into discrete political units. The first is simply this: one could simply construct the veil of ignorance in the original position so that the parties already *know* that the world is divided into states. Rawls's description of the original position postulates that the parties "know the general facts about human society. They understand political affairs and the principles of economic theory; they know the basis of social organization and the laws of human psychology." There are "no limitations on general information, that is, on general laws and theories."[32] So the existence of separate states can be seen as the "basis of social organization" or a given of

---

[30] *See supra* Chapter 2.

[31] *See* Taylor, "The Concept of Justice and the Laws of War," 13 *Colum. J. Transnat'l L.* 189, 191 (1974).

[32] Rawls, *Theory, supra* n. 18, at 137–138.

"political affairs," or a "general fact about human society." Neverthe-less, this obviously begs the question. The way we construct the veil of ignorance is a function of our considered moral judgments. In particular, the notion of the veil of ignorance is the result of our intuition that the distribution of burdens and benefits in society should not be affected by specific contingencies.[33] The question is then whether the *existence* of nation-states belongs to the class of circumstances that, if known by the contractors, would bias their decision one way or the other. But this is the question we are attempting to answer: indeed, in order to decide whether the system of nation-states should be considered as "given" or should instead be open to examination by the contractors, we need to have some prior moral intuition about the nature of the state. Since the original position is a stipulation, one could just as well construct the "veil of ignorance" to preclude the parties from knowing that the world will be divided into sovereign states. With that restriction, perhaps the parties in the original position would choose to create a world federation instead of a system of discrete nation-states.[34] It is therefore at least plausible to require that the moral credentials of the state should be open to examination like those of any other social insti-tution.[35]

But there is a better Rawlsian argument for the existence of states. In the original position, the contractors will have a powerful reason to establish separate states after all. If the parties established a world federation, there would be no safe harbor if the political system degener-ated into a tyranny: as Walzer and Nardin point out, there would be no refugees or political asylum for the victims of oppression.[36] Instead, human nature being what it is, the diversity generated by a world di-vided into states would presumably provide the balance that would enable freedom to survive, perhaps in some few societies, even in the

---

[33] Id. at 136.

[34] The point is made by Simon, "Global Justice and the Authority of States," 66 *Monist* 557, 559–60 (1983).

[35] *See* Pogge, "Globalizing Justice as Fairness" 12 (1987) (unpublished manu-script). 1987).

[36] *See* T. Nardin, *Law, Morality and the Relations of States* 238–239 (1983); Walzer "The Moral Standing of States," 9 *Phil. & Public Aff.* 209, 228 (1978–79. *See also,* Bull, "The State's Positive Role in World Affairs," 108 *Daedalus* 114 (1979).

case of widespread obscurantism and persecution. While these calculations are always problematic, it is not implausible to think that the parties in the original position, when choosing basic institutions, will divide the world into discrete political units for the purpose of maximizing the overall probabilities of global human rights observance.

Be it as it may, the basic principles would have been chosen not by representatives—i.e., governments—of the several groups, but by the people of all of them in one joint act.[37] Thus, the existence of states and their representatives is not a precondition of the original position, but rather a result at which the parties arrive by applying their criterion of rational choice—*maximin*. So assuming that the parties have concluded in the original position that it would be better to live in a world fragmented into separate states, they cannot be characterized as representatives of nations. As Rousseau once claimed, for the contractual justification to work it is essential that each citizen in the original position speak for himself, and not by representatives.[38] The parties of course know they will live in some nation, but they do not know which, and therefore they do not represent anything. Their task is to devise global principles of international justice that are rational and fair.[39]

Yet the main flaw in Rawls's theory of the law of nations is not related to whether or not the parties in the original position are representatives of states. The main problem with Rawls's account is that, representatives or not, the parties in the original position would not rationally choose an unqualified principle of nonintervention. Crucially, that principle cannot possibly be justified under the *maximin* rule. It will be recalled that the first principle they would agree on is that of equal

---

[37] *See* Pogge, *supra* n. 33, at 12–13; and Taylor, *supra* n. 29, at 191.

[38] J. Rousseau, 2 *Du Contrat Social*, ch. 3, at 196 (J.P. Siméon trans. 1977) ("*Il importe donc pour avoir bien l'enoncé de la volonté générale qu'il n'y ait pas de société partielle dans l'Etat, et que chaque citoyen n'opine que d'après lui.*")

[39] Professor Pogge writes:

The individualistic basis of Rawls's view as embodied in his concern for background justice supports then an interpretation of the original position on which the global parties are *persons from* the various societies who would thus decree that transnational institutions be designed toward protecting the basic liberties of all persons. . . .

Pogge, *supra* n. 33, at 10.

liberty, which roughly corresponds to civil and political human rights.[40] Now one could ask why the parties in the original position would agree to an absolute rule of nonintervention that would leave them at the mercy of dictators.[41] If the parties believed that some societies were likely to be grossly unjust, then it is plausible to conclude that, in following the *maximin* rule, they would prefer a principle of limited intervention on behalf of human rights. And this is so because the first aim of the parties in the original position is to see that the fundamental rights of *individuals* within every state are recognized and observed.[42] The purpose of the state organization is to protect the rights of individuals.[43] Because the parties in the original position agree to terms of cooperation that are mutually acceptable and fair, the aim of the international community thus created, that is, divided into states, should also be the protection of the rights of individuals, and not the prerogatives of princes.[44] Therefore, it is doubtful that the parties in the original position would agree to an unqualified rule of nonintervention that would jeopardize the very rights the original position is primarily supposed to secure—those that form the content of Rawls's first principle of justice.

The foregoing objection to the nonintervention rule holds even if it is conceded that Rawls is correct in characterizing the parties in the original position as representatives of nations. Professor D'Amato aptly articulates Rawls's dilemma in the following terms: "[S]hould just and unjust nations be given equal liberty in the original position?"[45] If they

---

[40] In Rawls's words:

The basic liberties of citizens are, roughly speaking, political liberty (the right to vote and be eligible for public office) together with freedom of speech and assembly; liberty of conscience and freedom of thought; freedom of the person along with the rights to hold (personal) property; and freedom of arbitrary arrest and seizure as defined by the concept of the rule of law.

Theory, supra n. 18, at 61.

[41] *See* Wicclair, "Rawls and the Principle of Non-Intervention," *in* J. Rawls, *Theory of Social Justice* 289, 299–300 (G. Blocker & E.H. Smith, eds. 1980).

[42] *See* id. Wicclair, however, unnecessarily concedes Rawls's requirement that the parties in the original position be representatives of nations.

[43] *See* R. Nozick, *Anarchy, State and Utopia* 1–53 (1974).

[44] *See* 1 K. Popper, *supra* n. 12, at 288 n. 7.

[45] A. D'Amato, "International Law and Rawls' Theory of Justice," 5 *Denv. J. Int'l L. & Pol'y* 525 (1975), *reprinted in* A. D'Amato, *Jurisprudence* 259, 270 (1984) (quoted from the latter).

should, then the consequence is that some persons will be deprived of equal liberty (those persons in unjust nations); if they should not, then Rawls's principle of "equal liberty" of nations cannot be maintained as the moral basis of international law. Again, it seems that the parties in the original position would agree to some rule of humanitarian intervention as an insurance against tyranny, in the same sense as the parties in an original domestic position would agree to a right to revolt against tyranny.[46] Moreover, as D'Amato points out,[47] Rawls himself seems to accept humanitarian intervention without realizing the contradiction. In his discussion of the justification of military conscription Rawls writes:

> Conscription is permissible only if it is demanded for the defense of liberty itself, including here not only the liberties of the citizens of the society in question, *but also those of persons in other societies as well.*[48]

If the government is morally justified to draft individuals for a war waged in defense of the liberties of persons in other societies, it analytically follows that such a war, i.e., humanitarian intervention, is morally just. Nowhere does Rawls attempt to reconcile his view about conscription with the rule of nonintervention that the parties in the original position would allegedly choose.

The same objection may be reformulated by focusing on the credentials of the nations' representatives in Rawls's account of the original position. Who are the nations' representatives? Is the representative in the original position representing the *government* or the *people* of that nation? If the former, should dictators be accepted as representatives? The way we set up the conditions and restrictions of the original position is morally significant.[49] It would seem therefore reasonable, and more consistent with Rawls's own theory of domestic justice, to require as "credentials" for this international conference at least the democratic character or *true* representativeness of each party.[50] The only way the

---

[46] By limiting the duty to obey the law to nearly just societies, Rawls implicitly recognizes the right to revolution against grossly unjust and corrupt regimes. *See Theory, supra* note 18, at 363.

[47] *See* A. D'Amato, *Jurisprudence, supra* n. 43, at 269.

[48] Rawls, *Theory, supra* note18, at 380 (emphasis added).

[49] See id. at 17–21.

[50] "Representation" theory discussed in detail in Chapter 4.

international original position makes sense is when the parties who are representatives of nations represent just states, and so genuinely speak for their respective constituencies.

There are two ways to defend Rawls's adoption of a flat nonintervention rule. It can be claimed that the individuals in the original position would include, as part of their liberty interests, concerns for loyalty, or a personal identification with the community.[51] If this is true, the argument runs, then the parties in the original position would after all agree on a rule of nonintervention. But this begs the question by assuming that the original parties value these communal rights over everything else. Admittedly, the parties in the original position would value some form of group identification or communal values once their basic rights have been secured. But this is different from maintaining that the nonintervention rule, prompted by the interest of the original parties in preserving their loyalties and their communal life, would have primacy over their interest in the establishment of just institutions. It seems intuitively more plausible and in accordance with the *maximin* rule to say that the parties in the original position would agree to a rule of nonintervention provided that their eventual domestic society will observe basic liberties, that is, of a rule of nonintervention applicable only among minimally just states. Assuming the parties agree on a world divided into separate states, they will further agree on an international principle that will put them in the best position *should they happen to be citizens of the worst possible state.* The most plausible rule is therefore one that contains an exception to state sovereignty allowing for humanitarian intervention in those nations at the bottom of the human rights scale. It would be irrational for the parties to agree to an absolute rule of nonintervention that would irremediably condemn them to oppression should they be unfortunate enough to be born in an oppressive society rather than in a free one.[52]

---

[51] *See* Kraiem, "Book Review," 21 *Harv. Int'l L. J.* 322, 326 (1980)

[52] The irrationality (and implausibility) of "desiring" tyranny was put into delightful words by Jorge Luis Borges in 1944:

Ser nazi . . . es, a la larga, una imposibilidad mental y moral. El nazismo adolece de irrealidad . . . Es inhabitable; los hombres sólo pueden morir por él, mentir por él, matar y ensangrentar por él. Nadie en la soledad central de su yo, puede anhelar que triunfe.

In translation:

To be a Nazi . . . is, in the last analysis, a mental and moral impossibility.

The second and, I think, more powerful, Rawlsian defense of nonintervention (one, however, that Rawls does not expressly make) would have to run as follows:[53] The parties in the original position know that governments tend to abuse those international law principles that allow for intervention. They know this as part of the "general facts about human society" which are not covered by the veil of ignorance. Therefore, even though they may recognize that in a few cases it would be beneficial for the human rights cause to allow military intervention, they fear that nations will abuse, that is, that they will use the humanitarian intervention exception as a rhetorical pretext to wage unjust wars. All things considered, then, the parties in the Rawlsian original position will conclude that a flat nonintervention rule best serves the human rights purposes, that is, the global maximization of the rights embodied in the first principle of justice. I deal generally with the "abuse" argument in Chapter Five, so I will confine myself here to a few remarks in the context of Rawls's theory.

There are several reasons to doubt that the parties in the original position will be persuaded to outlaw humanitarian intervention because of the danger of abuse, assuming that for the reasons suggested above they acknowledge that but for such danger humanitarian intervention is morally justified in appropriate cases. First, one could reply that when the parties agree upon international principles of justice they have an expectation of compliance. This has some support in Rawls's writings: "The general recognition of [the fairness of the initial agreement] would provide the basis for a public acceptance of the corresponding principles of justice."[54] In devising a theory of justice we must concentrate on ideal theory. It is thus a mistake to build a theory of international justice by focusing on delinquent governments, that is, on those that will abuse the right of humanitarian intervention for selfish purposes. The self-defense exception to the prohibition of the use of force is often

---

Nazism suffers from irreality . . . It is uninhabitable; men can only lie for it, kill and murder for it. Nobody, in the central loneliness of his self, can possibly want it to succeed.

J. L. Borges *Obras Completas* 727, 728 (1974).

[53] This point was shown to me by Jeffrie Murphy and Thomas Pogge.

[54] *Theory*, supra n. 18, at 13. *See also* Rawls, "The Basic Liberties and Their Priority," *in* 3 *The Tanner Lectures on Human Values* 1, 19–20 (1982) (the parties are expected to have the capacity to honor fair terms of social cooperation).

abused, and no one has suggested that it should be eliminated for that reason. Someone may challenge the validity of this analogy by noting that the reason why the right of self-defense cannot be eliminated, even if it is abused, is because no state would fail to defend itself against aggression. This is of course correct, yet what is the moral rationale of the right of self-defense? It is, I suggest, precisely *to grant the right to governments to wage war in defense of the rights of the citizens of the state that is being attacked.*[55] So self-defense also is a form of war on behalf of human rights. It is indeed hard to distinguish between the justice of war on behalf of the rights of a certain group of individuals (our citizens), and wars on behalf of the rights of a different group of individuals (the foreign human rights victims), *only* on the grounds that in the former case (self-defense) war cannot be avoided anyway.

Moreover, the empirical assumption that most governments would abuse if humanitarian intervention were allowed is itself doubtful if a recent study is correct in suggesting that constitutionally secure liberal states *have never engaged in wars against each other.*[56] This seems to suggest that if the parties in the Rawlsian original position agree upon the first principle, the greater the global compliance with that principle the smaller the probability of aggressive war. In short: liberal states will not intervene in other liberal states. (That is not to say that interventions by liberal states in illiberal states are always justified on humanitarian grounds.)

Now let us concede, *gratia argumentandi*, that the original contractors assume that governments will make such mistakes, either in good or bad faith, and intervene in situations where humanitarian intervention is not justified. If so, the parties also must suppose that *governments will make mistakes in the opposite direction*, that is, that they will refrain from intervening in egregious cases of oppression and genocide.[57] If that is so, arguably allowing for humanitarian intervention will not tend to increase the probability of human rights violations. The cases where

---

[55] For a full discussion, *see infra* Chapters 5, 6, and 7.

[56] *See* Doyle, "Kant, Liberal Legacies, and Foreign Affairs, Part I," 12 *Phil. & Public Aff.* 205, 213 (1982).

[57] A dramatic example of nonintervention was the passivity of the international community in the 1969 Nigerian civil war. *See generally* Reisman, "Humanitarian Intervention to Protect the Ibos," in *Humanitarian Intervention and the United Nations* 167 (R. Lillich ed., 1973).

abuses occur will presumably be balanced out in the long run by the cases in which states refrain from intervening where they could have done so. There is no reason why the parties in the original position, when attempting to devise principles of international justice that will foster the globalization of the first principle, i.e., of human rights, will only take into account abuse, and not also underuse, the right of humanitarian intervention.

Another reason to doubt that the original contractors would agree on a flat nonintervention rule is that the parties in the original position know that governments will have a powerful incentive not to abuse the humanitarian intervention exception: simply, that governments that intervene for humanitarian reasons become potential targets for similar actions. The equation thus has to take into account the *deterrent* effect on those less powerful states whose governments will avoid gross human rights violations for fear of intervention. Governments have to live up to their words and deeds. They cannot intervene for humanitarian reasons and then consider themselves shielded from similar interventions; therefore, they will presumably be cautious in availing themselves of the rule. This, of course, is another example of the universalizability implicit in normative discourse discussed in the preceding chapter.

In conclusion: Assuming that a right of nations to intervene for humanitarian purposes is mandated by a proper application of the *maximin* rule, from the perspective of the parties in the Rawlsian original position the danger of abuse does not seem to be a sufficient reason to prohibit such interventions. Arguably many governments will be deterred from violating human rights if they know they are not protected by the principle of sovereignty. Governments are not likely to abuse the exception, and even if they do, they will also often refuse to intervene and stop genocide and mass murders.

There is another intriguing feature of Rawls's account of the ethical basis of international law that is partly relevant for our purposes. Few would dispute his assertion that a state's conduct in international relations should be guided by a duty to defend and uphold its own just institutions.[58] But should this be a just state's paramount duty?[59] A strict

---

[58] *See supra* text accompanying nn. 26–27.

[59] Rawls writes that the just state will aim "above all" to maintain and preserve its just institutions, so perhaps he is thinking that this is an international *primary* duty, in the same sense as a parent has a duty to look after her children first. *See supra* text

application of this principle seems to justify two types of international conduct that many intuitively regard as immoral. First, the principle justifies giving support to repressive régimes on the grounds that they are the allies of the just state against other (presumably worse) totalitarian and repressive states. In this hypothesis, the just state supports the dictators in the belief that in so doing it is maximizing the long-term enjoyment of *its own* just institutions. Second, the principle seems too selfish, because it prescribes isolationism in face of genocide in those instances where the genocidal government does not threaten the state's free institutions. Suppose Nazi Germany would have confined itself to exterminating the German Jews within Germany, without engaging in foreign military aggression. Rawls's standard would entail a duty of nonintervention on the part of the democratic West, since the Nazi genocide would not have threatened their just institutions. On the contrary, I submit that the Allies had at least a right[60] to intervene by force in Germany between 1933 and 1939, even though their just institutions were arguably not yet in jeopardy. Some form of forcible intervention was probably justified in Germany sometime before their treatment of the Jews and other groups reached genocidal proportions. It seems more consistent with the universal nature of human rights, then, to say that a state's conduct in international relations should be guided by the principle of upholding *global* human rights, including, perhaps primarily, those within its own borders.

One final comment on the relationship between intervention and Rawls's theory. It seems plausible to say that intervention should not be allowed to remedy violations of the *second* principle of justice—roughly corresponding to socio-economic rights[61]—except perhaps in the case of starvation where the government has it in its power

---

accompanying nn. 28, 29. But the objection in the text remains for those cases where the defense of domestic human rights is carried out by means which necessitates the impairment of other peoples' human rights.

[60] Indeed, the case can even be made for a *duty* to intervene, at least in cases of genocide. Chilstrom forcefully suggests that the Second World War itself was a humanitarian effort. Chilstrom, "Humanitarian Intervention under Contemporary International Law," 1 *Yale Studies in World Public Order* 93, 120 (1974).

[61] Rawls's second principle of justice provides:

Social and economic inequalities are to be arranged so that they are both:

(a) to the greatest benefit of the least advantaged, consistent with the just savings principle, and

(b) attached to offices and positions open to all, under conditions of fair equality

to prevent it, as was the case recently in Ethiopia.[62] Aside from the fact that Rawls's second principle of justice is much more controversial than the first,[63] the intuitive idea here is that the priority of liberty agreed upon in the original position will not allow the sacrifice of lives entailed by war for the sake of upholding economic rights in another society. This is an extension of the general principle according to which "liberty can be restricted only for the sake of liberty."[64] The limitation has the important consequence that while different economic structures and systems are not morally indifferent for devising general principles of international justice,[65] they are morally indifferent for the purposes of ascertaining normative principles regulating the use of military force.

The conclusion of the foregoing discussion is that nonintervention in international law has a more limited scope than the one Rawls envisaged. As Kant argued, because a principal aim of the parties in the original position is to secure freedom, they will agree on a rule of nonintervention applicable only among *just* states.[66] If a system of separate nation-states is established by the contractors, they will acknowledge an exception allowing intervention to prevent or suppress serious human rights abuses. This solution is suggested by Rawls's own text, when he indicates that the representatives of nations deliberate on the law of nations after they have *already* agreed on the two principles of justice.[67] While, as I indicated above, this account is somewhat inadequate, it should naturally lead to the solution suggested here. It is therefore surprising that Rawls should place so much emphasis on nonintervention. Perhaps the explanation of such anomaly is Rawls's reluctance to extend justice as fairness to non-Western societies, discussed in the preceding chapter. For the reasons indicated in this and the preceding chapters,

---

of opportunity.
Rawls, *Theory, supra* n. 18, at 302.

[62] *See* Bazyler, "Stopping the Bloodshed: The Doctrine of Humanitarian Intervention Reexamined in Light of the Atrocities in Kampuchea and Ethiopia," *Stan. J. Int'l L.* (1987).

[63] *See* the famous critique by R. Nozick, *supra* n. 41, at 183–231.

[64] *See* Rawls, *Theory, supra* n. 18, at 302.

[65] *See* Beitz, *Political Theory, supra* n. 1, at 127–176.

[66] *See* I. Kant, "Eternal Peace" [1795], in *The Philosophy of Kant* 430, 434–441 (C. J. Friedrich, ed.1949).

[67] Rawls, *Theory, supra* n. 18, at 377–78.

this solution is unsatisfactory, and social contract theory can and should be able to explain not only the principles of constitutional law, but international human rights and the international legitimacy of governments as well. Rawls's own original-position devise supports the intuitive idea that strict nonintervention is justified only among states where basic civil and political rights are respected—where liberty is given its priority. Where that is not the case, where governments turn against their citizens depriving them of their rights, where the priority of liberty is drastically eliminated, justice as fairness must allow foreigners to help revolutionary efforts. The reason, simply put, is that it is reasonable to assume that human rights concerns will be present in the minds of the original parties when deciding the moral principles of the law of nations. Only with that important amendment can justice as fairness account for such principles.

III. STATE AUTONOMY AS THE SUM OF INDIVIDUAL AUTONOMIES

Another way of defending the moral autonomy of the state is to characterize it as the sum of individual autonomies. Gerald Elfstrom has argued that the reason why it makes sense to predicate moral autonomy of the nation-state is that it is founded upon the "collected moral autonomy of each of the individual citizens."[68] Part of what we mean by individual autonomy, writes Elfstrom, is that "in areas in which others have no specific authority over [a person] or have no particular responsibility for him, he ought to be free to follow his own lights."[69] Similarly, Elfstrom concludes, states should be left alone in the pursuit of their own institutions. Elfstrom's thesis can thus be summarized in two propositions:

(1) state autonomy is the result of the sum of individual autonomies of the citizens; and

(2) because foreigners do not stand in any special relationship with the citizens (do not have any responsibility for what occurs

---

[68] Elfstrom, "On Dilemmas on Intervention," 93 *Ethics* 709, 713 (1983) (hereinafter "Dilemmas").

[69] Id. at 712.

within the state's borders), they have no business intervening to remedy human rights violations, especially in the absence of an international authority.[70] Only the citizens are entitled to do so.

The argument is not convincing. First, the claim that humanitarian intervention automatically violates the individual autonomy of each citizen is empirically false and logically unsound. It is false because the oppressed population will ordinarily welcome foreign help in their struggle for freedom. It is implausible to maintain that men and women in torture chambers will reject outside intervention aimed at overthrowing their tormentors. The argument is logically flawed because the idea of individual autonomy is not accurately conveyed by the alleged right to have a state ruled by fellow citizens, regardless of how they rule.[71] Rather, individual autonomy is intrinsic to the notion of human rights, and so its thrust is best described as that of barriers to governmental authority, of claims against the state—in terms of the inviolability of each person,[72] "moral trumps,"[73] or "side constraints."[74] To use the notion of individual autonomy in the sense of a right of each individual to have his or her tyrannical rulers protected against outside encroachment is to distort that notion beyond all recognition. Indeed, it is hard to see how the collection of individual moral autonomies can result in a shield of protection for a tyrannical government which, by definition, is violating the individual autonomy of its citizens.

Elfstrom's second claim, that foreigners do not have responsibility for what happens within state borders, and that therefore they do not

---

[70] Elfstrom writes:

[O]utsiders can have no general responsibility for the citizens of a particular nation-state. The reason for this is that such a responsibility could not exist independently of the authority to carry it out. But since this authority would impinge on the authority of the citizens of the nation-state, it is not justified.

Id. Note that Elfstrom does *not* say that state autonomy rests on the citizen's consent, that is, on a delegation of rights effectuated by the individual in favor of the government. I consider this explanation much closer to the truth, and I discuss it in Chapter 6.

[71] As Luban rightly observed, noninterventionism only recognizes the rights emphasized by nationalism: to fight for the homeland and to live in institutions formed by one's fellow nationals. They are rights to a nation-state, not claims against it. *See* Luban, "The Romance of the Nation State," 9 *Phil. & Pub. Aff.* 392, 396 (1980).

[72] Rawls, *Theory, supra* n. 18, at 3 ("Each person possesses an inviolability founded on justice that even the welfare of society as a whole cannot override").

[73] R. Dworkin, *Taking Rights Seriously* 94 (1978).

[74] Nozick, *supra* n. 41, at 33.

have any authority to act to remedy human rights violations, is also unpersuasive. His emphasis on the need of external authority presupposes relativism, because the implication is that foreigners cannot pass judgments about human rights violations outside their borders.[75] One could ask why the determination by a centralized authority is preferable to that made by a foreign government: if relativism is true, then it surely holds for the international authority as well. But even if one concedes that foreigners do not have any responsibility for what happens within a nation-state, that only proves that they do not have a *duty* to intervene, not that they do not have a *right*. Elfstrom, after having argued for the nonexistence of a duty to intervene, jumps to the conclusion, unwarranted by his own arguments, that there is a duty *not* to intervene.[76] In truth, Elfstrom's denial of a right of humanitarian intervention relies on a different, though related, assumption: that governments necessarily represent the individuals in international relations. I discuss this argument in the next chapter.

IV. TOWARD A FUNDAMENTAL REVISION OF THE HEGELIAN MYTH

Engrained as it is in international law doctrine, the Hegelian Myth cannot survive critical scrutiny. The first objection is conceptual. The analogy of state to individual fails because words such as "freedom," "autonomy" and "equal liberty" are used with a different (and unclear) meaning when they are predicated of nation-states than when they are predicated of individuals. While we know approximately what "free person" means, we do not know what the notion of "a free government"[77] is supposed to convey. This essential indeterminacy gives rise to a number of problems.[78] First, who is the bearer of the state's right

---

[75] *See,* e.g., "Dilemmas," *supra* note 68, at 713, n. 7. For a rebuttal of this argument, *see* Beitz, "Democracy in Developing Societies," *in Boundaries—National Autonomy and Its Limits* 176,178 (P. G. Brown & H. Shue eds. 1981). Unfortunately, Beitz himself defends a form of relativism. Id. at 203 (rejecting "human rights orthodoxy").

[76] *See* Elfstrom, "Dilemmas," *supra* n. 68, at 718.

[77] Significantly, in ordinary speech we use the expression "free state" to denote a state in which human rights are respected, and not one in which the government has discretion *vis-à-vis* the external world.

[78] *See* Doppelt, "Walzer's Theory of Morality in International Relations," 8 *Phil. & Pub. Aff.* 3, 4–5 (1978–79).

to freedom, the government or the people? Second, by virtue of what features does the state have this right? As these puzzling questions show, this is another instance of the use of normative language in a context in which it does not, and cannot, retain its original descriptive meaning, although those words retain, of course, their emotive connotations.[79] The notion of individual autonomy, "in the sense fundamental to the idea of human rights, is a complex assumption about the capacities, developed or undeveloped, of persons, which enable them to act on . . . higher-order plans of action which take as their self-critical object one's life and the way it is lived."[80] Needless to say, these are human qualities. It is therefore impossible to articulate a concept of the state as a moral being analogous to a person.[81] Only persons can pursue rational ends and be autonomous in a moral sense, and we indeed have a moral duty not to interfere with their choices (unless those choices violate someone else's rights). But states are not persons, and although governments are made of persons, their moral rights *qua* governments are not grounded in any mystical quality of the state, as Hegel thought, but in the consent of their subjects. The rulers are agents of the people; therefore they do not hold, *qua* government, any independent right of autonomy.

But the problem is more than linguistic. A close examination of the notion of "state's choice" or "state's freedom" reveals the true facts denoted by that abuse of normative language. In truth, a defense of the "freedom" of the state amounts to a defense of *a right of individuals in power to exercise whatever methods of government they choose to exercise, including authoritarian methods.* Thus the assertion of a "fundamental right" of the state to "choose its political system" is no more than a defense of the legitimacy of *any* use of political power. The transmutation of words has now become a rationalization for oppression; the "freedom" ("independence," "sovereignty," "equal liberty") of the state means *carte blanche* for tyrants to exercise arbitrary power and deny individual freedom, that is, "freedom" in its original sense. The invariable consequence of the Hegelian Myth in international legal

---

[79] *See generally* G. Carrio, *Sobre Los Limites Del Lenguaje Normativo* (1973).

[80] Richards, "Rights and Autonomy," 92 *Ethics* 6 (1983). *See also* Benn, "Freedom, Autonomy and the Concept of a Person," 66 *Proceedings of the Aristotelian Soc'y* 109 (1976).

[81] *See* Beitz, *Political Theory, supra* n. 1, at 76.

discourse is the confusion between government and people—*le peuple, c'est moi!*[82] But, as one commentator put it, "[i]t is not the case that for the same reasons individual autonomy is in itself a good thing, state autonomy is also in itself a good thing even when the state thwarts individual autonomy—this is the contradiction at the heart of the morality of the state."[83] Thus John Rawls is mistaken in assuming that the parties in the original position would choose "equal liberty" of nations just because they have chosen "equal liberty" for individuals: the expression "equal liberty" here is fundamentally ambiguous: when it is unqualifiedly applied to states, it contradicts "equal liberty" as applied to individuals. Any coherent theory of international law has to reconcile both. It is here submitted that state autonomy is philosophically grounded on, and subordinated to, individual autonomy, that is, human rights.

This suggestion, however, reveals that state autonomy remains a useful concept in an important and obvious sense: apart from self-defense, there is a general duty not to intervene in states where human rights are observed.[84] Strategical considerations, quest for power and territorial aggrandizement are immoral reasons to wage war. In these instances, Walzer's powerful argument against war fully comes into play. His argument is convincingly grounded on human rights: war is a crime, teaches Walzer, because the aggressor forces men and women to fight and risk their lives for their rights.[85] That is not the case, however, of citizens in tyrannical states. External intervention aimed at overthrowing the tyrants and liberating the oppressed does not force men and women to fight for their rights, because those rights are being denied by their government in the first place. They have no rights to fight for.

---

[82] For a striking example of the use of judicial reliance on the Hegelian Myth, *see* the discussion of the *Nicaragua* case in Chapter 9.

[83] Shue, "Book Review," 92 *Ethics* 710 (1982).

[84] Following Kant, *supra* n. 64, both Wicclair ("Rawls and the Principle of Non-Intervention," *supra* n. 39, at 298) and Beitz (*Political Theory*, supra n. 1, at 83–92), reach a similar conclusion. A democratic state that commits aggression (non-humanitarian intervention) is violating the rights of the citizens of the target state. *Cf.* Walzer's definition of aggression in M. Walzer, *Just and Unjust Wars* 21–33 (1977). In a sense, then, that state becomes less democratic. The invader, while democratic within its borders, has ceased to observe global human rights because it has forced the citizens of the invaded state to fight for their rights.

[85] M. Walzer, *Just and Unjust Wars, supra* n. 84, at 51.

The Hegelian Myth, therefore, should be rejected. Its failure stems not so much from the historical fact that it is a product of German idealism, and thus an ideological source of authoritarian doctrines from the right and from the left. The theory does not work because it is incompatible with human rights.[86] Noninterventionists are forced to deny the priority of human rights because they regard the moral autonomy of the state as a cluster of state rights that are held over and above individual rights. Nor can the Hegelian Myth be salvaged by appealing to a collection of individual autonomies. By definition, a tyrannical government is already violating individual autonomy. It follows that if nonintervention is to have some moral content, it should be conceived as protecting the rights of individuals (for example, against foreign invasion which threatens their rights by forcing them to fight), and not the prerogatives of tyrannical governments.

While John Rawls's appeal to hypothetical consent is a step in the right direction, the principles of justice among nations that he suggests do not seem to follow from the premises of his own theory. Yet social contract theory, properly defined, provides a defensible foundation of international law. By preserving the priority of human rights, social contract theory is able to explain both domestic and international schemes of social justice as part of a single process of hypothetical rational choice. And the only way to effect that harmonization is to recognize that the rule of state sovereignty is ultimately subordinated to the recognition of fundamental human rights.

---

[86] Luban captures this same idea by characterizing the concept of state sovereignty as morally impotent. Luban, "Just War and Human Rights," 9 *Phil. & Pub. Aff.* 160, 171 (1979–80).

CHAPTER 4

THE INTERNATIONAL LEGITIMACY OF GOVERNMENTS

I. THE DOCTRINE OF REPRESENTATION IN TRADITIONAL INTERNATIONAL LEGAL THEORY

It is hardly disputed in specialized literature and in ordinary discourse that the government of a state necessarily represents the individuals in international relations. This "representation" theory is a key notion in international legal thought. Traditional international law lays down a standard of effective political power as the criterion for statehood and consequent international personality.[1] A government is deemed internationally legitimate when it rules effectively over a population located in a territory. No ethical requirement is attached to this notion of international legitimacy. More than twenty years ago Charles Fenwick summarized the state of the law:

---

[1] An exhaustive list of authorities for this proposition would exceed the scope of this work. De Visscher, for example, teaches that governments consider themselves entitled to recognize a new government when it seems to be more or less solidly established. *See* de Visscher, *Théorie et réalité en droit international public,* 255 (4th ed. 1970). I need not distinguish here between recognition of states and recognition of governments: The representation theory holds for both. When international lawyers say that in order to recognize an entity as a "state" it needs to have *some* government, they are dismissing the relevance of what kind of government that may be. Any effective government will validly turn a "community" into a state. Similarly, international law tells us that an individual or group of individuals are the legitimate government of a state (already existing) when they exercise effective political authority over most of the territory. Here again, traditional international law does not care about methods of

Whether a totalitarian dictatorship, coming into power by methods of violence and maintaining itself into power by suppression of the fundamental liberties of a people, could be regarded as having the "stability" required for recognition is a question with which international law has not yet concerned itself.[2]

Yet historically there have been attempts to temper the rigor of the traditional rule by articulating theories of recognition of government that relied on human rights and constitutional legitimacy. Woodrow Wilson attempted to implement a policy of non-recognition of tyrannical and unconstitutional governments.[3] His challenge to the international legitimacy of dictators went back to the famous Mobile speech, where he asserted that international cooperation was possible "only when supported by the orderly processes of just government based upon law, not upon arbitrary or irregular force."[4] Wilson further specified this human rights-based view of legitimacy by emphasizing that a government's just powers were derived from the consent of the governed.[5] Similar in scope was Tobar's doctrine, according to which only constitutionally elected government deserves recognition.[6]

Yet, with one important exception discussed below,[7] these theories of legitimacy were soon rejected in favor of the thesis of effectiveness mentioned above.[8] A distinguished specialist on recognition justifies the

---

government. *See*, e.g., the Tinoco arbitration (*Costa Rica v. Great Britain*), 1 *U.N. Rep. Int'l Arb. Awards* 369 (1923) (Taft, Sole Arb.).

[2] C. Fenwick, *International Law* 180 (4th ed. 1965).

[3] *See* 1 Hackworth, *A Digest of International Law* 180–192. The new policy was announced in connection with the issue of recognition of the government of Mexican dictator Huerta.

[4] *See* the speech in 7 *A.J.I.L.* 331 (1913).

[5] *See* Instruction to his Minister in Santo Domingo, Sept. 9, 1913, in 1 Hackworth, *supra* n. 3, at 183. The policy was also embodied in the 1907 treaty among Central American Republics. Id. at 186.

[6] *See* Letter of Minister Tobar to the Consul in Brussels, 1914 *Revue de droit international* 483.

[7] This is the case of South Africa. *See infra*, text accompanying nn. 19–20, and Chapter 7.

[8] *See*, e.g., the famous holding in the Tinoco arbitration:

[W]hen recognition *vel non* of a government is by those nations determined by inquiry, not into its de facto sovereignty and complete governmental control, but into its illegitimacy or irregularity of origin, their non-recognition loses something of evidential weight on the issue with which those applying the rules of international law are alone concerned.

principle of effective political power by reminding us that it prevents interventions in the domestic affairs of the recognized government.[9] An additional supposed virtue of the theory, at least for international law-yers, is that it lays down an "objective" standard (i.e., the citizens' general obedience) for international legitimacy, as opposed to the "sub-jective" standards of democracy, real representativeness and respect for human rights. Any government that succeeds in exacting obedience must be considered as presumptively legitimate. While from a philo-sophical perspective the domestic legitimacy of governments may de-pend on respect for rights and political consent, the representation theory links international legitimacy only to political power.

The representation theory, understood as the proposition that gov-ernments that succeed in subduing the people are to be considered as representing that people vis-à-vis the world community, is the result of applying the political philosophy of Thomas Hobbes to the issue of international legitimacy. The notion of state sovereignty is Hobbesian because it underscores the citizens' obedience toward the sovereign, based on fear, as the only effective means of ending the internal state of nature.[10] In a sense, then, while political theory and constitutional doctrine may support the idea that governments should be Lockean, or Kantian, to be *internally* legitimate, international law teaches that they need only be Hobbesian to become honorable members of the interna-tional community. International law, like Hobbes, teaches that political legitimacy is determined by the success of the sovereign in exacting obedience from the subjects, in imposing order and thus creating the conditions that make civil society possible. Writes Hobbes:

> The only way to erect such a common power, as may be able
> to defend them from the invasion of foreigners, and the injuries

---

Tinoco Arbitration, *supra* n. 1, at 3369. *See also* the discussion in I. Brownlie, *Principles of Public International Law* 95–97 (1979) (arguing that recognition dependent on the democratic character is "political").

[9] *See* J. Verhoeven, *La reconnaissance internationale dans la pratique contempor-aine* 607 (1975).

[10] *See* T. Hobbes, *Leviathan* [1651], ch. 18, and ff. (M. Oakeshott ed., 1946) ("Of The Rights Of Soveraignes by Institution"). Beitz discusses and rejects Hobbes's philoso-phy in a different and important sense. He argues convincingly against the view that nations are in an international state of nature and that consequently international moral-ity is impossible or meaningless. *See* Beitz, *Political Theory and International Relations* (1979), Part One. *See also* Cohen, "Moral Skepticism and International Relations," 13 *Phil. & Pub. Affairs* (1984).

of one another . . . is, to confer all their power and strength upon one man, or upon one assembly of men, that may reduce all their wills, by plurality of voices, unto one will. . . . This is more than consent, or concord; it is a real unity of them all, in one and the same person, made by covenant of every man with every man, in such manner, as if every man should say to every man, I authorize and give up my right of governing myself, to this man, or to this assembly of men, on this condition, that thou give up thy right to him, and authorize all his actions in like manner.[11]

What sets Hobbes apart from other social contract philosophers is the ruthlessness of the sovereign, of this "mortal god."[12] Hobbes's sovereign has full executive, legislative and judicial power.[13] Indeed, terror is the very basis of the state:

For by this authority, given him by every particular man in the Commonwealth, he hath the use of so much power and strength conferred on him, that by terror thereof, he is enabled to form the wills of them all, to peace at home, and mutual aid against their enemies abroad.[14]

Thus effective power based on terror is the foundation of both the domestic and international moral standing of governments. Hobbes was overly concerned with unifying individual wills, and he believed that this could only be done by the citizens agreeing to waive all their rights to a ruler with unlimited power. And other governments, living themselves in a state of nature,[15] will look only at this ruler, the recipient of the unified collective will, as the legitimate representative of the commonwealth.

Hobbes's political morality arises from a belief that absolute power is the only way to preserve peace at home and abroad. Thus his account of political legitimacy is largely instrumental. Peace and security are the supreme values; men have to waive the rights they hold in a state

---

[11] Hobbes, *supra* n. 10, at 112.

[12] *See* id.

[13] Id. at 114.

[14] Id. at 112.

[15] Id. at 83.

of nature in order to enable the sovereign to subdue everybody and thereby achieve peace. Hobbes's philosophy is therefore not amoral: His political morality consists in ranking peace and stability over all other values, especially those associated with rights and justice.

Under the influence of positivism, traditional international law, like Hobbes, values order and peace over justice and rights. Yet it is appropriate to ask whether the absolute priority of peace is defensible from a moral point of view. The question is whether peace, admittedly a very important value, should invariably be regarded as the supreme concern in international relations. Certainly we do not accept it as supreme in our justification of civil society. Political obligation depends upon whether a state is just or not, and this in turn is measured by how the state respects the boundaries set by the rights of individuals.[16] Where the state is tyrannical, the basis of obligation collapses, and justice and rights take precedence over peace and order. This is well expressed in the right of revolution: We consider ourselves entitled to revolt against tyrants. In Hume's words, "we may resist the more violent effects of supreme power, without any crime or injustice."[17] We do not, therefore, follow Hobbes in his unlimited justification of established political authority. Our domestic notions of justice are sensitive to the moral dimension of politics, sensitive to consent and human rights. Yet international legal thought has unjustifiably overlooked that moral dimension. Just as we place peace and order behind justice and rights in our domestic

---

[16] *Cf.* J. Rawls, *A Theory of Justice* 350–351 (1971). (We are bound to obey isolated unjust laws only when the basic structure of society is just and they do not exceed certain limits of injustice.)

[17] D. Hume, *A Treatise on Human Nature* [1739] (L. A. Selby-Bigge & P. H. Nidditch ed. 1978), Book III, Sec. IX, at 552. Hume is clear that the basis for political obligation is consent. Id., Sec. X, at 554 ("Government . . arises from the voluntary convention of men"). For a useful discussion, *see* J. Harrison, *Hume's Theory of Justice* 203–228 (1981).

John Locke's famous formulation of the right of revolution also relies clearly on consent:

When any one, or more, shall take upon . . . [the people] to make laws, whom the people have not appointed so to do, they make laws without authority, which the people are not bound to obey . . . being in full liberty to resist the force of those, who without authority would impinge any thing upon them.

J. Locke, *An Essay Concerning the True Original, Extent, and End of Civil Government* [1690], in *Social Contract* (Sir E. Baker ed. 1948), c. XIX ("On the Dissolution of Government"), at 124.

political thought, so justice and rights should prevail over peace and order when ascertaining the international legitimacy of states and governments.[18]

There is today an important exception to the representation theory, where most governments have applied the Wilsonian doctrine of parallelism between domestic and international legitimacy: South Africa. Here the majority of states have, for the first time, linked the international legitimacy of the South African government to its representativeness and its observance of human rights. Recent resolutions adopted by the United Nations General Assembly refer to the South African rulers not as the "South African Government," but as the "*Apartheid* regime," the "racist regime" or the "Pretoria regime."[19] But then there is no reason why the principle applied in the South African case should not be extended to challenge the international legitimacy of all serious human rights violators. While racial discrimination is a serious human rights violation, there is little doubt that, say, genocide and widespread torture are worse. Moral rationality dictates that the inspired refusal to recognize the South African regime should be extended to other dictatorial regimes.[20]

Regardless of how much the principle of state sovereignty (understood in the Hobbesian sense) may be encroached in international legal tradition, it is not acceptable from an ethical standpoint. The Hobbesian principle of political legitimacy is indifferent to the moral dimension of politics.[21] It shields from intervention governments that should not be protected on any acceptable philosophical account of the state. Governments are not above ethical constraints; their sovereignty must be rightly exercised.[22] When they fail in the proper exercise of sovereignty, they

---

[18] Of course, this conclusion alone does not entail the permissivity of humanitarian intervention: There are other constraints on war. *See infra*, Chapters 5 and 6.

[19] *See*, e.g., U.N. G.A. Res. 39–72 (XXXIX), adopted on Jan. 9, 1985, U.N.Doc.A/RES/39/72.

[20] For a detailed discussion, *see infra*, Chapter 7.

[21] Michael Walzer thinks that this disregard for political morality is one of the *merits* of his vindication of state sovereignty: He wishes to take the defense of politics against the traditional "philosophers' dislike of politics." *See* Walzer, "The Moral Standing of States," 9 *Phil. & Pub. Aff.* 209, 228–229 (1978–79) (hereinafter "Moral Standing").

[22] Writes Hume:

Few persons can carry on this train of reasoning: "Government is a mere human invention for the interest of society. Where the tyranny of the governor

cease to represent the people and are no longer entitled to the protection afforded by state sovereignty. In sum, the Wilsonian proposition that human rights are the proper basis of international legitimacy flows naturally from the assumption that governments should be, internally and internationally, mere agents of the people.

II. THE PARENT-CHILD ANALOGY

In his argument against humanitarian intervention, Professor Elfstrom defends the representation theory by appealing to the parent-child analogy:

[I]nternational affairs have proceeded on the assumption that the governments of particular nation-states have the *legitimate* authority to speak and act for the citizens of those nation-states. . . . In the eyes of the larger world community, the government of a nation-state stands in a special relationship somewhat similar to the special relationship between parent and offspring.[23]

Elfstrom then goes on to assert that just as "the values and interests of the child are what the parent determines them to be," so governments "are charged with overseeing the interests of its citizens."[24] Only governments are "authorized" to interpret the interests of its citizenry vis-à-vis the international community.[25] When a government obviously misinterprets the interests of its citizenry, only the citizens themselves have primary responsibility for taking action.[26]

---

removes this interest, it also removes the natural obligation to obedience."

D. Hume, *supra* n. 17, at 552.

This simple point—that the sovereign is not above the law—is rightfully emphasized by Chilstrom, "Humanitarian Intervention under Contemporary International Law," 1 *Yale Studies in World Public Order* 93, 99 (1974).

[23] Elfstrom, "On Dilemmas on Intervention," 93 *Ethics* 709, 714 (1982–83) (emphasis added).

[24] Id. at 715.

[25] Id. at 716.

[26] Id.

Elfstrom deserves credit for having used the right domestic analogy. Neither Brownlie's choice of euthanasia[27] nor Reisman's example of self-help in the Far West[28] are helpful to illuminate the problem of humanitarian intervention from a philosophical perspective. The parent-child situation seems more to the point: The tension between state sovereignty and the international community's claim to protect individual rights in international relations is quite similar to that between the rights of parents to raise their children and society's claim to protect the children's basic rights against abuse by their parents.

However, Elfstrom's own analogy undercuts his argument. As Professor D'Amato points out in the same connection, it is widely accepted today that society may and must intervene to protect children against parental mistreatment.[29] There is, of course, ample room for parental autonomy, and just as we ought not to intervene in domestic affairs of states where basic human rights are not involved, so we have a duty to refrain from intervening in a parent-child relationship where the basic rights of the child are not at stake. But where parents abuse children we feel morally compelled to intervene, even sometimes to "overthrow" the parent as a guardian of the abused child. Similarly, when governments mistreat citizens, we have a right, if not a duty, to come to their rescue. This is especially true when they are helpless against the military power of the rulers.

Elfstrom's response to this objection is that only the citizens are entitled to determine whether or not their government should be overthrown.[30] Otherwise, he claims, we would be violating the autonomy of those individual citizens.[31] But as I indicated above, this is an implausible proposition. First, the government is already depriving individuals of their rights, and therefore violating their autonomy. Second, to assume that they prefer being mistreated to being freed by foreigners is to rely too much on nationalism and irrationality. But even conceding

---

[27] See Brownlie, "Humanitarian Intervention," in Law and Civil War in the Modern World 217, 223 (J. N. Moore ed. 1974).

[28] See Reisman, "Coercion and Self-determination: Construing Article 2(4)," 78 A.J.I.L. 642, 643 (1984).

[29] See D'Amato, International Law: Process and Prospect 226 (1987).

[30] Elfstrom, supra n. 23, at 715.

[31] Id.

that intervention is wrong where some of the oppressed individuals, perhaps a majority, oppose foreign humanitarian intervention (maybe their nationalist feelings are stronger than their dislike for the government), Elfstrom's thesis is nevertheless indifferent to that issue. His suggestion is much harsher: For him, only the citizens are entitled to act, whether or not they would welcome outside help, and even if they are bound for disaster. Helpless as they may be, they have no right to ask for, and foreigners have no right to give, military assistance. This conclusion runs counter to some of our intuitions about the reaction to request for help by persons in need. But whatever our position may be regarding our *duty* to rescue, it can hardly be disputed that we have a *right* to act in that situation.[32]

In sum: Elfstrom's analogy of states and citizens to parents and children, while correct, is devastating for his own argument. We regard children as having some fundamental rights that not even parental authority may override, and so we consider ourselves entitled to intervene in cases of serious abuse. Similarly, citizens have certain rights that governments may not ignore, and consequently foreigners are entitled to provide help to individuals whose rights are being violated by their government.[33] Just as the parent's representation of the child is a function of the parent's respect for the rights of the child, so the government's representation of its citizens is a function of its observance of human rights.

III. THE "RIGHTS" OF THE CITIZENS WHO SUPPORT OR TOLERATE THE DICTATORS

A related objection to humanitarian intervention is that even if a government engages in serious human rights violations there will always

---

[32] That this is so is proved by Elfstrom's own discussion of the Good Samaritan principle as applied to international relations. Elfstrom, *supra* n. 23, at 718–724. The only issue is whether third parties *ought* to help people in need. There is no question that, absent a refusal by the victim, they have a *right* to do so.

[33] Writes Professor Przetacznick:

When freedom is lost a man has the duty to fight for his own freedom, for freedom of his own country and for the freedom of other men. A man has a moral duty to help all other men who fight for their freedom against foreign and domestic oppressors. In the defense of freedom . . . and in the fight for the recovery of freedom, men, people or nations should use all legitimate

be a number of citizens, perhaps a majority, whose rights are not violated, or at least not seriously. If nothing else, intervention violates *their* right of autonomy; that is, their right not to be invaded. Writes Elfstrom:

> In most cases of human rights violations by governments, the rights of all citizens are usually not directly affected. The most serious violations of rights are rarely directed at an entire population, but rather at a small minority . . . [I]f the majority is complacent . . . then intervention will constitute a violation of their right of autonomy.[34]

This conclusion is surprising in view of Elfstrom's concession that "it cannot be thought that the minority ought to sacrifice its rights for the interests of the whole."[35] Like Walzer, however, Elfstrom believes that a government that extends its inhumane treatment to more than a fraction of the entire population cannot possibly survive for long.[36] Walzer even insists that the request for outside help by the victimized citizens amounts to an admission of weakness, and that for that reason they should not be assigned by foreign nations.[37]

Aside from the fact that there are obvious examples of human rights violations directed at the whole or the majority of the population,[38] this argument is not convincing. Again, the claim depends on the implausible assumption that there is something worth protecting in self-determination regardless of the outcome in terms of human rights and democratic values. As shown above, there is no such thing as "collective" right of autonomy or, in Walzer's words, "communal integrity."[39] Each citizen holds an individual right of autonomy, and apart from

---

means to achieve the sacred task to liberate everywhere men from a domestic and foreign deprivation of freedom.

Przetacznick, "The Philosophical Concept of Freedom as a Basic Human Right," 63 *Revue de droit international, de sciences diplomatiques et politiques* 93, 157 (1985).

[34] Elfstrom, *supra* n. 23, at 717. Elfstrom goes so far as to say that the right of autonomy of the *victims* (and not only of the "complacents") is violated by humanitarian intervention. Ibid. This I have shown to be at best empirically false, and at worst self-contradictory.

[35] Id.

[36] Id.

[37] Walzer, "Moral Standing," *supra* n. 21, at 220.

[38] South Africa and Pol Pot's Cambodia are two cases that come readily to mind.

[39] *See generally* Walzer, "Moral Standing," *supra* n. 21.

consent there can be no philosophical transmutation of individual autonomies into the social body. Therefore, *unless the victims themselves prefer to tolerate their government rather than see their state invaded,* there is no right of autonomy of the complacents worth protecting. It may be that, under social contract principles, "[t]he members of the community are bound to one another."[40] But it is equally certain that victims of human rights deprivations cease to be bound to those of their fellow citizens who support their tormentors. I do not deny that sometimes victimized citizens may prefer domestic tyranny to benign outside intervention. In that case, it is correct to say that foreign states should refrain from intervening. A moral requirement for humanitarian intervention, I argue below, is that victimized citizens welcome the intervention.[41] This requirement follows logically from the characterization of humanitarian intervention as an extension of the domestic right to revolution. But in order to reject the moral propriety of humanitarian intervention on those grounds *it is necessary to collect the refusals of each oppressed citizen.* This is so because, as Elfstrom himself concedes, it is morally unacceptable to condone human rights violations just because the majority wants it. Therefore, oppressed minorities are entitled to receive outside help, even if a majority of citizens opposes the intervention.

More important, those citizens who support the tyrants in the repression of a segment of the population do not have any moral claim to defend that government against foreigners. To some extent *they are accomplices* of the government in its criminal enterprise. If they decide to take arms to defend the dictators against foreign humanitarian intervention, they are guilty of, and have to take the responsibility for, fighting an unjust war. They have a moral duty to support the benign intervention against the tyrants. If they do not do so, they are almost as responsible as their government for the murders, executions, tortures, and imprisonments. Therefore, Walzer is wrong to claim that "it is the expectation of resistance which establishes the ban on invasion."[42] Resistance may or may not be morally justified. Roughly, it is justified when it is in defense of just governments; it is unjustified when it is in

---

[40] Id. at 211.

[41] *See infra,* Chapter 6.

[42] Walzer, "Moral Standing," *supra* n. 21, at 212.

defense of tyrants. To be sure, Walzer concedes that citizens do not have an *obligation* to defend their tyrannical government against foreigners.[43] But the crucial point is that, contrary to Walzer's claim, individuals who decide to defend the tyrannical government also do not have a *right* to do so. Those who are morally accomplices of the dictators (the supporters) and those bystanders who are not necessarily accomplices (the complacents) do not have a right to fight in order to prevent outside forces from freeing the victimized population. They are not morally entitled to resist the struggle on behalf of the victims of oppression.

Humanitarian intervention must therefore be regarded as an *extension of the right to revolution.* If it is morally justified violently to resist oppression, then there is at least a prima facie justification for *assisting* the revolutionaries in their quest for freedom. Noninterventionists are forced to argue that there is some moral quality of the state, or "communal integrity," or necessary legitimacy, that morally precludes foreign intervention even in cases where violent overthrow is perfectly justified on the merits; that is, even in those cases where revolution is morally justified. But this is pure mysticism. A tyrannical government is no more justified vis-à-vis other governments than it is vis-à-vis its own subjects, and once it loses its legitimacy the subjects may request foreign help for the purposes of restoring free institutions. Aid given to a just revolution amounts to a just war.

IV. MICHAEL WALZER'S "FIT" THEORY

Michael Walzer has defended a modified version of the representation theory. In his 1980 article he departed from the thesis he had developed in his book *Just and Unjust Wars.* In the book Walzer had correctly grounded state autonomy in the individual rights of its citizens.[44] However, in his *Moral Standing of States* he shifted ground significantly by formulating his "dualist" thesis. Governments are *domestically* legitimate, writes Walzer, when there is a "fit" between

---

[43] Id. at 211.

[44] *See* M. Walzer, *Just and Unjust Wars* 53 (1977) (hereinafter *Wars*).

the government and "the political life of its people."[45] We may call this relationship "fit₁." If there is no "fit₁," each citizen has an individual right to revolution, which of course may be exercised by groups of citizens.[46] But it is not the case, claims Walzer, that humanitarian intervention is justified whenever revolution is.[47] The right to overthrow the dictators does not easily transfer to foreign states and governments; it does not become a right of invasion.[48] It is only when the absence of "fit" is *radically apparent*, that is, in cases of genocide, enslavement or mass deportation, that foreigners acquire a right of humanitarian intervention.[49] So although "fit₁" might be absent, there is still some "fit" between people and government if the latter is not engaged in genocidal or equivalent practices. We may call this relationship "fit₂."[50] In all other cases of "ordinary oppression," that is, where only "fit₁" is absent, foreign governments must act as if the dictators were legitimate. While a government may be illegitimate from the standpoint of appropriate principles of domestic justice (because it has turned against its own citizens), unless human rights violations reach genocidal proportions, foreign states ought to regard that government as internationally legitimate. Therefore, Walzer concludes, it is entirely plausible to say that foreign invasions with revolutionary purposes violate the rights of the citizens of dictatorial states.[51]

As a preliminary matter, Walzer's view goes a long way toward justifying intervention in cases where many legal scholars would deny such legitimacy.[52] The problem now becomes one of setting the threshold for intervention. For Walzer, only genocidal or equivalent action justifies intervention. The arguments he marshals, however, are grounded on the Hegelian Myth—the moral reality of the state. But once he has accepted what he calls the "rules of disregard," one could

---

[45] Walzer, "Moral Standing," *supra* n. 21, at 212.

[46] Id. at 214, 215.

[47] Walzer, *Wars, supra* n. 44, at 89; id., "Moral Standing," *supra* n. 21, at 214.

[48] Id.

[49] Id.

[50] Doppelt also noted this twofold meaning of "consent" in *Wars. See* Doppelt, "Walzer's Theory of Morality in International Relations," 8 *Phil. & Pub. Aff.* 3, 14–16 (1978).

[51] Walzer, "Moral Standing," *supra* n. 21, at 215–17.

[52] For references, *see infra*, Chapter 7.

ask why the exceptions cannot be extended to cover other cases of serious oppression. It seems that Walzer's arguments would support, if anything, a noninterventionist rule with no exceptions—a step, however, that he, quite rightly, refuses to take.

There are several ways of interpreting Walzer's claim. It is possible to see it as a test for legitimacy defining "fit₂" as a relationship of *cultural* correspondence between the people and its government. Even though there is no "fit₁"—because the government is not democratic—there is still enough "correspondence" between government and people to justify the latter's existence in the eyes of the world community. In several passages Walzer emphasizes shared history, hidden political currents, religious beliefs and local loyalties as factors that determine the presence or absence of "fit₂." He even claims that the emergence of dictators is not a mere coincidence or the result of misfortune: "Indeed, the history, culture, and religion of the community may be such that authoritarian regimes come, as it were, naturally, reflecting a widely shared world view or way of life."[53] Walzer believes that a government may be ruthlessly authoritarian and repressive and yet somehow be consistent with the (authoritarian) traditions of that people, and consequently deserving of international respect.[54]

There is a disturbing elitist overtone in Walzer's "fit" theory, understood in this sense.[55] The suggestion here is that people get the government they deserve, that somehow the oppression they suffer is their

---

[53] Id. at 224–25.

[54] Walzer imagines Swedish officials administering to all Algerians a wondrous chemical that will turn them into liberal democrats à la Swedish. Walzer, "Moral Standing," *supra* n. 21, at 225–26. He concludes that such action—which he constructs in that fanciful way to avoid all the issues related to the use of force—would be unjustified. Walzer expressly says that the Algerian people "have a right to a state within which their rights are violated." Ibid. Professor Beitz rightly pointed out that the administration of the chemical in that hypothetical example is wrong because it violates *individual* autonomy, not "communal integrity." *See* Beitz, "Nonintervention and Communal Integrity," 9 *Phil. & Pub. Aff.* 385, 389–90 (1979–80). While I agree with Beitz's forceful critique of Walzer's notion of "communal integrity," we apparently differ on the moral correctness of humanitarian intervention. *See* id. at 390.

[55] I have discussed this elitist theory of human rights in Chapter 2, and in my article "International Human Rights and Cultural Relativism," 25 *Va. J. Int'l L.* 869, 895–896 (1985).

own fault. This doctrine smacks of historicism. The emergence of tyrannical rulers is seen as the inevitable result of the "blind forces of history," similar to the occurrence of an earthquake or a flood.[56] The conclusion is harsh indeed: If there is nothing the citizens alone can do to carry out a successful revolution against the tyrants, then it must be because the laws of history, or historical development, have so determined. We foreigners should leave the citizens to "work out their own salvation."[57]

There is no need yet to recite the theoretical inadequacies and disastrous political consequences of such a view of history and society.[58] From the point of view of the victims, there is no such thing as dictators coming to power "naturally," as Walzer would want us to believe.[59] Asks Doppelt:

> Why assume that the mere balance of existing forces expresses true self-determination or anything *worth* preserving (for example, the "general will") rather than the fortuitous distribution of military skill, experience, ruthlessness, or equipment between the contending parties in the struggle?[60]

But even conceding, for the sake of argument, that dictators sometimes come "naturally" in the sense of enjoying the support of the majority of the population, the crucial point is that *they are still illegitimate with regard to the oppressed minority*. This minority has a right to revolt against such government, with or without outside help; and foreigners have a right to furnish that help.

A second interpretation of Walzer's claim is that there is "fit$_2$" when citizens are prepared to defend their tyrannical government against foreign intervention.[61] How can we explain the fact, asks Walzer, that

---

[56] For a comprehensive critique of historicism, *see* K. Popper, *The Poverty of Historicism* (1957).

[57] This phrase belongs to S. I. Benn & R. S. Peters, *Social Principles and the Democratic State* 362–363 (1959).

[58] *See generally* K. Popper, *The Poverty of Historicism, supra* n. 54.

[59] David Luban ironizes: "Surely all those strapped to the torture table are not misfits in their own culture." Luban "The Romance of the Nation-State," 9 *Phil. & Pub. Aff.* 392, 395 (1980).

[60] Doppelt, *supra* n. 50, at 13. Emphasis in the original.

[61] "[A]s long as substantial numbers of citizens believe themselves bound and are prepared, for whatever reasons, to fight, an attack upon their state would constitute aggression." Walzer, "Moral Standing," *supra* n. 21, at 213.

tyrannical governments are able to rally the citizens again and again against foreign invasion? His response is that "[i]n all such cases, though the 'fit' between government and community is not of a democratic sort, there is still a 'fit' of some sort, which foreigners are bound to respect."[62] But that is tantamount to saying that foreigners should not intervene to protect human rights when the victims genuinely do not want to be protected. If this is all there is to the "fit" theory, then, as I show below, it is correct, although I do not think it yields the results desired by Walzer.[63]

However, in spite of strong indications to the contrary, Walzer is not really espousing any of these two positions. Rather, what he claims is that if a government is not engaged in genocide, enslavement or mass deportation of its people, then it is *always* legitimate. Thus, despite Walzer's repeated emphasis on cultural and historical factors and on the expectation of resistance as reasons to bar foreign intervention, those considerations are irrelevant for purposes of determining the government's international standing. By definition, any non-genocidal government automatically "fits" (in the sense of "fit_2") the people and must therefore be treated as legitimate by the international community. In other words, even if in a particular case we found that a non-genocidal dictator did not "fit" the people in terms of culture, history, and shared traditions; and even if we predicted that the citizens would not resist, that would not be enough for declaring that government's international illegitimacy. Walzer's only test is whether or not the government engages in genocide or its equivalents. "Fit_2" means absence of genocide or its equivalents.

I discard the interpretation of this position as relying on a stipulation of what "fit" means. Again, surely no normative conclusions may be drawn from stipulative definitions. Rather, as Walzer says, it is a presumption.[64] But if so, it lacks factual support and runs against common sense. As Doppelt observes, "a state may be extremely tyrannical and unfree even though it does not exhibit any of these three kinds of exceptional conditions [genocide, enslavement or massive deportation]."[65] A

---

[62] Id. at 216.

[63] See *infra*, Chapters 5 and 6.

[64] See Walter, "Moral Standing," *supra* n. 21, at 212.

[65] Doppelt, "Walzer's Theory," *supra* n. 50, at 17.

typical situation of ordinary oppression, where Walzer's theory would not allow intervention, is well described by David Luban:

> Each year there are a few score executions, a few hundred tortures, a few thousand political imprisonments, a few million people behaving cautiously because they know that a single slip will bring the police.[66]

Walzer defines the state as "a union of people and government,"[67] and argues from there that foreign military intervention against governments is almost always wrong, even if its purpose or effect is to establish liberal or democratic institutions.[68] Walzer's definition of "state" would be correct if "union" had only descriptive meaning, conveying the obvious idea that all states must have *some* government. But in advocating respect by foreigners toward this "union," Walzer gives "union" moral, not just descriptive, meaning. It simply violates common sense to presume, as Walzer does, that the citizens put up with such a government because they somehow feel there is a "fit" between them and their rulers, that somehow it is "their" tyranny. Rather, citizens fail to revolt because they are afraid. "The government fits the people," concludes Luban, "the way the sole of the boot fits a human face: After a while the patterns of indentation match with uncanny precision."[69] Walzer gives only one reason to support his presumption: that foreigners are in no position to know what goes on within the state.[70] This, however, is not a reason of principle; it depends instead on the truth of that particular empirical claim. As I will try to show below, that contention is devoid of foundation as well.[71]

The "fit" theory fails because of its unsatisfactory account of the idea of political representation. Representation of the people by the government is a contingent rather than a necessary fact. Either the government represents the people or it does not. Either it observes minimal human rights or it does not. We cannot escape the need for such an

---

[66] Luban, *supra* n. 58, at 395.

[67] Walzer, "Moral Standing," *supra* n. 21, at 212.

[68] *See* Doppelt, *supra* n. 50, at 7.

[69] Luban, *supra* n. 58, at 395–96. I have tried partially to depict the climate of terror in Argentina during 1976–83 in "Book Review," 79 *A.J.I.L.* 259 (1985).

[70] Walzer, "Moral Standing," *supra* n. 21, at 212.

[71] *See infra*, Chapter 5.

inquiry by saying that where there is no genocide or its equivalents we must act "as if" the government is legitimate. There is only one notion of political legitimacy, and if it holds, it holds for domestic and international relations as well. A government is legitimate in internal and international relations when it observes a certain human rights standard determined by objectively valid (although not self-evident) principles of political justice.[72] The notion of agency or representation in a philosophical sense is exactly the same outside as within national boundaries. Because protection of human rights is the justification of having states in the first place, only governments that represent the people (in the sense of having their consent and respecting their rights) are entitled to the protection afforded by international law. Another way of conveying the same idea is to say that the state has the international rights of territorial integrity and political independence if, and only if, it is a legitimate state from the standpoint of domestic justice—when it protects and guarantees the rights of its subjects.[73]

Of course, the assertion that a government is illegitimate does not entail the assertion that armed intervention to depose it is morally justified. Wars may be unjust for other reasons; for example, they may be disproportionate or their ends unjustifiable.[74] The point here, however, is that the invaded government does not enjoy the protection of the rights associated with sovereignty. In view of the inadequacies of the traditional legalist paradigm, noninterventionists may abandon the attempt to prove that there is some philosophical principle in international relations that would shield all governments, including tyrannical ones, from humanitarian intervention. They may give up the attempt to articulate a rights-based defense of noninterventionism and rely instead on a utilitarian justification of that doctrine. They can take the position that the use of military force exhibits some empirical features, or that there are some particular factual traits in international relations, which advise

---

[72] Beitz arrives at a similar conclusion, although I differ from him on the criteria for identifying those principles of justice. See C. Beitz, *Political Theory, supra* n.10, at 83. Unlike mine, Beitz's notion of "appropriate" principles of justice" is clearly relativistic. See Beitz, "Democracy in Developing Societies," in *Boundaries, National Autonomy and Its Limits* 177 (P. C. Brown & H. Shue eds. 1982).

[73] Thus, "[t]he autonomy of states is the outer face of their legitimacy." C. Beitz, *Political Theory, supra* n. 10, at 81. *See also* Doppelt, *supra* n. 50, at 16.

[74] *See* Doppelt, *supra* n. 50, at 7.

against humanitarian intervention even in the absence of any independent philosophical justification for oppressive governments.

In the next chapter, I examine, first, the place of utility in international relations, especially in connection with the preservation of human rights. I then discuss two utilitarian arguments commonly put forward against humanitarian intervention: that foreigners should not intervene on behalf of human rights because they are most likely to abuse; and that foreigners should not intervene because they do not have enough knowledge about the political life in the target state.

CHAPTER 5

UTILITY, RIGHTS, AND HUMANITARIAN INTERVENTION

I. RIGHTS AND UTILITY IN INTERNATIONAL RELATIONS

In the preceding chapters I examined philosophical arguments for nonintervention rooted in the idea of autonomous rights of nation-states. In rejecting that notion, I suggested that international law must be wed to human rights and political legitimacy. However, an alternative is possible: Strict noninterventionism may be defended on utilitarian grounds. The general difficulties of utilitarian theory are well known, and I cannot deal with them at length here.[1] Mervyn Frost has recently discussed some of the problems faced by a utilitarian theory of international relations.[2] In particular, because of its indifference to distribution, utilitarianism may justify human rights deprivations of peoples, say in the Third World, if that maximizes aggregate utility, measured for example in terms of global economic prosperity.[3] More generally, as has often been said, if human rights are conceived as moral thresholds, their violation cannot be justified by utilitarian calculations.[4] In contrast to utilitarianism, from the standpoint of a theory of international justice

---

[1] For an introduction, *see* J. Smart & B. Williams, *Utilitarianism, For and Against* (1973).

[2] *See* M. Frost, *Toward a Normative Theory of International Relations* 137–144 (1986).

[3] *See* id. at 139–140.

[4] *See* J. Rawls, *A Theory of Justice* 3–4 (1971).

based on human rights, there is a moral duty of democratic governments to value these rights over everything else when dealing with other nations. No utilitarian calculation—for example, the belief that a dictator will better protect the foreigners' investments, or that he is a "vital strategic" piece in the world's chessboard—may serve as justification for according him political legitimacy.

Aside from the general question of whether utilitarianism can justify the system of nation-states, there are two kinds of arguments that utilitarians can make against humanitarian intervention. First, benign military interventions cause deaths and suffering of innocent persons that have to be weighed against the death and suffering caused by tyrannical methods of government. It is by no means certain, it is argued, that the disutility produced by political oppression is greater than the one caused by the invasions. (This is said to be true both in most individual cases and in the long run.) Second, having an (humanitarian) exception to the nonintervention rule will in the long run provide incentives to aggressive governments to invade under humanitarian pretexts, thus causing death and suffering that will not even be counterbalanced by the achievement of any true humanitarian objective. The exception to the prohibition of using force will thus be abused. When measured in terms of utility and desires (or in terms of suffering and pleasure), the cumulative consequences of recognizing a right of humanitarian intervention are thought to be undesirable. International law should not, therefore, recognize such a general right, even conceding the moral appeal of intervening in individual cases. I shall examine these arguments in turn.

II. UTILITARIANISM OF RIGHTS

A plausible justification of the doctrine of humanitarian intervention is that recognizing it would maximize human rights enjoyment. Under a theory of international law based on human rights, it may be thought, the morality of intervention will be judged by consequences in terms of the enjoyment of rights. Here, the rights-based theorist cannot avoid relying on calculations that are suspiciously similar to utilitarian calculations. A military intervention will be morally right if, and only if, it maximizes the respect for human rights of everybody affected by the intervention.[5]

A theory of international law based on human rights faces a serious problem here. Let us suppose that the intervenor's war is genuinely aimed at stopping rights deprivations, at rescuing innocent people from their oppressors. It is obvious that many *innocent* people will die in the war. Yet if rights are seen as moral thresholds, how can one justify the deaths of some innocent persons in order to rescue other innocent persons, i.e., those who will be liberated by the intervention? Utilitarians can argue, first, that under utilitarian theory humanitarian interventions often are immoral, because the death or suffering of innocent persons is not compensated by the utility experienced by rescued persons. Second, and more crucially, that the rights theorist cannot, consistently with his position (i.e., the sacredness of rights), justify the death and suffering of innocent persons in wars aimed at restoring human rights.

In order to meet this objection, a theory of intervention based on human rights must offer a refined notion of rights and of the concept of rights violation.[6] According to one definition of *violation* of human rights, the focus should be solely upon the victim's interests: a right is infringed when the interests protected by the right are thwarted or frustrated. Thus someone's right to life is violated, say, *both* by an assassination ordered by the government and by the accidental although foreseeable death caused by street demonstrators protesting against that same government. What matters under this conception is the victim's enjoyment of rights in terms of frustration of his/her interests and expectations. The *intention* of the violator is irrelevant. Applied to the problem of intervention, the test is one of *utilitarianism of rights*.[7] An intervention will be justified if, and only if, it maximizes the enjoyment of rights of everybody affected by the intervention.[8]

Such a position, however, seems to be inconsistent with a theory based on individual rights. In most cases of forcible intervention, a

---

[5] This is David Luban's position; *see* "Just War and Human Rights," 9 *Phil. & Pub. Aff.* 160 (1979–80).

[6] I adopt here the argument made by Daniel Montaldi in his article "Toward a Human Rights Based Account of the Just War," 11 *Social Theory and Practice* 123 (1985).

[7] *See* Wasserstrom, "Book Review," 92 *Harv. L. Rev.* 544 (1978).

[8] In this sense, *see* Luban, *supra* n. 5, at 176.

nation going to war for a prima facie just cause cannot avoid inflicting suffering and death. Utilitarianism of rights only takes into account the welfare of innocent persons in the aggregate, just as classic utilitarianism does. The deprivation of rights of innocent persons is seen as justified by the aggregate result—a view diametrically opposed to a rights-based notion of justice. Innocent persons (bystanders and children, for example) have not surrendered their rights. How can we then justify a war that kills innocent people and thus overrides their individual autonomy, just because they have chosen not to fight, or they cannot fight? An international ethical theory thus must face the challenge of providing a nonutilitarian account of those interventions in which, although we expect that innocent persons will die, we still claim that the war effort is morally justified.

A solution suggested by Daniel Montaldi distinguishes between the *infringement* and the *violation* of rights. An infringement of rights is characterized by a frustration of the interest of the victim, as described above. Only the *kind* of rights and the *number* of the victims are relevant for the purpose of calculating the infringement of rights.[9] Indeed, the size of the infringement determines the presence of one of the moral requirements of just war, its *proportionality*. But not all infringements of rights are *violations* of rights. Perhaps one well-known example will help clarify this assertion. Why was it morally justified for the Allies to fight Nazism? If we adopt the test suggested by utilitarianism of rights, it is at least plausible that yielding to Hitler's demands would have caused fewer deaths and less suffering, and consequently more human rights enjoyment than the alternative. Under that test, therefore, the Allies were not justified in declaring war on Germany! Yet our moral intuitions regarding World War II strongly suggest that counting alone cannot be the answer. As Walzer has written:

> In the choice between Nazi victory and resistance through war (when victory is possible), there is human degradation and enslavement on the one side and dignity, courage, and solidarity on the other. Here it is not possible simply to count.[10]

Waging war against the Nazis resulted in a state of affairs which seriously impaired the situation of many innocent persons. A justification

---

[9] *See* Montaldi, *supra* n. 6, at 127.

[10] Walzer, "World War II: Why Was This War Different?" 1 *Phil. & Pub. Aff.* 3, 10 (1971).

of the war can only rest on the recognition that protecting innocents is a moral concern, but not the *only* moral concern.[11] The war against Nazism was fought not only for the alleviation of suffering of many people, but also against a state apparatus and an ideology that amounted to an evil "so potent and apparent that there could never have been anything but fight against it,"[12] even if doing so resulted in loss of lives greater than there would have otherwise been.

There is a subclass of infringements of rights that can be characterized as the class of rights *violations*. All violations are of course infringements, but not the other way round. A violation of rights is an infringement caused in such a way as to entail *disrespect* (in a Kantian sense) for the victim.[13] Disrespectful violations of rights are violations caused by human agents willfully and with the knowledge that they are failing to accord respect to the victims. Thus in evaluating the justice of wars we must look not only at the harm caused by the wrongdoers but at *their reasons* for causing it. It is here that the Kantian notion of respect for persons provides us with a plausible criterion. Respect for persons, as part of the definition of right action, includes right motive, and not simply states of affairs involving interests. It follows that sometimes innocent persons may be "morally bound to suffer extreme burdens for the sake of an end higher than protecting anyone's interest."[14] The basic contempt for individual autonomy, and not just the consequences in terms of lives and suffering alone, justified fighting against Nazism:

> It is . . . conceivable that in situations in which stopping persons from being grievously disrespected is of greater importance than merely ensuring that persons enjoy the freedom to pursue their interests.[15]

Respectful treatment owed to persons is thus not derived simply from the utility of maximizing persons' welfare or interests.

---

[11] *See* Montaldi, *supra* n. 6, at 138.

[12] Walzer, *supra* n. 10, at 4.

[13] *See* Montaldi, *supra* n. 6, at 139.

[14] Id.

[15] Id. at 145.

Generalizing from the Nazi lesson, we can say that *human rights violations by governments are disrespectful violations of rights par excellence*. As has often been said, there is something particularly evil in the institutionalized violations of human rights by individuals who have monopolized the use of force in a political community. From a philosophical perspective, governments that engage in human rights deprivations fail to respect persons in two ways. They frustrate the individual autonomy of the victims, just as a common criminal (say, a private murderer) does. But they also fail to respect persons in a deeper sense: They fail to honor the purpose of their office—to protect and enforce the rights of everybody. Tyrants are disrespectful human rights violators, then, not only for willfully interfering with the exercise of the citizens' individual autonomy, but because they are betraying their *raison d'être* qua rulers of the state—the protection and enforcement of the rights of persons. The common criminal also violates victims' rights in the sense of failing to accord them the respect they are due. But the tyrant, in addition to doing that, and doing it on a much larger scale, uses the means put at his disposal by his fellow citizens to turn against them and deprive them of their rights. These means include not only sheer physical force but also institutional and ideological tools, such as legislation and propaganda.

We can now formulate one requirement that genuine humanitarian interventions must satisfy. Just cause for war is stopping the willful violation of human rights. An intervention directed at stopping government-directed violations of human rights is, in appropriate cases, just. Humanitarian intervention can be just even if the intervenor infringes the rights of innocents, and even if, in rare cases, more necessary infringements will occur than the intervention will prevent. Indeed, as Luban, Montaldi, and others have suggested, *all* just wars, including wars in self-defense, are human rights-based wars.[16]

Montaldi's argument can be made even more forcefully by considering the case of *domestic* resistance against oppression. If utilitarianism of rights were the ultimate test for evaluating the correctness of political action, then only bloodless revolutions would be justified. Yet, once again, it seems that citizens are justified to take arms against a tyrant

---

[16] *See infra*, Chapter 6.

even in those cases where more innocent people will die and suffer than would in the absence of revolution. I am not addressing here the difficult question of determining what degree of disrespectful violations of human rights is needed to give rise to the citizens' moral right to revolt against the government.[17] The point is rather that *more* is needed than just calculations of consequences in terms of frustration of interests or rights of innocent persons. Rights are sometimes worth fighting for, even if we, or other innocent persons, succumb in the process. Utilitarianism of rights seems inconsistent with some of our considered judgments about the justification of domestic political violence. Montaldi's standard can be generalized to explain the justice of political violence, and not only the justice of wars. Indeed, humanitarian intervention is but an extension of the moral right of individuals to revolt against oppression. Because individuals hold rights *qua* individuals, and not as citizens of particular states, the justice of both their revolutionary efforts and of foreign help (humanitarian intervention) should be judged by the same standard.

It is possible at this point to raise the following objection: Indiscriminate political violence, for example terrorism, is often justified by the perpetrators by appealing to the justice of the ends. Yet we feel that what is wrong with terrorism is that it uses the victims as means. The terrorist's bomb kills innocent persons in the pursuit of a just cause, say, to overthrow a tyrannical government. Does then the theory defended here, which provides a moral justification for deaths of (some) innocents in just wars, justify terrorism for a just cause? The response is clearly negative. For, the *means* used in justified revolutions (and wars) must be directed as narrowly as possible to suppress the evil. The just revolutionary does not plant bombs to kill innocents. He conducts his fight against the unjust ruler, and tries as hard as possible to respect persons, that is, to avoid using them as means.[18] The same can be said of humanitarian intervention. Here there are moral constraints upon the forms of transboundary violence, which are well codified in the laws

---

[17] *See* the collection of essays by Richards, Greenawalt, Terrell, Reisman, and Paust, "Human Rights and Human Wrongs: Establishing a Jurisprudential Foundation for a Right to Violence," 32 *Emory L.J.* 383 (1983).

[18] *See* Murphy, "The Killing of the Innocent," 57 *Monist* 528, 538 (1973).

of war, or humanitarian law. Deliberate indiscriminate killing of civilians is always unjustified, even if the war is, in principle, justified.[19] An act of terrorism is an act of violence which the perpetrator *knows* is immediately directed at innocent persons. His purpose is to use the victim as a means for achieving the (just) political end. In contrast, the just warrior does everything possible to avoid hurting the innocent. The deaths of innocent persons in justly conducted just revolutions and wars, as for example in World War II, are instead unwanted yet sometimes uavoidable consequences of morally justified violence. In turn, violence is morally justified if, and only if, it is the only means to restore human rights and liberal institutions.

III. THE DANGER OF ABUSE

The second and quite popular utilitarian argument against humanitarian intervention emphasizes the danger of abuse and partiality by the intervenors. Benn and Peters, in an influential work, capture that idea well:

> Within its own jurisdiction, a state has a claim to interfere with other associations as umpire, providing it does so impartially. But in international affairs, states are very rarely impartial, and their own interests are bound to weigh heavily in shaping their policies. When one state meddles in another's affairs, the nationals of the victim are rarely considered on the same footing as those of the interfering state. The latter treats them rather as means for its own end.[20]

Most legal scholars who are opposed to humanitarian intervention as a matter of morality or policy have done so almost exclusively on the same grounds.[21] As a preliminary matter, it is crucial to note that

---

[19] For example, that lack of respect for the laws of war is one of the factors that sheds doubt on the justice of the war waged by the Nicaraguan rebels. *See infra,* Chapter 10.

[20] S. I. Benn & R. S. Peters, *Social Principles and the Democratic State* 361 (1959).

[21] *See,* e.g., Henkin, "Remarks," 66 *A.S.I.L. Proceedings* 89, 96 (1972); Brownlie, "Humanitarian Intervention," in *Law and Civil War in the Modern World* 217, 226 (I. N. Moore ed. 1974) (it is nearly impossible to discover an aptitude of governments in general for carefully moderated, altruistic, and genuine interventions to protect human rights); Schachter, "The Legality of Pro-Democratic Invasion," 78 *A.J.I.L.* 645, 649 (1984). After conceding that "the will and consent of the governed is (or at least should

this is an empirical rather than a principled claim. It depends on the truth of the empirical proposition that governments always, or almost always, abuse when they intervene abroad, even if they say they are intervening on grounds of humanity, and even if the actual result of the intervention is to restore human rights. Starting from this premise, noninterventionists make an argument along rule-utilitarian lines: It is better to have a rule of absolute nonintervention in order to minimize abuses. The rule-utilitarian is not concerned with the consequences of a particular act—such as, for example, the 1979 French intervention in Central Africa—but rather with the consequences of adopting some general rule, such as the rule allowing for humanitarian intervention.[22] Rule-utilitarians claim that we ought to adopt that rule the general observance of which is likely to have the best overall consequences (for example, in terms of preservation of lives or maximization of rights). Given the danger of abuse, it is argued, an international legal rule against intervention will yield better results in the long run, even if in particular cases intervention would maximize human rights enjoyment. General obedience to an absolute rule of nonintervention will thus save more lives and prevent more suffering, it is claimed, than a rule allowing for the so-called humanitarian exception.[23]

I have partially addressed the argument of abuse in the discussion of the philosophy of John Rawls.[24] There I showed that global rational contractors, when agreeing upon principles of international justice, would weigh *both* the dangers of abuse and underuse of the right of humanitarian intervention. I also argued that to some extent governments will be deterred from abusing the doctrine because their stability

---

be) a key principle for political legitimacy" (id. at 647), Professor Schachter rejects humanitarian intervention because it "would introduce a new normative basis for recourse to war that would give powerful states an almost unlimited right to overthrow governments alleged to be unresponsive to the popular will. . . ." But the right of humanitarian intervention is no more "unlimited" than, say, the right to self-defense. Both of course can be abused, but legally and morally both rights are articulated as capable of exercise under certain conditions. States that do not respect the constraints of humanitarian intervention are guilty of aggression, just as are those states that do not respect the constraints of article 51 of the U.N. Charter.

[22] *See* Smart, "Utilitarianism," in 7 *Encyclopedia of Philosophy* 206 (1967).

[23] *See,* e.g., Brownlie, Humanitarian Intervention, *supra* n. 21, at 226 (intervention has high price in human terms).

[24] *Supra,* Chapter 3.

would be threatened if they did so. Some additional objections to this argument should be noted here. First, the rule-utilitarian is advocating the nonintervention principle because it is presumably most conducive to human happiness. But she is inconsistent if she then recommends that we should obey the rule of absolute nonintervention even in those cases (such as when governments are engaged in serious human rights violations) in which she knows that it will *not* be most beneficial to obey, that is, after subtracting the disutility caused by the "erosion" of the rule from the benign effects of the intervention.[25] If utilitarians are really concerned with beneficial consequences (for example, maximization of rights), then they are logically committed to the proposition that governments may disobey the nonintervention rule in those rare cases where humanitarian intervention will maximize rights enjoyment and the general rule prohibiting war will not be significantly eroded.[26]

Second, there is a problem which is common to rule-utilitarianism generally. Rule-utilitarians argue that (1) if everybody refrained from violent actions, good consequences would result; (2) humanitarian interventions are violent actions; (3) therefore, governments should refrain from performing humanitarian interventions. But the class of violent actions is not the appropriate class to consider when deciding whether humanitarian intervention belongs to the class of actions which would have good or bad consequences if generally performed.[27] The reason is that the class of violent actions *can relevantly be made more specific.* The class of violent actions contains as subclasses the violence of parent against child, the violence of a police officer toward a criminal, the violence of a criminal toward a householder, the military reaction in self-defense, military aggression, violence in human rights violations, humanitarian intervention, and so on. Because the consequences of the general practice of each of these subclasses will be different from those

---

[25] *See* McCloskey, "An Examination of Restricted Utilitarianism," 66 *Phil. Rev.* 466, 475 (1957).

[26] Writes Ewing: "Why on earth should I be debarred from doing something, not because my doing it produces bad consequences, but because, if everybody did it, which I know will not be the case, the consequences *would* be bad?" Ewing, "What Would Happen If Everybody Acted Like Me?" 28 *Philosophy* 16 (1953).

[27] *See* Harrison, "Utilitarianism, Universalisation and Our Duty to Be Just," 53 *Proceedings of the Aristotelian Soc'y* 105, 117 (1953).

of the general practice of violent actions, we should consider the consequences of the general practice of the *species*, not of the *genus*.[28] Therefore, the relevant question from a rule-utilitarian standpoint is what consequences would follow if states generally engaged in *humanitarian* intervention. If part of the definition of the class of actions "humanitarian intervention" is that states do not abuse, then it is difficult to resist the conclusion that the adoption of a rule allowing for humanitarian interventions will have beneficial consequences.[29]

So even conceding that there is a danger of abuse, the argument does not address the issue of the philosophical status of humanitarian intervention. An intervention in which foreign troops abuse their power is not an instance of *humanitarian* intervention. Part of the definition of humanitarian intervention is that it be narrowly aimed at putting an end to human rights violations, if necessary by overthrowing the tyrants. Proponents of this objection must concede that *if* in a particular case the intervening state does not abuse and the rest of the conditions of humanitarian intervention are fulfilled,[30] then the intervention is morally justified. If the state abuses, on the contrary, it is not. This is perfectly correct, but it leaves the philosophical argument intact. Objectors might reply that it is the case that military intervention *always* ends up in abuses. There seem to be, however, instances of intervention which have effectively restored human rights and where intervenors have not abused their power.[31] Whether foreign armies abuse, therefore, is a contingent question.

There is an additional weakness in Benn's and Peters's argument. They assume that governments are justified in intervening in conflicts among citizens because they have a *domestic* commitment to impartiality among them. Because they do not have such commitment with regard to foreigners, the assumption continues, they cannot be impartial

---

[28] Id.

[29] Of course, the rule allowing for the humanitarian exception must be formulated in such terms as to include the requirement of prohibition of abuse. If in all likelihood prospective intervenors will abuse (because, for example, they are notorious for not respecting human rights at home) then *they* are morally banned from intervening. See *infra*, Chapter 6.

[30] In addition to disinterestedness, the conditions for the moral and legal correctness of humanitarian intervention are necessity, proportionality, and welcome by the victims of human rights deprivations. See *infra*, Chapters 6 and 8.

[31] See examples *infra*, in Chapter 8.

when intervening in another state's affairs.[32] Now, why must we assume that governments are *always* impartial when intervening in their citizens' affairs and *never* so when intervening in foreigners' affairs? Some governments are partial and abusive in both situations, that is, when dealing with their citizens and in their foreign adventures; some are more or less impartial with their citizens and abusive abroad; a few are known to have been less abusive when intervening than in their domestic policies; finally, some are relatively impartial both inside and outside their borders. I do not suggest that governments never abuse when intervening for alleged humanitarian motives. Again, the point is that this is an empirical matter. Therefore, the morality of a particular intervention should be appraised in the light of whether or not, in that case, intervenors have in effect aimed their efforts at stopping human rights violations. If they have not, if they have abused, then the intervention is morally unjustified. The moral argument for humanitarian intervention is left intact.

In any case, it is not clear what is meant by "abuse" and "partiality" in this argument. One possible interpretation is that the intervening state abuses when it does not aim its action at stopping human rights violations. As I indicated above, this is enough to turn the intervention into aggression in Walzer's sense. But there is an alternative interpretation. Some legal scholars approach this problem as one of disinterestedness. In this view a necessary condition for the justification of humanitarian intervention is that the intervenors act out of purely humanitarian concerns.[33] A state acts abusively by this standard if it entertains a hidden agenda—if its principal motives are selfish. Noninterventionists, however, are much too ready to stigmatize as abusive every intervention on behalf of human rights whenever they find collateral non-humanitarian reasons behind the intervention. To that end, they usually engage in shrewd and convoluted second-guessing of the intentions of the intervenors, and so they are often able to find the "real" reasons ("power politics" reasons) behind the action.[34] This

---

[32] *See supra* text accompanying n. 19.

[33] *See*, e.g., Moore, Toward an Applied Theory of Intervention, in *Law and Civil War in the Modern World* 3, 24–25 (N. Moore ed. 1974).

[34] This is, of course, a mark of the "realist" school of international politics, according to which states can, or should, only act for reasons of national interest. *See generally*, H. Morgenthau, *Politics Among Nations*, 5–12 (5th ed. 1978). For a philosophical critique, *see* M. Walzer, *Just and Unjust Wars*, 3–19 (1977); and Cohen,

methodology is unacceptable. If we are concerned with human rights we should look most primarily at whether the intervention has rescued the victims of oppression, and whether human rights have subsequently been restored. The intervenor must also employ *means* that are consistent with the humanitarian purpose.[35] But unless other motivations have resulted in further oppression by the intervenors (including political subjugation), they do not necessarily count against the morality of the intervention. It is not immoral for a government to act out of humanitarian *and* self-interested motives at the same time. The true test is whether the intervention has put an end to human rights deprivations. That is sufficient to meet the requirement of disinterestedness, even if there are other, non-humanitarian reasons behind the intervention. There is nothing wrong in a government trying at the same time to rescue foreign victims of oppression and legitimately to advance the interests of its own citizens, provided that the self-interested action does not impair the main humanitarian objective. Humanitarian intervention is thus justified not because the motives of the intervening government are pure, but because "its various motives converge . . . on a single course of action that [is] also the course of action called for by [the victims of oppression.]"[36]

IV. THE FOREIGNERS' LACK OF KNOWLEDGE

Similar considerations can be adduced in reply to the claim that foreigners are in no position to really know what is happening within a state, an argument much emphasized by Walzer and Benn and Peters. Writes Walzer:

> Foreigners are in no position to deny the reality of [the] union [of people and government] . . . They don't know enough about its history, and they have no direct experience, and can form no

---

"Moral Skepticism and International Relations," 13 *Phil. & Pub. Affairs* 299 (1984). For a critique of realism from the standpoint of epistemology and social science, *see* Ashley, "The Poverty of Neo-realism," 38 *Int'l Organization* 225 (1984).

[35] For an application of this standard to the United States intervention in Nicaragua, *see infra,* Chapter 10.

[36] Walzer, *supra* 34, at 105. Walzer here is defending the morality of India's intervention in Bangladesh because the human rights violations by the Pakistani army had reached genocidal proportions.

concrete judgments, of the conflict and harmonies, the historical choices and cultural affinities, the loyalties and resentments, that underlie it. Hence their conduct . . . cannot be determined by either knowledge or judgment.[37]

This assumption is unwarranted. There is no intrinsic reason why foreigners should not know what is happening within the state, especially in terms of human rights abuses. "[W]hy presume we are ignorant?" writes Luban. ". . . There are, after all, experts, experienced travelers, expatriates, scholars and spies; libraries have been written about the most remote cultures."[38] As Luban observes, Walzer's claim sounds like an *a priori* assumption of the philosophy of nationalism, of "you don't really know what it is like" to be a member of one culture.[39] The truth is that we usually do know; we ordinarily make true judgments about other countries, other cultures, and other governments' abuses. Again, this is a contingent matter. If foreigners do not actually know, then they should not intervene. But once they learn about the conditions in the dictatorial society (including history, loyalties, and the rest of the factors mentioned by Walzer) then their conduct is governed by ordinary principles of morality, especially by the right to rescue individuals in need.

Perhaps an example will illustrate this point. During the military dictatorship in Argentina (1976–1983) the rulers undertook a systematic repression, including murder, torture, kidnapping, and imprisonment against all those suspected of being "subversives."[40] Those who were not directly persecuted, while saving their lives, suffered a drastic curtailment of their basic rights, such as freedom of speech, freedom of religion, freedom of thought and conscience, right to privacy, and academic freedom among others. Everybody experienced an ever-present fear of being spied upon and threatened. But the astonishing fact was that during the first two years or so, most ordinary citizens of the second

---

[37] Walzer, "The Moral Standing of States," 9 *Phil. & Pub. Aff.* 209, 212 (1978–79).

[38] Luban, "The Romance of the Nation State," 9 *Phil. & Pub. Aff.* 392, 395 (1980).

[39] Id.

[40] *See generally, Comisión Nacional por los Desaparecidos, Nunca Más* (1984) (Report to President Alfonsín by the Commission of the Disappearance of Persons); and Organization of American States, Interamerican Commission on Human Rights, *Report on the Situation of Human Rights in Argentina* (1981).

group *were not fully aware* of the murders, kidnappings, disappearances, and imprisonments suffered by the first group. It was a frighteningly efficient machinery of underground repression, concealed behind the government's propaganda instrumented by their control of the electronic media and their intimidation of the private press.[41] As a result, *foreign governments and organizations (such as President Carter's administration and Amnesty International) knew more about the atrocities (at least during the first two-and-a-half years) than those who happened to live in Argentina.* We know the reason too well: In free societies, the truth (including the truth about foreign lands) is much more likely to surface than in closed, repressive societies. It is almost a truism to say that a free market of ideas and lack of restrictions on speech are not only formidable counterbalances to arbitrary power, but also our best chance to reach the truth.[42] Conversely, when those values are ignored or suppressed, individuals can hardly perceive or understand what is happening before their eyes. Any educated Frenchman or American knew more about the disappearances in Argentina than their Argentine counterparts, who had to rely on rumors about someone (perhaps a relative or friend) who had mysteriously vanished, or draw inferences from seeing unlicensed cars patrolling the city of Buenos Aires.[43]

In short, Walzer's assumption is unfounded. There may be reasons for not intervening in particular cases of human rights violations, but lack of knowledge will rarely be one of them. As Beitz says, "it is a contingent matter whether a state is in a better position than any other state to assess its members' interests and resolve their claims."[44] Thus the assumption about the lack of knowledge of foreigners is not plausible enough to warrant a general prohibition of intervention.

---

[41] *See* Mignone, Estlund & Issacharoff, "Dictatorship on Trial: Prosecution of Human Rights Violations in Argentina," 10 *Yale J. Int'l L.* 118, 121 (1985).

[42] *See* J. S. Mill, *On Liberty* (1859).

[43] It is true that most people were afraid to know, that many refused to believe, and that many others kept silent, mostly out of fear. The point made in the text does not address the difficult issue of the moral responsibility of the silent majority who, out of fear, did not speak out or act against the tyrants.

[44] C. Beitz, *Political Theory and International Relations* 84 (1979).

CHAPTER 6

A MORAL FRAMEWORK FOR HUMANITARIAN INTERVENTION

The considerations in support of the moral justification of humanitarian intervention in appropriate cases emerge, I hope, from the foregoing critique of the noninterventionist model. In this chapter I shall summarize the ethical theory of international law defended here, in the light of which international legal materials should be interpreted. Our normative theory should be able to perform two tasks. It must try to explain in a consistent manner those norms of international law that are well settled, and it must provide guidance in difficult cases.[1]

1. From an ethical standpoint governments are, internationally and domestically, mere agents of the people. Consequently, their international rights derive from the rights of the individuals who inhabit and constitute the state.

International law has been traditionally articulated as a cluster of inter-state principles and norms. However, since states do not have the same moral status as individuals, discourse about rights of states must be reduced to discourse about rights held by individuals. Propositions

---

[1] *See generally* R. Dworkin, *Taking Rights Seriously* 81 (1978). I extend his argument, originally conceived to account for domestic adjudication, to international legal discourse. *See also* J. Rawls, *A Theory of Justice* 20 (1971) (normative theory must accommodate our firmest convictions and provide guidance where guidance is needed).

about international rights of states can be translated into propositions about individual rights without any loss of meaning. I have suggested that, from a philosophical standpoint, only governments that are representative and respect human rights have these international rights. This is the idea conveyed by the claim that state autonomy can only be predicated of governments that conform with "appropriate principles of justice."[2] The state's rights to political independence and territorial integrity, therefore, derive from the rights of individuals; governments do not have any independent or autonomous moral standing. This suggestion requires further elaboration.

The thesis advanced in this book ultimately rests on a fundamental philosophical assumption: that the reason for creating and maintaining states and governments is precisely to ensure the protection of the rights of the individuals. A necessary condition to justify political power exercised by human beings over their fellow human beings is that the rights of everybody be respected. Thus states and governments do not exist primarily to ensure order, but to secure natural rights. Accordingly, my defense of humanitarian intervention presupposes some form of social contract as the proper philosophical justification of the state.[3] States and governments exist because individuals have consented, or would ideally consent, to transfer some of their rights in order to make social cooperation possible.[4] I need not deal here with the issue whether the

---

[2] C. Beitz, *Political Theory and International Relations* 80–81 (1979). As I indicated in previous chapters, I part company with Beitz in two important respects. First, he seems to endorse a form of relativism, and so the notion of "appropriate principles of justice" becomes meaningless. *See supra*, Chapter 4. Second, he refuses to include humanitarian *military* intervention in his analysis of state autonomy. *See* id. at 72. Thus, unfortunately, Beitz is defending a proposition that almost nobody challenges today: that governments may criticize and condemn other governments' human rights practices. The crucial issue, however, is whether a *war* waged in defense of human rights is a just war.

[3] *See generally* Rawls, *supra* n. 1 (hypothetical consent). In the same sense, Beitz, *supra* n. 2, at 80–81. *See also* R. Nozick, *Anarchy, State and Utopia* (1974) Chapters 1 and 2 (state of nature-invisible hand consent); M. Walzer, *Just and Unjust Wars*, 54 (1977) (actual consent over time); Luban, "Just War and Human Rights," 9 *Phil. & Pub. Aff.* 160, 167 (1979–80).

[4] "Thus the rights of political communities are explained by two rather harmless assumptions: that people have rights, and that those rights may be transferred through freely given consent." Luban, *supra* n. 3, at 167. *See also* Doppelt, "Walzer's Theory of Morality in International Relations," 8 *Phil. & Pub. Aff.* 3, 5–6 (1978).

consent is actual[5] or hypothetical.[6] While lines are sometimes hard to draw, in most cases the oppressive nature of a regime is apparent. In an appraisal, both actual and hypothetical consent play a role: actual consent, as reflected in the presence or absence of democratic institutions and effective protection of individual rights; hypothetical consent, as a philosophical standpoint from which to improve and perfect those free institutions.

Rights of governments are solely the result of a consensual transfer by the citizens of some of their rights. That "vertical contract"[7] establishes the legitimate boundaries of political conduct. States and governments that are generally faithful to that original purpose are fully protected, in a moral sense, against foreign intervention—they hold against foreigners the rights of political independence and territorial integrity. To wage war against such states (except in self-defense) is a crime. But governments who turn against their citizens are on a different moral footing. By denying human rights they have forfeited the protection afforded them by international law. They are no longer justified *qua* governments, they no longer represent or are entitled to represent the citizens vis-à-vis the outside world, and therefore foreigners are not bound to respect them.[8] In sum, dictators lose their international rights by virtue of the violation of the terms of the original contract—by betraying their *raison d'être*.

The theory of international law defended here—rights of states as derived from human rights—applies beyond the justification of the doctrine of humanitarian intervention. *All* international rights of states are ultimately derived from the rights of individuals. Article 51 of the United Nations Charter, which recognizes the right of self-defense against armed attack, is a forceful illustration of the humanitarian underpinnings

---

[5] As Walzer suggests; *see* his "The Moral Standing of States," 9 *Phil. & Pub. Aff.* 209 (1978–79).

[6] As Rawls and Beitz suggest, *supra* n. 1.

[7] The term was coined by Luban, "Just War," *supra* n. 3, at 168.

[8] Writes Wasserstrom:

If the basic rights of individuals . . . are crucial, then once again the unanswered question is why war is necessarily wrong if it is begun in order to bring about the recognition and protection of those rights presently unprotected and unrecognized in any particular state.

Wasserstrom, "Book Review," 92 *Harv. L. Rev.* 536,544 (1978).

of international law. Why is a war in self-defense morally justified? Under a human rights-based theory of international law, a war in response to aggression is justified as *governmental action to defend the rights of its subjects, that is, the rights of individuals as victims of the foreign aggression.* The use of force in self-defense, therefore, is a use of force in defense of human rights. But, unless one accepts the notion (rejected in Chapter Three) of an autonomous right of the state, there is no substantial moral difference between the rights of citizens and those of foreigners, at least where basic human rights are at stake. Persons have rights as persons, not as citizens of particular states. Therefore, the same principle that justifies self-defense justifies humanitarian intervention in appropriate cases. The resistance to accept this simple conclusion springs from the continuing adherence, especially in international legal discourse, to some version of the Hegelian Myth—of the moral autonomy of the state.[9]

Even areas of international law that seem quite limited to exclusive intergovernmental relations can ultimately be traced to human rights. When the Law of the Sea Convention grants rights to coastal states, say, to an Exclusive Economic Zone of 200 miles,[10] it is not conferring privileges to governments. The purpose (the only defensible philosophical purpose) of this and any other international legal rule, is to allocate

---

[9] Thus, Professor Kahn is mistaken when he asserts that

Humanitarian intervention and self-defense, as categories of justification for the use of violence, represent two fundamentally different approaches to international law. The former appeals to the notion that the individual is the bearer of morally cognizable and legally relevant rights: the latter appeals to the domestic analogy and the conventional system within which the state is the bearer of legal rights.

Kahn, "From Nuremberg to The Hague: The United States Position in *Nicaragua v. United States* and the Development of International Law," 12 *Yale J. Int'l. L.*2, 50 (1987). As Walzer and others have shown, self-defense is morally justified as a defense of the rights of individuals who are forced to fight by the aggressor, not as a defense of some mystical collective entity with life and rights of its own. To dissociate individual rights from wars against aggression results in a strange two-faced moral-political theory. Professor Kahn and like-minded commentators cannot have it both ways: either they believe in human rights with the consequences that self-defense is also justified by an appeal to them, or they must adhere to some version of the Hegelian Myth (in Professor Kahn's words, "the domestic analogy"), with the nefarious consequences analyzed in Chapter 3.

[10] *See generally* arts. 55–75, U.N. Convention on the Law of the Sea, done at Montego Bay, December 10, 1982, U.N. Document A/CONF. 62/122, October 7, 1982, reprinted at 22 *I.L.M.* 1261 (1983).

resources to, and demarcate spheres of competence between, human beings organized in political communities in a manner consistent with their natural rights. From a philosophical standpoint, international law may not transgress the limits of the individual consent which justifies governments in the first place. While it is true that governments implement and carry out the policies of political communities toward the outside world, they can only act in that capacity as mere agents of the members of the group, and not for their own benefit or interest.

2. A justifiable intervention must be aimed at dictators for the purpose of putting an end to human rights violations.

A military intervention must be truly humanitarian to be justified. The problem is to formulate standards to measure the humanitarian purpose of the intervention. I suggest the following reformulation of this requirement of disinterestedness: First, the intervening state must aim its military action at stopping human rights deprivations by governments. This includes overthrowing dictatorial governments where necessary. Second, collateral non-humanitarian motives (such as desire for border security and strengthening of alliances) should be such as to *not impair or reduce the first paramount human rights objective of the intervention.* Third, the *means* used must always be rights-inspired. This requirement is violated where the intervenor acts in such a way as to impair human rights along the way (for example in third nations), even if its true overall aim is to protect human rights in the target state.[11]

Disinterestedness should not be measured by reference to some mythical "state will" as evidenced in statements by government officials. Rather, the authenticity of the humanitarian purpose must be ascertained by examining the *concrete actions* taken by the intervenor in the light of the human rights objective mentioned above. Some of the questions we must ask in order to assess the morality of the intervention are the following: Did troops occupy the territory longer than necessary?

---

[11] With respect to the U.S. intervention in Nicaragua, there were press reports that the U.S. government, in its anxiety to put pressure on Argentina to get that state to join U.S. policy, threatened President Alfonsín with destabilization of the young Argentine democratic institutions. *See* Chardy, "White House Reportedly Threatened 5 Latin Nations to Support Contras," *Arizona Republic,* May 10, 1987, at 1, col. 4. No humanitarian objective in Nicaragua could possibly justify such immoral foreign policy.

Has the intervenor demanded advantages or favors from the new governments? Did the intervenor seek to dominate the target state in some way unrelated to humanitarian concerns? The test I suggest here avoids the difficulties of trying to determine what state officials really had in mind when they decided to intervene, whether they said that they were acting out of humanitarian concerns or for some other reason. Their actions, not their words, must count. And the final test will be whether human rights have been effectively restored as a result of the intervention.

3.   Humanitarian intervention is governed by the interplay of the principles of proportionality and restoration of human rights.

The principle that applies here is the well-known rule of proportionality. The seriousness of the reaction against human rights abuses must be proportionate both to the gravity of the abuses and to the probability of remedying the situation. If an oppressive government can be forced to enact democratic reforms through economic or political pressure, then those measures are preferable to forcible action and should be tried first. Military intervention, as a remedy against human rights violations, should only be resorted to when all peaceful means have failed or are likely to fail.[12] The reason is simple: war is devastating; innocent people die, countries are ravaged and destroyed. By the same token, the intervention should be as surgical as possible: To be morally acceptable it must be narrowly aimed at the delinquent government and its military supporters, and not at the general population.

The test of proportionality, however, is not a utilitarian test. In some cases of humanitarian intervention more lives will be lost than saved. The moral imperative to fight evil sometimes overrides calculations in terms of death and sufferings.[13] Proportionality must be measured in terms of the size of forcible means used compared to the evil it is designed to suppress. As shown in a previous chapter, such evil is not measured only in terms of individual utility, of human rights enjoyment,

---

[12] This requirement is emphasized by many legal scholars. *See*, e.g., Moore, "Toward an Applied Theory for the Regulation of Intervention" in *Law and Civil War in the Modern World* 3, 24–25 (J. N. Moore ed. 1974).

[13] *See supra* Chapter 5.

but in terms of the disrespectful nature of the dictatorial regime which is being targeted by the intervention. Under the approach suggested here, rights of innocent persons may sometimes be infringed, but only to restore human rights in a society where they are being ignored in a widespread, consistent and patent manner. In Rawls's terms, "a less extensive liberty must strengthen the total system of liberty shared by all."[14] Extending this principle to international relations, one might say that the hardships that result from intervening can only be justified if the intervention has strengthened the total system of liberty, i.e., human rights, shared by all, where liberty is defined in a nonutilitarian way. Yet it is important to stress that, other things being equal, humanitarian interventions that are likely to cause substantially disproportionate additional suffering should not be initiated. As indicated above, consequences in terms of suffering are important, although they should not be the only concern. There will always be need of a prudential calculation on the part of governments; indeed, this is the reason why humanitarian intervention is a right and not a duty of governments.[15]

The principle of proportionality also dictates that human rights violations must be serious enough to justify foreign intervention. As explained in the previous chapter, human rights deprivations that justify war are disrespectful violations in the Kantian sense, that is, governmental infringements aimed at thwarting individual autonomy. This proviso has two dimensions. Quantitatively, human rights deprivations must be extensive, although they need not reach genocidal proportions. Qualitatively, only the violation of basic civil and political rights warrants humanitarian intervention. As to the quantitative element, where the violation of human rights is not systematic, force should not be used. Violations of human rights may occur even in democratic societies. The test, however, is whether human rights violations are sufficiently widespread and pervasive as to justify classifying that society as a repressive state. There are many well-known indicators of freedom. Is the government representative? Does it practice arbitrary detention or

---

[14] Rawls, *supra* n. 1, at 302.

[15] Indeed, there is a strong case for a duty (and not just a right) of humanitarian intervention once the intervening government has cleared all of the prudential hurdles. I cannot, however, pursue the point here: I am content to show that there is at least a right to intervene.

torture? Is there freedom of speech? Are political opponents allowed? How are they treated? Is there a minimally fair judicial system? Are people being kidnapped by government forces? It is a conjunction of these and other similar factors that turn governments into illegitimate, outlaw dictatorships.

While cases like Amin's Uganda and Pol Pot's Cambodia are clear instances of situations warranting humanitarian intervention, oppression need not reach those proportions to warrant foreign-supported over-throw. As shown above, all dictators guilty of disrespectful human rights deprivations are equally illegitimate, and so people have a right to revolt against them and, to that end, to seek and receive outside help. We saw that Walzer argues for the permissibility of humanitarian interven-tion only in cases of genocide, enslavement and mass deportation.[16] But once he has allowed for those cases his own argument for state autonomy falls apart. Why only those cases and not others? Why should self-determination have priority over freedom from terror, torture, or suppressed speech?[17] We are all too well acquainted with dictatorial methods not to know that individuals can be denied their basic rights even if no genocide or enslavement is taking place.[18] Governments that engage in rule by terror have no more claim to legitimacy than Amin or Pol Pot.

As to the qualitative element, I suggest that only willful violations of civil and political rights warrant humanitarian intervention. I part company here with David Luban in two respects. The theory he devel-oped in his article "Just War and Human Rights" is at the same time under-inclusive and over-inclusive. It is wanting because it restricts hu-manitarian intervention to remedy deprivations of "security rights," that is, the rights not to be subject to torture, killing, arbitrary arrest, and so on.[19] He thus excludes pro-democratic intervention. In contrast, I have suggested that governments that are not representative are not interna-tionally legitimate. However, two possible situations must be carefully distinguished with regard to the correctness of intervention aimed at

---

[16] See Walzer, supra n. 3, at 89–90.

[17] See Doppelt, "Statism without Foundations," 9 Phil. & Pub. Aff. 398, 403 (1980).

[18] See Wasserstrom, "Book Review," supra n. 8, at 544.

[19] Luban, "Just War," supra n. 3, at 175.

overthrowing unrepresentative governments. Either a non-elected government plans to grant free elections in the reasonably near future or it is permanently encroached into power. If the former, the principle of proportionality dictates restraint, because there is no need to intervene to restore human rights. If the government is instead permanentl, denying individuals their right to participate in political affairs, political consent is by definition absent. Such undemocratic government is therefore illegitimate and the citizens have a right to revolt; and in doing so they have a right to request and receive foreign support.

Luban's theory is also over-inclusive because it allows intervention in defense of "subsistence" rights, which include the rights to healthy air and water, adequate food, clothing, and shelter.[20] There are two alternative decisive reasons for restricting the right of humanitarian intervention to cases of serious violations of civil and political rights. First, one can take the position that problems of distributive justice often involve issues of policy, not of rights. In this view, individuals have consented to transfer to the majoritarian process the decision-making power regarding economic policies (recall that this is the hypothesis where political rights are observed). Alternatively, one can defend the view that, while distribution of wealth and power does raise issues of rights, liberty has a lexical priority over economic justice.[21] Such priority is reflected in the fact that while the majoritarian process cannot justify the violation of civil and political rights, it can and often does yield disparate conceptions of economic justice about which reasonable men and women may disagree. Therefore, foreign intervention to protect socio-economic rights in states where civil and political rights are observed violates the territorial integrity and political independence of those states. The only exception, more apparent than real, is where the government willfully fails to take action to prevent the starvation or death by disease of the population. Intervention then is justified. But this can best be described as a case of violation of the right to life.[22] In most cases the priority we accord to liberty indicates that it is the

---

[20] Id. at 175.

[21] See Rawls, *supra* n. 1, at 243–251, 541–548.

[22] See generally Bazyler, "Stopping the Bloodshed: The Doctrine of Humanitarian Intervention Reexamined in Light of the Kampuchea and Ethiopia" (1987 in the *Stanford J. Int'l L.*).

safeguarding of civil and political rights, and not of a particular pattern of wealth distribution, that legitimizes governments.

4. The victims of oppression must welcome the intervention.

A necessary condition for humanitarian intervention is that the victims of human rights violations welcome the foreign invasion. This requirement is met when subjects are actually willing to revolt against their tyrannical government. This definition, however, must be refined further.[23] For there are situations where tyrants exercise extreme forms of terror that hypnotize their victims into "willing" submission. Because individuals in those extreme situations have lost their moral autonomy, the moral correctness of humanitarian intervention cannot depend on their expressed will to revolt. We must therefore qualify the requirement as follows: *Humanitarian intervention is forcible help to individuals who are willing to revolt against their tyrannical government, or who would be willing to revolt if they were fully autonomous.* It must be stressed that only extreme forms of submission of the will should trigger the applicability of this model of ideal, as opposed to actual, rationality.[24] In most cases the victims of oppression must actually be willing to receive outside help.

This important requirement helps us put humanitarian intervention in its proper moral perspective. The aim of intervention is to rescue individuals from their own government. If the citizens whose rights are being violated do not wish to be rescued—if they consent to their government—then foreigners should not substitute their judgment for that of the citizens. Traditional critics have portrayed humanitarian intervention as unilateral action taken by foreign governments to remedy what those governments subjectively perceive as human rights deprivations.[25] Indeed, even the word "intervention" wrongly emphasizes the

---

[23] I am indebted to Jeffrie Murphy on this point.

[24] Thus it is not enough to say that the "dominant ideology" by definition keeps people in submission, and that therefore we should always appeal to their ideal, rather than actual, desires.

[25] Walzer's argument in "The Moral Standing of States," *supra* n. 5, is weakened by his assumption that humanitarian intervention is always, or almost always, carried out against the wishes of the people. But what justifies this presumption? It is more natural to adopt the contrary presumption: that people who are persecuted, tortured, arrested, and spied on by their government would prefer to be liberated.

standpoint of the intervenor rather than that of the victims of human rights deprivations. The definition suggested here underscores instead the essential moral link between the will of the citizens who revolt against their tyrants and the foreigners who are willing to help them. The task, then, is to determine the scope of this requirement.

Michael Walzer concedes that if "the invaders are welcomed by a clear majority of the people, then it would be odd to accuse them of any crime at all,"[26] a statement that seems to be inconsistent with his views about communal integrity.[27] More important, the claim that only majoritarian approval legitimizes humanitarian intervention is morally weak. Such claim rules out intervention to protect minorities whose rights are being systematically denied by the government with majoritarian acquiescence. To be sure, Walzer concedes that intervention on behalf of minorities who are victims of genocide, enslavement or mass deportation is justified.[28] But in all other cases where minorities are persecuted short of genocide Walzer's theory would deny the right of minorities to seek and receive outside help. This view is unacceptable from a natural rights perspective. There are certain limits that not even political action validated by the majoritarian process or general acquiescence may override. The requirement of local support for the intervention cannot be measured by an opinion poll among the citizens of the state.

The view suggested here instead is that the *victims themselves* must welcome the intervention.[29] If the victims of oppression (whether or not they are a majority of the population) reject foreign intervention and prefer instead to tolerate their situation, then foreigners should exercise restraint. Conversely, if the victims of oppression welcome the intervention they are entitled to receive help, provided that the other requirements obtain, even if a majority of the population is ready to join the tyrants against the foreigners. It is worth noting that, contrary to what Walzer and others suggest, there is evidence that in recent instances of

---

[26] Walzer, *supra* n. 5, at 213–214, n. 7.

[27] For a full discussion of Walzer's theory, *see supra*, Chapters 2 to 6.

[28] *See supra*, n. 13 and accompanying text.

[29] Of course, the requirement that the violation of rights be substantial still holds. It would not be enough that, say, some few persons welcome the intervention. That is ruled out by the principle of proportionality.

humanitarian intervention local populations have welcomed the inter-venors.[30] Similarly, in cases where the victims rejected the (benign) intervenors, as the Mexicans did during Woodrow Wilson's intervention in 1914, the results were disastrous.[31] While the presumption should be that the oppressed people wish to be liberated from the tyrants, democratic governments must make sure as best they can before they decide to intervene that such is indeed the case.

In many situations the local support for intervention will be evidenced by a request to intervene from local leaders. In this context, it is necessary to mention here Walzer's theory of counter-intervention. Following Mill and Montague Bernard, Walzer claims that foreign intervention is justified in a civil war when it is designed to offset prior or simultaneous intervention by another foreign state.[32] The aim of counter-intervention, he argues, is to restore the balance of forces in the indigenous struggle—to protect the integrity of the process of self-determination.[33] Gerald Doppelt has forcefully responded to this amoral theory of counter-intervention:

> But this is a very strange doctrine. . . . [I]f one side clearly represents the democratic or liberal forces . . . and gets the external military intervention it needs and requests, would another state have the right to intervene on the side of the tyrannical government and its supporters merely to restore the original balance of forces?[34]

Walzer answers this question in the affirmative. So not only does he reject humanitarian intervention (except for genocide, enslavement or mass deportation) but he accepts pro-dictatorship intervention when the democratic forces are receiving outside help! I need not, at this stage

---

[30] *See* the cases examined *infra*, in Chapter 8.

[31] *See* Gilderhus, *Diplomacy and Revolution* 11 (1977).

[32] Walzer, *Wars, supra* n. 3, at 96–97.

[33] In his reply, Walzer merely restates his position:

Counter-interventions . . . can be defended without reference to the moral character of the parties. Hence it may be the case that a foreign state has a right to intervene even when, given certain political principles, that would not be the right thing to do.

Walzer, "The Moral Standing of States," *supra* n. 5, at 217.

[34] Doppelt, "Walzer's Theory of Morality in International Relations," 8 *Phil. & Pub. Aff.* 3, 13 (1978).

in my argument, reiterate that this "neutral" rule of counter-intervention disregards the moral dimension of the internal struggle.[35] Because in civil wars the correctness of foreign intervention cannot be disentangled from the justice of the cause, intervention in favor of tyrants is *always* unjustified, regardless of whether it is in response to prior intervention on behalf of the democratic, or prohuman rights, forces.[36] Walzer's astonishing defense of foreign intervention in favor of tyrants where the democratic forces have already received, or are receiving, outside help, reveals the implausibility of Walzer's conception of self-determination as the highest value of international morality.[37] It underscores the exalted and primary status enjoyed by the rights of states, and not of individuals, in his theoretical scheme. Put simply, noninterventionism is a doctrine that strongly supports the international status quo; it is, therefore, blind to the moral dimension of politics.[38] Such a view cannot possibly have a place in an ethical theory of international law rooted in human rights.

---

[35] *See* S. Hoffman, *Duties Beyond Borders* 71 (1981). Cf. Coste, "Réflexion philosophique sur le problème de l'intervention," 71 *Revue générale de droit international public* 369, 373 (1967) (arguing that failure to intervene amounts to adopting a value judgment toward the internal conflict).

[36] Walzer's reference to the laws of war is irrelevant. *See* Walzer, *supra* n. 5, at 217. Of course, all parties in a civil war, including the "Forces of Good," have to abide by those rules. However, that does not address the crucial moral issue; namely that one of the parties in the civil war is waging a just war and the other is not. They cannot be *both* waging a just war. Of course, intervention in favor of illiberal *rebels* is also immoral. Democratic, rights-loving governments should always be supported, even militarily, if their existence is threatened.

[37] *See* Doppelt, *supra* n. 29, at 13.

[38] *See* Wasserstrom, *supra* n. 8, at 544.

PART TWO

HUMANITARIAN INTERVENTION IN
INTERNATIONAL LAW

CHAPTER 7

THE CONCEPT OF HUMANITARIAN INTERVENTION IN INTERNATIONAL LAW

I. SOFT, HARD, AND FORCIBLE INTERVENTION

The customary meaning of prohibited intervention in international law denotes "dictatorial interference . . . in the affairs of another state for the purpose of maintaining or altering the actual condition of things."[1] Prohibited intervention in international law involves, therefore, some kind of coercive action. The International Court of Justice has confirmed this definition of prohibited intervention. According to the Court, acts of prohibited intervention must be coercive, and they must be aimed at thwarting choices by the target state that under international law must remain free.[2] Thus the *means* of the intervention must be coercive (although not necessarily *forcible*) and the *ends* of the intervention must be to influence another state (by effect of the coercion exercised) on a matter falling under the state's domestic jurisdiction. Both requirements must be met for an action to be called "prohibited intervention" in this traditional sense. The Charter of the United Nations in turn prohibits the Organization from intervening "in matters which

---

[1] 1 L. Oppenheim, *International Law* 305 (H. Lauterpacht ed. 1955); *see also,* C. Arellano García, *Derecho Internacional Público* 465–66 (1983).

[2] Case of Military and Paramilitary Activities In and Against Nicaragua (*Nicaragua v. U.S.*), Merits, Judgment of June 27, 1986, 1986 *I.C.J. Rep.* 14 (hereinafter *Nicaragua case*), 107–108.

are essentially within the domestic jurisdiction of any state."[3] This limitation does not apply to the enforcement measures taken by the United Nations Security Council under Chapter VII of the Charter. The prohibition in Article 2(7) is but one instance of a broader duty of international organizations and states not to intervene in matters that fall within the domestic jurisdiction of sovereign states.[4] It is safe to assume that the legal principles that govern *unilateral* intervention will differ from those that govern *collective* intervention, especially intervention authorized by international organizations such as the United Nations or the Organization of American States.[5]

Yet obviously the word "intervene" in article 2(7) cannot possibly embody the idea of coercion. Rather, that article merely prohibits any United Nations organ from *discussing, examining, or issuing recommendations* on matters that fall within the state's domestic jurisdiction.[6] The prohibition in article 2(7) thus covers *noncoercive* action by the United Nations: the word "intervene" is used here in its ordinary, nontechnical sense, not as a legal term of art. This is confirmed by the fact that article 2(7) expressly *exempts* from the prohibition those cases where the Organization is otherwise entitled to take coercive enforcement measures under Chapter VII of the U.N. Charter. Thus we need to ask three disctinct legal questions. First, what is the present scope of domestic jurisdiction removed from the scrutiny of the international community, and the United Nations in particular? Second, can individual states use force to protect human rights? Third, can the United Nations validly adopt coercive measures (including force) against a state

---

[3] Art. 2(7), U.N. Charter.

[4] The traditional Cold War view of nonintervention is reflected, *inter alia,* in the Declaration of Principles of International Law Concerning Friendly Relations and Cooperation Among States in Accordance with the Charter of the United Nations, U.N. G.A. Res. 2625 (XXV) 25, U.N. G.A.O.R., Supp. No. 28, U.N. Doc. A/8028, at 121 (1970) (hereinafter Resolution 2625).

[5] For a classic overview of the principle of nonintervention, *see* A. Thomas & A. J. Thomas, *Nonintervention* (1956). *See also* T. Farer, "The Regulation of Foreign Intervention in Civil Armed Conflict," 142 *R.C.A.D.I.* 291 (1974); the essays collected in *Intervention in World Politics* (Hedley Bull ed. 1984); and those in *To Loose the Bands of Wickedness: International Intervention in Defence of Human Rights* (N. Rodley ed. 1992).

[6] *See* H. Lauterpacht, *International Law and Human Rights* 166–173 (1950); *see also* D. Nincic, *The Problem of Sovereignty in the Charter and in the Practice of the United Nations* 161–170 (1977); and Gilmour, "The Meaning of 'Intervene' within

to remedy a situation *other* than a breach of the peace or act of aggression? In this section I discuss the first question. The second question is examined in the next section. The third question will be discussed in Chapter 9.

As a preliminary matter, it is necessary to distinguish between three different meanings of "intervention," according to the degree of coercion utilized in the attempts to influence other states. The first is the sense in which the word is used in article 2(7). In this sense, "intervention" means simply discussion, examination, and recommendatory action: this I will call *soft* intervention. The second meaning of the word "intervention" refers to the adoption of measures that (unlike soft intervention) are coercive but do not involve the use of force, such as economic and other kinds of sanctions: this I will refer to as *hard* intervention. And finally, the word "intervention" is often used to refer to acts involving the use of force (as in "humanitarian intervention"): this I call *forcible* intervention. The important issue regarding forcible intervention is that the use of force is subject to independent legal constraints. Therefore, a situation which could qualify for collective soft or hard intervention may nevertheless not be appropriate for collective forcible action.

The distinction between the different forms of intervention according to their degree of coercion leaves intact a common requirement: prohibited intervention has to be action aimed at influencing a government on an issue where the target state has legal discretion. This is plain in the case of soft intervention, where the only issue is an issue of *ends*, not of means, since the means (discussion, recommendation) are perfectly permitted in principle. But the same is true in cases of hard and forcible intervention. If state A violates, say, a fishing treaty with state B, and B adopts economic sanctions in retaliation, B's action will not be deemed "intervention," because A was not legally free to violate the treaty; that matter did not fall within A's exclusive jurisdiction. The legality of B's retaliation will be determined by the law of countermeasures, in particular by the principle of proportionality. If, however, state A decides, say, to nationalize certain natural resources, and B responds by declaring an economic embargo against A, this action amounts to prohibited hard

Article 2(7) of the United Nations Charter—An Historical Perspective," 16 *Int'l & Comp. L.Q.* 330 (1967).

intervention, because B's action is coercive (although not forcible) and the question of nationalization of natural resources is one over which A has, in principle and absent an international commitment, exclusive jurisdiction. In this example, B has no right to coerce A into reversing the nationalizations.

The same analysis applies to forcible intervention. Applying the general requirements that define unlawful intervention, prohibited forcible intervention will occur when two conditions are met: first, the action by the intervenor can be described as indirect or direct use of force, and second, the "choices" that the intervenor attempts to influence should remain "free" for the target state—the choices have to fall under its exclusive jurisdiction.[7] Here again, the two requirements must be met. If a state violates a trade agreement with another state, and the latter retaliates with a limited forcible mesaure, this will of course be a violation of the prohibition on the use of force (since treaty breaches of this kind do not justify the use of force) but not a violation of the principle of nonintervention, because actions concerning a treaty are not within the legal discretion of the target state.[8] The need to determine whether or not a subject-matter falls within the domestic jurisdiction of a state arises, therefore, in the assessment of all three forms of intervention.

II. THE CONCEPT OF EXCLUSIVE DOMESTIC JURISDICTION

The concept of exclusive domestic jurisdiction has been the subject of controversy both during the life of the League of Nations and in the United Nations era. Two schools of thought competed. According to

---

[7] I use "exclusive domestic jurisdiction" or "domestic" jurisdiction interchangeably, although technically those areas where the state is legally "free" may or may not concern "domestic" matters. For example, choices regarding foreign policy are not "domestic," but they may be legally discretionary and thus within the exclusive jurisdiction of the state. Thus, for example, Resolution 2625, *supra* n. 4, prohibits intervention in the *internal or external* affairs of other states. Although the issue is a general one of the permissible limits of state influence, technically only intervention in internal affairs gives rise to issues of *domestic* jurisdiction.

[8] If the aggrieved state responds instead by invading the wrongdoer (as opposed to merely retaliating) this will of course be a violation of the principle of nonintervention as well.

the first one, there are matters that *necessarily* fall within the domestic jurisdiction of states. For this view, the *essence* of sovereignty requires that certain matters, in particular matters broadly referred to as *domestic policy*, be left outside the reach of international law.[9] In particular, such matters ought not be subject to action undertaken by international organizations. On this view, the concept of domestic jurisdiction does not depend on the development of international law; it is not relative but fixed, at least as long as we continue to live in a world of sovereign states. The essential attributes of the sovereign state require that certain matters be left to the state's own sovereign judgment. There are, therefore, matters that fall *essentially* within the domestic jurisdiction of states—just as the language of article 2(7) suggests. Those who defend the essentialist view give various versions of the content and scope of domestic jurisdiction, but the common theme is that matters pertaining to exclusive domestic jurisdiction are those that are closely related to the sovereignty of the state.[10]

The second position is the *legalist* view of domestic jurisdiction. For this view, whether or not a matter falls within the state's *domaine reservé* cannot be determined by appealing to the notion of sovereignty. This is instead a relative matter which depends on the state of international law at any given time in history.[11] Thus, to cite the most notorious example of such evolution, human rights were a matter of exclusive domestic jurisdiction before 1945; but this is no longer the case today. Where a rule of international law regulates an issue, it automatically ceases to be a matter of exclusive domestic jurisdiction for the states formally bound by the rule.

There are problems with both positions. The essentialist view can only be defended by appealing to an abstract and autonomous *normative* conception of state sovereignty. The gist of the essentialist argument

---

[9] Thus, for example, a commentator opines that: [it] has always been considered that the constitutional, political, and social organization of a state is essentially a matter coming under the latter's sovereignty, i.e., within its domestic jurisdiction." Nincic, *supra* n. 6, at 186. *See, e.g., Nicaragua case, supra* n. 2, at 107–108.

[10] Most of the scholars in the pre-United Nations era favored this view. *See,* e.g., T. Woolsey, *International Law* 50 (4th ed. 1874); P. Fauchille, *Traités de droit international public* 396–97 (1922).

[11] The classic citation for this proposition is the dictum by the Permanent Court of International Justice in the Nationality Decrees case: "The question whether a certain matter is or is not solely within the jurisdiction of a state is an essentially relative

is that certain matters *ought not* be regulated by international law, come what may. But this cannot be defended without providing a justification of state sovereignty in the first place; otherwise the argument becomes circular ("exclusive domestic jurisdiction derives from the attributes of sovereignty, and sovereignty consists of matters that are within the state's exclusive domestic jurisdiction"). So the essentialist view is less a theoretical explication of domestic jurisdiction than a *moral* injunction to international actors not to intervene in matters that are thought to be closely bound with the sovereignty of the state.[12]

At first blush, the legalist position seems closer to the truth. Indeed, international law *defines* the boundaries of state sovereignty. Yet the problem with the legalist position is that, without more, it is tautological. It simply says that domestic jurisdiction ends where international jurisdiction begins. This is true but trivial: *Where exactly* does international jurisdiction take over? At least the essentialist view had some (perhaps unattractive) suggestions about substance. Legalism needs to provide a criterion to decide which matters fall within the state's exclusive domestic jurisdiction, and the answer will depend on the operational definition of international law. On a strictly positivist view of international law, only custom and treaty count. In contrast, on a more teleological view of international law, moral principles, purposes, and policies will count as well. Domestic jurisdiction will then swell or shrink accordingly.[13]

---

question; it depends upon the development of international relations." 1923 *P.C.I.J. Rep.* (ser. B.), at 23.

[12] The essentialist view of domestic jurisdiction is thus a version of anti-cosmopolitan nationalism, and it will stand or fall with it. If, for example, one believes that state sovereignty is not autonomous or original but rather derivative from more basic moral principles such as individual dignity and human rights, then the essentialist view of domestic jurisdiction in this all-or-nothing form is harder to defend. I defend a derivative concept of sovereignty in F. R. Tesón, *The Philosophy of International Law* (Westview Press, forthcoming). If one has a derivative definition of state sovereignty, one can make distinctions regarding state sovereignty and the conditions under which it has normative weight against foreign intervention. These distinctions will be based, perhaps, on different degrees of domestic legitimacy.

[13] Some writers clearly saw this weakness of the legalist position. It is not enough to say that domestic jurisdiction ends where international jurisdiction starts; nor is it possible to say that the United Nations organs may decide the issue on a case-by-case basis. A policy or principle is needed to decide in individual cases whether or not a matter is within the domestic jurisdiction of states. Professor Rosalyn Higgins, in her seminal discussion of domestic jurisdiction thirty years ago, proposed the policy that "states must be made responsible when their actions cause substantial international

Whatever the answer may be to this jurisprudential question, this much seems true today: the "substantial international effects" policy is outmoded, and the international community is legally entitled to pass judgment and take action on matters that used to be deemed as purely internal. To buttress this conclusion, I will review a number of areas where the concept of domestic jurisdiction has undergone spectacular transformations in recent years. Areas which have traditionally been claimed by states as falling within their *domaine reservé* are now unequivocally subject to review by international bodies, in particular to soft and hard intervention by international organizations.

III. HUMAN RIGHTS

Human rights have long been subtracted from the exclusive domestic jurisdiction of states, notwithstanding the fact that they seem to constitute the paradigm of an "essentially" domestic matter since they define the relationship between government and subjects. Already in the early discussions of the concept of domestic jurisdiction in the U.N. Charter writers had reached this conclusion, citing not only the well-known provisions of the U.N. Charter, but also a number of human rights cases that had been addressed by the various organs of the United Nations.[14] The proposition that human rights are no longer a matter of exclusive domestic jurisdiction is indisputable. This is so, independently of the legal grounds for the obligation of states to respect human rights.[15] The General Assembly routinely adopts resolutions concerning human rights. Many are addressed to the membership in general, but some are addressed directly to particular states. Thus recently the General

---

effects." R. Higgins, *The Development of International Law Through the Political Organs of the United Nations* 62 (1963).

[14] *See,* e.g., Higgins, *supra* n. 13. Felix Ermarcora, "Human Rights and Domestic Jurisdiction," 124 *R.C.A.D.I.* vol. II, 371, 436 (1968). The most famous case is that of South Africa which, contrary to the widespread opinion that the basis for the exercise of United Nations powers was the "international effects" test, is and was a human rights case. Maintaining and enforcing a system of *apartheid* is not a valid "domestic jurisdiction" choice for a state, *regardless* of whether or not it is deemed to produce international effects.

[15] *See generally,* B. Weston, "Human Rights," in *Human Rights in the World Community* 14 (B. Weston & P. Claude eds., 2d ed. 1992).

Assembly has passed resolutions on the human rights situation in Bosnia-Herzegovina;[16] El Salvador;[17] Iraq;[18] Myanmar (formerly Burma);[19] Afghanistan;[20] territories occupied by Israel;[21] Haiti;[22] and Iran.[23] Some of these cases (e.g., the "intifada" in the territories occupied by Israel or the situation in Afghanistan) do produce substantial international effects and can therefore be explained by reference to the traditional test, but this rationale is seldom offered by the General Assembly. In the case of Myanmar (Burma), the General Assembly simply recalled that states have an obligation to promote and protect human rights in accordance with the applicable international human rights instruments. In the case of El Salvador, where a civil war of serious regional repercussions was taking place, the General Assembly could not emphasize enough the importance of observing human rights, "full respect of which is essential to the attainment of a just and lasting peace." No references to international repercussions are cited in the case of Haiti either. In those cases of human rights violations that do threaten international peace and security, such as *apartheid* in South Africa, the action by the United Nations is legally *overdetermined*: the "international effects" test *and* the human rights violations provide equally valid grounds for soft intervention.

That human rights violations warrant United Nations soft intervention has ceased to be a matter of controversy. Governments singled out by the General Assembly very rarely claim nowadays that such action violates article 2(7) of the U.N. Charter. Because the General Assembly treats the Charter and the Universal Declaration of Human Rights as establishing definite obligations for members, violations of such obligations can trigger action by the appropriate United Nations body.

---

[16] A/Res/46/242.

[17] A/Res/46/133.

[18] A/Res/46/134.

[19] A/Res/46/132.

[20] A/Res/46/136.

[21] A/Res/46/76.

[22] A/Res/46/7.

[23] A/Res/45/173.

IV. FORM OF GOVERNMENT: DEMOCRACY

Many writers and governments who accept the premise that observance of human rights, in the sense of *treatment* by a government of its own citizens, is now an appropriate subject for international scrutiny, nonetheless draw the line on the question of the *legitimacy* of the government itself. They argue that *this* is a question of domestic jurisdiction, if there ever was one. In the absence of widespread human rights violations, the international community should not be in the business of passing judgment on the legitimacy of *origin* of a government.[24] The question of internal political legitimacy is, in this view, a matter falling under the exclusive jurisdiction of the state and thus exempt from even soft intervention by international organizations or, indeed, the international community as a whole.

There are *a priori* reasons to doubt the conclusion that international law is or should not be concerned with democratic legitimacy. First and fundamental is the question of *agency*. If international law is largely created by nation-states, then the international community needs some criterion to determine when some official actually *represents* the state. Traditional international law has proposed the criterion of *effectiveness*. A government internationally represents a people living in a territory if that government has effective political control over that people.[25] Traditional international law is indifferent to how that political control has been acquired. Whether political power has been consensually granted to the government or usurpers rule instead through fear and terror is of little interest to supporters of the traditional doctrine of effectiveness.

Such view is indefensible. If the international system is going to be the result of what the "peoples of the United Nations" want it to be,[26] then it makes sense to require that governments which participate in the creation of international law be the real representatives of the people

---

[24] This was the virtually unanimous view before 1948. *See* G. H. Fox, "The Right to Political Participation in International Law," 17 *Yale J. Int'l L.* 539, 549–69 (1992).

[25] The classical view is summarized in Restatement of Foreign Relations (Third), §201 (d).

[26] *See* Preamble, U.N. Charter.

who reside within the boundaries of the state. A rule requiring democratic legitimacy in the form of free adult universal suffrage seems the best approximation to actual political consent and true representativeness.

Second, there are strong grounds for believing that democratic rule is a necessary condition for enjoying other human rights. While it is always possible to imagine a society where human rights are respected by an enlightened despot, this has never occurred in practice. This is why the right to political participation is included in the major human rights conventions.[27] The right to participate in government is a very important human right in itself; it is also crucially instrumental to the enjoyment of other rights. Its violation should therefore trigger appropriate international scrutiny.

The third reason for requiring democratic rule is the one indicated by Kant: democracies are more peaceful, and therefore a rule requiring democratic rule is consonant with the ideal of a lasting world peace, in a way that the rule of effectiveness or pure political power, which countenances tyrannies, is not.[28] This is so because tyrannies tend to be more aggressive *and* because the difference in regimes is a major cause of conflict. Democracies have built-in mechanisms that cause them to avoid war with one another altogether. The reason why democracies are sometimes belligerent is that they often perceive threats by illiberal regimes to their democratic institutions. These threats are sometimes real and sometimes imaginary, which is why democracies also get involved in unjustified wars. But these wars are always against illiberal regimes. Democracies *do not* make war against one another. So if the aim of international law is to secure a lasting peace where the benefits of international cooperation can be reaped by all, then it has to require democratic legitimacy.

---

[27] *See* International Covenant on Civil and Political Rights, U.N.T.S. 171, 179 at art. 25; American Convention on Human Rights, 36 O.A.S. T.S. 1, OAE/Ser L/V/II.23, doc. 21, rev. 6, 9 *I.L.M.* 673, 682, at art. 23 (1970); Protocol (No.1) to the European Convention for the Protection of Human Rights and Fundamental Freedoms, 213 U.N.T.S. 262, 264; and African Charter on Human and Peoples' Rights, 9 *I.L.M.* 58, 61, at art. 13 (1981).

[28] I summarize here the argument I made in F. R. Tesón, "The Kantian Theory of International Law," 92 *Colum. L. Rev.* 53, 74–81 (1992). The argument relies on the seminal research by M. Doyle, "Kant, Liberal Legacies, and Foreign Affairs (pt.1)," 12 *Phil. & Pub. Aff.* 205, 213 (1983); id., "(pt. 2)," 12 *Phil. & Pub. Aff.* 323 (1983).

But even if none of this were true, even if there were no correlation between democracy and peace, international law should require democratic rule simply because that is the right thing to do. I do not need a complicated philosophical defense of democracy: a simple comparison with the traditional rule of effectiveness will suffice. Traditional international law *authorizes* tyranny. It gives *carte blanche* to anyone who wishes to bypass popular will and seize and maintain power by sheer political force. This is delicately described by pertinent international materials as a state's right to "choose" its political system.[29] Such a state-centric view suffers from acute moral and conceptual poverty. Both ordinary commonsense morality and the structure of international law, which presupposes agency and representation, require that governments should be recognized and accepted in the international community only if they genuinely represent their people.

These arguments suffice, I believe, to demonstrate why international law must recognize an individual and collective right to democratic rule. It has become abundantly clear, moreover, that the principle is supported by contemporary state practice.[30] Professor Thomas Franck's findings are well-known and I am content to rest on them here. I will briefly discuss, however, two precedents: the International Court of Justice's discussion of democracy in the *Nicaragua* case and the resolution on democracy adopted by the U.N. General Assembly.

In spite of some remarkable precedents,[31] until quite recently the principle of democratic rule has been slow to make headway as a universally accepted principle. The main reason, was, of course, the Cold

---

[29] *See,* e.g., U.N. Res. *supra* n. 4 ("Every State has an inalienable right to choose its political . . . system. . . .").

[30] *See generally,* Fox, *supra* n. 24; *see also* T. M. Franck, "The Emerging Right to Democratic Governance," 86 *Am. J. Int'l L.* 46 (1992).

[31] *See,* for example, the International Covenant on Civil and Political Rights, Dec. 16, 1966, 999 U.N.T.S. 171, reprinted in 6 *I.L.M.* 368 (1967), and its Optional Protocol, opened for signature Dec. 19, 1966, art. 1, 999 U.N.T.S. 302. . . . Under the Optional Protocol, the Human Rights Committee held that Uruguay's military regime was in violation of art. 19(2) of the Covenant (which states that everyone shall have the right to freedom of expression, including the freedom to seek, receive, and impart information) when it denied a petitioner the right to freely engage in political and trade union activities. *Alba Pietroria v. Uruguay,* Communication R. 10/44, Report of the Human Rights Committee, 36 U.N. G.A.O.R. Supp. No. 40, at 153–59, U.N. Doc. A/36/40 (1981). For further examples, *see* Franck, *supra* n. 30, at 62–65.

War.[32] The uncertainty and ambivalence of the principle of democratic rule during the Cold War years was demonstrated by the International Court of Justice as recently as 1986.[33] The Court, while accepting that a state may bind itself by treaty or other formal commitment to hold free elections, held that every state "is free to decide upon the principle and methods of popular consultation," this being part of a "fundamental right to choose and implement its own political, economic, and social systems."[34] This includes the "freedom" to be undemocratic (which was precisely the issue the Court was addressing). If other states suspect that a country is sliding toward totalitarianism, there is not much they can do, according to the Court, because "adherence by a State to any particular doctrine does not constitute a violation of customary international law; to hold otherwise would make nonsense of the principle of state sovereignty."[35] As I argue in more detail in Chapter 9, the Court's position is indefensible today.[36] Its rejection of the principle of democratic rule in the Americas was outdated even in 1986; it is bad *general* international law in 1994. Whatever the other merits of the decision, the Court's discussion of democracy in the *Nicaragua* case should be buried along with other Cold War relics.

In the United Nations the movement toward recognition of democratic rule was cautious but unmistakable. On February 21, 1991, the General Assembly adopted Resolution 45/150, entitled "Enhancing the Effectiveness of the Principle of Periodic and Genuine Elections."[37] While this resolution still reflects some ambivalence associated with the tension between sovereignty and human rights, it is an important document. The resolution reaffirms the Universal Declaration of Human

---

[32] In addition to the precedent indicated *supra*, n. 31, the other important Cold War precedent is also found in the Americas. It is the historical resolution by the Council of Ministers of the Organization of American States in 1979 declaring the illegality of the Somoza regime in Nicaragua and calling for its immediate replacement. *See* OEA/Ser.F/II.17, doc. 40, rev. 2 (1979).

[33] *See, Nicaragua* case, *supra* n. 2.

[34] Id. at 131.

[35] Id. at 133.

[36] *See,* F. R. Tesón, "Le Peuple, C'est Moi! The World Court and Human Rights," 81 *Am. J. Int'l L.* 173 (1987).

[37] A/Res/45/150 (Feb. 21, 1991).

Rights, not just in the sense of providing (somewhat vaguely) that "everyone has the right to take part in the government of his or her country," but also, more fundamentally, by affirming that "the will of the people shall be the basis of the authority of government," and that "this will shall be expressed in periodic and genuine elections which shall be by universal and equal suffrage and shall be held by secret vote or by equivalent free voting procedures." This very specific and detailed content of the principle of democratic rule is reiterated throughout the resolution.

The document, however, also warns that these efforts to enhance democracy "should not call into question each State's sovereign right freely to choose and develop its political, social, economic, and cultural systems, whether or not they conform to the preferences of other states." Members have a duty, according to the resolution, to respect the "decisions taken by other states in freely choosing and developing their electoral institutions." The word "freely" in this context seems to mean "free from *foreign* coercion," not necessarily "free from *domestic* coercion." How can this statement be squared with the requirement of democracy and free elections? While on one hand a state has the right to choose its own political system without interference from other states, on the other hand it seems obvious that under the terms of the resolution a state cannot "freely choose" to be undemocratic, even though an undemocratic regime is a "political system."

The way to reconcile these two parts of the resolution is this: the "sovereignty" limitation contained in this resolution refers to the need to tolerate a diversity of *actual electoral procedures* in the domestic practice of members. The core of the principle remains intact, however: states have an obligation to make sure that governments are elected by the people in free elections. Many electoral systems and methods are compatible with this principle, but an undemocratic regime is not. Thus tyranny (meaning by this word an undemocratic regime) cannot be validly "chosen" by a state.

To summarize: There can be little doubt that a principle of democratic rule is today part of international law. While in a universal context the recognition of the principle has had, perhaps, only the effect of subtracting the question of democratic rule from the exclusive jurisdiction of states, the nations in Europe and the Americas have elevated the principle of democracy to the category of a rule which is fully enforce-able through appropriate regional collective mechanisms.

V. HUMANITARIAN INTERVENTION AND THE U.N. CHARTER

1. Article 2(4) of the United Nations Charter and Treaty Interpretation

Establishing the proper scope of the prohibition against the use of force in international law has proved to be a particularly difficult task.[38] Article 2(4) of the United Nations Charter provides:

> All Members shall refrain in their international relations from the threat or use of force against the territorial integrity or political independence of any state, or in any other manner inconsistent with the Purposes of the United Nations.

Whether article 2(4) should be understood to ban virtually all uses of force is the central question. Certain particular exceptions are formally recognized by Article 51 and Chapter VII of the U.N. Charter.[39] Other asserted exceptions, however, are more problematic. Should the use of force to remedy serious human rights violations, or to protect nationals

---

[38] General works include: I. Brownlie, *International Law and the Use of Force by States* (1963) [hereinafter *Use of Force*]; Y. Dinstein, *War, Aggression and Self-Defense* (1994); Council on Foreign Relations, *Right v. Might: International Law and the Use of Force* (1991); *Law and Force in the New International Order* (L. Damrosch & D. Scheffer eds. 1991); J. Stone, *Aggression and World Order* (1958); J. Zourek, *L'Interdiction de L'Emploi de la Force en Droit International* (1974); D. Bowett, *Self-Defence in International Law* (1958); A. Rifaat, *International Aggression* (1979); Waldock, "The Regulation of the Use of Force by Individual States," 81 *R.C.A.D.I.* 457 (1952); Higgins, "The Legal Limits of the Use of Force by Sovereign States: United Nations Practice," 37 *Brit. Y.B. Int'l L.* 269 (1961); Schachter, "The Right of States to Use Armed Force," 82 *Mich. L. Rev.* 1620 (1984) (hereinafter "Armed Force"); Reisman, "Criteria for the Lawful Use of Force in International Law," 10 *Yale J. Int'l L.* 279 (1985); Rostow, "The Legality of the International Use of Force by and from States," 10 *Yale J. Int.l L.* 286 (1985); Wallace, "International Law and the Use of Force: Reflections on the Need for Reform," 19 *Int'l Law.* 259 (1985).

[39] Art. 51 provides:

Nothing in the present Charter shall impair the inherent right of individual or collective self-defence if an armed attack occurs against a Member of the United Nations, until the Security Council has taken measures necessary to maintain international peace and security. . . .

Chapter VII of the U.N. Charter provides for a range of coercive measures against states that refuse to comply with the Council's decisions. *See* U.N. Charter, arts. 39–50.

abroad, or to secure some other legal right—for example, to take territory which the state considers rightfully hers—be included in the prohibition?[40] In Part One I defined humanitarian intervention as the use of international force to help victims of serious human rights deprivations.[41] In the previous section I made some general observations about intervention and domestic jurisdiction. The question with which I shall be concerned in this chapter is whether article 2(4) of the Charter prohibits unilateral or collective humanitarian intervention. Writers are acutely divided on this issue. Some object to all forms of humanitarian intervention. Others object to unilateral humanitarian intervention, but favor collective humanitarian action, especially when authorized by the U.N. Security Council. Others believe that humanitarian intervention is unlawful but sometimes morally justified. Opponents of humanitarian intervention maintain that article 2(4) cannot be interpreted as allowing the doctrine, either because that norm bans virtually all uses of force (with the only two exceptions noted above), or because allowing the exception would open the door to unacceptable abuse, or because, regardless of text, it is just bad policy.[42] Some support for this position

---

[40] *See* Schachter, "Armed Force," *supra* n. 38 at 1620, 1627–1628.

[41] *See supra,* Chapters 1 and 6.

[42] Writers who are generally opposed to the doctrine of humanitarian intervention include Dinstein, *War, Aggression, and Self-Defence, supra* n. 38 , at 86–90; N. Ronzitti, *Rescuing Nationals Abroad and Intervention on Grounds of Humanity* 89–113, 108–110 (1985); Akehurst, "Humanitarian Intervention," in *Intervention in World Politics* 95, 107–112 (H. Bull ed., 1984); Brownlie, "Humanitarian Intervention," in *Law and Civil War in the Modern World* 217 (J. N. Moore ed., 1974); Schachter, "The Legality of Pro-Democratic Invasion," 78 *A.J.I.L.* 645 (1984) (hereinafter "Invasion"); Rodley, "Collective Intervention to Protect Human Rights," in *To Loose the Bands of Wickedness* 14, 39–40 (Nigel Rodley ed., 1992) (generally unsympathetic, with a reluctant nod, however, to the possibility of United Nations intervention); Franck & Rodley, "After Bangladesh: The Law of Humanitarian Intervention by Military Force," 67 *A.J.I.L.* 275 (1973); Tom Farer, "The Regulation of Foreign Intervention in Civil Armed Conflict," 142 *R.C.A.D.I.* 291 (1974); Farer, "An Inquiry Into the Legitimacy of Humanitarian Intervention," in Damrosch & Scheffer, *Law and Force, supra* n. 38, at 185, 188–99 (but see his most recent views, *infra* n. 44); Verwey, "Humanitarian Intervention under International Law," 33 *Neth. Int'l L. Rev.* 357 (1985); Donnelly, "Human Rights, Humanitarian Intervention and American Foreign Policy: Law, Morality and Politics," 37 *J. Int'l Aff.* 311, 314, 317–325 (1984); Fairley, "State Actors, Humanitarian Intervention and International Law: Reopening Pandora's Box," 10 *Ga. J. Int'l & Comp. L.* 29 (1980); Kartashkin, "Human Rights and Humanitarian Intervention," in Damrosch & Scheffer, *Law and Force, supra* n. 38, at 202, 208–09; Henkin, "Use of Force: Law and U.S. Policy," in *Right v. Might: International Law and the Use of Force, supra* n. 38 , at 37, 41–43; Meron, "Commentary on Humanitarian Intervention," in Damrosch & Scheffer,

is provided by resolutions of the United Nations General Assembly.[43] Supporters of unilateral humanitarian intervention claim instead that forcible intervention to protect human rights is or should be an exception to the general prohibition of article 2(4). They rely partly on pure moral grounds, partly on state practice, and partly on an interpretation of the Charter based upon the purposes of the United Nations.[44] The

---

Law and Force, supra n. 38 , at 212–14; Nanda, "Commentary on International Intervention to Promote the Legitimacy of Regimes," in Damrosch & Scheffer, *Law and Force, supra* n. 38 , at 180, 183; Chaterjee, "Some Legal Problems of Support Role in International Law: Tanzania and Uganda," 30 *Int'l & Comp. L.Q.*755 (1981); Chimni, "Towards a Third World Approach to Non-Intervention: Through the Labyrinth of Western Doctrine," 20 *Indian J. Int'l L.* 243, 256 (1980); Jhabvala, "Unilateral Humanitarian Intervention and International Law," 21 *Indian J. Int'l L.* 208 (1981); and Hassan, "Realpolitik in International Law: After Tanzanian–Ugandan Conflict, 'Humanitarian Intervention' Reexamined," 17 *Willamette L. J.* 859 (1980–1981).

[43] For example, the Declaration on Principles of International Law provides that "No state or group of states has the right to intervene, directly or indirectly, *for any reason whatever*, in the internal or external affairs of another state." U.N. G.A. Res. 2625 (XXV), *supra* n. 4 (emphasis added). Similarly, the 1974 U.N. Definition of Aggression, after defining "aggression" as "the use of armed force by a State against the sovereignty, territorial integrity or political independence of another State. . . .," proclaims that "no justification *of whatever nature, whether political, economic, military or otherwise*, may serve as a justification for aggression." U.N. G.A. Res. 3314 (XXIX), 29 U.N. G.A.O.R., Supp. (No. 31) 142, U.N. Doc. A/9631 (1975), art. 1 and 5(1) (emphasis added).

[44] In the first edition of this book I wrote that those writers who favored the legitimacy of humanitarian intervention were "a substantial minority." In my view, that is no longer the case: at the very least, those who favor the doctrine number as many as those who oppose it. Writers who defend humanitarian intervention in some form include John Rawls, "The Law of Peoples," 1993 *Critical Inquiry* 20, 47; L. Brilmayer, *American Hegemony: Political Morality in a One Superpower World* 147–66 (1994); Michael Walzer, *Just and Unjust Wars* 101–108 (1977); Reisman, "Humanitarian Intervention and Fledgling Democracies," 18 *Fordham Int'l L.J.* 794 (1995); "Sovereignty and Human Rights in Contemporary International Law," 84 *Am. J. Int'l L.* 866 (1990); id., "Coercion and Self-Determination: Construing Article (4)" (hereinafter "Coercion"); id., "Humanitarian Intervention to Protect the Ibos," in *Humanitarian Intervention and the United Nations* (R. Lillich ed., 1973) 167 (hereinafter *Humanitarian Intervention*); McDougal, "Response" (with Reisman), 3 *Int'l Law.* 438 (1969); Lillich, "Humanitarian Intervention: A Reply to Ian Brownlie and a Plea for Constructive Alternatives," in *Law and Civil War in the Modern World* 229 (J. N. Moore ed., 1974) (hereinafter "Humanitarian Intervention;" reference to two previous articles); Farer, "A Paradigm of Legitimate Intervention," in *Enforcing Restraint* 316 (L. F. Damrosch ed., 1995); D'Amato, "The Invasion of Panama Was a Lawful Response to Tyranny," 84 *Am. J. Int'l L.* 516 (1990); id., "Nicaragua and International Law: The 'Academic' and the Real," 79 *A.J.I.L.* 657, 659–664 (1985), republished in A. D'Amato, *International Law: Process and Prospect* 223–232 (1987) (hereinafter *Process*); Moore, "Toward an Applied Theory for the Regulation of Intervention," in J. N. Moore (ed.), *supra,* at 3; Burmester, "On Humanitarian Intervention: The New World Order and Wars to Preserve Human Rights," 1994 *Utah L. Rev.* 269; Kylov, "Humanitarian Intervention: Pros and Cons,"

moral case for humanitarian intervention has already been discussed. State and United Nations practice will be examined in the next two chapters. The purpose of this section is to determine whether the analysis of the Charter denies or confirms the existence of the exception.

I argue that conventional methods of treaty interpretation, when applied to article 2(4), are incapable of yielding a solution to the hard case of humanitarian intervention. That solution can only be reached by presupposing an ethical theory of international law. Only then shall we be able to dissolve the tension between the two principles that underlie international legal doctrine—the entitlement to fundamental human rights and the prohibition of war. I have developed a normative theory in the first part of this book. In the light of the conclusions reached there, article 2(4) should be construed as allowing a right of humanitarian intervention.

The principles of treaty interpretation are laid down in articles 31 and 32 of the Vienna Convention on the Law of Treaties.[45] These norms represent a fairly accurate summary of customary law on this matter. Since the United Nations Charter is a treaty, its interpretation is governed by those principles as well. Accordingly, one may focus first on

---

17 *Loy. L.A. Int'l & Comp. L.J.* 365 (1995); Alberts, "The United States Invasion of Panama: Unilateral Military Intervention to Effectuate a Change in Government—A Continuum of Lawfulness," 1 *Transnat'l L. & Contemp. Prob.* 259 (1991); Harrington, "Operation Provide Comfort: A Perspective in International Law," 8 *Conn. J. Int'l L.* 635 (1993); Tyagi, "The Concept of Humanitarian Intervention Revisited," 16 *Mich. J. Int'l L.* 883 (1995); Sornarajah, "Internal Colonialism and Humanitarian Intervention," 11 *Ga. J. Int'l & Comp. L.* 45 (1981); Chilstrom, "Humanitarian Intervention under Contemporary International Law," 1 *Yale Studies in World Public Order* 93 (1974); Fonteyne, "The Customary International Law Doctrine of Humanitarian Intervention: Its Current Validity under the United Nations Charter," 4 *Cal. W. Int'l L.J.* 203 (1974); Umozurike, "Tanzanian Intervention in Uganda, 20 *Archiv des Völkerrecht* 301 (1982); Aroneau, "La guerre international d'intervention pour cause d'humanité, 19 *Revue internationale de droit pénal* 173 (1948); Levitin, "The Law of Force and the Force of Law: Grenada, the Falklands, and Humanitarian Intervention," 27 *Harv. Int'l L.J.* 621 (1986); Bazyler, "Reexamining the Doctrine of Humanitarian Intervention in Light of the Atrocities in Kampuchea and Ethiopia," 23 *Stan. J. Int'l L.* 547 (1987); and Behuniak, "The Law of Unilateral Intervention by Armed Force: A Legal Survey," 79 *Mil. L. Rev.* 157 (1978). The standard pre-Charter defenses of humanitarian intervention are E. Stowell, *Intervention in International Law* (1923); and Rougier, "La théorie de l'intervention d'humanité," 17 *Revue de droit international* 468 (1910).

45 On treaty interpretation under the Vienna Convention, *see generally* I. Sinclair, *The Vienna Convention on the Law of Treaties* 114–154 (2nd. ed. 1984); and Yasseen, "L'interprétation des traités d'après la Convention de Vienne sur le Droit des Traités," 151 *R.C.A.D.I.* 20 (1976–II).

the ordinary meaning of the words in article 2(4) in their context and in the light of the Charter's object and purpose.[46] Second, the inquiry could stress the original intent of the drafters of the Charter.[47] The third way to proceed is to examine article 2(4) in the light of subsequent state practice, as well as any "subsequent agreement" regarding the interpretation of the treaty, and any other "relevant rules of international law."[48] I shall examine the legal status of humanitarian intervention under article 2(4) in the light of each of these methods of treaty interpretation.

2. Language and Original Intent

A flat prohibition against the use of force is *not* supported by the plain language of article 2(4). The article requires states to refrain from using force *only* when that is against the territorial integrity and political independence of other states or "in any other manner inconsistent with the purposes of the United Nations." These words must qualify the prohibition, unless one reads them out of the Charter.[49] If the drafters wanted to prohibit all transboundary force, they would have done so.[50] Instead, in their ordinary meaning, these words seem to suggest that the drafters established three target prohibitions. The use of force is banned: a) when it impairs the territorial integrity of the target state; b) when it affects its political independence; or c) when it is otherwise against the purposes of the United Nations. As to the first two tests, recent research has revealed that the meaning of "force against territorial and integrity and political independence," as was known to the 1945 drafters, is

---

[46] *See* Vienna Convention on the Law of Treaties, May 23, 1969, entered into force on Jan. 27, 1980, U.N. Doc. A/CONF. 39/27, at art. 31, (1969), reprinted in 8 *I.L.M.* 679 (1969).

[47] *See* id. at art. 32.

[48] Id. at art. 31.

[49] Professor Stone was probably the first to make this observation. *See* Stone, *supra* n. 38, at 95. Some opponents of humanitarian intervention nevertheless concede that it would be arbitrary to ignore this qualifying clause. *See,* e.g., Schachter, "Armed Force," *supra* n. 38, at 1625. *But see,* e.g., Rifaat, *supra* n. 38, at 121–122 (the prohibition in art. 2(4) is all-embracing).

[50] This is overlooked, in my view, by Tom Farer in his article "Human Rights in Law's Empire: The Jurisprudence War," 85 *Am. J. Int'l L.* 117 (1991).

quite technical and does not encompass all uses of force.[51] A genuine humanitarian intervention does not result in territorial conquest or political subjugation. Hence, if one takes seriously ordinary meaning of the words as understood by the drafters of the Charter, tests a) and b) are satisfied.

The remaining task is to determine whether humanitarian intervention can survive the "purposes" test. At first blush, that clause provides a rather strong literal argument in favor of accepting a right of humanitarian intervention in appropriate cases.[52] It need hardly be emphasized that the promotion of human rights is a main purpose of the United Nations.[53] Writers who support a right of humanitarian intervention have forcefully contested the invariable priority of the purpose of maintaining international peace in the system created by the Charter.[54] It is urged along these lines that a purposive reading of article 2(4), a reading that is mandated by its very wording, indicates that the use of force to overthrow despotic regimes cannot be included in the blanket prohibition. The promotion of human rights is as important a purpose in the Charter as is the control of international conflict. Therefore, the use of force to remedy serious human rights deprivations, far from being "against the purposes" of the U.N. Charter, serves one of its main purposes. Humanitarian intervention is in accordance with one of the fundamental purposes of the U.N. Charter. Consequently, it is a distortion to argue that humanitarian intervention is prohibited by article 2(4).[55]

In order to be fully persuasive, however, this line of argument necessitates a demonstration of why concern for human rights should prevail over state-centered conceptions of the Charter. An argument based on the purposes of the Charter has to offer independent reasons for ranking human rights over other purposes articulated in Article 1. For example, economic cooperation is also a purpose in the Charter, yet it would be

---

[51] See, A. D'Amato, International Law: Process and Prospect 57–73 (1987).

[52] See the discussion in Lillich, "Forcible Self-Help by States to Protect Human Rights," 53 Iowa L. Rev. 325, 336 (1967) (hereinafter "Forcible Self-Help"). C. Farer, supra n. 50.

[53] Art. 1(3) states as one of the purposes of the U.N. "to achieve international cooperation . . . in promoting and encouraging respect for human rights and fundamental freedoms for all without disctinction as to race, sex, language, or religion."

[54] See Reisman, "Humanitarian Intervention," supra n. 44, at 171–173.

[55] Id. at 177. See also Lillich, Humanitarian Intervention, supra n. 44, at 237–244.

absurd to maintain that a state can resort to force to compel another state to cooperate.[56] An adequate theory has to show that the value of preserving human rights supersedes the prohibition of the use of force, itself based on another essential purpose, the maintenance of peace. Those independent reasons can only be articulated by an appeal to higher philosophical principles. In an eloquent passage, Professor Reisman himself underscores the moral-philosophical dimension of humanitarian intervention:

> The validity of humanitarian intervention is not based upon the nation-state-oriented theories of international law; these theories are little more than two centuries old. It is based upon an antinomic but equally vigorous principle, deriving from a long tradition of natural law and secular values: the kinship and minimum reciprocal responsibilities of all humanity, the inability of geographical boundaries to stem categorical moral imperatives, and ultimately, the confirmation of the sanctity of human life, without reference to place or transient circumstance.[57]

The reference to the purposes of the Charter, therefore, must be supplemented by an independent articulation of the hierarchy of the various purposes that inform the pertinent norms of the Charter. The important point here is that, absent any reference to a normative theory, the language in article 2(4) does not in itself prohibit states from using force to remedy serious human rights deprivations.

In support of the doctrine of humanitarian intervention it has also been argued that there is a necessary link between the maintenance of peace and the respect for human rights.[58] Human rights deprivations "would be internationalized as soon as it was demonstrable that they engendered a threat to the peace."[59] Since a breach of the peace provides sufficient legal reason to intervene, at least by the U.N. Security

---

[56] *See* Akehurst, "Humanitarian Intervention," *supra* n. 42, at 105–106.

[57] Reisman, "Humanitarian Intervention," *supra* n. 44, at 168.

[58] *See* McDougal & Reisman, "Rhodesia and the United Nations: The Lawfulness of International Concern," 62 *A.J.I.L.* 1, 15 (1968).

[59] Reisman, "Humanitarian Intervention," *supra* n. 44, at 172. Brownlie also accepts the legality of humanitarian intervention when there is a threat to peace. *See* Brownlie, "Humanitarian Intervention," *supra* n. 42, at 227. For a full discussion of the legal basis of the Security Council-authorized humanitarian intervention, and United Nations practice after the Cold War, *see infra,* Chapter 9.

Council, serious human rights deprivations, it is argued, should give rise to an analogous permission. This rationale may provide an additional reason to intervene in some cases, namely, where human rights deprivations have resulted in a breach of, or threat to, international peace.[60] Nevertheless, this justification of humanitarian intervention is insufficient. It shields from intervention cases of gross human rights violations that do not produce transboundary effects. More importantly, this argument unnecessarily concedes the main point of noninterventionism: that the preservation and stability of governments are the main values in international relations. The enhancement of human dignity would be just an accessory to the supreme value of preserving international stability. A defense of humanitarian intervention, however, must rest on an assessment of the intrinsic value of human rights in the international legal system, independently of their instrumental value to effect other purposes.

Similarly, an analysis of the Charter's Preamble read in conjunction with the purposes of the Organization listed in Article 1 yields no solution to our problem. The Preamble states the determination "to save succeeding generations from the scourge of war," but simultaneously urges states to establish "conditions under which justice" can be maintained. The language in the Preamble to the effect that "armed force shall not be used, save in the common interest," which is more in point for humanitarian intervention, breeds a similar uncertainty. There is no reason why "common interest" should mean only "interest in preserving the stability of governments," and not, say, "interest in eliminating oppression and tyranny." The expression "common interest" in that phrase can reasonably signify "common to all individuals on Earth," as opposed to "common to all established governments."[61] As already indicated, Article 1 includes both purposes—maintaining peace and promoting human rights. The primary method for treaty interpretation codified in the 1969 Vienna Convention on the Law of Treaties, the textual method, does not yield an unequivocal result. One cannot but agree

---

[60] *See,* e.g., the Security Council resolutions on *apartheid, see infra* text accompanying nn. 109–113, in this chapter.

[61] Professor Reisman rightly observes: "The repeated emphasis upon the common interest in human rights indicates that the use of force for the urgent protection of such rights is no less authorized than other forms of self-help." Reisman, "Humanitarian Intervention," *supra* n. 44 at 172.

with the late Professor Stone that, as a matter of exegesis, both the extreme and the narrow views of article 2(4) are possible.[62] The choice between the two, therefore, must depend on factors extrinsic to the text of the Charter.

Nor are the *travaux préparatoires* any more revealing in this regard. Resort to the *travaux préparatoires* is a supplementary method of treaty interpretation. There is a more general question whether the determination of original intent is feasible or relevant for our purposes.[63] That international law should be interpreted today in the light of the 1945 intentions of the drafters of the Charter is a venturous proposition. One could argue, as Professor McDougal and his associates have done for many years, that international treaties, especially organic ones like the U.N. Charter, should be interpreted in accordance with present purposes and expectations in the international community.[64] But even conceding the relevance of the inquiry into original intent, an examination of the *travaux préparatoires* does not answer the question whether the framers intended to maintain the customary exceptions to the use of force, including humanitarian intervention.[65] Professor Bownlie has been a prominent supporter of the view that Article 2(4) prohibits virtually all forms of use of force, including humanitarian intervention.[66] Yet, as Professor Lillich observed, Brownlie's own account of the *travaux préparatoires* does not support his conclusion that the final clause of article 2(4) does not qualify the prohibition.[67] As Professor Brownlie himself acknowledges, a Norwegian suggestion to omit the qualifying clause was *not* adopted in San Francisco.[68] Nor is there an indication

---

[62] *See* Stone, *supra* n. 38, at 97.

[63] The Vienna Convention authorizes recourse to the *travaux préparatoires* only when the application of the textual method either (i) leaves the meaning ambiguous or obscure; or (ii) leads to a result which is manifestly absurd or unreasonable. Vienna Convention, *supra* n. 46, at art. 32.

[64] *See supra* Chapter 1. *See also* M. McDougal, H. Lasswell & J. Miller, *Interpretation of Agreements and World Order* 3–77 (1967).

[65] *See* the discussions in Brownlie, *Use of Force, supra* n. 38, at 264–268; Thomas & Thomas, "The Dominican Republic Crisis 1965—Legal Aspects," in *Hammarsjkold Forum* 22 (1966); Fonteyne, *supra* n. 44, at 242–246 (1974).

[66] *See* Brownlie, "Humanitarian Intervention," *supra* n. 42.

[67] *See* Lillich, "Humanitarian Intervention," *supra* n. 44, at 236.

[68] *See* Brownlie, Use of Force, *supra* n. 38, at 264–268. This aspect of the *travaux préparatoires* is overlooked by Professor Farer in his conclusion that they do not support the legality of humanitarian intervention. *See* Farer, *supra* n. 50, at 120–21.

that the framers expressly contemplated and rejected the hypothesis of armed intervention for humanitarian purposes.[69]

Moreover, if original intent is taken seriously, one can even argue that the fresh memories from the Holocaust would have led the framers to *allow* for humanitarian intervention, had they thought about it.[70] Critics of humanitarian intervention have consistently overlooked the all-important humanitarian thrust of World War II and its sequel, the Nuremberg trials.[71] For example, Professor Schachter, in his defense of a broad prohibition of the use of force, emphasizes *only* the Tribunal's condemnation of aggressive war.[72] He summarily rejects the legality of the doctrine of humanitarian intervention without even mentioning Nuremberg's critical concern with crimes against humanity. Professor Schachter correctly describes the rationale for humanitarian intervention as one falling within the conception of just war, that is, a war "to achieve major political or moral ends."[73] Those higher ends, far from being absent in Nuremberg, matched in importance the purposes of controlling international conflict. Professor Schachter, however, concludes that "neither the U.N. Charter nor the extensive government commentary thereupon supports an interpretation subordinating the basic prohibition against unilateral use of force to ends other than self-defense or U.N. enforcement action."[74] Apart from the fact that the ethical end of self-defense is none other than the protection of human rights,[75] Professor Schachter seriously underestimates Nuremberg's human rights message. An early commentator on Nuremberg artfully summarized the thrust of the trials:

---

[69] *See* Lillich, "Intervention to Protect Human Rights," 15 *McGill L.J.* 205, 207–210 (1969) (hereinafter "Human Rights"). *But see,* Giraud, "L'interdiction du recours à la force—La théorie et la pratique des Nations Unies," 67 *Révue générale de droit international public* 501–512, 513 (1961) (narrow interpretation does not correspond to intent of framers).

[70] *See* Lillich, "Humanitarian Intervention," *supra* n. 44, at 236.

[71] I have already indicated that the fight against Nazism was much more than a fight against an aggressor. *See supra,* Chapter 6.

[72] *See* Schachter, "In Defense of International Rules on the Use of Force," 53 *U. Chi. L. Rev.* 113, 113–119 (1985) (hereinafter "Defense").

[73] Id. at 142–144.

[74] Id. at 143.

[75] *See supra,* Chapter 6.

No government any longer possesses an undisputed right to treat its subjects as it pleases. The very least of these could incriminate the very highest in a trial before an international court of justice. The officials of every nation must now be aware that they too may be condemned as international criminals, if they offend against the law of nations, if they instigate or prepare wars of aggression, if they apply laws that are in violation of the laws of humanity, or if they persecute groups or persons whose rights are recognized by most civilized nations. That is the meaning of Nuremberg.[76]

A complete account of the Nuremberg judgment must therefore underscore *both* dimensions, especially if one wishes to use them as a springboard for determining the content of the principle of non-use of force. Because World War II was itself a humanitarian effort, it is hard to see how the Nuremberg Tribunal would have condemned a war in defense of human rights as an *aggressive* war. To sum up: an examination of original intent cannot determine the present status of the humanitarian intervention doctrine. The *travaux préparatoires* of the United Nations Charter can be read either way. The principles laid down at Nuremberg are even less supportive of a state-centered view of international law. The Nuremberg trials, like the Charter, vigorously assert both the prohibition against aggressive war and the principle that individuals are entitled to fundamental human rights. Regardless of how one reads the drafting history, it is implausible to assume that the drafters of the Charter intended to repeal the whole corpus of customary law. Indeed, in the *Nicaragua* case, the Court expressed the view that the customary law regarding the use of force coexisted with the law of the United Nations Charter.[77] If this is correct, then textual analysis alone is not dispositive. Whether or not there is a right of humanitarian intervention in international law depends on the content of customary law, and that can only be determined by examining state practice in the light of an appropriate substantive moral theory.

Critics of humanitarian intervention also argue that, even if customary law recognized humanitarian intervention prior to 1945, the U.N.

---

[76] R. Woetzel, *The Nuremberg Trials in International Law* xiv (1961).

[77] *See Nicaragua* case, *supra* n. 2, at 94. I discuss the Court's view of humanitarian intervention in Chapter 10.

Charter with the broad prohibition in article 2(4) had such a decisive impact on customary law that the doctrine can no longer be accepted. But this argument faces two serious objections. First, one has to prove that subsequent state practice is consistent with the absolute prohibition. As we will see, this is not the case.[78] Further, those who take that view—that the Charter radically changed the law in 1945—must also deal with the equally revolutionary impact of the law of human rights upon traditional international law. This is not the place to trace the history of what has rightly been styled "the human rights revolution" in international law.[79] The point here is that anyone who in the face of the impressive rise of human rights concerns simply asserts that post-1945 international law must be seen as one containing a rigid prohibition of war, *even* to remedy serious human rights deprivations, carries a considerable burden of proof. One simply cannot select article 2(4) as the only norm that had a revolutionary impact in international law. After all, article 2(4) is part of a steady evolution that started with the Kellogg-Briand Pact. There was a customary principle prohibiting the use of force at the time the Charter was adopted.[80] In contrast, the human rights articles of the Charter opened the door to a much more innovative development: a concept of the law of nations as centered on the individual, not the nation-state.

3. The Problem of the Ineffectiveness of Collective Mechanisms

If literal analysis and intent do not yield a solution, the way to proceed is to examine Article 2(4) in the light of subsequent state practice. An argument for humanitarian intervention in this mode may take two forms which are not mutually exclusive. One can argue that article 2(4) must be linked to the collective security arrangements in the United Nations Charter. It has been claimed that in view of the failure of those

---

[78] *See infra,* Chapter 8.

[79] *See* Sohn, "The New International Law: Protection of the Rights of Individuals Rather than States," 32 *Am. U. L. Rev.* 1,9 (1982). *See generally* L. Henkin, *The Rights of Man Today* (1978); and P. Sieghart, *The International Law of Human Rights* (1983). A useful comprehensive bibliography is *Human Rights: An International and Comparative Law Bibliography* (J. Friedman & M. Sherman eds. 1985).

[80] *See* Brownlie, *Use of Force, supra* n. 38, at 112.

arrangements, the customary right of humanitarian intervention has survived under the Charter, or has reverted to states.[81] This is an application of the theory of *rebus sic stantibus* (fundamental change of circumstances).[82] In this view, when nations agreed in 1945 to renounce the use of force, they thought that the United Nations would take effective action to enforce international law. The fundamental change of circumstances, then, is the total inaction of the United Nations to remedy serious human rights violations. Such circumstance seems to meet the two requirements of being an "essential basis of the consent of the parties" to renounce force,[83] and producing the effect of radically transforming "the extent of the obligations still to be performed under the treaty."[84] The prohibition of article 2(4) only makes sense, in this view, provided that the collective security arrangements contemplated in the Charter are also effective. This argument carries considerable force.[85] It is indeed unlikely that states would have given up self-help to enforce their rights had they known that the U.N. Security Council would have been unable to adopt the enforcement measures contemplated in the Charter.

It may be objected that the International Court of Justice apparently has twice rejected the argument based on United Nations' ineffectiveness. Leaving aside the issue of the precedential force of the Court's

---

[81] *See* Reisman, "Coercion," *supra* n. 44, at 642. Along the same lines, Professor Lillich writes:

> Surely the abject inability of the United Nations to take effective action to terminate the genocidal conduct and alleviate the mass suffering in Bangladesh necessitates a fundamental reassessment . . . of the role of self-help, and especially of humanitarian intervention, in international affairs today.

Lillich, "Humanitarian Intervention," *supra* n. 44, at 230. This argument, and the discussion in the text, have become somewhat moot in the light of the revitalization of the Security Council since 1990, see *infra*, Chapter 9. The new question is: given that the Security Council is sometimes willing to intervene to protect human rights, do individual states still retain the right to intervene unilaterally? I am inclined to answer in the affirmative, at least until the Security Council can fully discharge its responsibilities in the alleviation of human suffering. For example, the intervention of NATO in the Bosnian crisis would have been lawful, in my judgment, even if the Security Council would have witheld its authorization. For a full discussion, see *infra*, Chapter 9.

[82] *See* Vienna Convention on the Law of Treaties, *supra* n. 46, at art. 62.

[83] Id. at art. 62 (1) (a).

[84] Id. at art. 62 (1) (b).

[85] *See*, e.g., the criticisms against the U.N. inaction in the Bangladesh crisis, *infra* Chapter 8.

decisions, the objection does not carry much weight. In the *Corfu Channel* case, the Court refused to consider the "defects in the present organization" as sufficient to validate British violation of Albanian sovereignty.[86] This passage, however, was specifically related to forcible gathering of evidence, and so the reference to the "defects in the present organization" may refer to the judicial shortcomings regarding discovery of pieces of evidence for the purposes of litigation, rather than to the failure of Chapter VII of the U.N. Charter to prevent aggression or gross human rights deprivations. In the recent *Nicaragua* opinion the situation was more complicated, and I will fully address it in a subsequent chapter.[87] A point, however, should be noted here. In *Nicaragua* the Court was applying the customary law on use of force, not Article 2(4) of the Charter. The Court, rejecting the United States' argument that customary and treaty law on the use of force were identical, wrote:

> In a legal dispute affecting two States, one of them may argue that the applicability of a treaty rule to its own conduct depends on the other State's conduct in the application of other rules . . . also included in the same treaty. . . . But if the two rules in question also exist as rules of customary international law, the failure of the one State to apply the one rule does not justify the other State to decline to apply the other rule.[88]

This Court is referring here to *breach* of a treaty, rather than fundamental change of circumstances.[89] Applying this rationale to the argument from United Nations inaction, the objection is that even if the Security Council has failed to remedy human rights deprivations in violation of the Charter and has thereby freed states from complying with article 2(4), states are still bound by the *customary* prohibition on the use of force. That prohibition does not depend upon the effectiveness of the institutional arrangements of the Charter, and so states are virtually banned from using force even if the United Nations has shown an "abject failure" in taking action to counter aggression or remedy gross human

---

[86] *Corfu Channel* case, Judgment of Apr. 9, 1949, 1949 *I.C.J. Rep.* 4, 35.

[87] *Infra* Chapter 10.

[88] *Nicaragua* case, *supra* n. 2, at 97.

[89] Vienna Convention, *supra* n. 46, at art. 60.

rights violations.[90] The demise of Chapter VII and other mechanisms thus does not entail the demise of the principle prohibiting the use of force.

The Court's reasoning, however, leads to the questionable result that the customary prohibition of using force is more stringent than the treaty obligation imposed by article 2(4). For while the obligation in article 2(4) may be apparently conditioned to the effectiveness of the institutional arrangements in the Charter, the customary principle cannot be so conditioned. Yet there is authority for the view that the customary law of use of force is either more permissive than, or identical with, the law of the Charter.[91] One may certainly say that the impact of the U.N. Charter has reinforced the customary prohibition against the use of force. But it is doubtful that the obligation of article 2(4) is conditioned to the security arrangements in the Charter, while the customary principle of nonuse of force is not conditioned to anything else. Indeed, the existence of customary mechanisms of self-help seem to weaken, rather than reinforce, the customary prohibition.[92]

Be it as it may, the argument for humanitarian intervention defended here is not inconsistent with the Court's holding on the relationship between Charter and customary law. The question of whether or not the customary principle prohibiting the use of force recognizes the exception of humanitarian intervention is independent from the argument based on the ineffectiveness of the United Nations. Suppose that customary law does recognize a right of humanitarian intervention. If a state is bound by customary law but not by the Charter, that state is not legally preempted from intervening for humanitarian purposes by the mechanisms of Chapter VII, *even if such mechanisms are functioning effectively.* A fortiori, states are not so preempted when the mechanisms are ineffective (as they actually are). So if the customary prohibition is

---

[90] Cf., the Court's assertion that "both the Charter and the customary international law flow from a common fundamental principle outlawing the use of force in international relations." *Nicaragua* case, *supra* n. 2, at 97.

[91] Professor Brownlie, for example, writes that "the difference between Article 2, paragraph 4, and "general international law" is the merest technicality." Brownlie, *Use of Force, supra* n. 44, at 113.

[92] Anthony D'Amato argues, provocatively, that proportionate retaliation is precisely the way in which the international system tends to preserve itself by seeking its equilibrium. D'Amato, *supra* n. 51, at 98–103.

independent from treaty obligations and is therefore not affected by the undeniable failure of the United Nations, it is still necessary to determine the content of that customary prohibition. And it may well be that the customary principle recognizes humanitarian intervention as an exception. The Court's argument can be read most naturally as expressing the view that Article 2(4) coexists with customary law and does not subsume it. Therefore, the law regarding the use of force, that is, *both* article 2(4) and customary law, must be ascertained in the light of the practice of states. This conclusion is consistent with the principle, discussed below, that treaty obligations may be modified by subsequent practice. A demonstration of the proper scope of the principle of non-use of force thus necessitates an evaluation of the customary law on the matter, including the precedents regarding humanitarian intervention. The argument defended here—that the *best* reading of the Charter and subsequent practice is that the prohibition of the use of force contains an exception allowing states to use force to stop serious human rights deprivations—is therefore unaffected by a rejection of the thesis of the inseparability of Charter provisions, whether it takes the form of *rebus sic stantibus* or termination or suspension for breach.

If one wants instead to take seriously the objection raised by the Court's reasoning in *Nicaragua*, one may argue that humanitarian intervention: (a) is not outlawed *by the Charter* because the broad prohibition of article 2(4) (assuming that that article indeed establishes a broad prohibition) was conditioned to the effectiveness of the enforcement mechanisms of the Charter; and (b) is not prohibited by the *independent customary principle* because the practice of states has carved out a humanitarian exception. The better view, however, is that the practice of states, construed in the light of appropriate values, determines *both* the scope of article 2(4) and the content of the customary counterpart.

We are then left with an evaluation of state practice. Supporters of humanitarian intervention claim that diplomatic practice has created an exception to article 2(4), or maintained a previously existing exception, legitimizing the use of force to remedy serious human rights deprivations. Critics claim that subsequent practice must be interpreted as forbidding humanitarian intervention. It is beyond doubt that subsequent practice may help ascertain the meaning of, and even modify, treaty provisions, the U.N. Charter being no exception. The Vienna Convention on the Law of Treaties provides that any subsequent practice in the application of a treaty should be taken into account to interpret that treaty.[93] This is a well-established principle of treaty interpretation. It has been upheld even in case of a practice that was plainly contradictory with the words of the Charter.[94] In order to sustain that argument, One must show that genuine cases of humanitarian intervention are not to be treated as violations of international law, or at least that they are not to be thrown in the same category as other clear-cut, non-humanitarian, uses of force. State practice related to humanitarian intervention will be examined in the following chapter. In the next section I shall briefly analyze the consequences for the doctrine of humanitarian intervention of the growing acceptance of an alleged exception to the prohibition of war: the material assistance to peoples fighting racist regimes.

4. Humanitarian Intervention and "Wars of National Liberation"

In recent years some have articulated and defended the lawfulness of a type of use of force not expressly contemplated in the Charter on prior customary law. Governments and scholars, mostly from the Third World, have claimed that force used by peoples fighting "wars of national liberation" should be considered lawful in international law.[95] Although the meaning of "war of national liberation" is unclear, there are at least two instances that have been identified in the pertinent instruments. The first is that of peoples fighting colonial wars, that is, peoples struggling to achieve national independence from a foreign power.[96] The second is the struggle of peoples fighting against racist regimes. I argue that if such an exception is allowed, it can only mean

---

[93] Vienna Convention, *supra* n. 46, at art. 31(3)(b).

[94] *See* Legal Consequences for States of the Continued Presence of South Africa in Namibia (Advisory Opinion), 1971 *I.C.J. Rep.* 22 (rejecting South Africa's argument that Security Council resolutions were invalid because of violation of voting provision). *See also* the Air Service Agreement Arbitration (*U.S. v. France*), 38 *I.L.R.* at 249 (1963) (subsequent practice may be a source of modification of the treaty).

[95] *See,* e.g., Tekane, "Reflections on Apartheid and the Legal Status of National Liberation Movements," in *New Perspectives and Conceptions of International Law—An Afro-European Dialogue* 181, 183 (1983).

[96] *See* Declaration on Principles of International Law, *supra* n. 4, section on the Self-Determination principle, para. 5 and 6 (peoples fighting colonialism entitled to fight and seek and receive support).

the recognition, in international law, of the right of "peoples" (that is, groups of individuals) to revolt against oppressive regimes generally- the right of revolution.[97] Furthermore, the assertion of the legitimacy of foreign help to "peoples" fighting "wars of national liberation" against colonial or racist regimes, properly entails legitimacy of *foreign help* to groups of individuals fighting civil wars against tyrannical governments generally.

Initially, the legitimacy of "wars of national liberation" was asserted in connection with colonial wars.[98] Peoples who fought wars against colonial powers were said to be fighting legitimate wars. Thus the use of force to gain independence was, not without resistance by the colonial powers, deemed legitimate by the international community.[99] In the United Nations, much of the effort was spent in characterizing colonial wars as international, as opposed to civil, wars.[100] The purpose was twofold. First, to place colonial wars under the "international relations" clause of article 2(4), thus avoiding their inclusion in the category of civil wars.[101] Second, and more radically, to legitimize the use of force by colonial peoples in their struggle for independence and, conversely, to outlaw the force used *against* peoples waging such wars.[102] The design of the United Nations majority was to except colonial wars from

---

[97] *See* Paust, "The Human Right to Participate in Armed Revolution and Related Forms of Social Violence: Testing the Limits of Permissibility," 32 *Emory L.J.* 545, 560–567 (1983).

[98] *See* Declaration on Principles of International Law, *supra* n. 4. *See generally,* N. Ronzitti, *Le Guerre de Liberazione et Il Diritto Internazionale* (1974); Charpentier, "Autodetermination et decolonisation," in *Le Droit des Peuples a Disposer d'Eux Mêmes—Méthodes d'Analyse du Droit International—Mélanges Offerts a Charles Chaumont* 117 (1984).

[99] *See generally,* Grahl-Madsen, "Decolonization: The Modern Version of a 'Just War'," 22 *German Y.B. Int'l L.* 255 (1979).

[100] *See,* e.g., art. 7 of the U.N. Definition of Aggression:

Nothing in this Definition, and in particular Article 3, could in any way prejudice the right to self-determination, freedom and independence . . . of peoples forcibly deprived of that right . . . particularly peoples under colonial and racist regimes or other forms of alien domination; nor the right of these peoples to struggle to that end and to seek and receive support, in accordance with the principles of the Charter and in conformity with the [1970 Declaration].

G.A. Res. 3314 (XXIX), *supra* n. 43. For a discussion of the meaning of this article, *see* Rifaat, *International Aggression, supra* n. 38, at 277.

[101] *See* Virally, "Art. 2, para. 4," in *La Charte des Nations Unies* 122 (J. P. Cot & A. Pellet eds. 1985).

[102] *See* Tekane, *supra* note 95.

the general permissive rule embodied in international law regarding the use of force by parties in a civil war. Traditionally, international law was generally silent as to which side in a civil war had a just cause.[103] A distinctive trait of this new normative scheme is that in a colonial war only the peoples fighting for independence have a just cause. If the colonial power uses force to repress the war of independence, it is waging an unjust, illegal war.

A parallel development was the increasing assertion of the legitimacy of foreign *assistance*, including "material" assistance, to peoples fighting against colonial domination.[104] The lawfulness of such assistance was contested by some commentators.[105] Nevertheless, the idea gained momentum in the United Nations, perhaps due to the ambiguity of the term "material assistance." In the *Nicaragua* case, the Court, in an aside, seemed to suggest that the use of indirect force to rebels fighting for decolonization would have been considered by the Court as additional exception to the prohibition against the use of force.[106] Since decolonization was not an issue, however, the importance of the Court's dictum should not be exaggerated. Yet the Court's ad-hoc exception contradicts its own theory of state practice: why does this exception count and not others, such as humanitarian intervention?[107]

By the 1970s, the endorsement of foreign help to certain types of struggle against established governments was widened to include "racist regimes." An example is the assertion in the 1970 Declaration that peoples, in their forcible action in pursuit of self-determination, "are entitled to seek and receive support in accordance with the purposes and principles of the United Nations Charter."[108] Recent pronouncements of the United Nations General Assembly have been much more

---

[103] *See* Pinto, "Les règles du droit international concernant la guerre civile," 114 *R.C.A.D.I.* 451, 477 (1965–I).

[104] *See* the series of U.N. General Assembly Resolutions cited by Van Boven, "Partners in the Promotion and Protection of Human Rights," 24 *Neth. Int'l L. Rev.* 55, 60, n. 5 (1977).

[105] *See,* Schwebel, "Aggression, Intervention and Self-Defence in Modern International Law," 136 *R.C.A.D.I.* 411 (1972).

[106] *Nicaragua* case, *supra* n. 2, at 108. In his dissent, Judge Schwebel acknowledged the legitimacy of the struggle of peoples in furtherance of self-determination, but denied the legitimacy of foreign help to such peoples. Id. at 351, (Schwebel, diss.).

[107] *See* D'Amato, "Trashing Customary Law," 81 *Am. U. J. Int'l L.* 102–103 (1987).

[108] Declaration on Principles of International Law, *supra* n. 4, under The Principle of Equal Rights and Self-Determination of Peoples, para. 5, in fine.

explicit. For example, a recent resolution urges all governments "to provide maximal moral, political and *material* assistance to the South African national liberation movements . . . and all those struggling for freedom in South Africa in uncompromising opposition to *apartheid,*" while at the same time reaffirming the legitimacy of the *armed struggle* of the South African people.[109] Leaving aside the question of the binding force of these resolutions, it is unquestionable that there was at the time a vigorous trend in the United Nations to legitimize both the struggle of the people in South Africa against their racist government and foreign armed assistance provided to them. There is little doubt that international pressure was decisive in ending *apartheid* in South Africa.

Proponents of this view, including the International Court of Justice (assuming that it would extend the rationale for decolonization to *apartheid*), are perhaps unaware of its consequences. There is no doubt that racism is a paradigmatic violation of human rights. The imperative of nondiscrimination is the only substantive human rights prescription in the United Nations Charter.[110] Most of the international pronouncements condemning *apartheid* acknowledge that it is a flagrant violation of human rights (and not just something that threatens peace and security).[111] All human rights conventions in force likewise include racial discrimination as an independent violation of human rights.[112] The question then becomes why should international law legitimize foreign material assistance *only* to peoples fighting racial discrimination, and not assistance to peoples fighting oppressive regimes generally. For racial discrimination, odious as it is, is certainly not the most egregious human rights violation. Mass murder, torture, genocide, enslavement, and even arbitrary imprisonment, when practiced on a massive scale, are indeed more serious deprivations than *apartheid* schemes. This conclusion is reinforced by the fact that while most human rights conventions *allow* derogation from the nondiscrimination provisions in case of emergency, they prohibit derogation from the articles that recognize the more fundamental rights and freedoms mentioned above.[113]

---

[109] A/Res/39/72 (XXXIX), at 2, 8.

[110] *See* arts. 1(3) and 55, U.N. Charter.

[111] *See, e.g.,* A/Res/39/72, *supra* n. 70 , at 5.

[112] *See* International Convention on the Suppression and Punishment of the Crime of *Apartheid,* U.N. G.A. Res. 3068 (XXVIII), 13 *I.L.M.* 50 (1974) art. I. (*apartheid* a crime against humanity *and* a serious threat to peace and security).

[113] *See, e.g.,* European Convention for the Protection of Human Rights and Fundamental Freedoms, 213 U.N.T.S. 221, E.T.S. 5, art. 15, Nov. 4, 1950, *entered into force*

A necessary characteristic of legal principles and rules is that we should be ready to apply them to all situations that are relevantly similar. The United Nations majority cannot consistently claim that "material assistance" to non-whites fighting *apartheid* in South Africa should be recognized as an exception to article 2(4), and that similar aid to pro-human rights rebels fighting a tyrannical regime is prohibited. To hold otherwise would mean that *apartheid* and racism are somehow unique human rights deprivations, the only ones that warrant armed assistance. This is an indefensible position. If one asserts the legitimacy of material help to the non-white South African majority, one must likewise recognize the legitimacy of assistance to the Ugandan rebels fighting Idi Amin or the Chilean people resisting dictator Pinochet. There is no indication in the law of human rights that racism enjoys a "preferential" status as the only human rights deprivation that would warrant foreign material assistance. In short, the legality of material (including military) support to victims of *apartheid* entails the legality of humanitarian intervention. The better explanation is that in case of widespread violation of human rights, including, but not limited to, pervasive and institutionalized racial discrimination, proportionate intervention should be accepted as an exception to the rule banning the use of force in international relations.

5. Political Philosophy and the Analysis of the United Nations Charter

The arguments from the text of the Charter are not decisive for determining the status of humanitarian intervention. Furthermore, one of the alleged exceptions to the prohibition of nonuse of force seems to confirm, rather than deny, the validity of the customary right of humanitarian intervention. But if Charter text and state practice may be interpreted either way, how can we discern what the law is on this matter? I have suggested here that the only way to reach a conclusion of law is to appeal to moral-political values. I have argued, following Ronald Dworkin, that hard cases can only be decided by an appeal to *both*

Sept. 3, 1953; American Convention on Human Rights, Nov. 22, 1969, *entered into force* June, 1978, O.A.S. Off. Rec. OEA/SER. K/XVI/1.1, art. 27 DOC. 65, REV. 1, CORR.1, Jan. 7, 1970, 9 *I.L.M.* 101, 673 (1970).

institutional history (i.e., state practice, treaties, and so forth) and political philosophy, in this case a normative theory of international relations.[114] I have suggested in the first part of this book that the theory that will serve to provide guidance in those cases where state practice or treaty analysis do not yield an unequivocal solution is a human-rights-based theory of international law.[115] The rights secured by article 2(4) are thus not rights held by states autonomously, that is, independently of their moral legitimacy. The protection of human rights is not just a value that is merely superior to state sovereignty. State sovereignty *derives* from individual rights.[116]

It will be recalled that an objection to the "purposes" argument was that there were several other purposes in the Charter, such as economic cooperation, and that it would be absurd to recognize the legality of forcing states to cooperate. A reply to this objection necessitates a philosophical demonstration of the proposition that human rights (unlike economic cooperation) form the philosophical basis of any justified legal order, including international law.[117] Any determination of the "purposes" of a legal instrument requires substantive moral assumptions. This is particularly true of the United Nations Charter, which is rightly seen as the organizational foundation of the international community. Our considered judgments about international justice, including state sovereignty and human rights, cannot therefore be absent from our interpretation of the Charter. I have suggested in the first part of the book that under the most satisfactory background theory, undisturbed state sovereignty cannot be the paramount political and philosophical value. To be sure, it is an important derivative value that ought to be preserved. Yet when state sovereignty clashes with minimal human dignity, the former must yield. A contrary solution would ignore the fact that all legal systems, including international law, are aimed at regulating human conduct in consonance with ethical ends.

---

[114] *See supra,* Chapter 1. The same method is followed by Professor Mervyn Frost in his work *Toward a Normative Theory of International Relations* chs. 3, 4 and 5 (1986). The background theory that I suggest, however, radically differs from his. Not surprisingly, our respective normative conclusions differ as well.

[115] *See supra,* Chapters 1 and 6.

[116] *See supra,* Chapter 6.

[117] *See supra,* Chapter 1.

There is yet another decisive consideration to support this conclusion. Those who defend an absolute prohibition on the use of force by denying the legitimacy of an appeal to values are themselves making a value choice. The efforts to lay down a flat prohibition on the use of force are not value-neutral as they often portray themselves to be.[118] For example, in the light of the language of article 2(4), an appeal to original intent is an interpretive device designed to enlarge the scope of the prohibition. The search for the intent of the framers thus is not a neutral procedure. For example, under standard rules of treaty interpretation, one could stick strictly to the ordinary meaning of the words of the Charter.[119] Noninterventionists are, *malgré eux*, making a value choice; they are giving priority to the rights of states over the rights of individuals. The controversy between supporters of a flat prohibition against the use of force and supporters of a right of humanitarian intervention is not a dispute between "positivists" and "teleologists." Rather, it is an authentic moral dispute, a dispute about values.

An example of this concealed value choice is offered in a book by Professor Natalino Ronzitti. He rejects the argument that the value of human rights must sometimes prevail over the prohibition against using force:

> [This] argument . . . gives rise to even more criticism. . . . Firstly, while it is quite sure that the obligation to refrain from the use of force is embodied in a peremptory norm of international law, it is not at all sure that the duty to promote human rights is set forth in a *ius cogens* rule. Consequently, it is difficult to agree that the value protected by the duty to safeguard human rights should prevail over the value protected by the rule which forbids the use of force . . . Second, [this] opinion is not supported by State practice.[120]

This argument is flawed. There is a growing trend in state practice and the literature in support of the proposition that the prohibition

---

[118] See Coste, "Reflexion philosophique sur le problème d'intervention," 71 *Revue générale de droit international public* 369 (1967).

[119] *See,* Vienna Convention, *supra* n. 46, at art. 31.

[120] Ronzitti, *supra* n. 42, at 15.

against massive human rights deprivations is indeed a rule of *ius co-gens*.[121] The definition of a rule of *ius cogens* has a specific meaning in the law of treaties: it is a norm accepted and recognized by the community of states as a whole as one from which no derogation is permitted.[122] Surely Professor Ronzitti is not prepared to say that states may agree by treaty to engage in gross human rights violations. If the obligation to observe human rights is indeed part and parcel of contemporary international law, the question of its priority vis-à-vis the principle of nonuse of force remains unresolved. As a result, Professor Ronzitti's argument begs the question. For it is the *value* assigned to a rule that determines its status as *ius cogens*, and not the other way round. Ronzitti fails to discuss any independent reasons why the preservation of peace (the value protected by the rule of nonuse of force) prevails against, say, the prevention of serious and widespread human rights deprivations (the value protected by the exception of humanitarian intervention).[123] The only way to reach a conclusion is to focus the inquiry on the most appropriate moral-political theory of international law. The theory must account for both state sovereignty and human rights. It will then guide us in deciding whether state practice should be interpreted as confirming or denying the existence of humanitarian intervention. Absent a value choice, there is little merit to Ronzitti's conclusion that "[t]he view that the Charter puts human rights before the maintenance of international peace and security remains . . . unfounded."[124]

That value choices are unavoidable is illustrated by a number of debates following instances of intervention. In the aftermath of the Grenada intervention, Professor Reisman eloquently argued that states may

---

[121] *See,* e.g., the *Barcelona Traction* case, 1970 *I.C.J. Rep.* 32 (human rights give rise to obligation *erga omnes* in which all states have interest). See the analysis in Sinclair, *supra* n. 45, at 209–224, and references therein.

[122] Vienna Convention, *supra* n. 46, at art. 53.

[123] Professor Ronzitti attempts to refute instead other legal arguments supporting the doctrine of humanitarian intervention. Those arguments are: that humanitarian intervention is based on self-defense; that it can be justified by Article 56 of the Charter; and that the armed protection of human rights may be justified because they are essential to the maintenance of peace and security. Ronzitti, *supra* n. 42, at 16–17. None of those other arguments is defended in this book. They are just straw men, easy to refute but also ineffective: the real issue is how we choose to interpret the Charter and state practice. And, as I try to show in Chapter 8, in my view Professor Ronzitti misreads that practice.

[124] Ronzitti, *supra* n. 42, at 16–17.

use force in furtherance of democratic values.[125] His argument has two stages. First, he regards article 2(4) of the U.N. Charter, not as an "independent ethical imperative of pacifism," but as an integral part of the institutional mechanisms laid down by the Charter to react to unlawful uses of force.[126] Because those mechanisms have conspicuosly failed, a "curious legal gray area extended between the black letter of the Charter and the bloody reality of world politics."[127] Professor Reisman's conclusion is that the scope of the prohibition of the use of force cannot be disentangled from the undeniable ineffectiveness of the United Nations peacekeeping and security mechanisms. Therefore, it is not possible to assert the automatic unlawfulness of all uses of force; rather, the challenge for international lawyers is to articulate a set of criteria for appraising the legality of unilateral resorts to coercion.[128]

The second stage in Professor Reisman's argument is as follows. It is wrong to blindly follow any legal rule, that is, without regard "for the policy or principle that animated its prescription."[129] And the principle that underlies article 2(4), according to Professor Reisman, is one of political legitimacy: the ongoing right of peoples to determine their own destinies.[130] Thus Professor Reisman reads the principle of self-determination as embodying a requirement of internal democracy and observance of human rights, and not just as forbidding external or colonial domination.[131] For example, one cannot justify "treating in a mechanically equal fashion Tanzania's intervention in Uganda to overthrow despotism, on the one hand, and Soviet intervention . . . to overthrow popular governments and to impose an undesired regime on coerced populations, on the other."[132] In short, the prohibition on the use of force must be read in the light of "community order and basic

---

[125] Reisman, "Coercion," *supra* n. 44.

[126] Id. at 642–43.

[127] Id.

[128] Id.

[129] Id. at 644.

[130] Id.

[131] For a distinction between external and internal self-determination, *see* M. Pomerance, Self-Determination in Theory and Practice 1–28 (1982). *See also* the discussion in my article "International Human Rights and Cultural Relativism," 25 *Va. J. Int'l L.* 869, 879–884 (1985).

[132] Reisman, "Coercion," *supra* n. 44, at 644.

policies." Article 2(4) is just the means, and so the lawfulness of any instance of use of force will then depend on whether force was used for or against those aims. Professor Reisman concludes that it is a "rape to common sense" to legally allow aid to repressive regimes while denying the right of forcible intervention to help the oppressed people overthrow their tyrants.[133]

Characteristically, scholarly criticism of Reisman's suggestion has emphasized the preeminence of the maintenance of peace and the prevention of aggression.[134] Professor Schachter's analysis, in particular, merits close scrutiny because of his well-known commitment to human dignity.[135] He first disputes Reisman's contention that the failure of the U.N. enforcement system has legitimized uses of force in self-help for nondefensive purposes.[136] Professor Schachter observes that from the undisputed fact that not all uses of force should be automatically condemned it does not follow that force for nondefensive (in this case, prodemocratic) purposes should be allowed. While the failure of the U.N. system to contain aggression makes self-defense necessary, that is not necessarily the case for the use of force for other purposes, however good.[137] But this criticism is inapposite, because self-defense has *not been made necessary because of the failure of the U.N. system.* The right of self-defense was understood to be an inherent right, one that would subsist even if the Chapter VII mechanisms worked well. Therefore, while it is true that the argument from the failure of Chapter VII alone does not prove Reisman's thesis,[138] it is nevertheless pertinent for two reasons. First, one can still say that when the achievements of the United Nations are measured against the promises of the Charter, the system has failed miserably. Those promises were born out of the fascist horrors undisclosed during the Second World War. The failure of the

---

[133] Id. at 645.

[134] *See* Schachter, "Invasion," *supra* n. 42. *See also,* Nowaz, "What Limits on the Use of Force? Can Force Be Used to Depose an Oppressive Government?," 24 *Indian J. Int'l L.* 406 (1984).

[135] *See,* e.g., Schachter, "Human Dignity as a Normative Concept," 77 *Am. U. J. Int'l L.* 848 (1983).

[136] Schachter, "Invasion," *supra* n. 42, at 646–47.

[137] Id. at 646.

[138] *See supra,* section v(A) of this chapter.

United Nations, therefore, is not just that it has not prevented aggression, but that it has not deterred oppression or reduced the human suffering associated with it. From *that* failure one could argue, with Professor Reisman, that at least in some cases states have retained their right to use force to eliminate oppressive regimes.[139] Second, and more generally, Professor Reisman's insistence upon the need to read article 2(4), as any other legal rule, in the light of the reasons and principles that support it, is unexceptionable. Schachter's true disagreement, then, is with Reisman's views on the policy and moral principles that underlie and support article 2(4) and, more generally, the whole corpus of international law. Professor Schachter rejects Reisman's views on the relative value and weight of human rights, consent of the governed and democracy, on one hand, and maintenance of peace and order, on the other. While expressing sympathy with democratic notions of political legitimacy, he reads article 2(4) as a shield protecting governments, even despotic ones, from outside intervention.[140] It is significant that Professor Schachter's objection to Reisman's thesis relies on what he perceives as the absence of grounds for the preeminence of democracy and human rights.[141] It is to his credit that he has not articulated the common relativistic objections to the injection of values in international legal discourse. Instead, he regrets the failure of supporters of the right of humanitarian intervention "to present a philosophical analysis that would be based either on deontological grounds or on a consequentialist utilitarian approach." He does not say that such arguments cannot or should not be made. Professor Schachter's point is well taken, and I have attempted to meet his challenge by presenting a philosophical defense of humanitarian intervention in the first part of this book. As I have tried to show, Professor Reisman is correct in asserting that some form of political consent is the only philosophically defensible basis of international law and state sovereignty. Whether his argument proves that forcible intervention is justified to further democratic values—and not just to remedy

---

[139] For a brief survey of customary law prior to 1945, see *infra,* Chapter 8.

[140] Schachter writes: "[I]t is almost startling to be told that Article 2(4) is now only a means and that such aims as the maintenance of peace and the prevention of aggression are secondary to the enhancement of popular rule." Schachter, "Invasion," *supra* n. 42, at 648.

[141] Id. at 647.

more serious human rights deprivation—is another matter.[142] The point here is that the limits that international law imposes upon the use of transboundary force depend on a value choice. Inescapably, the Schachter-Reisman controversy is an authentic dispute about values, one that cannot be solved by the sole appeal to diplomatic history and U.N. Resolutions, in short, to positivistic devices.[143]

The foregoing review of the scope and meaning of the prohibition of the use of force has led to the following conclusions. First, neither the words nor the *travaux préparatoires* of the Charter are dispositive of the issue whether the doctrine of humanitarian intervention, if it could be found in customary international law, has survived after 1945. Second, the failure of the collective security arrangements lends some support to the thesis that states have retained their customary right to act in self-help against violations of their rights under international law. Third, a proper determination of the meaning of article 2(4) necessitates an assessment of state practice. That assessment can only be made in the light of an appropriate moral theory, a normative theory of international law. No choice in this regard can possibly remain free of an articulation of moral values. Positivism has traditionally ignored or concealed this necessary moral dimension of international legal analysis.

In the first part of this book I provided a philosophical argument in favor of humanitarian intervention based on an ethical theory of international law. It is under that theory that the different purposes of the United Nations Charter should now be ranked. The response, at this stage in my argument, should not be surprising. The human rights imperative underlies the concepts of state and government and the precepts that are designed to protect them, most prominently article 2(4). The rights of states recognized by international law are meaningful only on the assumption that those states minimally observe individual rights. The United Nations purpose of promoting and protecting human rights found in article 1(3), and by reference in article 2(4) as a qualifying clause to the prohibition of war, has a *necessary* primacy over the respect for state sovereignty. Force used in defense of fundamental human rights is therefore *not* a use of force inconsistent with the purposes of

---

[142] *See* the discussion in the context of the *Nicaragua* case *infra,* Chapter 9.

[143] A similar dynamic can be observed in the debates that followed the United States invasion of Panama. *See* the discussion *infra,* Chapter 8.

the United Nations. We have created the institution of state sovereignty to provide a shield for groups of individuals to organize themselves freely in political communities. State sovereignty presupposes, however, that the rights of everybody will be respected. When human rights are instead violated, delinquent governments forfeit the protection afforded by article 2(4). The recognized and uncontroversial exception to the prohibition of article 2(4), article 51 on self-defense, confirms this conclusion. A war in self-defense is also a war to restore human rights. A distinction between self-defense and humanitarian intervention, therefore, can only rest on questionable distinctions between the rights of nationals and those of foreigners. Such distinctions are inconsistent with the universality of human rights and their derivation from the idea of individual autonomy, itself linked to universal traits of persons.

In the two next chapters I survey the practice of states and the United Nations on humanitarian intervention. I shall analyze in some detail several cases applying the moral-political theory developed so far. State and United Nations practice will be thus *interpreted* in the light of a normative theory of international relations firmly grounded on human rights.

CHAPTER 8

HUMANITARIAN INTERVENTION: STATE PRACTICE

I. HUMANITARIAN INTERVENTION SINCE 1945

The survey of state practice in this chapter will be limited to the post-1945 period. There are two reasons for focusing on the post-United Nations era. The first is that there is considerable authority for the proposition that the right of humanitarian intervention was a rule of customary law prior to the adoption of the United Nations Charter.[1] At the same time, it is commonly acknowledged that the prohibition of the use of force enshrined in article 2(4) of the Charter had a dramatic impact upon classic international law.[2] By examining the practice of states since 1945, we will be in a position to ascertain the relationship between article 2(4) and the right of humanitarian intervention. In particular, we will be able to decide whether state practice has carved out an exception to the prohibition on the use of force embodied in the United Nations Charter.

The second reason for focusing on contemporary history is that prior to 1945 there was no meaningful law of human rights. In Oppenheim's famous words, individuals were then only "objects" and not "subjects" of international law.[3] If customary law arguably recognized the right of

---

[1] See 1 Oppenheim, *International Law* 312 (H. Lauterpacht ed. 1955). *See infra,* text accompanying n. 10–19.

[2] *See supra,* Chapter 7.

[3] *See,* e.g., Oppenheim, *supra* n. 1, at 640–41, 736–38.

unilateral humanitarian intervention even before there was any law of human rights, the impressive development of human rights law in the post-United Nations era seems to reinforce the case for preserving that institution. The impact of the law of international human rights thus must be taken into account when assessing state practice and other relevant legal materials.

The method of examining state practice is generally in line with the traditional inductive approach to the determination of customary international law.[4] I adopt, however, a modified approach. First, the concept of custom that underlies my inquiry is claim-oriented, along the lines suggested by Anthony A. D'Amato.[5] My efforts will be directed to showing that there is a strong case for the existence of the right to humanitarian intervention on the basis of precedents. This claim, I suggest, is in turn stronger than the opposite position—the absolute noninterventionist doctrine. The proposition that a certain customary rule exists is partly a function of the number of instances a state can invoke in support of such rule.[6] Thus, it will not be necessary to show a practice that is completely consistent, uniform, and immemorial.[7] The claim-oriented approach is also better suited to the exceptional nature of humanitarian intervention. The traditional approach to custom (that is, the requirements of complete consistency, uniformity, and ancient character of the practice) is well-suited to the relatively noncontroversial, everyday exchanges among governments, such as diplomatic or maritime relations. Interventions are exceptional events. Therefore, the decision as to whether "custom" exists in this regard should take that exceptionality into account and adopt a flexible standard for the analysis of state practice.

More fundamentally, as I suggested in Chapter 1, the approach to customary law is permeated by values. In that sense it is not purely

---

[4] *See generally* G. Scharzenberger, *The Inductive Approach in International Law* (1965).

[5] *See* D'Amato, *The Concept of Custom in International Law* 18–20 (1971).

[6] Id. at 33.

[7] *See North Sea Continental Shelf* cases, 1969, *I.C.J. Rep.* 3, 41–44. In the case of Military and Paramilitary Activities in and Against Nicaragua (Merits), the Court wrote:

It is not to be expected that in the practice of States the application of the rules in question should have been perfect.

1986 *I.C.J. Rep.* 98. I fully discuss the *Nicaragua* case in Chapter 10.

inductive. The moral imperative of enhancing human dignity defended in the first part of the book will be a framework for inquiry, the working hypothesis under which state practice will now be examined. The examination of state practice will thus inevitably be purposive, much in the same way as scientific experiments are. Just as there are no naked facts in science,[8] there is no such thing as "naked state practice" in international law, that is, practice having a meaning *per se* independently of our normative and descriptive theoretical assumptions.[9]

I will examine several instances in which military force has arguably been used for humanitarian purposes: Tanzania's intervention in Uganda, 1979; France's intervention in Central Africa, 1979; India's intervention in East Pakistan, 1971; and the United States' intervention in Grenada, 1983. The purpose of studying these cases will be to discern a pattern of humanitarian intervention in the practice of states. In doing so, I hope to spell out the conditions that define genuine, legitimate humanitarian interventions.

II. A NOTE ON PRE-CHARTER PRACTICE

There is authority for the proposition that the doctrine of humanitarian intervention was accepted before 1945. Writers have hotly argued this point, and the validity of precedents has repeatedly been challenged.[10] There is little doubt, however, that the doctrine received considerable acceptance in the practice of states and in scholarly writings.[11] The pre-Charter practice crystallized throughout the 19th and 20th centuries when states, either collectively or unilaterally, intervened for humanitarian purposes. An early example occurred in 1827 when Great

---

[8] *See generally*, K. Popper, *Objective Knowledge: An Evolutionary Approach* (1972).

[9] The fact that in science theories are descriptive while in law and morality they are prescriptive does not affect this epistemological point. Cf. John Rawls's suggestion of "reflective equilibrium" as a way of checking our normative principles against our moral intuitions and vice versa. J. Rawls, *A Theory of Justice* 48–51 (1971).

[10] *See*, e.g., Brownlie, "Thoughts on Kind-Hearted Gunmen," in Humanitarian Intervention and the United Nations 139, 141–142 (R. Lillich ed. 1973) (hereinafter "Gunmen").

[11] *See* the authorities cited in Fonteyne, "The Customary International Law Doctrine of Humanitarian Interventions: Its Current Validity under the United Nations Charter," 4 *Calif. West. Int'l J.* 203, 214–226 (1974).

Britain, France, and Russia, under the auspices of the Treaty of Locarno of 1827, took military action to protect Christians in a conflict between Turkey and Greece that ultimately led to Greek independence.[12] In 1860 thousands of Christians were massacred in Syria. With the consent and approval of other Western powers, France dispatched six thousand troops to put an end to the atrocities.[13] Harsh treatment of Christians by Turkey in Bosnia, Herzegovina, and Bulgaria in 1877 led to a Russian declaration of war after the Turkish leaders rejected the London Protocol of 1877 (an agreement affirming the European concern for the oppressed people of the Balkans).[14] When the people of Cuba rebelled against Spanish domination in 1898, President McKinley and the Congress of the United States declared their right to intervene and later sent an armed force to assist the rebels. Within two years, the Republic of Cuba was established.[15] In 1913, Bulgaria, Greece, and Serbia intervened in response to the brutal "Turkification" program carried out by the Porte against Macedonian Christians.[16] The list would be incomplete without mentioning Woodrow Wilson's intervention in Mexico in 1914, discussed above.[17] Wilson's action, while flawed in other respects, was undoubtedly prompted by humanitarian concerns.

The most important pre-Charter precedent for humanitarian intervention, however, is the *Second World War itself*. That war, the paradigm of a just war, was without any doubt a humanitarian effort. The Allies did not fight Fascism just because Hitler and Mussolini were militarily aggressive with their neighbors. The thrust of that fight was dignity, reason, human rights, and decency on one side, against degradation, authoritarianism, irrationality, and obscurantism on the other.[18] It is therefore paradoxical, to say the least, to take the view that the

---

[12] *See* Oppenheim, *supra* n. 1, at 312–13.

[13] *See* Behuniak, "The Law of Unilateral Intervention by Armed Force: A Legal Survey," 79 *Mil. Law Rev.*157 (1978) and references therein.

[14] Fonteyne, *supra* n. 11, at 211–12.

[15] *See* Behuniak, *supra* n. 13, at 163. *See generally* Bogen, "The Law of Humanitarian Intervention: U.S. Policy in Cuba (1898) and in the Dominican Republic (1965)," 7 *Harv. Int'l L. Club J.* 296 (1966).

[16] *See* Fonteyne, *supra* n. 11, at 212, 213.

[17] *See* supra, Chapter 4.

[18] *See* Walzer, "World War II: Why Was This War Different?" 1 *Phil. & Pub. Aff.* 3 (1971).

United Nations Charter, the principal legal instrument of the present international society, which was the direct result of World War II, outlaws the very type of war to which the Charter owes its existence—a war for human rights.

Be that as it may, in this book I defend the view that a right of humanitarian intervention has been established *since* 1945, independently of what was the customary law prior to the United Nations Charter. The right of humanitarian intervention is thus a natural corollary of a return to the original concept of *ius gentium*; that is, of an international law based on human rights, and not centered on nation-states.[19] If anything, the pre-1945 precedents are reaffirmed by post-Charter practice. The notion that states could intervene to uphold "a minimum degree of civilization" has now matured: The "uncivilized" of yesterday are the tyrants of today.

III. THE TANZANIAN INTERVENTION IN UGANDA, 1979

In April 1979 the brutal rule of President Idi Amin of Uganda came to an end as a result of his overthrow by Tanzanian troops.[20] The Tanzanian action was the result of a series of events that took place in the context of strained relations between the two nations over the preceding years. In October 1978, Ugandan troops invaded Tanzanian territory and occupied the Kagera salient, an area located between the Uganda-Tanzania border and the Kagera River.[21] Amin attempted to justify this maneuver by pretending that Tanzania had previously invaded Ugandan territory.[22] The situation was complicated at the time by the simultaneous presence of anti-Amin groups in various regions of Uganda.[23] On November 1, Amin declared the annexation of the territory north of the Kagera salient.[24] President Nyerere considered the annexation tantamount to war and expressly stated his intention to act energetically

---

[19] *See* A. D'Amato, *International Law, Process and Prospect,* 217–22, 223–32 (1987).

[20] 1979 *Keesing's* 29669.

[21] Id.

[22] Id.

[23] Id.

[24] Id.

against Amin's forces.[25] At this point there were several efforts aimed at reaching a peaceful solution. Kenya tried to mediate; so did the Secretary General of the United Nations and the president of Mali.[26]

In view of the statement of President Nyerere that he was determined to use force against Uganda, Amin appealed to the Organization of African Unity and to the United Nations. Most significantly, a group of African states reportedly dissuaded Amin from pursuing the matter before the United Nations.[27] Libya seemed to be the only supporter of Amin,[28] while Zambia strongly sided with Tanzania.[29] The rest of the African states remained silent, apparently in deference to the dogma of nonintervention in internal affairs.[30] Amin then offered to withdraw from the occupied territories on the condition that Tanzania cease to support Ugandan dissidents. The offer was rejected by Nyerere, who announced his intention to expel the aggressor.[31] Amin then informed the United Nations Secretary General that he had ordered his troops to withdraw to the recognized borders of Uganda, but it was too late. Tanzanian sources stated that Amin could not be "let off" in view of the fact that during two weeks the Ugandan army had engaged in "pillage, massacre, destruction and rape" and had created a state of war between the two countries.[32]

On November 15, Tanzania launched an offensive from the southern bank of the Kagera River. Amin, sensing the defeat, offered once again to withdraw from occupied territories if the Tanzanian government guaranteed to stop trying to overthrow him.[33] Nyerere, for the first

---

[25] Nyerere declared: "We have the capacity to hit him; we have the reason to hit him; and we have the determination to hit him." 1979 *Keesing's* 29669.

[26] Id.

[27] Id.

[28] It was reported that Amin would have been ready to accept Khadaffi's mediation, but seemingly this was not acceptable for President Nyerere. Id. Later, when Tanzanian troops progressed over Ugandan territory, Khadaffi even issued an ultimatum to Julius Nyerere, threatening to declare war on Tanzania if its troops were not removed in twenty-four hours. This was ignored by Tanzania. *New York Times*, Mar. 27, 1979, at 2, col. 3.

[29] 1979 *Keesing's 29670*.

[30] *See* Umozurike, "Tanzanian Intervention in Uganda," 20 *Archiv des Völkerrecht* 301, 305 (1982).

[31] 1979 *Keesing's 29670*.

[32] Id.

[33] Id.

time, made clear in his response that his intention was to overthrow Idi Amin. He added that it would be a dangerous precedent if matters were allowed to rest at a point where Tanzania had to pay for the massacres and destruction caused by Amin's troops in the Kagera salient.[34] It seems, however, that Nyerere had decided as early as December that Amin would be toppled from power. That decision was apparently not part of his original plan but was to be entrusted, instead, to the Ugandans themselves, with the support of Tanzania.[35] Nyerere insisted that Tanzania harbored "no claim to an inch of Ugandan territory."[36] On January 26, Tanzania acknowledged for the first time that they had penetrated into Ugandan territory.[37] On February 23, Tanzania announced the capture of Masaka while Amin desperately called for help.[38] While the Ugandans joyously welcomed the Tanzanian troops, Amin threatened in a broadcast to punish his subjects for supporting the enemy.[39] Here, humanitarian considerations again played an important role: Withdrawal would have meant a certain genocide by Amin of numerous Ugandans. Consequently, President Nyerere declared that while it was not his responsibility to overthrow the Ugandan president, the Amin government was a government of "thugs" and the Ugandans had the right to overthrow him.[40]

In the meantime, renewed mediation efforts were taking place. The Organization of African Unity created a Committee which flew to Kampala and Dar-es-Salaam for talks with both presidents. The conditions specified by President Nyerere were that Uganda be condemned for invading Tanzania, that Amin renounce his claim to Tanzanian territory, and that Uganda pay compensation for loss of life and property during the occupation.[41] It is disputed whether President Nyerere was sincere, since he appeared to be determined to settle matters militarily with

---

[34] Id.

[35] 11 *Africa Contemporary Records* 395 (C. Legum ed. 1978–79).

[36] 1979 *Keesing's* 29670.

[37] Id.

[38] Id. at 29671.

[39] *See* Wani, "Humanitarian Intervention and the Tanzania-Uganda War," 3. *Horn of Africa* 18, 25 (1980).

[40] 1979 *Keesing's* 29671.

[41] Id.

Uganda.[42] It has been argued that because the O.A.U. has the practice of never condemning member states, Nyerere should have known that his conditions were unacceptable.[43] However, Tanzania was more than justified in claiming a departure from the O.A.U. practice of non-condemnation, in view of the atrocious nature of the Amin regime and his initial invasion of Tanzanian territory. Indeed, Nyerere had complained about the tendency in Africa to ignore what some of its leaders were doing, especially with regard to human rights violations.[44] He protested against the idea of the O.A.U. as a "trade union of heads of state" which automatically protected tyrants.[45]

On March 11, the Amin troops suffered a decisive defeat in Lukaya, 65 miles from Kampala.[46] As the Tanzanian forces continued to make progress, Kampala reportedly had become a ghost city where deserters of the Ugandan army were killing and looting at will. Amin's retreating forces plundered and destroyed everything they could.[47] In the meantime, Libyan aircraft and troops were helping Amin.[48] Finally, on April 11, a combined force of 4,000 Tanzanians and 3,000 Ugandan rebels took Radio Kampala and announced that the oppressive regime of Idi Amin was no longer in power.[49] The situation remained confused for a few days, but the Tanzanian control of the capital was complete by April 22.[50]

A new government headed by Professor Yusuf Lule was formed. In his first speech on April 11, Professor Lule reaffirmed his commitment to human rights and the rule of law.[51] Meanwhile, the whereabouts of

---

[42] *See* Hassan, "Realpolitik in International Law: After Tanzanian Ugandan Conflict, 'Humanitarian Intervention' Reexamined," 17 *Willamette L.J.* 859 (1980–81), n. 79.

[43] Id.

[44] Said Nyerere: "There is a strange habit in Africa: an African leader, as long as he is African, can kill Africans just as he pleases." *African Contemporary Records, supra* n. 35, at 394.

[45] Id. at 395.

[46] 1979 *Keesing's 29671.*

[47] *See* Southall, "Social Disorganisation in Uganda: Before, During and After Amin," *1980 J. of Modern African Studies* 627, 645.

[48] 1979 *Keesing's* at 29671–72.

[49] Id. at 29672.

[50] *See* Hassan, *supra* n. 42, at 880–81.

[51] 1979 *Keesing's* 29672.

Amin were not known. The reported casualties of the war were the following: fewer than 1,000 Ugandans and 400 Libyans killed in five months of fighting, as well as a smaller number of Tanzanians.[52] The cost of the war for Tanzania was estimated at $500,000 a day.[53]

Despite his strong determination to overthrow Amin, President Nyerere was cautious throughout the whole process to underscore the need for consent and participation of the Ugandan people in the change of government. He stressed from the beginning that the overthrow was the ultimate responsibility of Ugandans,[54] and from the start he supported groups of Ugandan dissidents and invited them to join in the common effort of ousting the Amin regime.[55] The two main groups opposed to Amin, the Forces of National Revolt and the Save Uganda Movement, met in Tanzania on March 23–25 and formed a Ugandan National Liberation Front.[56] This broad alliance represented more than eighteen exile groups and was headed by Professor Lule.

Restoring human rights in Uganda was a cardinal goal of the opposition. Already, two months before the Tanzanian victory, Milton Obote had praised the Tanzanian action because it had allowed the Ugandan people to rise against Amin's "institutionalized gangsterism." Similarly, the U.N.L.F. reaffirmed its commitment to the observance of human rights.[57] As already observed, the army that took Kampala included 3,000 Ugandan rebels. Professor Lule, in his first speech as President of Uganda, announced the resolve never again to allow a dictator to rule Uganda.[58]

---

[52] Id.

[53] Id.

[54] Id at 29671.

[55] *Africa Contemporary Records, supra* n. 35, at 429. It seems that Nyerere had outlined his plan to Milton Obote as early as October. He then emphasized the need to involve all Ugandans who were able and willing to contribute. Id. at 395.

[56] 1979 *Keesing's* 29671.

[57] Id.

[58] The Ugandan people's sufferings were not over, however. After an initial return to the rule of law in Uganda immediately after the overthrow of Idi Amin by Tanzanian troops, the human rights situation dramatically worsened. *See* 10 *Human Rights Internet Reporter* 658 (1985). It is estimated that during Milton Obote's next five years in power (1980–1985) more than 200,000 people died. The Economist, *World Human Guide* 289 (1986).

Many facets of the Uganda case are most relevant for an accurate juridical assessment of the Tanzanian action under humanitarian intervention principles. A judgment of international legality must take into account the human rights situation in Uganda, the motivation of the Tanzanian leaders, and the reaction of the international community.

Even those who have characterized the Tanzanian action as unlawful agree that the atrocities committed by the Idi Amin regime justified foreign intervention.[59] With few possible exceptions, the crimes committed by Amin probably have no parallel in modern history.[60] The arbitrariness, ruthlessness, and cruelty of Amin's rule can hardly be overstated.[61] Reliable estimations put the toll in human lives at 300,000.[62] When the Tanzanian troops reached Kampala they uncovered a horrid tale, which did no more than confirm what the world already suspected.[63]

It is not surprising, then, that the Tanzanian intervention was hailed as an act of liberation by the Ugandans, the rest of African nations, and the outside world.[64] In the words of a specialist:

> The defeat of Amin and the liberation of Uganda by Nyerere's Tanzania is the most significant African event of the last decade. With it Africa came of age, able to criticise itself, no longer determined to support the honour of corrupt rulers against the world simply because they are black.[65]

As noted above, there is no doubt that the Tanzanian leaders had humanitarian considerations in mind. The aversion that Tanzania's President Julius Nyerere felt for the murderous practices of the Ugandan

---

[59] *See*, e.g., Hassan, *supra* n. 42, at 882.

[60] *See* Ullman, "Human Rights and Economic Power: The United States v. Idi Amin," 56 *Foreign Aff.* 529 (1978).

[61] *See*, in addition to reference in preceding note, Richardson, *After Amin, the Bloody Pearl* (1980); Uganda and Human Rights, *Reports of the International Commission of Jurists to the U.N.* (1977).

[62] *See* H. Kyemba, *State of Blood* 9 (1977).

[63] It was reported that at the offices of the State Research Bureau the Tanzanians had found not only papers, but also the decomposing bodies of detainees. Many of the victims had been tormented and killed in the presence of Amin himself. 1979 *Keesing's* 29673.

[64] *See* Wani, *supra* n. 39, at 24.

[65] Southall, *supra* n. 47, at 627.

dictator is well documented. Nyerere was the first African leader ever to condemn Amin.[66] Several times he had referred to Amin as a "murderer" and had consistently refused to sit with him on the Authority of the East African Community.[67] Admittedly, Nyerere most probably would not have invaded Uganda had not Amin engaged in his frivolous aggressive enterprise. It is also possible that Nyerere was upset over the overthrow of his friend Milton Obote, and was committed to help reinstate him in power.[68] Yet considerations of humanity are the only conceivable legal justification for the Tanzanian overthrow of Amin. Reasons of humanity lie at the root of Tanzania's disregard for sovereignty-related inhibitions.

Noninterventionists are forced to take one of two positions: If they wish to justify the Tanzanian intervention—presumably because they correctly sense that international law just *cannot* protect rulers like Amin—then they must resort to some alternative legal explanation, such as self-defense. As mentioned below, article 51 of the U.N. Charter cannot possibly justify overthrowing the Ugandan government, because self-defense is not a punitive action.[69] The alternative argument is to declare the illegality of the Tanzanian action, in which case they would have to accept that international law does protect genocidal rulers. An interpretation of the U.N. Charter and State practice that yields such a result is unacceptable. We must attempt to reconcile international instruments and practice both with the primary place of human rights in international law and with some minimal moral constraints.

The international community was remarkably assertive in expressing the relief with which the fall of the Amin regime was received. The United States government supported Tanzania from the outset, although on self-defense grounds.[70] Tanzania also received strong support from

---

[66] *Africa Contemporary Records, supra* n. 35, at 393.

[67] Nyerere's own words indicate that Amin's human rights record was determinative of the Tanzanian's attitude: "Jomo [Kenyatta] is speaking for the people who elected him. I am speaking for you. Who will Amin be representing? I cannot sit with murderers." Id., at 393.

[68] Wani, *supra* n. 39, at 24 (1980).

[69] *See* Bowett, "The Interrelation of Theories of Intervention and Self-Defence," in *Law and Civil War in the Modern World* 38–40 (J. N. Moore ed. 1974).

[70] Secretary of State Cyrus Vance declared: "Our position is very clear; there is a clear violation of Tanzania's frontier by Uganda. We support President Nyerere's posi-

Zambia,[71] Ethiopia, Angola, Botswana, and Mozambique.[72] The Soviet Union, although it had not condemned Amin's policies,[73] announced the withdrawal of a military contingent from Uganda and the suspension of arms supplies after Amin's initial invasion.[74] While Kenya at first tried to remain neutral, it later offered its cooperation with the newly established Ugandan government.[75]

Even more significant was the deliberate inaction of the Organization of African Unity and the United Nations. The Africans themselves persuaded Amin not to appeal to the United Nations. That conduct is indicative of the probability that in that forum human rights considerations would have been a serious obstacle to the eventual condemnation of the alleged Tanzanian aggression. It is also possible that the African governments were uneasy over their past failure to condemn the barbaric rule of Amin in the name of the nonintervention dogma.[76]

The new Ugandan government was immediately recognized by Tanzania and her allies and by the United Kingdom.[77] The leading Western states warmly welcomed Mr. Lule's new regime. The British sent a mission to explore the needs of the new government and to reopen the British Embassy, which had been closed since 1976.[78] Claude Cheysson, then Commissioner for the European Economic Community, announced the Commission's readiness to send a mission to Kampala to discuss emergency aid measures under the Lomé Convention.[79] A member of the United States Embassy in Nairobi arrived on April 23 to reopen the embassy, which had been closed since 1973.[80] It is unlikely that these

---

tion according to which Ugandan troops must withdraw immediately." 1979 *Keesing's* at 29669.

[71] Id. at 29670.

[72] *Africa Contemporary Records, supra* n. 35, at 394.

[73] *See* Chaterjee, "Some Legal Problems of Support Role in International Law: Tanzania and Uganda," 30 *Int'l & Comp. L.Q.* 755, 755–56 (1981).

[74] *Africa Contemporary Records, supra* n. 35, at 394.

[75] *See* 1979 *Keesing's* 29674.

[76] *See* Umozurike, *supra* n. 30, at 305.

[77] 1979 *Keesing's 29673.*

[78] Id.

[79] Id. The EEC had decided on June 1977 to link aid to Uganda to the observance of human rights. *See* 1977 *Keesing's* 28928.

[80] 1979 *Keesing's* 29673.

actions would have been carried out had the Tanzanian invasion been perceived as an aggression.

While the reaction of international scholars was mixed,[81] on the whole the Tanzanian action was legitimized by the international community. And the main reason for international acquiescence was undoubtedly the repulsion felt by world opinion toward the Amin regime. A distinguished Ugandan writer who harbors misgivings about the legality of the Tanzanian intervention accurately summarized the world reaction: "[T]he Tanzanian invasion came as some kind of blessing. Though it was charged as a violation of certain peremptory norms of international law, it was never seriously censored."[82] Nigeria and Morocco expressed their concern about the danger of the precedent established by the Tanzanian intervention,[83] to which Nyerere answered:

> What we did was exemplary at a time when the Organization of African Unity found itself unable to condemn Amin. I think we have set a good precedent inasmuch as when African nations find themselves collectively incapable of punishing a single country, then each country has to look after itself.[84]

Indeed, the Tanzanian intervention is a powerful precedent for the reinforcement of human rights in a continent much too attached to an absolutist noninterventionist conception of international law.[85] A further point of interest in Nyerere's response is his emphasis on the position, which has been suggested by many writers, that the United Nations Charter has not suppressed self-help remedies for a number of cases, even where no direct self-defense is involved.[86]

---

[81] Writers who have argued for the legality of the intervention include Umozurike, supra n. 30, and Reisman, "Coercion and Self-Determination: Construing Article 2(4)," 78 A.J.I.L. 642, 644 (1984) (hereinafter "Coercion"). Professors Hassan, supra n. 42, and Wani, supra n. 39, have written against the intervention. Professor Hassan has even characterized the action as a "blatant aggression of Uganda's sovereignty" which "obviously disregarded the established principle of international law regarding the inviolability of a state's territorial autonomy." Hassan, supra n. 42, at 866.

[82] See Wani, supra n. 39, at 24 (1980).

[83] 1979 Keesing's 29673.

[84] Id.

[85] See Umozurike, supra n. 30, at 301.

[86] See the discussion in Chapter 7.

The Tanzanian overthrow of the Ugandan government cannot be justified on self-defense grounds. Although arguably the Ugandans engineered an "armed attack" within the meaning of article 51 of the United Nations Charter, it is well settled that a response in self-defense must be proportionate to the wrong inflicted.[87] If the only justification for the Tanzanian action had been self-defense, the overthrow of Amin would have been presumably condemned by the international community as disproportionate to the initial Ugandan aggression. Instead, the widespread feeling that the human rights cause had been served caused the international community to refrain from criticizing the Tanzanian intervention.

In sum, the Tanzanian intervention in Uganda is a precedent supporting the legality of humanitarian intervention in appropriate cases. Had the noninterventionist model been applied in this instance, it would have meant the continued suffering of millions of human beings at the mercy of Amin. There must be something deeply wrong with an international legal system that protects tyrants like Amin.[88] As I have tried to show, the answer is not that international law is wrong. Rather, the answer is that absolute noninterventionism resulting from a broad construction of article 2(4) of the United Nations Charter simply does not, and should not, represent international law. The Ugandan case is perhaps the clearest in a series of cases that have carved out an important exception to the prohibition of article 2(4).

The relevance of the Ugandan precedent is challenged in a recent work by Professor Natalino Ronzitti.[89] He argues that Tanzania's intervention in Uganda is not an authoritative precedent for the existence

---

[87] *See generally* D. Bowett, *Self-Defence in International Law* (1958). *See also* the *Nicaragua* case, 1986 *I.C.J. Rep.* 4, 122 (rejecting the proportionality of the U.S. mining of Nicaraguan harbors).

[88] This intuition is not shared by writers who have criticized the Tanzanian action. An extreme example is Professor Hassan, who, after acknowledging the support in classic international law for the doctrine of humanitarian intervention, writes:

> Even though this doctrine satisfies all the usual formalities of the jurisprudence of international law, we instinctively know that this could not be the *law*; it is simply a cloak of legality for the use of brute force by a powerful state against a weaker one.

Hassan, *supra* n. 42, at 862 (emphasis in the original). The instinct that dictators like Idi Amin should be protected by the law is a strange instinct indeed.

[89] N. Ronzitti, *Rescuing Nationals Abroad and Intervention on Grounds of Humanity* (1985).

of a right of humanitarian intervention.[90] Professor Ronzitti's well-documented account of the Tanzania-Uganda conflict deserves to be examined in some detail because it is a paradigmatic example of the dry, legalistic mode of prevailing literature about humanitarian intervention and about international law generally.

Professor Ronzitti's rejection of the Tanzania-Uganda case as an authoritative precedent for humanitarian intervention is supported, as I understand it, by three arguments. The first is that Tanzania never relied on humanitarian reasons. Professor Ronzitti draws the conclusion that "[h]umanitarian justifications would seem . . . to have been totally lacking in the Tanzanian intervention."[91] Although conceding that less than a month later the Tanzanian government did articulate humanitarian justifications,[92] he concludes that "the overthrow of the government in Uganda was not the main justification put forward by Tanzania."[93] The second argument is that Tanzania relied upon a theory of the "two wars," coupled with self-defense considerations.[94] This theory, also invoked by Vietnam in its invasion of Cambodia,[95] attempts to justify military intervention by asserting the existence of two distinct and legitimate wars against the Amin regime. One would be a "continuation" of the war of self-defense between Tanzania and Uganda.[96] The second war would be a "war of liberation" fought by the Ugandans themselves against the dictator.[97] The theory of the "two wars" attempts to explain and presumably justify the Tanzanian invasion by appealing to two already familiar and relatively well-established principles: self-defense and the legitimacy of at least some wars of "national liberation."[98] In this view there would be no need to resort to the more controversial and, it is thought, dangerous doctrine of humanitarian intervention. The

---

[90] Id. at 102–106, 110.

[91] Id. at 103.

[92] Id.

[93] Id.

[94] Id. at 102.

[95] *See* id. at 98–101.

[96] Id. at 102.

[97] Id. at 103.

[98] The relationship between "wars of national liberation" and humanitarian intervention is examined *supra*, Chapter 7.

third argument put forward by Ronzitti is that the Tanzanian intervention, when measured by official statements of governments, was not well received in the international community.[99]

As a preliminary matter, Ronzitti's account suffers from the same congenital defect as most current international legal scholarship: a persistent and deliberate failure to account for appropriate principles of political morality. The underlying methodological program of this form of positivism is that a legal scholar must scientifically (objectively) find the law. Objectivity requires, in this view, that the legal scholar should not allow ideology or value judgments to influence his task. That means that the only valid way to ascertain the true meaning of a precedent such as the Uganda case is to examine only diplomatic exchanges and the language of international instruments.[100] This dry legalistic approach should be rejected in favor of a methodology that accounts for politics in the broad sense of political morality. I have suggested a normative theory of international law in the first part of this book. The philosophical preeminence of human rights defended here is enough to legitimize the Tanzanian action.

But there is more. The application of the positivist paradigm to the Uganda case is mistaken by its own standards. None of Ronzitti's three arguments can withstand scrutiny. As to the first—that the Tanzanian intervention was not really humanitarian—Ronzitti assigns decisive weight to the fact that the Tanzanian government did not unequivocally state humanitarian motives as a justification of its action. However, the foregoing account shows that the Tanzanian authorities did have humanitarian considerations in mind. A review of the immediately previous history of bilateral relations reveals that the inhuman nature of the Amin regime was a determinant factor of Tanzanian hostility. As indicated before, the Tanzanian leader had repeatedly and publicly expressed his revulsion for the Ugandan dictator.[101] Therefore, Professor Ronzitti's reading of President Nyerere's statements seems to be unduly narrow. Many of those statements can indeed be interpreted as articulating humanitarian concerns.

---

[99] Ronzitti, *supra* n. 89, at 105–106.

[100] Cf. Dworkin's description of positivism as relying on a pedigree of rules. R. Dworkin, *Taking Rights Seriously* 17 (1978).

[101] *Supra*, text accompanying nn. 66–67.

More importantly, even conceding that such a reading of Tanzanian statements is correct, the view that places all probative value on governments' words fails to account for the whole picture of the Uganda case. The truth is that the world does not present itself nicely packaged in labels that read "humanitarian intervention," "self-defense," and so on. We try to impose order on diplomatic history. Humanitarian intervention is the best explanation of the Tanzanian action; it is the one that *interprets* that piece of history in its best light.[102] The question we ask is about the *meaning* of the Uganda affair in terms of world order. What really happened here? What does the incident tell us about the competing principles of promoting human rights and avoiding the use of force? From that perspective, the Uganda case tells us much more than what can be concluded by just examining the politicians' speeches. The world sighed with relief at the fall of Idi Amin. Uganda did not even succeed in reaching the United Nations. The international community refused to react against the use of military force by Tanzania in any of the ways in which nations may react against unwanted uses of military force. If, as Ronzitti claims, article 2(4) of the U.N. Charter is the paramount controlling provision, one would have expected states to react emphatically against this seemingly flagrant violation of Ugandan sovereignty. Instead, the international community virtually approved the Tanzanian intervention. It is thus pertinent to ask why nations reacted so passively in face of a military intervention that resulted in the overthrow of an established government—indeed, a violation of political sovereignty and territorial integrity *par excellence*. The answer is not hard to find: *the human rights record of the Amin government was such that it prevented governments of the world from assuming Uganda's defense.* But this surely is tantamount to saying that the international community as a whole recognized in this case the primacy of a modicum of human dignity over sovereignty considerations. So Tanzania's deeds and the world's reaction, much more than any words, underscored the humanitarian reasons which alone could justify the intervention.

Professor Ronzitti's reading of the Uganda case is illustrative of a problem with most current positivist international legal scholarship. Positivist writers incur a double confusion. In the first place, they confuse *motives* with *reasons*. Perhaps an analogy with the philosophy of

---

[102] *See* R. Dworkin, *Law's Empire* 87–113 (1986); and *supra*, Chapter 1.

science will exemplify this crucial difference. When a scientist articulates a new theory his motives for doing so are largely irrelevant. Why the scientist decided to elaborate the theory or how that theory psychologically came about are matters of no interest to science.[103] Rather, what matters is how the scientist can *justify* the theory, what *reasons* he can supply for defending it. Those reasons or justifying statements will have to do with some form of correspondence of the theory with physical facts, either in the form of potential counter examples, as Popper believes, or in the form of appropriate inductive assertions, as some other philosophers think.[104] Similarly, President Nyerere's hidden motivations, if any, matter little here. What matters instead are the legal *reasons* that can possibly justify the Tanzanian action on these facts. And the only reasons are human rights considerations. Only the restoration of human rights in Uganda can justify the Tanzanian action in the eyes of the world. Those reasons were articulated by the Tanzanian authorities and by the Ugandan rebels on behalf of whom the Tanzinian action was ultimately undertaken. So even if President Nyerere had a selfish motivation for overthrowing Amin (say, to enthrone his friend Obote), that does not speak to whether Nyerere was legally justified in doing so.

The second confusion is much more frequent. It is the view that what really matters is what governments *say*, regardless of what they *do*. It may be asserted along those lines, for example, that the fact that Tanzania did not say, or did not emphasize enough, that it was in fact liberating the Ugandan people from a bloody tyrant means that it was not really doing that.[105] Conversely, the argument runs, if Tanzania relied expressly upon self-defense principles, then the action must be appraised in their light. According to this view, the only reasons that qualify are those that the government in question actually invokes, even if they are inapplicable or mistaken, and even if there are other, more

---

[103] *See generally* Popper, *supra* n. 8. *See also* K. Popper, *Conjectures and Refutations: The Growth of Scientific Knowledge* (1963).

[104] I do not want to enter the debate about the value of inductive logic, or push the analogy with science too far, mainly because it functions differently for law. *See* M. Golding, *Legal Reasoning* 1–6 (1984).

[105] *See*, e.g., Ronzitti, *supra* n. 89, at 103–104 (an examination of Tanzania's justifications shows that they were not really humanitarian).

fitting, available principles of international law upon which that government failed to rely.[106] This way of ascertaining the value of state practice for the purpose of articulating customary international law is mistaken. As Professor D'Amato persuasively put it:

> given the simplicity of verbal invention, and the infinite variety of sentences that can be used to explain or mis-explain events, I find it unpersuasive to base a theory of customary law upon what states *say*.[107]

This view is buttressed by the fact that we (courts, writers, governments, historians) impose order on history. Finding customary law is trying to provide an interpretation of a largely amorphous diplomatic material. Indeed, we read historical events in the light of a complex set of empirical and normative assumptions. That complexity is poorly conveyed by the theory that customary law is determined by the speeches of politicians. A theory of law devoid of any moral underpinnings, one whose only currency is the sanctimonious language of government officials, is hardly deserving of that name. It matters little that the Tanzanians (wrongly) thought that they were acting in self-defense or said that they were so acting. The *logic of the situation*, revealed by world reaction, tells a different story: that the observance of a minimum of human rights is a precondition of the protection afforded governments by article 2(4) of the United Nations Charter.

The second argument advanced by Ronzitti to disqualify the relevance of the Ugandan case—that the real justification was a theory of "two wars"—rests on a misconception of the doctrine of humanitarian intervention. It will be recalled that Ronzitti argues that Tanzania justified its invasion and overthrow of Amin by positing the existence of two separate and equally legitimate conflicts. First, a continuation of the war of self-defense undertaken by Tanzania in response to the initial Ugandan aggression; and second, a civil revolt of Ugandan citizens

---

[106] Thus, for example, Professor Akehurst writes:

I would submit that the descriptions of a state's actions which are legally relevant are those which the state itself chooses to give of its actions; customary law is created by states, not by academics.

Akehurst, "Letter," 80 *A.J.I.L.* 147 (1986).

[107] D'Amato, "Response," 80 *A.J.I.L.* 149 (1986).

against Amin.[108] Professor Ronzitti (if he endorses the alleged Tanzanian justification) must contend that each of these principles justifies an aspect of the Tanzanian action. Self-defense justifies the initial Tanzanian armed response, while the civil war justifies the overthrow of the Ugandan government. Thus, the argument runs, we do not need to postulate a right of humanitarian intervention. The Tanzanian action can be justified as self-defense. The overthrow of Amin was in turn an internal Ugandan matter that was settled by the Ugandans themselves.[109] It is not clear whether Professor Ronzitti claims that the Tanzanian help to the rebels was legitimate or was instead impermissible intervention in Ugandan affairs. If the latter, presumably the Tanzanian government pretended that the overthrow of Idi Amin was an exclusively internal Ugandan enterprise—a claim so obviously contrary to the facts that it is hard to assume that the Tanzanian government would seriously defend it.

The "two wars" theory cannot withstand examination. The Tanzanian overthrow of the Ugandan government cannot be justified as an act of self-defense because it was disproportionate. Ugandan troops had already withdrawn and Amin had offered to reach a peaceful settlement. A use of force in self-defense is not punitive in character and therefore cannot have a "continuation." Had Tanzania acted in self-defense it would have had to stop after repelling the Ugandan initial attack. Instead, the Tanzanian troops did not stop until the fall of Kampala. So the only possible legal basis for the Tanzanian intervention is that it constituted *military aid provided to the Ugandan rebels.* Of the "two wars," only the second appears as a plausible ground for the Tanzanian action.

If the foregoing conclusion is correct, the principle that emerges from the Uganda affair is that states may provide support to individuals who are revolting against oppressive governments. Ronzitti and likeminded commentators make the mistake of assuming that humanitarian intervention is always a unilateral action by the intervening state with no participation of the local population.[110] This is a serious misconception about the nature of humanitarian intervention. Post-1945 state

---

[108] *See* Ronzitti, *supra* n. 89, at 102–106.

[109] Id. at 103.

[110] *See,* e.g., Brownlie, "Humanitarian Intervention," in *Law and Civil War in the Modern World* 217 (J. N. Moore ed. 1974). Implied throughout Brownlie's argument

practice unequivocally crystallizes a requirement for the legality of humanitarian intervention in addition to necessity and proportionality: The intervention must be welcomed by the victims of human rights violations, by those who are supposed to be rescued by the intervention.[111] Thus humanitarian intervention is best defined as military help for those who fight oppression, not as a unilateral action of the intervening state.[112] In this light, no appeal to self-defense is necessary. The only justification in the Uganda case is the assumed lawfulness of the military aid supplied by the Tanzanians to the Ugandan rebels. This element is present in all modern instances of genuine humanitarian intervention.

The third assertion made by Ronzitti—that the world reaction was negative—simply distorts the facts. He describes the reactions of various governments to the Tanzanian action and concludes that they were hostile to the legality of the intervention. Professor Ronzitti makes a selection of governments' statements that seems designed to prove what he has set out in advance to prove—that humanitarian intervention violates article 2(4) of the U.N. Charter.[113] The account provided in this section, however, abundantly shows that the reaction of the international community was largely positive.[114] The conjunction of those positive reactions and the international passivity in the face of the Tanzanian intervention far outweighs the isolated expressions of concern.

The Tanzanian intervention in Uganda was a legitimate use of force to stop ongoing serious deprivations of the most fundamental human rights. The Ugandan ruler had failed to exercise sovereignty within appropriate moral limits. The acquiescence by the international community incorporated the moral judgment that no rights of territorial integrity or political independence, no rule of nonintervention, can possibly shield tyrants like Amin. And rightly so: To hold otherwise would amount to corrupting our foundations of moral good—and evil.

---

against humanitarian intervention is the idea that such action is, almost by definition, unilateral.

[111] See supra, Chapters 6 and 7.

[112] As I indicated, this requirement is in harmony with the philosophical underpinnings of humanitarian intervention. See supra Chapter 6.

[113] Ronzitti, supra n. 89, at 105–106.

[114] See supra, text accompanying nn. 70–84.

IV. THE FRENCH INTERVENTION IN CENTRAL AFRICA, 1979

On September 20–21, 1979, the dictator Jean-Bedel Bokassa, self-proclaimed emperor of the Central African Republic, was overthrown by a group of citizens with the active support of a contingent of 1,800 French troops.[115] The French deposition of Bokassa was bloodless, unlike the Tanzanian intervention in Uganda. The French made their move while the Central African emperor was absent from the country.[116] Central Africa had been a French colony since 1900, and the relationship between the two governments had always been close. For example, Charles De Gaulle presided over a state ceremony in 1969.[117] French economic interests in the tiny landlocked African state remained strong after independence in 1960. In 1975, an international consortium had signed an agreement to study the exploitation of uranium in the southeastern part of the country.[118] In December of 1977 Bokassa crowned himself Emperor in a lavish ceremony largely financed by the French government.[119]

The atrocities committed by Bokassa during his reign are well documented. Amnesty International reported that schoolchildren had been tortured and murdered early in 1979 on Bokassas's personal orders, following riots in January.[120] The international outrage over this action marked the beginning of the emperor's downfall. In May 1979, the French-African Conference established a Commission of Inquiry (*Commission de constatation*) composed of judges of five African states (Senegal, Ivory Coast, Rwanda, Togo and Liberia).[121] The commission was charged with traveling to Bangui with Bokassa's agreement to investigate the massacre. The report of the commission confirmed beyond doubt Bokassa's personal participation in the massacre.[122] Bokassa subsequently took reprisals against those who had provided evidence to the commission.[123]

---

[115] See Rousseau, "Chroniques de faits internationaux," 83 *R.G.D.I.P.* 1058 (1979).

[116] Id. *See also* 1979 Keesing's 29933.

[117] Rousseau, *supra* n. 115, at 362.

[118] Id.

[119] 1979 *Keesing's* 29933.

[120] Id.

[121] Rousseau, *supra* n. 115, at 364.

[122] Id.

[123] 1979 *Keesing's* 29933.

In September 1979, a group of citizens headed by David Dacko, with the support of French troops, seized power in a bloodless coup. The French government took advantage of Bokassa's visit to Tripoli—where presumably he had gone to request military aid—to launch "Operation Barracuda."[124] French commandos were flown along with David Dacko to Banjui and the Republic was restored.[125] Although some early French statements may have given the impression that the French sent their troops after the coup,[126] it was soon apparent that the French troops had participated directly in the maneuver. The French Minister of Cooperation, Mr. Robert Galley, recognized three days later that France had "accompanied" the coup.[127] French and foreign commentators at the time uniformly labeled the French participation as military intervention.[128]

Before surveying the international reaction to the French intervention, it is instructive to dwell briefly on the prior *lack* of reaction of international organizations toward Bokassa's human rights violations. As in the case of Idi Amin, the United Nations and the Organization of African Unity remained silent during the massacres themselves. This exasperating passivity was vividly put in evidence by the speech of the Central African ambassador subsequent to the French intervention:

> I cannot conceal the bitter disappointment of my country over the culpable silence of the United Nations and of the Organization of African Unity regarding the suffering of the people of the Central African Republic in face of massive and flagrant violations of human rights in the name of the sacred principle of nonintervention in the internal affairs of states. Those institutions, whose basic principles depend on the protection of human rights and freedoms . . . , will never be able to do anything

---

[124] Wauthier, "France in Africa: President Giscard d'Estaing's Ambitious Diplomacy," 12 *Africa Contemporary Records* 120, 121 (C. Legum ed. 1978–79).

[125] Id.

[126] The French government immediately welcomed the coup as "an extremely happy event" and confirmed that at the request of Mr. Dacko a contingent of troops had been sent to Banjui to help the new regime maintain order. 1979 *Keesing's* at 29934.

[127] Statement of September 24, 1979, to the French television, cited by Rousseau, *supra* n. 115, at 365.

[128] *See*, e.g., Rousseau, *supra* n. 115, at 365; Wauthier, *supra* n. 124, at 120. Professor Michael Akehurst is therefore mistaken in denying the relevance of the Central African precedent on the grounds that the French "tried to pretend" that the troops had

useful until they stop being a syndicate of dictatorial oppressive governments.[129]

However, as in the Uganda case, few voices were heard in condemnation of the French intervention. Apart from the predictable hostility of Libya, only Benin and Chad condemned the French action.[130] Moreover, the basis upon which France acted was the multinational report prepared by eminent African magistrates. This fact authorizes the conclusion that France had the encouragement, and perhaps even the approval, of the leading French-speaking African nations.

The humanitarian motives of France can hardly be doubted. To be sure, the French determination to overthrow Bokassa arose out of a guilty conscience for having supported the tyrant in the past.[131] But the course of events showed an unmistakable shift of policy by the French government. That shift was directly caused by the reports about Bokassa's schoolchildren massacre and by the generally atrocious nature of the emperor's regime. The evolution of the French position from a non-interventionist to a pro-human rights stance took place in three steps. Following press reports, the French government first appointed the Commission of Inquiry. After the Commission's report was made public, the French Minister of Cooperation announced that French financial aid would be cut off, while the United States, Senegal, and the newly liberated Uganda broke off diplomatic relations.[132] The first step was "Operation Barracuda." Statements by French officials and President Dacko immediately after the coup confirm that humanitarian concerns were crucial to the French decision to overthrow Bokassa.[133]

Oddly enough, neither Professor Ronzitti nor Professor Verwey, in their recent work on humanitarian intervention, mentions the deposition of Central African Emperor Bokassa as a candidate for precedent of humanitarian intervention. Only Professor Akehurst alludes to it briefly

---

been sent after the coup. *See* Akehurst, "Humanitarian Intervention," in *Intervention in World Politics* 95, 98 (H. Bull. ed. 1984).

[129] 4 U.N. G.A.O.R., U.N. Doc. A/34/PV 32, at 41 (1979).

[130] Rousseau, *supra* n. 115, at 365.

[131] *See* Wauthier, *supra* n. 124, at 120–21.

[132] *See* 1979 *Keesing's* 29934.

[133] Id. at 29934.

in his article, only to point out that although French troops did over-throw Bokassa, France tried to pretend that her troops had arrived in the Central African Empire after Bokassa had been overthrown.[134] But Akehurst's account does not accurately reflect what happened. The French did not conceal the fact that their troops had "accompanied" the coup.[135] More generally, Akehurst makes the mistake, discussed above, of relying exclusively on the statements of politicians. Again, one has to look instead at the whole situation and decide what is the best interpretation we can supply. And there is no doubt that, as in the Uganda case, the French intervention to depose the bloody African ruler was hailed with relief almost unanimously by the concert of nations.[136] Moreover, the null cost in human lives makes the Central African case an instance of humanitarian intervention *par excellence.* French troops provided the necessary and proportionate help the Central African citizens needed to depose a dictator who had undoubtedly rendered himself guilty of the gravest crimes against humanity.

It may be objected that because the Central African coup was blood-less it does not qualify as a precedent for an exception to the prohibition of the use of *force* embodied in article 2(4) of the U.N. Charter. But this objection fails to take into account the accepted definition of the use of force banned by article 2(4). Sending troops to another nation without the consent of the sovereign for the purpose of helping rebels or dissent-ers overthrow that government is prohibited by international law, absent one of the exceptions to article 2(4).[137] Consequently, the French inter-vention can only be justified as a use of force *permitted* by international law as an exception to article 2(4), rather than as an incident that is empirically or conceptually different from the kind of conduct envis-aged by that provision. The French action would have been unlawful but for the humanitarian reasons—the existence of a serious and persis-tent pattern of human rights violations in Central Africa—that justified

---

[134] Akehurst, "Humanitarian Intervention," *supra* n. 128, at 99. *Cf.* Verwey, "Hu-manitarian Intervention under International Law," 32 *Neth. Int'l L. Rev.* 357 (1985); and Ronzitti, *supra* n. 89 (neither of these two writers lists Central Africa as a possible instance of humanitarian intervention).

[135] *See supra* n. 125–27 and accompanying text.

[136] *See supra,* text accompanying nn. 129–132.

[137] For a full discussion, *see infra,* Chapter 9.

that action in the eyes of the international community.[138] Unlike the Uganda case, self-defense analysis is obviously irrelevant here. Only the recognition of a right of humanitarian intervention, defined as the right of states to provide armed help to individuals in another state who are revolting against an oppressive government, can accommodate our intuition that the French action was morally justified.

V. THE INTERVENTION OF INDIA IN EAST PAKISTAN, 1971

On December 16, 1971, India achieved victory in a war against Pakistan. That war had as a result the independence of Bangladesh, previously called East Pakistan.[139] Among India's justifications was the protection of the Bengalis from the atrocities undertaken systematically against them by the Pakistani army.[140] For that reason, some commentators saw the Indian action as a valid instance of the exercise of the right of humanitarian intervention.[141] Others, however, thought that the Indian intervention had been unlawful.[142]

When Great Britain withdrew from the Indian peninsula, two separate nations, India and Pakistan, came into existence.[143] Pakistan was a nation geographically and ethnically divided into two entities, West Pakistan and East Pakistan. These two communities had sharply different characteristics. The Urdu-speaking West Pakistanis were closer to Middle Eastern countries than to the Hindustan. The East Pakistanis spoke

---

[138] With the very few exceptions noted above, I have seen no government or commentator arguing that the French intervention in Central Africa violated international law.

[139] *See generally, International Commission of Jurists, The Events in East Pakistan,* 1971 (1972) (hereinafter *Int'l Comm. Jur. Report*).

[140] *See infra,* n. 140 and accompanying text.

[141] *See* Reisman, comment in "Conference Proceedings," Lillich (ed.) *supra* n. 10, at 17–18; Nawaz, "Bangla-Desh and International Law," 11 *Indian J. Int'l L.* 459 (1971). Professor Farer described Bangladesh as a "morally irresistible case for intervention." Farer, "Humanitarian Intervention: The View from Charlottesville," in Lillich (ed.), *supra* note 10, at 149, 157. Similarly, the late Professor Friedmann thought that the Indian intervention was morally justified. *See* "Conference Proceedings," id. at 114.

[142] *See* e.g., Franck & Rodley, "After Bangladesh: The Law of Humanitarian Intervention by Military Force," 67 *A.J.I.L.* 275 (1973); Brownlie, "Thoughts on Kind-hearted Gunmen," in *Humanitarian Intervention and the United Nations* 139 (R. Lillich ed. 1973).

[143] *See Int'l Comm. Jur. Report, supra* n. 139, at 1–14.

Bengalese and considered themselves closer to the Hindu civilization (although not necessarily to India).[144] The main source of conflict between West and East Pakistan, however, turned out to be the nature of the political and economic ties between the two. West Pakistan achieved economic and military domination over a more populated East Pakistan.[145] Moreover, the political rights of the Bengali majority had been persistently frustrated by the West Pakistani leaders. For example, East Pakistani representation in central government services of Pakistan was barely 15 percent; their presence in the army never comprised more than 10 percent; and only one Bengali minister had been briefly appointed to the government. All this after fifteen years of independence.[146]

The Pakistani government remained a military dictatorship completely dominated by West Pakistani officials, notwithstanding some attempts to negotiate with the Bengalis. This situation caused growing social and political unrest during the 1960s, with the army refusing to yield to democratic pressures.[147] When Yahya Khan assumed the presidency in 1969, he promised a return to civilian rule. It is important to underscore that, until then, the Awami League (the autonomist political party of East Pakistan) had not urged outright political independence for East Pakistan.[148] Rather, their demands centered on observance of the one-man, one-vote principle and a framework for economic autonomy for East Pakistan. While the Pakistani government took the positive step of promising the former, both sides remained irrevocably split over the latter.[149]

Free elections were held in November 1970. The Awami League won 167 out of the 169 parliamentary seats reserved to East Pakistan, and the Bengalis thus obtained a comfortable majority in the Pakistani

---

[144] Id. Professor Nanda points out that "Islam and hatred to India were perhaps the only unifying factors between East and West Pakistan." Nanda, "Self-determination in International Law—The Tragic Tale of Two Cities: Islamabad (West Pakistan) and Dacca (East Pakistan)," 66 A.J.I.L. 323, 329 (1972), and references therein.

[145] See Int'l Comm. Jur. Rep., supra n. 139, at 7–14; Nawaz, supra n. 141, at 251.

[146] See Nanda, supra n. 144, at 328 and references therein.

[147] See Int'l Comm. Jur. Report, supra n. 139, at 15–23.

[148] See the Awami League Manifesto, in "Documents: Civil War in East Pakistan," 4 N.Y.U.J. Int'l & Pol. 524 (1971).

[149] See Int'l Comm. Jur. Report, supra n. 141, at 15–23.

National Assembly.[150] The central government immediately construed this result as a threat to the territorial integrity of Pakistan, and President Yahya Khan decided to postpone the National Assembly indefinitely.[151] The already serious situation in East Pakistan was then aggravated. Occasional claims of independence were added to claims for observance of democratic rights.[152] On March 23, Sheikh Mujibur Rahman, the Awami League leader, issued a "Declaration of Emancipation."[153] This was the final blow to any attempt to settle the conflict peacefully.

On March 25, 1971, the West Pakistani army struck Dacca and started an indiscriminate killing of unarmed civilians, Bengalis and Hindus, burning of homes and other property, using powerful military weapons. The mass murders and other atrocities committed by the Pakistani army during a period of several months are amply documented.[154] It seems that the motivation behind this genocidal action was simply to break the spirit of the Bengali people. The Awami League leaders were not the only victims; rather, the Pakistani ferocity was unleashed against *all* of the East Pakistani people. The Pakistani action thus can be legally characterized as genocide.[155] It is estimated that at least one million people died and millions more fled the country.[156] The Report of the International Commission of Jurists vividly summarizes the reign of terror:

> The principal features of this ruthless oppression were the indiscriminate killing of civilians, including women and children and the poorest and weakest members of the community; the attempt to exterminate or drive out of the country a large part of

---

[150] Mr. Bhutto's Pakistan People's Party obtained 88 out of the 144 West Pakistan seats. *See* Pakistan National Assembly Election Results, in "Documents: Civil War in East Pakistan," *supra* n. 148, at 550.

[151] *See* Nawaz, *supra* n. 141, at 254.

[152] *See* statement by Sheik Mujibur Rahman, March 7, 1971, in "Documents," *supra* n. 148, at 550.

[153] *See Int'l Comm. Jur. Report, supra* n. 139, at 20–21.

[154] *See* id. at 27–42; Salzberg, "U.N. Prevention of Human Rights Violations: The Bangladesh Case," 27 *Int'l Organization* 115, 116, n. 1 (1973) (list of eyewitnesses' accounts of atrocities); Schanberg, "Pakistan Divided," 50 *Foreign Aff.* 126, 126–27 (1971).

[155] *See* Mani, "The 1971 War on the Indian Subcontinent and International Law," 12 *Indian J. Int'l L.* 83, 85 (1972).

[156] *Int'l Comm. Jur. Report, supra* n. 139, at 24–26.

the Hindu population; the arrest, torture, and killing of Awami League activists, students, professional and business men and other potential leaders . . . ; the raping of women; the destruction of villages and towns; and the looting of property. All this was done in a scale [sic] which is difficult to comprehend.[157]

As a result of the massacres, Bengalis started to flee East Pakistan *en masse*. The number of refugees reached the millions, and included Moslem and Hindu Bengalis, many of them fleeing from their villages which had been destroyed by the Pakistani army.[158] As a Pakistani scholar put it, "never in the history of South Asia had there been such a mass exodus of population in one direction."[159] There is no doubt that the exodus was directly caused by the brutal Pakistani repression.[160] The exact number of refugees is in dispute. The Pakistani government claimed that there were no more than 2 million,[161] while Prime Minister Gandhi put the number at 10 million,[162] an estimation that seems closer to the truth and is confirmed by independent sources.[163] What is undisputed, however, is that the flux of refugees caused extreme hardship to India's economy. Relief efforts proved inadequate and soon the suffering in the refugee camps reached horrifying proportions.[164] The refugee situation made it impossible for India to remain indifferent to the conflict. Moreover, the massacres had a profound effect on the Indian people, who viewed the military repression in East Pakistan as "nothing less than evil crushing good."[165]

---

[157] Id. at 26–27. Other sources confirm the truth of the Commission's findings. *See* references in Nanda, *supra* n. 144, at 322–23.

[158] *See Int'l Comm. Jur. Report, supra* n. 141, at 41–42. *See also* H. A. Rizvi, *Internal Strife and External Intervention* 13–41 (1981).

[159] Id. at 136.

[160] Id. The magnitude of the refugee problem was recognized by the Pakistani representative in the discussions of the U.N. Security Council. *See* 26 U.N.S.C.O.R., 1606th mtg., S/PV 1606, at 11 (1971).

[161] 1971 *Keesing's* 24990.

[162] *See* Gandhi, "India and the World," 51 *Foreign Affairs* 70–71 (1972).

[163] *See The Times* (London), Aug. 27, 1971 (more than 8 million); K. P. Misra, *The Role of the United Nations in the Indo-Pakistani Conflict, 1971* (1973), at 59 (more than 9 million). Rizvi suggests that both the Indian and Pakistani figures are inaccurate and that a realistic figure would be in the neighborhood of five million. Rizvi, *supra* n. 158, at 138.

[164] *See* Rizvi, *supra* n. 158, at 138.

[165] Schanberg, *supra* n. 154, at 126.

Following tensions and incidents along the border, the Indian army invaded Pakistan, and on December 6, India formally recognized Bangladesh as an independent state.[166] The war lasted 12 days, and on December 16 the Pakistani army surrendered in Dacca.[167]

The Bangladesh case raises two distinct legal issues. The first is whether Bangladesh was a political unit entitled to self-determination. Assuming a positive answer, a subquestion is that of the legality of the Indian armed intervention in aid of the Bengali people attempting to exercise the right of self-determination. A second issue is whether the Indian intervention can be justified as a response to the brutal repression undertaken by the Pakistani central government against the Bengali people (humanitarian intervention). A response to the humanitarian intervention issue is quite independent of the response given to the first issue—of the validity of East Pakistan's claims to statehood.

Commentators are divided on whether Bangladesh was a political unit entitled to self-determination. By recognizing Bangladesh as a state, however, the international community has acknowledged the status of the Bengalis as a people entitled to self-determination in unequivocal terms.[168] So have a majority of writers.[169] While it is fairly well established that self-determination generally does not apply in non-colonial contexts,[170] a combination of factors in the Bangladesh

---

[166] See Int'l Comm. Jur. Report, supra n. 141, at 43–44. It is disputed whether Pakistan launched the first attack.

[167] Id. at 43–44.

[168] More than 50 countries recognized Bangladesh within four months of its establishment. See Nanda, "A Critique of the U.N. Inaction in the Bangladesh Crisis," 49 Denver L.J. 53, 66–67 (1972) (hereinafter "Critique").

[169] See J. Crawford, The Creation of States in International Law 115–117 (1979); Frey-Wouters, in R. Lillich (ed.), supra n. 10, at 127–128; Mani, supra n. 155, at 92–93; Nawaz, supra n. 141, at 255–56. Nanda, supra n. 144, at 325–333; 336. Cf. Int'l Comm. Jur. Report, supra n. 139, at 65–75 (claiming that Bangladesh was not entitled to self-determination under the Charter but that the Pakistani army was not entitled either to impose by force a different constitution than that decided by the majority). Professor Salmon argues that the correct solution would have been to grant the Bengali people the right of self-determination but without breaking up Pakistan. Salmon, "Naissance et reconnaissance du Bangladesh," in 1 Multitudo Legus, Ius Unum: mélanges en honneur du Wilhelm Wengler 467, 487 (1973).

[170] For example, Section 6 of the Declaration on the Granting of Independence to Colonial Countries and Peoples, after establishing the right to self-determination of colonial peoples, provides:

Any attempt at the partial or total disruption of the national unity and the territorial integrity of a country is incompatible with the purposes and princi-

case distinguishes it from other non-colonial situations.[171] Those criteria are, first, the physical separation, the cultural differences and the economic disparity between East and West Pakistan.[172] They also include the refusal by the Pakistani central government to implement the results of free elections. Most importantly, a decisive factor was the genocidal conduct of the Pakistani army against the Bengali people.[173] So even if East Pakistan was not initially a self-determination unit entitled to secession, both the denial of their democratic rights by the Pakistani elite and the genocide attempted by the Pakistani army against the Bengali people sufficed to revert self-determination rights to the Bengali people. Thus the best legal position is that when a case is doubtful, brutal repression by the central government strengthens the self-determination claims.[174] As Michael Walzer wrote in his unsurpassed discussion of the Bangladesh case: "People who initiate massacres lose their right to participate in the normal (even normally violent) processes of domestic self-determination."[175]

Some commentators are puzzled by the following dilemma: How can Bangladesh be a legitimate state in view of the fact that it was originated from an illegitimate use of force by another state?[176] But this is a pseudo-problem, created by the use of a false premise: that the Indian intervention was illegal. If, as these authors recognize, Bangladesh was entitled to self-determination, and if the use of force by Pakistan against the Bengali people was a use of force contrary to article 2(4) of the Charter,[177] then assistance furnished to that people seems to

---

ples of the United Nations.

U.N. G.A. Res. 1514 (XV), 15 U.N. G.A.O.R., Supp. (No. 16) 66, U.N. Doc. A/4684 (1961).

[171] See Nanda, supra n. 144, at 328.

[172] See supra, text accompanying n. 143–149.

[173] See Nanda, supra n. 144, at 330–33.

[174] Thus Professor Nanda's views, supra n. 144, are entirely correct. In the same sense, see Nawaz, supra n. 141, at 260–63.

[175] Walzer, Just and Unjust Wars 106 (1977).

[176] See in this sense, Salmon, supra n. 169, at 467, 490; and Crawford, supra n. 169, loc. cit. Crawford concludes that Bangladesh was a unit entitled to self-determination and that for that reason India's alleged illegal intervention does not deprive Bangladesh of statehood.

[177] See Crawford, supra n. 169, at 117.

be lawful as well.[178] The counter-use of force against a use of force prohibited by article 2(4) is itself lawful. Once it has been established that the central government is unlawfully depriving a people of their self-determination rights, it matters little whether the situation is a colonial or non-colonial one. To hold otherwise—that the right to self-determination and therefore the lawfulness of material help is limited to colonial peoples—leads to unacceptable results.[179] Further, we have seen in Chapter 7 that it is unprincipled to extend the lawfulness of material help only to peoples fighting against racist regimes. If the law allows forceful intervention on behalf of individuals who are victims of racial discrimination, a fortiori it allows intervention on behalf of a people like the Bengalis who are deprived of their democratic rights by genocidal governmental conduct.

The characterization of the Indian action as humanitarian intervention can thus be made at two levels. First, as foreign assistance for a people engaged in a struggle for their right to self-determination, which is a (collective) human right. Second, the Indian action can be characterized as foreign intervention aimed at stopping acts of genocide, that is, humanitarian intervention proper.[180] The strength of the Indian claim to legality is that both aspects are combined here. Indeed, even a writer who has doubts about the legality of the Indian intervention recognizes that the international support for the self-determination of Bangladesh "seems justified" due to the "particular, indeed extraordinary, circumstances of East Bengal in 1971–72."[181] This is, of course, just a euphemism for the acts of genocide referred to above. To put it differently: Even if the Indian intervention had not aimed at helping Bangladesh to

---

[178] See Mani, supra n. 155, at 93–94. See also the discussion infra, Chapter 7.

[179] Professor Salmon, who has doubts about the legality of the Indian intervention, concludes that the Third World cannot limit the exercise of self-determination to colonies. Salmon, supra n. 169, at 489.

[180] Franck and Rodley, who vehemently challenged the legality of the Indian action, recognize that in the Bangladesh case two objectives of international law appeared to be in conflict: justice and peace. Contrary to the conclusion in the text, they accord priority to the prohibition of article 2(4) over self-determination and human rights. Their almost exclusive argument is the danger of abuse involved in recognizing a right of humanitarian intervention. Franck & Rodley, supra n. 142, at 275–276. The concern about the danger of abuse is also crucial for Brownlie. See Brownlie, "Gunmen," in Lillich (ed.), supra n. 10, at 146. I discussed the abuse argument in Chapter 6.

[181] Crawford, supra n. 169, at 117.

achieve independence, it would have been justified as humanitarian intervention *tout court.* The case under study, directed toward rescuing the Bengalis from the genocide attempted by Pakistan, is an almost perfect example of humanitarian intervention. It is not necessary to draw those distinctions, however, because each claim (self-determination and human rights violations) is strong on its merits, and both converge here.

The discussions in the United Nations are particularly revealing. Both the General Assembly and the Security Council were seized of the dispute.[182] Writers have unanimously criticized the total inability of the United Nations to even address, let alone stop, the massacres, and to prevent the Indo-Pakistani war.[183] That inaction is yet another omission in the exercise of the United Nations' responsibility to promote human rights, an express mandate of the United Nations Charter.[184] The lack of response to genocide supports the assertion of many qualified legal scholars that, unless the international community is ready to tolerate a return to the Nazi era, the right to prevent genocide has reverted to individual states, where the prevention can be undertaken with reasonable chance of success.[185]

Contrary to what some commentators assert,[186] India *did* articulate humanitarian reasons as justification for her military action.[187] However,

---

[182] 26 U.N.S.C.O.R. (1606 to 1621 mtgs.), U.N. Doc. S/PV., 1606–1621 (1971); 26 U.N. G.A.O.R. (2002–2003 mtg. and Corr. 1), U.N. Doc. A/PV2002 (1971); *see also* U.N. G.A. Res. 2793 (XXVI), 26 U.N. G.A.O.R., Supp. (No. 29), U.N. Doc. A/8429 (1971).

[183] *See* Nanda, "Critique," *supra* n. 168; Salzberg, *supra* n. 154; R. Lillich & F. Newman, *International Human Rights: Problems of Law and Policy* 487 (1979).

[184] Art. (3), and 55. *See* Salzberg, *supra* n. 154, at 117.

[185] *See* the discussion *supra,* Chapter 7.

[186] Akehurst, "Humanitarian Intervention," *supra* n. 128, at 96. Both Ronzitti and Verwey admit that humanitarian considerations were invoked by India, but claim that humanitarian intervention was not her main line of defense. *See* Ronzitti, *supra* n. 89, at 96, 108–109; Verwey, *supra* n. 134, at 401–402.

[187] The Indian representative in the General Assembly declared:

[T]he reaction of the people of India to the massive killing of unarmed people by military force has been intense and sustained. . . . There is intense sorrow and shock and horror at the reign of terror that has been let loose. The common bonds of race, religion, culture, history and geography of the people of East Pakistan with the neighbouring Indian state of West Bengal contribute powerfully to the feelings of the Indian people.

26 U.N. G.A.O.R. 2002th, U.N. Doc. A/PV 2002 (1971), at 14. *See also* the Indian

whether she did it or not, or whether, as Akehurst claims, India amended her initial pro-interventionist statements in the U.N.,[188] are matters of little importance. The important point here is not so much whether the Indian leaders harbored selfish purposes along with humanitarian ones, or in what proportion those purposes blended as an efficient cause of the intervention (how could anyone establish that anyway?), but rather that the whole picture of the situation was one that warranted foreign intervention on grounds of humanity. Humanitarian intervention is the best interpretation we can provide for the Bangladesh war. That reading puts the incident in its best light under both principles of international law and elementary moral commitments to human dignity. As Walzer put it, the appeal has to be to humanity as a whole; it is not the conscience of political leaders that one refers to in such cases.[189] Indeed, in the Bangladesh case, India's "various motives converged on a single course of action called for by the Bengalis."[190] The Bengali people joyously welcomed the Indian help, which not only freed them from genocidal repression but also gave them the first opportunity in modern times to rule their own homeland.[191]

It is true that the dominant concern of states who participated in the U.N. discussion was the restoration of peace, rather than the condemnation of one of the parties.[192] But even these statements and the wording

---

delegate's statement in the Security Council. 26 U.N.S.C.O.R. 1606th mtg. 26, U.N. Doc. S/PV. 1606 (1971), at 5 and especially at 14–15 (Pakistani military repressions were unleashed in a manner that would shock the conscience of mankind), and at 27. At the same meeting the Indian representative said:

> We are glad that we have on this particular occasion nothing but the purest of motives and the purest of intentions: to rescue the people of East Bengal from what they are suffering.

Id. at 18. Pakistan's attack on India in the Security Council relied heavily on the lack of disinterestedness on the part of Indian leaders. See, e.g., id. at 11; and id., 1607th mtg., U.N. Doc. 1607, at 15.

[188] See Akehurst, supra n. 128, at 96.

[189] Walzer, supra n. 175, at 107.

[190] Id. at 105.

[191] See Talbot, "The Subcontinent: Ménage à Trois," 50 Foreign Aff. 698, 700 (1971–72).

[192] See, e.g., the statement of the representative of Argentina, 26 U.N. G.A.O.R., supra 182, at 4. See also Nanda, "Critique," supra n. 168, at 60 (regretting the obsession of U.N. delegates with territorial integrity and cease-fire and the corresponding neglect of the human rights situation in East Pakistan).

itself of General Assembly Resolution 2793 (XXVI)[193] show that nations were also concerned with "the restoration of the conditions necessary for the voluntary return of refugees," an ultra-euphemism to urge Pakistan to renounce its genocidal policies.[194] Similarly, France urged the cessation of *all* hostilities, a clear reference to the Pakistani repression.[195] India's explanation of her negative vote rightly underscored the draft resolution's lack of emphasis on the Pakistani repression against the Bengalis.[196] At the very least, an examination of the discussion in the United Nations showed that a majority of states did not view the Bangladesh case as one involving *only* an inter-state problem. They did not regard the Bangladesh war as a situation framed entirely as a case of use of force by India against Pakistan. While falling far short of its responsibilities in a situation of egregious violation of human rights (as Secretary General U Thant himself readily recognized[197]), the majority did not react by flatly condemning India for a violation of article 2(4). Rather, the majority implicitly acknowledged that the normative force

---

[193] U.N. G.A. Res. 2793 (XXVI), 26 U.N. G.A.O.R., Supp. 29 (1971), at 3.

[194] In the General Assembly, to which the matter was referred by the Security Council after a failure to adopt any resolution, see the Argentine delegate's statement, at 26 U.N. G.A.O.R., *supra* n. 182, at 4 (Argentina drafted the resolution). In the same sense, stressing in various degrees the importance of achieving a satisfactory solution *within* Pakistan, see the statement of the representatives of Hungary, id., at 4–5 (reference to mass atrocities and gross violations of human rights); Tanzania, id., at 22; New Zealand, id., at 21; Greece, id., at 12; Yugoslavia, id., at 11 (special reference to human rights); Netherlands, id., at 9; Bhutan,id., at 4; Sri Lanka, id., at 2–3. Delegations flatly opposed to the Indian intervention included Togo, id., at 19; Portugal, id., at 24–25; Iran, id., at 5; Indonesia, id., at 7; Ghana, id., at 6; and Turkey, id., at 7.

In the Security Council, statements favoring a "political solution" including "solving" the internal Pakistani situation, included, apart from India, those of the U.S.S.R., 26 U.N. S.C.O.R., 1608th mtg., U.N. Doc. S/PV. 1608 (1971), at 5–6; the United States, id., 1611th mtg., U.N. Doc. S/PV 1611, at 2–3. (The United States, however, claimed that the "tragic mistake" by Pakistan did not entitle India to use force, id., at 2); Italy, id., 1606th mtg., U.N. Doc. S/PV. 1606, at 20; France, id., at 21; Syria, id., at 23; Poland, id., at 28; Belgium, id., 1607th mtg., U.N.Doc. S/PV. 1607, at 22. Statements against the Indian intervention included, apart from Pakistan and occasionally from the United States, those of China, id., 1606th mtg., U.N. Doc. S/PV. 1606, at 22–23; and Somalia, id., at 15.

[195] *See* 26 U.N. G.A.O.R., 2003 mtg., *supra* n. 194, at 32.

[196] Id. at 43.

[197] *See* the Secretary General's speech, 26 U.N. G.A.O.R., Supp. 1A, Doc. A/8401/ Add. 1, at paras. 146–147.

of that principle is attenuated where acts of genocide are concerned.[198] The priority of the condemnation of genocide is reinforced by Security Council Resolution 307, adopted after the fall of Dacca. That decision was far from condemning India as an aggressor or even implying such condemnation.[199]

VI. THE INTERVENTION OF THE UNITED STATES IN GRENADA, 1983

On October 25, 1983, a joint military force composed of a United States contingent of 8,000 troops and 300 men from six Caribbean countries, landed in the island of Grenada, located about 100 miles off the coast of Venezuela. After three days of fighting, the invaders deposed the newly self-appointed Revolutionary Military Council.[200]

The legality of the intervention in Grenada has been defended by the United States Government and some commentators under three headings. It has been claimed that the intervention was legitimized by a lawful invitation by the Grenadian Governor General.[201] The Grenada action has also been defended as a regional peace-keeping action authorized by the competent regional treaties, in turn grounded on Article

---

[198] Professor Ronzitti wrongly reads the action by the General Assembly and the statements by delegates quoted *supra*, at n. 194, as general statements against humanitarian intervention. *See* Ronzitti, *supra* n. 89, at 95–97.

[199] Resolution 307 (1971) called for "respect of cessation of hostilities" and "withdrawal of troops as soon as possible." U.N. S.C. Res. 307, U.N. Doc. S/Res/307, Dec. 21, 1971, reprinted in 11 *I.L.M.* 125 (1972). Professor Nanda points out that "as the eventual surrender of the Pakistani army became imminent, the tone of the Council debates shifted from an unrelenting emphasis on an immediate cease-fire to a fresh concern for a political settlement." Nanda, "Critique," *supra* n. 168, at 62. In my opinion, Professor Schachter misreads G.A. Res. 2793 (probably because India voted against it) and fails to explain the conspicuous lack of condemnation of S.C. Res. 307. *See* Schachter, "The Right of States to Use Armed Force," 82 *Mich. L. Rev.* 1620 (1984), at 1629, n. 19.

[200] For a complete factual account, *see* W. C. Gilmore, *The Grenada Intervention: Analysis and Documentation* (1984); and Gordon, Bilder, Rovine & Wallace, "International Law and the United States Action in Grenada: A Report," 18 *Int'l Law.* 331 (1984) (hereinafter "Gordon Report"). For a Caribbean view, *see* Fraser, "Grenada: The Sovereignty of a People," 7 *West Indian L.J.* 205 (1983).

[201] *See* Moore, "Grenada and the International Double Standard," 78 *A.J.I.L.* 145, 159–161 (1984). *See also infra*, text accompanying n. 281–220.

52 of the U.N. Charter.[202] And finally, the intervention was described as a lawful use of force in protection of nationals whose lives were threatened in the island.[203] Most of the critics of the intervention have also focused on those claims.[204]

The analysis here shall concentrate instead on the Grenada case as a possible instance of humanitarian intervention proper; that is, as an intervention aimed at rescuing Grenadians and others from actual or imminent human rights deprivations. The suggestion here is that the operation in Grenada was aimed at rescuing the Grenadians from an immediate threat to their lives and from deprivation of their democratic rights stemming from the imminent imposition on them of an unwanted authoritarian regime. The structure and design of that regime would have led, with all but absolute certainty, to a permanent denial of human rights.

Grenada was granted independence from British colonial rule in 1974. The country was controlled by a parliamentary government until 1979. At that time Maurice Bishop with the New Joint Endeavor for the Welfare, Education and Liberation (JEWEL) movement ousted Prime Minister Sir Eric Gairy in an almost bloodless coup. When Bishop overthrew Gairy he promised free elections and observance of human rights, a promise he never fulfilled.[205] Bishop held the position of Grenadian Prime Minister until mid-October 1983, when a rival faction of the New Jewel Movement staged a coup headed by Deputy Prime Minister Bernard Coard and the Commander of the Armed Forces, General Hudson Austin.

On October 14, 1983, reports of political upheaval and a possible military coup in Grenada began to circulate. It was unclear who was

---

[202] *See* Moore, *supra* n. 201, at 153–156. *See also infra*, text accompanying n. 218–220.

[203] *See* Moore, *supra* n. 201, at 156. *See also infra*, text accompanying n. 218–220.

[204] *See* Gilmore, *supra* n. 200, at 37–74; "Gordon Report," *supra* n. 200, at 340–378; Nanda, "The United States Armed Intervention in Grenada—Impact on World Order," 14 *Calif. W. Int'l J.* 395, 404–422 (1984) (hereinafter "Grenada"); Dore, "The U.S. Invasion of Grenada: Resurrection of the 'Johnson' Doctrine?" 20 *Stan. J. Int'l L.* 175, 180–189 (1984). Only Doswald-Beck discusses humanitarian intervention at some length. *See* Doswald-Beck, "The Legality of the U.S. Intervention in Grenada," 31 *Neth. Int'l L. Rev.* 35, 362–366 (1984).

[205] *See* Fraser, *supra* n. 200, a 207.

in effective control of the government. Because outside communication had been cut off, there was little information available on the effectiveness of Coard's attempt to replace Bishop. On October 17, General Hudson Austin announced that Mr. Bishop had been ousted from the central committee on the New Jewel Movement and been placed under arrest.[206] The army also took into custody three cabinet ministers and two trade union leaders. The Minister of Information described the episode as "an internal party matter" and prohibited the presence of foreign correspondents and photographers.[207] On October 19, a crowd of approximately 3,000 people marched on the army barracks in which the six prisoners were being held (Bishop, three ministers, two union leaders). Violence ensued and resulted in at least seventeen deaths with reports of up to two hundred. General Austin announced on state-run Radio Free Grenada that Bishop had been shot when "he had been freed by supporters and led a crowd of them to army headquarters to free others."[208] The three cabinet members and "many others" were also reported killed.[209] Austin and the Revolutionary Military Council (RMC) established on October 20, stated that the shootings occurred in self-defense in reaction to initial firing by Bishop and his supporters. Most reports, however, indicate that Bishop and his cabinet members were summarily executed (i.e., assassinated in cold blood) by a firing squad, and that the army open-fired on the crowd.[210] The presence of women and children in the crowd was apparently confirmed when the military council, while still asserting self-defense, condemned Bishop for the "irresponsible and crazy act" of leading women and children into a military installation.[211] In the wake of Bishop's death, the RMC imposed a 96-hour shoot-on-sight curfew. Schools and the airport were closed.

The news of the killing of Bishop and his cabinet members provoked widespread condemnation.[212] The RMC, responding to rumors of possible military intervention, sent a telex to the U.S. Embassy in Barbados.

---

[206] 1984 *Keesing's* at 32614. For details about the internal dissension, *see* Fraser, *supra* n. 200, at 206, 229.

[207] *N.Y. Times*, Oct. 17, 1983.

[208] *See* "Gordon Report," *supra* n. 200, at 337.

[209] *N.Y. Times*, Oct 20, 1983, Section 1, at 1.

[210] *See N.Y. Times*, Oct. 21, Section 1, p. 8; id., Nov. 1, at Section 1, p. 16.

[211] *N.Y. Times*, Oct. 22, Section 1, at p. 5.

[212] *See* 1984 *Keesing's* 32615.

It stated in relevant part: "Presently peace, calm and good order prevail in our country" and added that the RMC "has no desire or aspiration to rule the country" but was "beginning the process of establishing a fully constituted civilian government within ten to fourteen days." The State Department regarded these assurances as unreliable and later offered the telex as evidence of the lack of government authority in Grenada. The interpretation was that since a government was to be established, there was not one already established.[213]

On October 25, following requests by the Organization of Eastern Caribbean States and Grenada's Governor General Sir Paul Scoon, operation "Urgent Fury" began, with the arrival of 1,500 members of the 82nd Airborne Division and 400 U.S. Marines, as well as a 300-person security unit from neighboring islands.[214] After three days the military operation was completed. The U.S.-Caribbean force encountered resistance, mostly from part of the 800 Cuban personnel.[215] Casualties included 18 Americans, 45 Grenadians (among them 21 civilians killed in an accidental bombing of a hospital), and 34 Cubans.[216] December 15th, all United States combat troops had been withdrawn from Grenada, leaving only a small number of American and Caribbean support personnel on the island.[217]

As indicated above, the Reagan administration had three official justifications for the invasion of Grenada. First, they relied on an invitation from Grenadian Governor General, Sir Paul Scoon, to restore order on the island.[218] Second, they relied on a request from the Organization of Eastern Caribbean States (OECS) for collective security action.[219]

---

[213] See "Gordon Report," supra n. 200, at 339.

[214] Id. at 334.

[215] Id. For a detail of the Cuban involvement in Grenada, see Fraser, supra n. 200, at 222–23.

[216] "Gordon Report," supra n. 200, at 334. See also Grenada: A Preliminary Report, issued by the Departments of State and Defense, Dec. 16, 1983.

[217] "Gordon Report," supra n. 200, at 334.

[218] See statement of Deputy Secretary of State Kenneth Dam, 82 State Dept't Bull., No. 2081, Dec. 1983, at 79, 80–81 (hereinafter Dam Statement); letter of Legal Adviser, Davis Robinson, 18 Int'l Law. 381, 382–83 (1984) (hereinafter Robinson Letter).

[219] See Dam Statement, supra n. 218, at 80; Robinson Letter, supra n. 218, at 383–85.

Third, they relied on the right to protect United States nationals in Grenada.[220] While humanitarian intervention (apart from protection of U.S. nationals) was not officially listed among the legal justifications for the intervention, the whole logic of the situation, evidenced not only by the conduct of the United States and her Caribbean allies, but also by statements by the highest United States officials, denotes the humanitarian underpinnings of the mission.[221] Moreover, the three official reasons themselves can be explained by reference to an ultimate human rights objective.

Humanitarian justifications for the Grenada operation can be divided into two categories: references made to human rights violations and a concurrent state of chaos, and references made to the need to restore democracy in Grenada. On October 26, President Reagan announced the invasion, offering two reasons relevant to humanitarian intervention: "to protect innocent lives, including up to 1,000 Americans" and "to forestall further chaos." He stated that the United States had "no choice but to act strongly and decisively to oppose a brutal gang of leftist thugs."[222] This sentiment was mirrored in Secretary of State George Shultz's comment that there existed "an atmosphere of violent uncertainty." He supported his claim by mentioning the shoot-on-sight curfew, arrests, and sporadic firing. Shultz also described the situation as evidencing a "vacuum of legitimate government."[223] This was probably a reference to the October 23 letter from the OECS requesting intervention, which focused on the "current anarchic conditions, the serious violations of human rights and bloodshed" that had occurred and the threat to regional security created by "the vacuum of authority in Grenada."[224] The OECS letter in turn reflected a subsequently disclosed letter from Sir Paul Scoon, Governor General of Grenada, to Prime Minister Tom Adams of Barbados, requesting assistance in similar language.[225]

---

[220] Dam Statement, *supra* n. 218, at 81; Robinson Letter, *supra* n. 218, at 385.

[221] *See* D'Amato, *supra* n. 19, at 229–230 (1987) (real rationale for Grenada intervention was human-rights-based). *Cf.* Schachter, "In Defense of International Rules on the Use of Force," 53 *U. Chi. L. Rev.* 113, 143 (1985) (although the United States did not invoke humanitarian intervention, many have considered it the real and better reason).

[222] *N.Y. Times*, Oct. 26, 1983, Section 1, at 16.

[223] Id. at 18.

[224] Id. at 19.

[225] Reproduced in Moore, *supra* n. 201, at 148 (1984). For the important role played by Prime Minister Tom Adams, *see* "Gordon Report," *supra* n. 200, at 340–46.

The human rights theme was reiterated in a comment made by a State Department official declaring "I don't think we have to worry about saying we have restored democracy and human rights to a country that was clearly deprived of them."[226] Larry Speakes, the President's Press Secretary, cited "bloody anarchy on the island" as the reason why Grenadian leaders could not be dealt with.[227]

In response to harsh criticism directed at the United States in the United Nations, Jeane Kirkpatrick had this to say:

> The prohibitions against the use of force in the United Nations Charter are contextual, not absolute. They provide justification for the use of force against force, in pursuit of other values also inscribed in the Charter, such values as freedom, democracy and peace. . . . The Charter does not require that people submit supinely to terror, nor that their neighbors be indifferent to their terrorization.[228]

Ten days after the invasion, President Reagan began describing it as a "rescue mission" which "saved the people of Grenada from repression."[229] In a State Department policy statement, Kenneth Dam, Deputy Secretary of State, indicated that restoration of order and human rights had been an objective in the military action. Dam further stated that "the disintegration of political authority in Grenada had created a dynamic that spread uncertainty and fear and that made further violence likely."[230]

The second, long-term, humanitarian objective was to restore democratic rights to the Grenadians. President Reagan's initial announcement of the invasion included as a stated objective and desire "to help restore democratic institutions."[231] The President's statement was echoed by

---

[226] N.Y. Times, Oct. 27, 1983, Section 1, at 1.

[227] N.Y. Times, Oct. 27, Section 1, at 1. See also Rostow, "It Was Within Acceptable Nation-State Practice," L.A. Daily J., p. 4, col. 3, Nov. 17, 1983 (intervention can be justified when, as in Grenada, public order disintegrates and social life sinks below minimal standards of human decency).

[228] N.Y. Times, Oct. 28, Section 1, at 15. See also her statement in the Security Council, Oct. 27, 1983, reprinted in 83 Dep't State Bull., No. 2081, at 74–76.

[229] N.Y. Times, Nov. 4, Section 1, at 16.

[230] Dam Statement, supra n. 218, at 79.

[231] N.Y. Times, Oct. 26, 1983, Section 1, at 16.

Shultz's stated objective of establishing institutions "responsive to the will of the people,"[232] and by Jeane Kirkpatrick's address to the U.N. General Assembly:

> We believe that the use of force . . . was lawful under international law and the UN Charter . . . because it was carried out in service of the values of the Charter, including the restoration of the rule of law, self-determination, sovereignty, democracy, respect of the human rights of the people of Grenada.[233]

A discussion of the objective of restoration of democracy occurred during a press conference held by Secretary of Defense Caspar Weinberger. The Secretary of Defense described the chaos in Grenada as nothing "remotely resembling a democratic form of government." When questioned as to the possibility of Grenadians choosing a Marxist government, Weinberger retreated somewhat by saying: "The form of government we want to get into Grenada is the form of government that enables the people to choose the kind of government they wish."[234] This emphasis on popular choice was reiterated by Deputy Secretary of State Dam: "Our objectives do not involve the imposition on the Grenadians of any particular form of government. Grenadians are free to determine their institutions for themselves."[235]

While these statements are eloquent, it is true that the Reagan administration did not officially espouse humanitarian intervention for the protection of Grenadians as an explicit justification for intervention. The legal advisor to the U.S. Department of State said explicitly that the United States "did not assert a broad doctrine of humanitarian intervention"[236]—a statement that is inconsistent with those of executive officials examined above. However, once again the case has to be interpreted in light of all relevant circumstances. Consistently with the discussion of other precedents, the statements of politicians should not be

---

[232] Id. at 18.

[233] 83 *State Dep't Bull.*, No. 2081 (1983), at 76–77. Of course, one would have hoped that Professor Kirkpatrick's commitment to human rights would have been equally strong in the case of the Argentine Junta and other right-wing dictators. This reprehensible failure does not detract from the accuracy of her assessment of the human rights situation in Grenada.

[234] *N.Y. Times*, Oct. 26, 1983, Section 1, at 1.

[235] *See* Dam Statement, *supra* n. 218, at 81.

[236] Robinson Letter, *supra* n. 218, at 386.

regarded as decisive. This holds true both when leaders try to justify aggression as humanitarian intervention *and* when they fail to invoke the doctrine where appropriate. From the above-quoted statements, from the conduct of the United States, and, most importantly, from the results of the invasion, it is no longer possible to deny that the operation in Grenada can be justified as an intervention carried out to rescue the Grenadians and others from immediate threat from a brutal regime and to restore democratic institutions to them.[237]

That justification becomes clearer when we examine the reaction of the people of Grenada. All sources agree that the Grenadian people overwhelmingly welcomed the intervention.[238] It is symptomatic that armed opposition to the task force came not from Grenadians but from the Cubans.[239] Dr. Francis Alexis, a Grenadian exile and president of the Grenadian Democratic Movement, called the invasion a "freedom, a liberation from criminal dictatorship that is welcomed by the vast majority of the people of the Caribbean."[240] Thus, when a critic of the Grenada mission assuredly tells us that "[t]he most overriding value cherished by states (and by their citizens) in the world today is that of national sovereignty, and human rights considerations come a poor second,"[241] she chooses the least eloquent example—Grenada—to illustrate her state-centered thesis. The value cherished by the Grenadians, like the Bengalis, the Ugandans, and the Central Africans before them, was their individual autonomy and the rights derived therefrom,

---

[237] Professor Verwey, a critic of the intervention, acknowledges that its aim was humanitarian. Verwey, *supra* n. 134, at 357.

[238] Results from a CBS poll indicate that 91 percent of Grenadians welcomed the arrival of U.S. forces while 8 percent did not. A smaller majority of 81 percent said they had felt in danger under the government of General Austin. *N.Y. Times,* Nov. 6, 1983, Section 1, at 21. A poll taken during the last week of December and the first week of January by the St. Augustine Research Associates of Trinidad and Tobago which was reported in the Barbados newspaper *Nation* indicated 86 percent of Grenadians polled thought the invasion was a "good thing." Cited in U.S. Dept. of State, Bureau of Public Affairs, Washington, D.C., Policy No. 541.

[239] *See* Note, "The Grenada Intervention: 'Illegal' in Form, Sound as Policy," 16 *N.Y.U. J. Int'l L. & Pol.* 1167, 1200 (1984), and references therein.

[240] *N.Y. Times,* Oct. 27, 1983, Section 1, at 21. Similarly, Alister Hughes, a Grenadian journalist, thanked the American intervention and said that "at that stage we were back in the jungle." *N.Y. Times,* Oct. 30, 1983, Section 1, p. 21.

[241] Doswald-Beck, *supra* n. 204, at 376–377. In the same sense, *see* Gilmore, *supra* n. 200, at 73.

and not that of the inviolability of the territory. The thesis of the primacy of sovereignty exhibits a blind insensitivity toward the very individuals whose fate is at stake and, ultimately, who should have the last say about their destiny and about the correctness or wisdom of receiving help to restore their human rights.

There is no question that an acceptable level of human rights, pluralism, democracy, and the rule of law have been restored in Grenada. On December 3, 1984, the Grenadians held their first free, multi-party general elections since 1976, and the House of Representatives, which had been dissolved by the Bishop regime in 1979, was reconstituted.[242] In terms of their fairness, the elections in Grenada compared favorably with those in other countries, such as El Salvador, Panama, Nicaragua, and Uruguay.[243] There were no proscriptions, limitations, violence, or fraud.[244] The pro-Western New National Party, led by Herbert Blaize, won 14 of the 15 seats, which seems to confirm that the New Jewel Party, led by Bishop and then by the Revolutionary Council, did not represent the people but rather had simply established a dictatorship on the island.[245]

That the human rights situation of the Grenadians has been radically improved is not disputed by critics of the intervention. There are two groups of critics. The first either simply ignores human rights considerations or claims that nonintervention and article 2(4) take precedence over human rights. That position is defended by some commentators and by the United Nations majority who have flatly condemned the Grenada intervention as a violation of international law.[246] The Boyle letter, for example, simply insists that "chronic disorder in a country

---

[242] 1985 *Keesing's* 33327.

[243] *See generally* International Human Rights Law Group, *Elections in Grenada: Return to Parliamentary Democracy: a Report on the Dec. 3, 1984, Grenadian Election* (1985).

[244] Id.

[245] Id. The popular vote was closer than the result indicates. *See also* Fraser, *supra* n. 200, at 209–10 ("Maurice Bishop was the dictator of Grenada"). It is also significant that the United States strongly indicated to Sir Eric Gairy, the pre-Bishop corrupt ruler, that aid to Grenada would be jeopardized if he returned to office. *See* 1985 *Keesing's* 33327.

[246] *See* U.N. G.A. Res. 38/7, Nov. 2, 1983, reprinted in Gilmore, *supra* n. 200, at 107–108. *See also* Boyle et al., "Letter: International Lawlessness in Grenada," 78 *A.J.I.L.* 172 (1984); Doswald-Beck, *supra* n. 204.

does not permit neighboring states to intervene for the purpose of rees-tablishing minimum public security, let alone imposing a democratic form of government."[247] It is hard to see how a democratic form of government can be imposed (if it is imposed it is not democratic). But more importantly, the complete omission of any consideration to the rights and wishes of the Grenadians is striking. Other critics discard the humanitarian intervention argument because the mission, unlike the Entebbe mission, was not "surgical."[248] But this objection stems from a complete misunderstanding of the doctrine of humanitarian interven-tion. The requirement is that the intervention to protect human rights (including rescue of nationals) be both *proportionate* to the gravity of the human rights deprivations and *necessary* to effect the liberation of the victims. It follows that in some cases, precisely the most egregious cases, the only action that is proportionate and necessary is the over-throw of the tyrants. Viewed in this light, the Grenada intervention was proportionate and moderate.[249] Unlike other interventions which can hardly be called humanitarian, American troops withdrew promptly from Grenada.[250] It follows that the only argument that can be marshaled against the proposition that the Grenada mission was justified as hu-manitarian intervention is that international law does not recognize the doctrine, an argument that these writers certainly make. But assuming that international law does recognize a right of humanitarian interven-tion, the Grenada mission fulfills the twin requirements of proportional-ity and necessity.

There is a final objection to characterizing the Grenada mission as an exercise of the right of humanitarian intervention. Unlike the Uganda, Central Africa and Bangladesh cases, the rights violated by the deposed government did not reach proportions of mass murder or genocide. But the conditions in Grenada were such that a very serious deprivation of human rights was imminent.[251] Intervention to prevent

Boyle letter, *supra* n. 246, at 173.

[248] *See* Vegas, "International Law under Time Pressure: Grading the Grenada Take-Home Examination," 78 *A.J.I.L.* 169, 169–70 (1984); Nanda, "Grenada," *supra* n. 204, at 405.

[249] *See* Audéoud, "L'intervention américano-caraïbe à la Grenade," 29 *Annuaire Français de droit international* 217, 224 (1983) ("L'action collective peut être qualifée").

[250] *See supra*, text accompanying n. 217.

[251] *See supra*, text accompanying nn. 206–213. For a comparison with the *Nicara-gua* case, *see infra*, Chapter 9.

imminent, certain, and extensive human rights violations must be considered encompassed by the doctrine of humanitarian intervention.

The reaction of the United Nations majority and of this first group of critics does not do justice to the human rights cause. Such a position is another instance of the canonization of the Hegelian Myth—the notion that states and not individuals have rights, even where the "states," i.e., despotic rulers, have machine-gunned their way into power.[252] It completely ignores the wishes and rights of the people of Grenada—the very individuals that they purport to protect against real or imagined aggressive imperialism. In short, these critics are perfectly coherent: State sovereignty and the "rights" of dictators take precedence over human rights. They distort or ignore not only moral imperatives, but the very positive legal materials that they usually worship: state practice and U.N. Charter provisions.

The second group of critics, while declaring the illegality of the intervention, seem to believe, in view of the positive human rights results, either that the law is wrong or insufficient or that the intervention was sound as a matter of policy or morality. Thus, for example, the detailed Gordon Report analyzes the legality of the mission almost exclusively by reference to the regional powers of the OECS and the Governor General.[253] In the brief section on humanitarian intervention, the report summarily dismisses the claim with respect to the rescue of both Americans and Grenadians, stating that "[t]he judgment of the world community on this claim [i.e., humanitarian intervention] has not been kind."[254] The only authority cited by the report for this criptical proposition is Professor Ian Brownlie, a leading "Charter literalist" and supporter of an extreme view of the sacredness of state sovereignty.[255] The report thus unjustifiably overlooks an important segment of state practice as well as the arguments marshaled by proponents of humanitarian intervention. Yet the report shows some sensitivity to human rights imperatives. In the conclusions, the authors of the report recognize:

---

[252] The description belongs to D'Amato, "Intervention in Grenada, Right or Wrong?" *N.Y. Times*, Oct. 30, 1983, at E18, col. 3 (suggesting that intervention in Grenada might perhaps be described as within the Wilsonian tradition of humanitarian intervention).

[253] "Gordon Report," *supra* n. 200.

[254] Id. at 379–80.

[255] Id., n. 116. For a full discussion of Brownlie's views, *see supra*, Chapter 7.

There appears to be room to argue that the United Nations Charter does not deal adequately with externally supported subver-
sion or indirect aggression and anticipatory self-defense, *and
that it fails to place in proper perspective all the policies that
rightly bear upon decisions, made in good faith, to intervene in
the protection of human life and civil order.*[256]

Similarly, Professor Audéoud has claimed that although the intervention was illegal, condemnation of it was muted because of the limited
nature of the intervention and the return of democracy to the island.[257]
He correctly underscores the democratic intention of the intervenors:
"La restauration dès les premiers jours de l'intervention d'une autorité
montre le souci de redonner aux habitants de la Grenade la responsabi-
lité politique," and calls the intervention "action de maintien de la
paix informelle et subrégionnelle validée par l'effectivité du retour à la
démocratie dans l'île."[258] Characteristically, after reminding the readers
that the intervention was a violation of the O.A.S. and U.N. Charters,[259]
Professor Audéoud concludes:

[I]l faut constater que, en dépit de la condamnation internationale et de la violation de la Charte des Nations Unies, c'est la
population de l'île de la Grenade qui a, par son acceptation,
changé la nature de l'action militaire. Ceci confirme . . . l'importance de l'effectivité en droit international et le rôle fondamen-
tal des populations.[260]

Commentators in this second group apparently believe that the mission was inconsistent with international law, but that somehow international law is wrong, because "the Charter does not deal adequately"
with the protection of human life. There are two answers to the claim
that international law is wrong. The first is that if international law is
wrong or immoral, then governments ought not to comply with it, at
least in cases of conflict with moral principles of the first order, as

---

[256] "Gordon Report," *supra* n. 200, at 380 (emphasis added).

[257] *See* Audéoud, *supra* n. 249, at 219, 224.

[258] Id. at 224.

[259] Id. at 227.

[260] Id. at 227. The same position (illegal but right) is defended in a law review
note, "The Grenada Intervention: 'Illegal' in Form, Sound as Policy," *supra* n. 239,
at 1190–1203.

human rights principles are. A second, more constructive answer is that there is something fundamentally wrong with construing state practice and treaty language in such a way as to reach propositions of law that the interpreter believes are morally indefensible when applied to concrete cases. The better alternative, suggested here, is that state practice and treaties—like the U.N. Charter—*may be interpreted in a manner consistent with our basic moral perceptions.* Thus, the U.N. Charter does not "deal" or "fail to deal" with the protection of human life, as the Gordon Report suggests. It is *we,* governments, lawyers, writers, courts, who talk about, and invoke, international law, who attempt to impose coherence and order upon international materials, just as domestic courts and lawyers do with domestic legal materials. As Ronald Dworkin has suggested, propositions of law are interpretive in a fundamental sense, interpretive *both* of history—in the case of international law, of diplomatic history—and of our most basic moral intuitions, principles and convictions.[261] This methodological view should not be interpreted as recommending the abandonment of state sovereignty or the prohibition on the use of force. Rather, these well-established principles should be read in a manner consistent with other well-established principles—those that have to do with upholding a modicum of human dignity. In short: The problem of the legal status of humanitarian intervention is not a problem of fidelity to international law. Rather, it is one of *determination* of the law and of proper balance between competing principles.[262]

These case studies have demonstrated that the moral reality of international politics differs from the "paper world" of the United Nations Charter. The four precedents examined here stand for the proposition that governments owe their legitimacy to something more fundamental than sheer political power. Governments exist to make sure that human rights are respected. If we discount rhetoric, the international community has reacted eloquently toward these apparent breaches of international law. It is no longer possible to ignore these cases and dismiss them as not counting in the formation of customary rules. That method

---

[261] *See* R. Dworkin, *A Matter of Principle* 147–148 (1985). That view is now fully developed in his *Law's Empire* (1986). *See* the discussion in Chapter 1.

[262] *See* R. Dworkin, *Law's Empire* 6–11 (1986).

is even less appropriate where the fundamental ethical purpose of the international legal system is at stake—the preservation and protection of freedom and individual autonomy recognized in the present international human rights code.

CHAPTER 9

COLLECTIVE HUMANITARIAN INTERVENTION

I. INTRODUCTION

While, as we saw in the last two chapters, opinion is roughly evenly divided on the issue of *unilateral* humanitarian intervention, most international actors and writers are rallying behind the idea that the United Nations Security Council may, in appropriate cases, act forcibly to remedy serious human rights deprivations and their moral equivalents (e.g., situations of anarchy). The doctrine of humanitarian intervention, in its several forms, has experienced a dramatic *relance* with the end of the Cold War. The realignment of global political forces and the awareness of the crucial link between human rights and peace have produced a significant change of opinion among governments and writers on the subject. In this chapter I defend the legitimacy of collective humanitarian intervention, in particular (but not only) when authorized by the U.N. Security Council.

The Charter of the United Nations prohibits the Organization from intervening "in matters which are essentially within the domestic jurisdiction of any state."[1] This limitation does not apply to the enforcement measures taken by the United Nations Security Council under Chapter VII of the Charter. The prohibition in Article 2(7) is but one instance of a broader duty of international organizations and states not to intervene

---

[1] Article 2(7), U.N. Charter.

in matters that fall within the domestic jurisdiction of sovereign states.[2] Yet the principles that govern collective intervention are different from those that govern unilateral intervention, especially intervention authorized by international organizations such as the United Nations or the Organization of American States.[3] Unilateral humanitarian intervention must be evaluated in the light of the standard rules governing the use of force. Collective humanitaran intervention must instead be evaluated in the light of the powers of the international organization, which may well derogate from general international law.

In Chapter 7, I examined the different meanings of the notoriously ambiguous word "intervention," and the place of humanitarian intervention in the general scheme of use of force contemplated by the United Nations Charter. Here I will discuss humanitarian intervention authorized by the Security Council, both under Chapter VII and under the practice of the Security Council since the end of the Cold War. My conclusion is that international law today recognizes, as a matter of practice, the legitimacy of collective forcible humanitarian intervention, that is, of military measures authorized by the Security Council for the purpose of remedying serious human rights violations. While traditionally the only ground for collective military action has been the need to respond to breaches of the peace (especially aggression), the international community has accepted a norm that allows collective humanitarian intervention as a response to serious human rights abuses.

---

[2] The traditional Cold War view of nonintervention is reflected, *inter alia*, in the *Declaration of Principles of International Law Concerning Friendly Relations and Cooperation Among States in Accordance with the Charter of the United Nations,* G.A. Res. 2625, U.N. G.A.O.R., 25th Sess., Supp. No. 28, at 121, U.N. Doc. A/8028 (1970).

[3] For a classic overview of the principle of nonintervention, *see* A. Thomas & A. J. Thomas, *Nonintervention* (1956). *See also* T. Farer, "The Regulation of Foreign Intervention in Civil Armed Conflict," 142 *R.C.A.D.I.* 291 (1974); the essays collected in *Intervention in World Politics* (Hedley Bull ed., 1984); and those in *To Loose the Bands of Wickedness: International Intervention in Defence of Human Rights* (N. Rodley ed., 1992).

II. COLLECTIVE HUMANITARIAN INTERVENTION

1. General Principles

We saw in Chapters 7 and 8 that some writers reject the legitimacy of humanitarian intervention altogether, collective or unilateral.[4] For these authors, the intent of the intervenor is irrelevant, as are the *degree* of human rights violations and the attitude of the victims themselves (that is, whether or not the intervention is decided only by the intervenor, or requested instead by the citizens of the target state). Armed intervention for humanitarian purposes, for these authors, is flatly prohibited. Undeniably, the anti-interventionist position has the support of traditional state-centric conceptions of international law and relations.[5] It is also informed by the commendable moral purpose of reducing the permissible instances of war, of containing armed conflict. Yet this extreme position, highly protective of despotic regimes, cannot be maintained today. The content and purpose of state sovereignty have undergone, since 1945, and more dramatically since 1989, profound changes. Human beings have claims against their own states and governments that the international community cannot simply ignore. While of course war ought to be the remedy of last resort to redress human rights violations, there are some, admittedly rare, serious cases of human rights deprivations where a strong case can and should be made for forcible intervention authorized by the international community and even by individual states. Whether these cases are to be seen as extreme instances of "moral catastrophe" and thus *outside* the law, or whether they are instead genuine exceptions to the legal prohibition is a jurisprudential preference to which little weight ought to be attached. I cannot

---

[4] *See* L. Henkin, "Use of Force: Law and U.S. Policy," in *Right v. Might: International Law and the Use of Force* 37, 341–44 (Council on Foreign Relations, 2nd ed., 1991), Lori F. Damrosch, "Commentary on Collective Military Intervention to Enforce Human Rights," in *Law and Force in the New International Order* 215, 217–21 (Damrosch & Scheffler eds., 1991).

[5] *See,* e.g., T. Oppermann, "Intervention," in 3 *Encyclopedia of Public International Law* 233, 235 (R. Bernhardt ed., 1987): "[T]he raison d'etre of the nonintervention rule is the protection of the sovereignty of the State."

see much consequence to the proposition that an act is illegal but morally permitted (or obligatory),[6] as contrasted with the proposition that the act is legally permitted (or obligatory) in those rare instances. This is so because moral reasons are overriding. If anti-interventionists can agree on the kind of cases where the international community can or must intervene, their protestations that this is nevertheless illegal does not carry much credibility.

That states have a right to intervene in other states, even by force, to put an end to serious human rights violations, is demonstrated by an examination of state practice since 1945.[7] Yet here I wish to concentrate exclusively on *collective* humanitarian intervention. In more technical terms, the question is whether or not the U.N. Security Council may authorize article 42 measures to put an end to serious, or extreme, human rights violations. Some writers who are hostile to the legitimacy of unilateral action concede that the legal situation changes when the humanitarian intervention is authorized by the United Nations or an appropriate regional body.[8] This support for multilateral action may be prompted by the feeling that if a coercive action is authorized by some kind of formal international *process* (such as voting in the Security Council), then it acquires a legality that it would lack were the decision to intervene to be left to national governments acting unilaterally. Or they may think that collective humanitarian intervention is more apt to curb the danger of abuse posed by unilateral intervention.[9] More

---

[6] An example of this position is T. Farer, "Human Rights in Law's Empire: The Jurisprudence War," 85 *Am. J. Int'l L.* 117 (1991) (While sympathetic to intervention in cases of brutal repression, the U.N. Charter does not authorize unilateral humanitarian intervention.)

[7] See *supra,* Chapter 8.

[8] *See,* e.g., V. Kartashkin, "Human Rights and Humanitarian Intervention," in *Law and Force in the New International Order* 202, 208 (Damrosch & Scheffler eds., 1991); Jost Delbruck, "A Fresh Look at Humanitarian Intervention Under the Authority of the United Nations," 67 *Ind. L.J.* 887 (1993). While reluctantly believing that unilateral humanitarian intervention is banned by the U.N. Charter, Tom Farer has a more sympathetic view of collective humanitarian intervention. See, in addition to work, *supra* n. 46, Tom J. Farer, "An Inquiry into the Legitimacy of Humanitarian Intervention," in *Law and Force in the New International Order* 185, 191, 198–99 (Damrosch & Scheffler eds., 1991).

[9] *See,* e.g., B. M. Benjamin, "Unilateral Humanitarian Intervention: Legalizing the Use of Force to Prevent Human Rights Atrocities," 16 *Fordham Int'l L.J.* 120 (an inherent problem with unilateral intervention is that it may be done for self-interest or political gain (although this may be more closely monitored by modern technology)); N. D. Arnison, "International Law and Non-Intervention: When do Humanitarian Concerns

technically, some may argue that the Security Council, unlike individual states, has absolute discretion in deciding when to authorize the use of force. In this view, under article 39 of the U.N. Charter the Security Council *determines* the existence of a breach of the peace, threat to the peace, or act of aggression. Therefore, if the Security Council authorizes enforcement measures in a case of serious human rights deprivation, it has determined that such situation qualifies under article 39 as the kind of situation that *is* a breach of the peace.[10]

Anti-interventionists disagree. They argue that under article 39 the Security Council can only authorize collective forcible action in cases of threat to the peace, breach of the peace, and acts of aggression.[11] Serious human rights violations, even genocide, do not, if contained within state borders, constitute aggression or threat or breach of the (international) peace. In addition, anti-interventionists deny absolute discretion to the Security Council in this regard. For them, the Security Council is subject to standards imposed by the Charter and cannot lawfully overstep those constraints.[12] Unless a violation of human rights threatens international peace, the Security Council does not have the power to authorize forcible action. At most, these authors argue, the Security Council can criticize the dictatorial government, and demand peremptorily that the violations cease. Such a demand will be legally binding under article 25. The Security Council can even authorize *hard* intervention, such as economic or other sanctions, by members against the outlaw state.[13] But the Council may not authorize the use of force.

Supersede Sovereignty?'' 17 *Fletcher Forum World Aff.* 199, 201 (1993) (collective humanitarian intervention preferable to unilateral action, although collective action may also suffer from potential for abuse and mixed motives).

[10] *See,* e.g., P. Malanczuck, *Humanitarian Intervention and the Legitimacy of the Use of Force''* 26 (1993) (decision on what constitutes "threat to peace" a political one subject to Security Council's discretion).

[11] *See,* e.g., T. Meron, "Commentary on Humanitarian Intervention," in *Law and Force in the New International Order* 212–213 (Damrosch & Scheffler eds., 1991). In the same volume, Professor Damrosch finds the arguments for collective humanitarian intervention stronger than those for unilateral action, but still not free from doubt. *See* Damrosch, *supra* n. 4, at 219.

[12] This was the position taken by Libya in the *Lockerbie* case. *See* 1992 *I.C.J.* 114, 126; reprinted 31 *I.L.M.* 665, 671.

[13] This was the case of Haiti before Resolution 940. There the Security Council imposed economic sanctions under Article 41. The Haiti case is fully discussed below. *See infra,* section II (c).

The first question is whether the Security Council has complete discretion to interpret Article 39 and thus authorize the use of force without being formally constrained by the language of that article. As we saw, those who respond in the affirmative say that what the Security Council says is a breach of the peace *is* legally a breach of the peace. This position, however, must be rejected. The Security Council, like any other United Nations organ, is bound by the principles, rules, and standards set forth in the United Nations Charter. Its actions, therefore, are subject to legal scrutiny, both substantively and procedurally.[14] Those who vindicate the absolute discretion of the Security Council confuse two different meanings of discretion.[15] One meaning of discretion arises when an official's decision, authorized by law, is not subject to review by a higher body. This is a *weak* meaning of the word "discretion," because it does not presuppose that the law lacks standards to guide the official's decision. That decision is perhaps nonreviewable, but it may not be lawless; it is controlled by substantive legal standards. The second meaning of discretion is that the official's decision is not guided by any standards, that he has absolute power to decide one way or the other, unconstrained by law (except, of course, by the rule of competence that empowered *him* as the legitimate authority). This is discretion in a *strong* sense, because it conceives of the official as deciding the case anew, as creating fresh law. The difference between the two is very important. In the first case the official's decision is vulnerable to the criticism that he applied the law incorrectly, that the decision is legally wrong. In the second case, however, the official is not open to the criticism that he misapplied the law, because the official's decision is not substantively constrained. He is deemed to be authorized to create fresh law for the case.

It is reasonable to suppose that the Security Council under the Charter enjoys, at most, discretion in the first, weak, sense. Under the Charter, neither the General Assembly nor the International Court of Justice

---

[14] For a general discussion of the legitimacy of Security Council decisions (mostly from a procedural standpoint), *see* D. J. Caron, "The Legitimacy of the Collective Authority of the Security Council," 87 *Am. J. Int'l L.* 552 (1993).

[15] The discussion that follows is taken from the seminal work by R. Dworkin, *Taking Rights Seriously* 31–39 (1978).

have original or plenary jurisdiction to review the decisions of the Security Council (although, as the *Lockerbie* case demonstrates, the International Court of Justice may, in appropriate cases, be called to pass upon the legality of the Security Council's actions[16]). But the Security Council has no discretion in the strong sense. Its decisions *are* constrained by international law, in particular by the United Nations Charter, and thus subject to the judgment of legality by governments and international lawyers generally, even if its decisions are not formally subject to review. Anti-interventionists are right, therefore, in rejecting the view that the Security Council can decree a collective intervention for any reason. There *is* a substantive law of collective use of force, and the Security Council is bound to comply with it just like anyone else.

Nor is it possible, to respond to anti-interventionists, simply to echo, as some do, the uncontroversial proposition that human rights are no longer part of the exclusive domestic jurisdiction of states.[17] Anti-interventionists rightly respond that this affects only *soft* (and perhaps even hard) intervention. They happily concede that the United Nations organs, including the Security Council, may address human rights issues, even condemn states for their human rights abuses, *as long as no use of force is involved.* They correctly point out that the collective use of force is subject to *independent* constraints, which are to be found in Chapter VII. Thus, article 39, not the chameleon article 2(7), is the right place to look into when evaluating the legitimacy of collective *forcible* intervention.[18]

A complete answer to the anti-interventionist view draws from text, morality, history, and practice. The legitimacy of collective humanitarian intervention to remedy gross human rights violations irrespective of international effects finds some textual support in the Charter.[19] The Preamble declares that armed force should not be used "save in the

---

[16] Cf. Lockerbie case, *supra* n. 12, at 126–27 (ruling only that Security Council decisions prevail over contrary treaty obligations by virtue of Article 103 of the Charter; thus not excluding the possibility that the Council may act ultra vires).

[17] *See*, e.g., J. A. Gallant, "Humanitarian Intervention and Security Council Resolution 688: A Reappraisal in Light of A Changing World Order," 7 *Am. U. J. Int'l L. & Pol'y* 881 (1992).

[18] *See* Malanczuk, *supra* n. 10, at 25.

[19] I have argued that the text of the Charter is inconclusive on this issue. *See supra,* Chapter 7.

common interest," and there is no reason to assume that common interest excludes the interest in upholding human rights, particularly since in the Preamble itself the "Peoples of the United Nations" reaffirm "faith in fundamental human rights [and] in the dignity and worth of the human person." The Preamble also states the United Nations' determination "to establish conditions under which justice . . . can be maintained." It would be a very narrow definition of justice indeed which would not include human rights in any context, let alone in this one, where human rights are one of the pillars of the Organization.

In addition, the anti-interventionist's reading of article 39 and Chapter VII is just too narrow, and is not supported by the United Nations and state practice, as we shall see. Subsequent practice under the Charter, if unchallenged on the whole, may determine the more precise meaning of the words in the Charter.[20] Admittedly the language drafted almost fifty years ago contains the limitation that forcible action may be authorized only in case of threat or breach of the (international) peace or act of aggression. This limitation can be easily understood in historical terms, since the possibility of genuine collective action to respond to and prevent aggression was already a revolutionary step.

The legitimacy of collective humanitarian intervention in appropriate cases flows from an interpretation of the United Nations Charter that looks, beyond the letter, to the purposes and principles that animate, shape, and define legitimacy in the international community today. I am not simply suggesting the playing of verbal games on this very important issue. Indeed, it is always possible to *define* serious human rights violations as a *breach of the peace* and thus trigger enforcement action under article 39. I am suggesting that the substantive law of the Charter has now evolved to include human rights as a centerpiece of the international order, and *serious* human rights violations as one of the situations that *may* warrant collective enforcement action. This imperative prevails over unrestrained state sovereignty, and may be enforced, in rare cases of serious human rights violations and when other means have failed or are certain to fail, by the Security Council acting on behalf of the international community.

There is, of course, a case where even anti-interventionists would agree that serious violations of human rights can trigger enforcement

---

[20] A well-known example is, of course, the voting practice in the Security Council.

action: where those violations *do* constitute a "threat to peace."[21] This will be the case quite often, as in the cases of South Africa or Iraq's treatment of the Kurds (discussed below). It is possible to argue as a consequence that the basis for collective humanitarian intervention is the threat to peace, not the gravity of the human rights violations. In this view, only when the human rights deprivations cause international effects will the United Nations have a right to intervene.[22] Presumably, genocidal action which is purely internal, that is, contained within a state's borders, is beyond the reach of the Security Council's action.

There is no problem practically with the Security Council actually invoking the language of article 39 when deciding to authorize humanitarian intervention. In my view, the crucial question is what the Security Council *does*, not what it *says*. Suppose there is a massive human rights violation and the Security Council decides to intervene. When doing so, it uses the "threat or breach of the peace" language of article 39. This, let us suppose, becomes an institutional habit. It is intolerably formalistic to cling to the view, on such facts, that the Security Council is *not* authorizing humanitarian intervention, when a common sense reading of the situation by any unprejudiced observer will indicate that that is precisely what the Security Council is doing. The better interpretation is that, regardless of the language in which it cloaks its decision, the Security Council authorizes the use of force in two instances: to counter aggression and restore peace, and to remedy serious human rights abuses. In both situations the Security Council will authorize the use of force only in rare and extreme cases where everything else has proved ineffective or unavailable.

Moreover, the anti-interventionist position is peculiarly blind to history. The United Nations was created as a response to the horrors caused by one of the most tyrannical regimes in modern history. The Second World War was in great part (although not only) a humanitarian effort. It is therefore surprising to be told that the very crimes that

---

[21] *See, inter alia,* Damrosch, *supra* n. 4, at 218.

[22] *See* N. S. Rodley, "Collective Intervention to Protect Human Rights and Civilian Populations: The Legal Framework," in *To Loose the Bands of Wickedness: International Intervention in Defense of Human Rights, supra* n. 3 (although winds may be breathing in direction of collective humanitarian intervention, threat to international peace will probably be required).

prompted the massive, cruel, and costly struggle from which the United Nations was born, are now immune from action undertaken by the organ entrusted to preserving the fruits of the hard-won peace. The legalist technicality of anti-interventionists thus not only rewards tyrants: it betrays the purposes of the very international order that they claim to protect. Some may find the concerns of the anti-interventionists strong enough to severely limit or reject the lawfulness of unilateral humanitarian intervention. But those concerns have little force against humanitarian intervention properly authorized by the United Nations Security Council.

The reasons of political philosophy that support the legitimacy of humanitarian intervention are many and complex, and I have discussed them above at length.[23] The central point is that states derive their legitimacy, their sovereignty, from popular consent and the protection of basic human rights. The purpose of states is to protect human rights in the first place. Therefore, governments forfeit their legitimacy in the international arena when they turn against their citizens and betray the ethical end that justifies their existence. In some cases, therefore, forcible humanitarian intervention is morally permitted, subject to several constraints. These reasons gain in strength when the intervention is collective, for in that case a number of concerns about intervention are assuaged—in particular the concern about the dangers of unilateral abuse.[24]

2. The Case of Iraq's Treatment of the Kurds, 1991

These textual, historical, and moral arguments are validated by recent practice. The first, historic, instance of humanitarian intervention was authorization given by the Security Council to create "safe havens" for Kurds in Iraq, following the defeat of the Iraqi Army in the beginning of 1991.[25] On August 3, 1990, armored and mechanized units from the

---

[23] See supra, Part One.

[24] See, e.g., L. Hamilton, "When It's Our Duty to Intervene" Wash. Post, Aug. 9, 1992, at C2 143 ("multilateral consideration would guard against aggression, prevent hasty or capricious intervention and enhance the effectiveness of subsequent action").

[25] Even a long-standing opponent of the doctrine of humanitarian intervention grudgingly concedes that "the wind is breathing in the direction of collective humanitarian intervention." Rodley, "Collective Intervention to Protect Human Rights and Civilian Populations;" supra n. 22, at 14, 40. See also, in To Loose the Bands of Wickedness,

Iraqi Army's Republican Guard divisions invaded and occupied the neighboring nation of Kuwait. In early 1991 the United Nations Security Council authorized the use of force to terminate Iraq's occupation of Kuwait. While rather unique in its scope and intensity, the collective military action taken by U.N. member states in "Operation Desert Storm" can be addressed within the traditional interpretation of the principles set forth in articles 39, 41, and 42 of the U.N. Charter.

During the coalition military campaign President George Bush had publicly expressed optimism that Iraqi citizens would "take matters into their own hands" and remove Saddam Hussein from power.[26] The crushing defeat of the Iraqi Army in and around Kuwait, and public exhortations from foreign leaders to throw off Saddam Hussein's rule, reignited the long-simmering desire for independence among Kurds living in Northern Iraq.[27] Although the Iraqi Army was no match for the Allied coalition, it proved more than effective at suppressing the Kurdish revolt. Iraqi army troops and helicopter gunships relentlessly attacked Kurdish villages, forcing two million civilians to flee into the countryside. Almost one million of these Kurds fled north through the mountains in an attempt to reach safety in Turkey.[28]

The Security Council, faced with mounting atrocities committed by the Iraqi government against the Kurds and others,[29] adopted Resolution

---

supra n. 3, L. Freedman and D. Boren, " 'Safe Havens' for Kurds in Post-War Iraq," at 43 (in establishing those safe havens, Western governments created an important precedent for humanitarian intervention).

[26] R. Atkinson, *Crusade: The Allied Victory in the Persian Gulf* 24–26 (1993).

[27] H. Adelman, "Humanitarian Intervention: The Case of the Kurds," 4 *Int'l J. Refugee L.* 4, 5–7 (1992). Kurds constitute 23–27 percent of the Iraqi population and are concentrated in the northern area of Iraq. Conflict between Arabs and Kurds in Iraq is decades old. For example, a Kurdish revolt occurred in 1974 when a 1970 autonomy agreement between Iraqi Kurds and Saddam Hussein's Ba'ath regime broke down. The rebellion was finally crushed by Saddam Hussein in 1975 at a cost of 50,000 killed. Guerilla warfare resumed in the 1980s, however, and after the Iran-Iraq war ended in 1988, the Iraqi army killed thousands of Kurdish nationalists and used poison gas against the population of the Kurdish village of Hallabja. *Id.*

[28] Id. at 7.

[29] *See* K. McKiernan, "Kurdistan's Season of Hope," *L.A. Times Mag.*, Aug. 23, 1992, at 28; J. C. Randal, "Against All Odds: Resistance to Saddam," *Wash. Post,* Apr. 7, 1991, at A1. More recent evidence suggests that Iraq continues to violate this Resolution, inflicting serious human rights violations against the Shiite Muslim civilians in southern Iraq, as well as continuing to attack the Kurds in the north. A. Pine and R. Wright, "U.N. Aide Cites 'Serious' Violations of Human Rights in Southern Iraq," *L.A.*

688, initially proposed by France, on April 5, 1991 by a margin of ten to three, with two abstentions.[30] In that document, the Security Council first condemned "the repression of the Iraqi civilian population in many parts of Iraq," and demanded that "Iraq . . . immediately end this repression." The Security Council further urged Iraq to "allow immediate access by international humanitarian organizations. . . .", and appealed to "all member States . . . to contribute to these humanitarian relief efforts."[31] The Security Council also *demanded* that Iraq cooperate with the Secretary-General to these ends. The Security Council also added several provisos linking the resolution to the language of article 39, perhaps to make sure that its action was consistent with its powers under the Charter. In particular, the resolution stated that these human rights violations had consequences "which threaten[ed] international peace and security in the region" and characterized the requested Iraqi compliance with its human rights demands as "a contribution to international peace and security in the region." Also, Resolution 688 contained in the Preamble a rare reference to article 2 (7) of the Charter. It is therefore easy for anti-interventionists to claim that Resolution 688 was a lawful Security Council action in response to a "threat to the peace," thus well within the traditional paradigm of aggression. Again, this is excessively formalistic. The relevant issue is not whether the Security Council can do anything it wants, as long as it styles it a "threat to the peace." The question remains that, aside from word games, this *is* a human rights issue concerning Iraq's treatment of its own citizens.

Times, July 31, 1992, at A6. In addition, confiscated Iraqi materials have provided comprehensive documentation of massive human rights violations. Through paper, audio, and film records of interrogations, torture sessions, and executions detail atrocities perpetrated by the Iraqi government. A. Kaslow, "Documents Give Evidence of Atrocities Against Iraqi Kurds," *Christian Sci. Monitor,* June 10, 1992, at 1; J. C. Randal, "Iraqi Files Point to Mass Deaths," *Wash. Post,* Feb. 22, 1992, at A1; T. Hundley, "Iraq Plotted Genocide of Kurds," *Chi. Trib.,* Apr. 1, 1992, at 1; and J. Kirkpatrick, "It is Appropriate to Speak of Genocide," *Wash. Post,* Mar. 2, 1992, at A17. A report by Max Van der Stoel, special United Nations investigator, tells of "arbitrary executions of individuals, families, whole villages; of arbitrary arrests and unspeakable tortures, including electric shocks, burnings, beatings, rapes, and extractions of teeth and nails."

[30] U.N. Doc. S/Res/688, Apr. 5, 1991. *See generally, J. A. Gallant, supra* n. 17; *see also* D. J. Scheffer, "Toward A Modern Doctrine of Humanitarian Intervention," 23 *U. Tol. L. Rev.* 253 (1992); and *To Loose the Bands of Wickedness, supra* n. 3, at 28–34.

[31] U.N. Doc. S/Res/688, *supra* n. 30.

A reasonable interpretation of Resolution 688 is that the Security Council was centrally concerned with the human rights violations themselves, and that the reference to the threat to peace and security was added for good measure.

With Turkey resisting international appeals to provide aid and sanctuary for the one million starving and freezing refugees along its border with Iraq, the United States, Britain, and France announced that they would undertake a humanitarian relief effort to assist the Kurds. The term "humanitarian organization" referred to in Resolution 688 was interpreted by these states to include military forces with the limited and specific mission of humanitarian assistance. Dubbed "Operation Provide Comfort," the relief effort greatly expanded as the scope of the refugee problem in northern Iraq and southern Turkey became known. An initial count found 452,000 refugees in ten major and 30 to 40 smaller camps along the Iraq-Turkey border. Disease, starvation, and freezing temperatures led to an increasing mortality rate among those seeking sanctuary in Turkey.[32] Estimates of deaths from starvation and exposure among Kurdish refugees fleeing north were in the range of 1,000 per day during this period.[33] As Kurdish refugees made clear their fear of returning to Iraq without assurances of safety, the governments involved in Operation Provide Comfort decided it was necessary to establish protected "safe havens" inside northern Iraq in order to entice Kurdish refugees to return from the border area with Turkey.[34]

On April 12, 1991, U.S. Army Lt. Gen. John M. Shalikashvili met with Iraqi General Nashwan Tahoon and told him to remove all Iraqi ground forces to locations south of the 36th parallel and to cease all air operations north of the parallel or risk the potential use of allied offensive military force. By the next day, elements of the U.S. 24th Marine Expeditionary Unit and the 10th Special Forces Group had been airlifted into the town of Zakhu in northern Iraq to secure the surrounding area and prepare for the construction of refugee repatriation camps. Iraqi military and government officials quickly ceded control

---

[32] M. E. Harrington, "Operation Provide Comfort: A Perspective in International Law," 8 *Conn. J. Int'l L.* 635, 644 (1993).

[33] *See* P. Tyler, "U.S. Scouting Refugee Sites Well Inside Iraq's Border," *N.Y. Times,* Apr. 10, 1991, at A1.

[34] Harrington, *supra* n. 32, at 644–45.

over the area to the intervention force. Within weeks of the passage of Resolution 688, thirteen nations had sent almost thirty thousand military and civilian personnel to participate in the relief mission. U.S. forces numbered 18,285, while other states contributed an additional 10,962 personnel.[35] Military forces were not the only participants in the operation however. Thirty states contributed relief supplies and fifty nongovernmental organizations (NGOs) either offered assistance or participated in the operation. On May 13, 1991, Gen. Shalikashvili turned control of the operation over to the United Nations High Commissioner for Refugees,[36] and by July 15, 1991, the last allied troops had been withdrawn to Turkey and replaced by United Nations refugee officials and security forces,[37] pursuant to an agreement between the United Nations and Iraq.[38]

While the decision to operate with military forces within Iraqi territory was deemed necessary to avert a large-scale human disaster, the expansion of Operation Provide Comfort created some doubts in the international community. For instance, the United Nations' Secretary-General, Javier Perez de Cuellar, warned early on that the planned intervention would require approval of the U.N. Security Council and the Iraqi government and noted that it posed a clear legal problem, even if from a moral point of view there was no difficulty.[39] Although the Secretary-General may have had initial reservations about the scope of the humanitarian mission in northern Iraq, his September 1991 final report to the U.N. General Assembly argued forcefully for a change in the traditional view of state sovereignty in view of the universal international interest in responding to human rights emergencies:

---

[35] Id. at 645. The other nations that provided military forces to assist in Operation Provide Comfort include: Australia (75), Belgium (155), Canada (120), France (2,141), Germany (221), Italy (1,183), Luxembourg (43), Netherlands (1,020), Portugal (19), Spain (602), Turkey (1,160), United Kingdom (4,192). In addition, 117 civilians participated in the relief effort as well as 88 individuals from the Office of the United Nations High Commissioner on Refugees (UNHCR).

[36] Harrington, *supra* n. 32, at 646.

[37] J. M. Brown, "Last Allies Pull Out of North Iraq," *Fin. Times,* July 16, 1991, at A12.

[38] "Security Force Pact is Settled With Iraq, Official at U.N. Says," *N.Y. Times,* May 24, 1991, at A8.

[39] *See* S. Robinson, "The Middle East: Bush and the U.N. Chief Clash Over Legality of Military Move," *Daily Telegraph,* Apr. 18, 1991.

[Protection of human rights] now involves more a concerted exertion of international influence and pressure . . . and, in the last resort, an appropriate United Nations presence, than what was regarded as permissible under traditional international law.

It is now increasingly felt that the principle of non-interference with the essential domestic jurisdiction of States cannot be regarded as a protective barrier behind which human rights could be massively or systematically violated with impunity. . .

We need not impale ourselves on the horns of a dilemma between respect for sovereignty and the protection of human rights. . . . What is involved is not the right of intervention but the collective obligation of States to bring relief and redress in human rights emergencies.[40]

Perez de Cuellar's admission that state sovereignty must, on occasion, yield to human rights concerns, was an important step for the U.N. in accepting humanitarian intervention as a principle of international law. When the Secretary-General further notes that "the defense of the oppressed in the name of morality should prevail over frontiers and legal documents,"[41] it becomes increasingly apparent that the official U.N. view of state sovereignty underwent significant reevaluation in light of the Gulf War and Operation Provide Comfort.

Anti-interventionists argue that the Security Council resolution did not authorize *forcible* measures in the Kurdish crisis, but only non-forcible humanitarian relief action.[42] Once more, this is just blind adherence to words on paper. While apparently referring to non-forcible intervention, the context of this resolution reveals that the United Nations' effort relied upon a number of factors which demonstrate that actual or potential forcible action was contemplated. As David Scheffer has showed, those factors were: allied military intervention in northern Iraq in its efforts to create a security zone; allied threats to respond to

---

[40] *Report of the Secretary-General on the Work of the Organization,* U.N. G.A.O.R., 46th Sess., No.1, at 5, U.N. Doc. A/46/1 (1991).

[41] R. C. Longworth, "End of Sovereignty: Nations' Internal Affairs Now the World's Business," *Chi. Trib.,* Sept. 19, 1993, at 1.

[42] *See,* e.g., Malanczuk, *supra* n. 10, at 18.

any Iraqi operations; the deployment of a U.N. force to protect humanitarian relief efforts; and the existence of an agreement with Iraq that contemplated the possible use of force in case of noncompliance.[43] In the light of these facts, it is hard to avoid the conclusion that this was a genuine case of collective humanitarian intervention.

Another strategy to justify Resolution 688 within the old paradigm of aggression, that is, without introducing the concept of humanitarian intervention, is to claim that Resolution 688 was adopted in the context of the series of Security Council resolutions directed at countering Iraqi aggression. In this view, the action authorized by the Security Council to protect the Kurds is simply an extension of the enforcement measures authorized to counter aggression.[44] Resolution 688 would thus be analogous to Resolution 687, which authorized a sweeping range of measures on matters that normally would fall under the exclusive jurisdiction of Iraq (mainly regarding the disarming and denuclearization of that state). The argument is that the "intervention" to protect the Kurds is justified *because* it is a sequel to Chapter VII action, itself justified as a response to Iraqi aggression. Once again, this interpretation is highly contrived. The Iraqi government perpetrated at least two distinct violations of international law: the attack against Kuwait (a violation of article 2(4) which triggers Security Council action under Chapter VII), and a massive violation of the human rights of individuals in Iraq, most notably the Kurds. Resolution 688, by its very terms, was addressed to the latter. Not only did the resolution peremptorily demand that Iraq stop the repression; it authorized, as we saw, non-consensual relief measures. Moreover, from the fact that the Security Council decreed mandatory disarmament of the defeated aggressor (thus instituting coercive measures on matters that would normally fall within the exclusive jurisdiction of Iraq) it does not follow without more that the Security Council has authority to institute coercive measures on *any* matter that would normally fall within Iraq's exclusive jurisdiction. In other words, Resolution 687 does follow logically from the previous resolutions of the Security Council

---

[43] *See* Scheffer, *supra* n. 30, at 258.

[44] *See*, e.g., M. E. O'Connell, "Commentary on International Law: Continuing Limits on U.N. Intervention in Civil War," 67 *Ind. L.J.* 903, 907–08 (arguing that Resolution 688, together with Resolution 678, gave coalition members the authority to use "all necessary means" to secure peace in the area that included the Kurdish region).

(especially from Resolution 678 authorizing the use of force as a response to Iraq's refusal to withdraw from Kuwait). But we need the humanitarian intervention standard *in addition* to the "breach of the peace" standard to justify Resolution 688.

In short: "Operation Provide Comfort"was a truly landmark precedent for the lawfulness of humanitarian intervention authorized by the Security Council. As such, it complies with the formal requirements of a custom-originating act, in that it was not objected to by the international community, and in that it was followed by similar decisions and operations, in the cases of Somalia, Haiti, Rwanda, and Bosnia.

3. The Operation in Somalia, 1992-1993

On December 3, 1992, the U.N. Security Council unanimously passed Resolution 794, authorizing a U.S.-led military force to "use all necessary means to establish as soon as possible a secure environment for humanitarian relief operations in Somalia."[45] The Somali crisis was touched off by the power vacuum created when the country's longtime dictator, President Mohammed Siad Barre, fled the capital city of Mogadishu in January 1991.[46]

Barre's departure split the opposition. Forces under the command of General Mohammed Farrah Aidid controlled most of southern Somalia and the southern portion of Mogadishu. Soldiers loyal to Ali Mahdi Mohammed gained control of the northern section of Mogadishu and declared him the interim President of Somalia. Muhammed Said Hersi Morgan, the son-in-law of Siad Barre, controlled the city of Bardera in the main famine area. Colonel Omar Jess controlled the strategic port of Kismayu in southern Somalia. Finally, General Muhammad Abshir Musa, leader of the Somali Salvation Front, one of the first political movements to oppose Siad Barre, controlled an area in northeastern Somalia.[47]

---

[45] S.C. Res. 794, U.N. S.C.O.R., 47th Sess., 3145th mtg., at 3, U.N. Doc. S/Res/794 (1992).

[46] *See* D. Oberdorfer, "The Path to Intervention," *Wash. Post,* Dec. 6, 1992, A1, A35. The brief account that follows is borrowed from J. Clark, "Debacle in Somalia," *Foreign Aff.* 109 (America and the World, 1992/93).

[47] *See* "Who's Who," *Economist,* Jan. 23, 1993, at 41.

As the various clan militias turned on one another, the country was effectively divided into 12 zones of control. A so-called "reconciliation conference" between the warring factions was held in Djibouti in July 1991 resulting in the selection of Omer Arteh Qhalib as interim Prime Minister. In reality, however, Qhalib held no perceptible authority over the Somali faction leaders. By November 1991, the struggle between the warring factions had escalated to a full-scale civil war. On January 11, 1992, Qhalib sent a letter to the Security Council requesting an immediate meeting to address the rapidly deteriorating security situation in Somalia.[48] Responding to Qhalib's letter, the Security Council passed a series of resolutions citing Chapter VII of the U.N. Charter as the basis for U.N. action and implying that an article 39 justification, dealing with threats to international peace and stability, for collective military action could be invoked in the future. A complete weapons embargo was imposed on Somalia[49] and the United Nations Operation in Somalia (UNOSOM) was established in April 1992, with fifty U.N. observers to monitor a widely ignored ceasefire among the factions.[50]

In the summer of 1992, with the warring factions in Somalia continuing to disrupt desperately needed relief supplies, the Security Council passed increasingly aggressive resolutions, eventually asserting in Resolution 767 that "the situation in Somalia constitutes a threat to international peace and security."[51] In late August, the Security Council passed Resolution 775 approving airlifts of humanitarian aid and supplementing UNOSOM personnel levels with a battalion of Pakistani troops to assist in relief supply distribution.[52]

---

[48] *Letter Dated 20 January 1992 From the Chargé d'Affaires A. I. of the Permanent Mission of Somalia to the United Nations Addressed to the President of the Security Council,* U.N. S.C.O.R., 47th Sess., U.N. Doc. S/23445 (1992).

[49] S.C. Res. 733, U.N. S.C.O.R., 47th Sess., 3039th mtg., at 2 (1992) (resolution of Jan. 23, 1992).

[50] S.C. Res. 751, U.N. S.C.O.R., 47th Sess., 3069th mtg., at 2 (1992) (resolution of Apr. 24, 1992).

[51] S.C. Res. 767, U.N. S.C.O.R., 47th Sess., 3101st mtg. (1992) (resolution of July 27, 1992).

[52] S.C. Res. 775, U.N. S.C.O.R., 47th Sess., 3110th mtg. (1992) (resolution of Aug. 28, 1992).

The collapse of all governmental authority, combined with drought and the continuation of traditional clan and sub-clan warfare and growing chaos, led to a situation of mass starvation.[53] Although the United States supplied food aid through the International Committee of the Red Cross (ICRC) and private voluntary relief organizations, estimates were that up to three-quarters of the U.N. food supplies were confiscated or stolen by the various factions for their own use or to sell for profit. By September 1992, the ICRC estimated that 1.5 million Somalis faced imminent starvation, and three times that number were already dependent on external food assistance, even as tons of undistributed food piled up at the Mogadishu airport and waterfront.[54]

In late November 1992, U.N. Secretary General Boutros-Ghali reported numerous violations of humanitarian law against U.N. relief workers by forces of the various factions in Somalia, including attacks on the Pakistani troops by forces loyal to General Aidid, and the shelling of a World Food Programme ship as it attempted to enter Mogadishu's port.[55] On November 25, 1992, U.S. Secretary of State Lawrence Eagleburger conveyed an offer to Boutros-Ghali for the U.S. to lead a multinational force into Somalia to implement the Security Council's resolutions.[56]

One week later, the Security Council passed Resolution 794 and within days 24,000 U.S. troops had arrived in Somalia as part of Operation "Restore Hope" to establish, in the words of the Resolution, "a secure environment for humanitarian relief operations." The distribution of relief supplies went exceedingly well according to most reports and several hundred thousand Somalis, who otherwise would have perished, managed to survive.[57] On May 4, 1993, the United States formally turned the operation over to the United Nations.

---

[53] *See* J. Clark, *"Debacle in Somalia: Failure of the Collective Response,"* in *Enforcing Restraint: Collective Intervention in Internal Conflicts* 204, 207, 213 (L. F. Damrosch ed., 1993).

[54] C. A. Robbins et al., "Waiting for America," *U.S. News & World Rep.,* Dec. 7, 1992, at 26.

[55] *Letter Dated 24 November 1992 From the Secretary-General Addressed to the President of the Security Council,* U.N. S.C.O.R., 47th Sess., U.N. Doc. S/24859 (1992).

[56] D. Binder, "Bush Ready to Send Troops to Protect Somalia Food," *N.Y. Times,* Nov. 26, 1992, at A1.

[57] E. Schmitt, "U.N. Completes Withdrawal from Somalia," *N.Y. Times,* Mar. 5, 1992, at E2.

The operation in Somalia took a turn for the worse, however, when the U.N. mandate expanded to include "nation-building" projects such as disarming the factions and arresting recalcitrant or uncooperative faction leaders such as General Aidid.[58] One particular raid conducted on October 3, 1993, by U.S. Army Rangers and Special Forces soldiers turned deadly when the U.S. forces attempted to protect the crew of a downed U.S. helicopter pilot in a neighborhood tightly controlled by one of the factions. Eighteen U.S. soldiers died in the ensuing all-night firefight and 75 were wounded before U.N. armored units could come to their rescue.[59] In another incident, several dozen Pakistani peacekeepers were ambushed and killed by gunmen firing automatic weapons from behind human screens of women and children. In all, 100 U.N. peacekeepers died during the operation.[60]

Unwilling to sustain additional casualties, the U.S. withdrew its peacekeeping forces from Somalia in March 1994 and the U.N. mission contracted in scope from nation-building back to a focus on food relief and distribution. Frustrated by its inability to bring about the formation of a government in Somalia, and subjected to increasing hostility from the populace and the factional forces, the Security Council voted to gradually withdraw UNOSOM from Somalia. The last Pakistani U.N. peacekeepers left Somalia on March 4, 1995, escorted by 1,800 U.S. Marines.

In January 1995, as the U.N. operation in Somalia was drawing to a close, Secretary-General Boutros-Ghali issued a supplement[61] to his 1992 report entitled *An Agenda for Peace*. This supplement noted that U.N. operations were increasingly intrastate rather than interstate operations. For example, of the five peacekeeping operations underway in 1988 only one (20 percent of the total) involved an intrastate conflict. Of the 21 operations established since early 1988, 13 (62 percent) involved intrastate conflict. The trend is growing even more pronounced in the

---

[58] *See* M. R. Hutchinson, "Note, Restoring Hope: U.N. Security Council Resolutions for Somalia and an Expanded Doctrine of Humanitarian Intervention," 34 *Harv. Int'l L.J.* 624, 634 (1993).

[59] J. Adams, "A Farewell to Arms? *Sunday Times,* Jan. 15, 1995 at 1.

[60] Schmitt, *supra* n. 57, at E2.

[61] *Supplement to An Agenda for Peace: Position Paper of the Secretary-General on the Occasion of the Fiftieth Anniversary of the United Nations,* U.N. Doc. A/50/60, S/1995, Jan. 3, 1995.

U.N.'s most recent operations. Of the 11 operations established since January 1992, nine (82 percent) involve intrastate conflicts.[62]

The Secretary-General also recognized the emergence of a new type of U.N. military operation based on the type of mission of UNOSOM in Somalia:

> A second qualitative change is the use of United Nations forces to protect humanitarian operations. . . . This has led, in Bosnia and Herzegovina and in Somalia, to a new kind of United Nations operation. Even though the use of force is authorized under Chapter VII of the Charter, the United Nations remains neutral and impartial between the warring parties, without a mandate to stop the aggressor (if one can be identified) or impose a cessation of hostilities. Nor is this peace-keeping as practised hitherto, because the hostilities continue and there is often no agreement between the warring parties on which a peace-keeping mandate can be based.[63]

Unlike the case of Iraq, here there is not even the possibility of appealing to the catchall language of article 39 to justify this humanitarian mission. The civil war in Somalia did not pose any serious danger of breach of international peace. The main reason that prompted enforcement action by the Security Council was the extreme situation of famine, death, and disease caused by the civil war, by the breach of *humanitarian* law by the warring factions, and by the general situation of anarchy. The resolution referred to "the magnitude of the human tragedy caused by the conflict," and to "the deterioration of the humanitarian situation."[64] Most significantly, the Security Council mentioned the reports of "widespread violations of international humanitarian law" in Somalia, including violence against personnel participating in humanitarian relief there.[65] The Security Council summarized the situation as "intolerable," adding that it had become necessary to review "the basic premises and principles of the U.N. effort" in Somalia. This was, of course, a reference to the distinction between peacekeeping

---

[62] Id. at 3.

[63] Id. at 6.

[64] Res. 794, *supra* n. 45, at Preamble.

[65] Id.

action, which, among other things, is based on consent by the territorial state, and enforcement action based on Chapter VII of the Charter.[66]

After demanding a cease-fire in the civil conflict, the Security Council, "[a]cting under Chapter VII," authorized the Secretary-General and member states to use "all necessary means to establish as soon as possible a secure environment for humanitarian relief operations in Somalia."[67] Of course, "all necessary means" includes the use of force; this had already been established in the Gulf War precedent, but was specifically recognized in resolution 794 when the Security Council endorsed the recommendation of the Secretary-General to that effect.[68]

The import of Resolution 794 is thus not difficult to glean: the Security Council authorized member states to stop, by force if necessary, the egregious violations of humanitarian law that were occurring in Somalia. The Security Council expressly reaffirmed that it was not its task to dictate a solution to internal differences: the Somali people "bear ultimate responsibility for the reconstruction of their own country."[69] But the message of Resolution 794 was that in deciding their own political fate, political groups may not violate the constraints imposed by humanitarian law. This is, therefore, a pristine case of collective forcible intervention to put an end to a civil war in the course of which warring factions have rendered themselves guilty of serious violations of human rights. The reference in the resolution to the "call by Somalia" underscored that the goal was to rescue the Somali people from the horrors of the war. It is not just that the Security Council authorized states to intervene to make sure that humanitarian law was respected; it *demanded* a cease-fire. Under the powers granted to the Security Council by articles 25, 39, 41, and 42 of the Charter, this request is mandatory.

Some may challenge the validity of this precedent for humanitarian intervention on the grounds that this is not an action to overthrow a tyrannical government, which is the traditional (and contested) paradigm of humanitarian intervention. They may emphasize that there is

---

[66] For a recent description of the distinction, *see* Boutros Boutros-Ghali, "Empowering the United Nations," *Foreign Aff.*, 89, 89 (Winter 1992).

[67] Res. 794, *supra* n. 45, at para. 10.

[68] Id. at para. 7.

[69] Id. at Preamble.

not even a government in Somalia. Therefore, this is an intervention that, unlike the cases that supporters of humanitarian intervention cite, does not aim at stopping *government-directed* human rights violations. Therefore Resolution 794, it is argued, is not a valid precedent for the legitimacy of collective humanitarian intervention.

This argument is not convincing. For one thing, the fact that there is no government does not mean that there is no *state*. No one denies that Somalia is a state and that therefore Somalians have a right to their own state; indeed this point is expressly underscored by the Security Council. The intervention, however, punctures the sovereignty of Somalia as a state, and noninterventionists need to explain that, unless they concede that the purpose of the nonintervention rule is to protect *governments* per se. In addition, this is a case of *civil war*, which for the traditional doctrine is a typical domestic situation in which foreign intervention is banned.[70] And finally, it is important to underscore that what is called "humanitarian law" is no more than the body of *human rights* principles that must be respected by all parties in an armed conflict.[71] Therefore, an intervention to put an end to violations of humanitarian law is an intervention to uphold human rights—the human rights that parties in a war, civil or international, ought to honor. As I said, Resolution 794 goes further in that it demands not merely respect for the laws of war but an end to the civil conflict itself. And the reason it goes that far is because the "human tragedy" has been caused by the war. Human suffering thus has taken precedence over state sovereignty, which is precisely the policy that undergirds humanitarian intervention.

Here again, anti-interventionists will call attention to the language in the preamble of Resolution 794. There the Security Council determined "that the magnitude of the human tragedy caused by the conflict in Somalia" constituted "a threat to international peace and security."[72] Thus this is a case, the argument goes, that falls squarely within the terms of article 39 which defines the powers of the Security Council only in terms of breach of international peace or threat thereof. The answer is the same I gave before: this view wrongly focuses on what the

---

[70] *See* O'Connell, *supra* n. 44, at 908.

[71] *See generally,* R. Lillich, *International Human Rights: Cases and Materials* 767–83 (2d ed, 1991).

[72] Res. 794, *supra* n. 45, at Preamble.

Security Council says and not on what it does. The Security Council's decisions are governed by international law. The Security Council, therefore, runs afoul of the Charter if it determines that a situation is a threat to the peace when in reality it is not. The Council does not have discretion (in the strong sense of creating fresh law) to authorize enforcement measures to address *any* situation as long as it invokes, like a catchall, the language of article 39. Hence, a defense of Resolution 794 requires postulating a *preexisting* legal principle that justifies that resolution—a principle that the international community could invoke as grounds for the action in Somalia. That principle can only be the power of the Security Council to authorize forcible measures in the extreme situation of human rights violations. Anti-interventionists would be on surer footing if they would flatly challenge the legality of Resolution 794 because it falls outside article 39 standards, rather than claiming that the resolution is really about restoring international peace and not about protecting human rights. In fact, if they take the latter position, their anti-interventionism becomes empty: the Security Council can do as it pleases, provided it pays lip service to the language of article 39. There is only a jurisprudential difference between this position and the position defended in this book, that the Security Council may authorize humanitarian intervention in appropriate cases. The difference is that I argue that international law properly interpreted *did* authorize collective humanitarian intervention at the time the Security Council was called upon to act on the Somalian situation. That right, therefore, was not created afresh by Resolution 794.

Nor is the language in Resolution 794 to the effect that the situation in Somalia had a "unique character" of a "deteriorating, complex, and extraordinary nature"[73] a bar to this conclusion. That the situation was unique and extraordinary is obviously true, in the sense that only these kinds of extreme situations warrant the collective use of force. This is perfectly consistent with the doctrine of humanitarian intervention. The doctrine does not recommend the use of force to remedy any human rights problem, any more than the doctrine of self-defense recommends using force to repel any unlawful act. Only serious human rights violations that cannot be remedied by any other means warrant proportionate

---

[73] Id. The same language was used by the Security Council in its recent imposition of nonforcible sanctions against Haiti.

collective forcible intervention for the purpose of restoring human rights, provided further that the victims themselves welcome the intervention (as was the case in Somalia).[74] Thus for example, the Security Council would be exceeding its powers if it installed one of the leaders of the warring factions in power, because that would be inconsistent with the humanitarian character of the intervention.

That the situation is "unique" thus cannot mean that this is the only one case, the only exception where intervention in the domestic affairs of a state will ever be authorized, for that would mean that the Security Council did not act on principle. The reference to the uniqueness of the situation in Resolution 794 means instead that this is an extraordinary case covered by a principle that authorizes intervention only in this class of extraordinary cases, and that the Resolution should not therefore be construed as a precedent for a broad power of the Security Council to authorize intervention in less egregious cases. This interpretation of the "uniqueness" language was confirmed by the Haitian case.

4. The Case of Haiti, 1994

The case of Haiti is the most important precedent supporting the legitimacy both of an international principle of democratic rule and of collective humanitarian intervention. In 1987 the Organization of American States urged Haiti to resume the democratic process through free elections.[75] No "sovereignty" limitation or exception was attached to this resolution. In 1990, the Reverend Jean-Bertrand Aristide was elected President of Haiti with sixty-seven percent of the popular vote.[76] A military coup removed Aristide from office on September 30, 1991. While the U.N. Security Council assembled late on the day of the coup at the request of Haiti's Ambassador to the United Nations, it did not formally convene to consider the coup allegedly because a majority of its members saw the coup as an internal domestic matter, which did

---

[74] Id.

[75] OEA/Ser.G/CP/RES.489, Doc. 720 (1987).

[76] Douglas Farah, "Carter Makes Return Visit to Wary Haiti; Aristide's Government Fears Meddling in Vote," *Wash. Post,* Feb. 24, 1995, at A16.

not constitute a threat to the peace placing it within the competence of the Security Council.[77]

In contrast to the initial Security Council inaction, the Organization of American States (OAS) responded quickly to the coup. At an ad hoc meeting on October 2, 1991, the foreign ministers of OAS members formally condemned the coup and recommended imposition of economic and diplomatic sanctions on Haiti by OAS members.[78] The Security Council convened formally on October 3, 1991 to hear President Aristide address the Council. All members denounced the coup and expressed strong support for the OAS action. However the Council failed to adopt a formal resolution addressing the coup, reportedly because China and certain non-aligned states were concerned about increasing Security Council involvement in affairs traditionally considered domestic and thus beyond the realm of U.N. concern.[79]

When the U.N. General Assembly took up the issue of the Haiti coup it went further than ever before; it strongly condemned the "illegal replacement of the constitutional President of Haiti" and affirmed as "unacceptable any entity resulting from that illegal situation."[80] Here again, there is no mention of Haiti's "right" to "choose its political system," nor any reference to Haiti's sovereignty or self-determination.

Refusal of Haiti's de facto military dictators, Lt. Gen. Raoul Cedras and Brig. Gen. Philippe Biamby, to reinstate the democratically-elected Aristide government, and continued violent persecution of Aristede supporters, led the Security Council to finally adopt coercive measures against Haiti in June 1993. Acting under Chapter VII of the Charter, the Security Council imposed a mandatory economic embargo on Haiti.[81]

---

[77] See A. C. Arend, "The United Nations and the New World Order," 81 Georg. L.J. 491, 500–501 (1993). See also T. L. Friedman, "U.S. Suspends Assistance to Haiti and Refuses to Recognize Junta," N.Y. Times, Oct. 2, 1991, at A1.

[78] Support to the Democratic Government of Haiti, Organization of American States Res. 1/91, OEA/Ser. F/V.1, MRE/RES. 1/91 Corr. 1 (Oct. 3, 1991), reprinted in Letter Dated 3 October 1991 from the Permanent Representatives of Ecuador and the United States of America to the United Nations, U.N. Doc. S/23109, Annex at 2–3 (1991).

[79] See U.N. S.C.O.R., 46th Sess., 3011th mtg., U.N. Doc. S/PV.3011 (1991); P. Lewis, "U.N. Stops Short of Haiti Resolution," N.Y. Times, Oct. 4, 1991, at A8; Arend, supra n. 77, at 501–02.

[80] G.A. Res. 46/7, U.N. Doc. A/Res/46/7, at 2 (1991).

[81] S/Res/841 (1993). This resolution imposed a compulsory embargo on the delivery of oil and petroleum products, and arms and police equipment, and froze assets of

The Security Council's binding resolution expressly affirmed that the solution to the crisis in Haiti "should take into account the above-mentioned resolutions of the Organization of American States and of the General Assembly of the United Nations"—i.e., the restoration of democracy in the country.[82]

The strict U.N. sanctions induced the Haitian military junta to accept a U.N.-brokered agreement in July, 1993, known as the Governors Island Agreement, which would have returned Haiti to democratic rule under President Aristide.[83] Under the terms of Resolution 841 and the Governors Island Agreement, the U.N. lifted the economic sanctions on Haiti on August 27, 1993, because the junta had begun implementing the arrangements for the restoration of democractic rule.[84] The Governors Island Agreement collapsed, however, when violence against Aristide supporters resurfaced in September and October of 1993 and reached a crisis point when pro-junta mobs blocked the debarkation of troops assigned, under U.N. Resolution 867,[85] to assist in the monitoring and modernization of Haiti's police and military. On October 13, 1993, the Security Council unanimously passed Resolution 873 which reimposed the previously suspended economic sanctions,[86] and authorized member states, in another resolution passed on October 16, to use military force to enforce the sanctions.[87]

On July 31, 1994, the United Nations Security Council adopted Resolution 940. This resolution in its operative part authorized Member States "to form a multinational force and . . . to use all necessary means to facilitate the departure from Haiti of the military leadership."[88] Acting under this U.N. mandate, the United States and other U.N. members turned up the pressure on Haiti's military leadership. On September 15,

---

the Haitian government and its de facto leaders. Resolution 841 expressly relies on the previous OAS and U.N. General Assembly Resolutions.

[82] *See also* the reimposition of sanctions by the U.S. government, IO. *Int'l Trade Rep. (BNA)* 1756; available on LEXIS; and Resolution S/Res/841 (June 16, 1993).

[83] L. F. Damrosch, "Recent Security Council Actions Concerning Internal Conflicts: Economic Sanctions," *Am. Soc'y Int'l L. Newsletter,* Jan. 1994.

[84] S/Res/861 (1993).

[85] S/Res/863 (1993).

[86] S/Res/873 (1993).

[87] S/Res/875 (1993).

[88] *See* S/Res/940 (1994), at para. 4.

President Clinton delivered an ultimatum to Haiti's ruling junta via a television address to the American public. He indicated that diplomatic measures had been exhausted and that a U.S.-led military invasion was a near certainty.[89] September 18, former U.S. President Jimmy Carter, accompanied by Senator Sam Nunn (D-GA), and former Chairman of the Joint Chiefs of Staff General Colin Powell, persuaded the junta's leadership to agree to surrender power to President Aristide and leave the country by October 15. This agreement was reached only hours before an invading force of U.S.-led multinational troops was to land in Haiti.[90] The next day 2,000 U.S. troops from the Army's 10th Mountain Division landed in Port-au-Prince,[91] and the total swelled to over 15,000 troops within a matter of days.[92]

International reaction to the September 18th agreement and the subsequent U.S. occupation was almost universally positive. The new Secretary-General of the OAS voiced "deep satisfaction over the agreement, which assumes that political measures and diplomacy will prevail."[93] Venezuela was the only Latin American nation to condemn the U.S. action in Haiti.[94] After Haitian military and police administered public random beatings to pro-Aristide demonstrators in full view of U.S. troops during the first few days of the occupation, President Clinton ordered U.S. forces to abandon the original non-interference policy and prevent such violence by anti-Aristide forces.[95]

U.S. forces in Haiti met no armed resistance during the initial troop landings and suffered no casualties (through February 25, 1995) while restoring democracy and stability to Haiti.[96] The United States officially

---

[89] "Haiti's Military Junta Agrees to Step Down; U.S. Recalls Invasion Force," *Facts on File,* Sept. 23, 1994, at 673.

[90] Farah, *supra* n. 76, at A16.

[91] See "2,000 U.S. Troops Land Without Opposition and Take Over Haiti's Ports and Airfields," *N.Y. Times,* Sept. 20, 1994 at A1.

[92] Farah, *supra* n. 76, at A16.

[93] *Facts on File, supra* n. 89, at 673.

[94] Id. Venezuela's Foreign Minister, Miguel Angel Burelli Rivas, was quoted as saying "This is the 16th United States military intervention in Latin America, and it is lamentable." Id.

[95] Id.

[96] Farah, *supra* n. 76, at A16.

turned the mission over to the United Nations on March 31, 1995. Of the 6,000 U.N. troops, about 2,400 were U.S. personnel.[97]

An analysis of the resolution and of subsequent events confirms the conclusions reached in the cases of Iraq and Somalia. The resolution determined that "the illegal de facto regime" in Haiti had failed to comply with the Governor's Island Agreement and with previous resolutions of the Security Council. The Council expressed its concern with the "significant further deterioration of the humanitarian situation," in particular with the regime's "systematic violation of civil liberties." Thus the Security Council invoked human rights abuses as well as the illegitimacy of the regime as the operative reasons for authorizing military action. In contrast with the case of Somalia, in this resolution the Security Council *did not* determine that the situation in Haiti constituted a threat to international peace and security, while at the same time asserting that it was acting under Chapter VII of the Charter. Thus this case strengthens the interpretation of the Charter suggested in this book: that the practice of states has accepted serious violations of human rights as grounds for action by the Security Council under Chapter VII. Here again, Resolution 940 refers to the "unique character of the present situation in Haiti and its deteriorating, complex, and extraordinary nature, requiring an exceptional response." That the Security Council considered Haiti *another* "unique situation" confirms the interpretation of this language suggested in the discussion of the events in the Somalia case above, namely that Somalia was not strictly a "unique" case, but certainly an "extraordinary" one, and that subsequent equally "extraordinary" cases can occur—as shown by the fact that there have now been two such "unique" cases.

What are the possible counter-arguments against treating the Haitian case as a genuine precedent for collective humanitarian intervention? Noninterventionists may argue, again, that in fact the Security Council found a threat to the peace and thus authorized the military action under the classic terms of article 39. To the argument that Resolution 940 does not even try to characterize the situation in Haiti as a threat to the peace, they may reply that Resolution 940 refers to previous Security Council resolutions on Haiti and that in those resolutions the

---

[97] Id.

Council did determine that there was a threat to international peace and security in the region.[98] And again, the answer is that this is stubborn adherence to the noninterventionist thesis even when it flies squarely against the facts. No one can seriously argue that the Haitian situation posed a threat to international peace and security in the region. A more accurate reading of Resolution 940 is that the previous reference to threat to peace in the region in Resolution 841 was unpersuasive because it reflected neither the facts nor the normative context of the Haitian situation. For that reason the Council, in Resolution 940, sensibly abandoned the reference to the language of article 39.

Another strategy could be to maintain that the United States really acted out of purely selfish motives, not humanitarian ones, either to stop the flux of refugees or to get rid of a problem in the United States' "backyard." First of all, as I argued in Chapter 6, this view confuses psychological motivation with legal justification. Second, the view is inconsistent with the wording of Resolution 940—the legal grounds for the U.S.-led intervention. Anti-interventionists would have to say that the Security Council simply lied when it mentioned human rights abuses and the restoration of democracy in the resolution. More important, the humanitarian justification of the intervention was given by President Clinton in his address of September 15, 1994.[99] There the U.S. President referred repeatedly to the atrocities committed by the Haitian dictators (not just to the fact that they interrupted the democratic process in Haiti). The President did stress that such atrocities affected United States interests, but that begs the question of what is the legitimate U.S. national interest. If one asks why the atrocities affected U.S. interests, a plausible answer is that the national interest (defined in a broader sense, not just in terms of pure national egoism[100]) was affected precisely because the atrocities were morally intolerable. Someone could reply that

---

[98] *See,* e.g., Res. 841, *supra* n. 81, at Preamble.

[99] The complete text of the address is reprinted *Wash. Post,* Sept. 16, 1994, at A31. I quote from there.

[100] People who talk about the national interest tend to have, in my view, a noticeably narrow definition of what national interest should be and typically is in a democracy. Why would citizens of a democracy define national interest as only strategic, economic, or political advantages over other nations? It seems to me that typically, a democratic government also advances the national interest if it is responsive to the moral indignation that citizens feel when confronted with serious violations of human rights outside the state's borders.

the United States' interests were affected because of the flow of Haitian refugees into U.S. territory.[101] This is certainly true, but what that only means is that the United States had a self-regarding motive (stopping the flux of refugees) *in addition* to the humanitarian motives. The United States receives a huge flux of illegal immigrants from Mexico every year, and no one would suggest that such a "refugee problem" justifies armed action or even nonforcible action against Mexico. The "refugee problem" in Haiti is best defined as "the refugee exodus caused by oppression" and not as "the refugee exodus" *tout court*. Finally, there is no reason why the existence of mixed motives (and the Haitian case is one where the humanitarian motive is overwhelmingly predominant) should blight an otherwise justified intervention.

Another possible argument here is that the action by the multinational force is not a case of humanitarian *forcible* intervention, because the U.S.-led forces occupied the country either with the consent of the junta, that is, of the effective government as required by traditional international law, or alternatively with the consent of the legitimate government, represented by President Aristide, as required by modern international law. Thus this is, so the argument goes, a mere case of peacekeeping and not of enforcement action. But this position cannot be seriously maintained. The position that the junta's consent validates the intervention is deficient for two reasons. First, it begs the question of the junta as the legitimate government of Haiti, and thus as the valid consenting agent.[102] But secondly, no one can say, on these facts, that the junta validly consented to the occupation. Their "consent" was exacted by the U.S. envoys led by ex-President Jimmy Carter under the threat of military invasion.[103] A cursory reading of the Vienna Convention on the Law of Treaties shows that the agreement is internationally binding.[104] The correct legal position is that the overthrow of the junta was achieved by the threat of force, which would be prohibited by the

---

[101] This justification was cited by President Clinton in his address, *supra* n. 99.

[102] For a thorough discussion of intervention by consent, *see* David Wippman, "Treaty-Based Intervention; Who Can Say No?," 62 *U. Chi. L. Rev.* 607 (1995)

[103] *See* "On the Brink of War, a Tense Battle of Wills—Attack Was Imminent as the Junta Mediator Forced an Accord," *N.Y. Times,* Sept. 20, 1994, at A1, A13.

[104] *See* art. 52, Vienna Convention on the Law of Treaties.

U.N. Charter,[105] but for the existence of a justification such as humanitarian intervention. And because the language of Resolution 940 ("all necessary means"), includes the use of force, *a fortiori* it includes the threat of force. The method followed by the United States is, in addition, in compliance with the requirements of necessity and proportionality, since it was the least intrusive action necessary to achieve the result mandated by Resolution 940.[106] And from a moral and political standpoint, the United States government must be commended for having achieved the desired result (restoration of human rights in Haiti) without having to resort to open combat.

The argument that President Aristide consented to the intervention is more colorable, yet it is questionable on several grounds. First, it is not clear that such consent was actually given.[107] Second, the position is in contradiction of one of the most cherished noninterventionist dogmas—the principle that the internationally legitimate government is the one that has effective control. (This is of course not fatal to the noninterventionist, because she may reject the principle of effective control and endorse instead the right to democratic governance, while opposing the legitimacy of forcible humanitarian intervention.) Third, a fair reading of Resolution 940 and the statements of President Clinton and others shows that the legitimacy of forcible action did not depend on the position that Aristide represented the legitimate government. Because the situation in Haiti was much more serious than mere illegitimacy of origin of the government, a denial of consent by Aristide would not have sufficed to foreclose the legality of the collective action, nor was such consent required by Resolution 940. And finally, even if the consent by Aristide is considered valid, that would only mean that the intervention was, here again, overdetermined, that is, justified under more than one principle.

The only argument denying the validity of this precedent consistent with the facts (and internally consistent) is simply to take the position

---

[105] *See* U.N. Char. art. 2, paragraph 4.

[106] *See generally* J. G. Garden, "Proportionality and Force in International Law," 87 *Am. J. Int'l L.* 391 (1993).

[107] For an account of the changes of opinion by Aristide, *see* D. Zabarenko, "Aristide Thanks U.S., Gets Assurances on Haiti," BC Cycle, Sept. 21, 1994, available on LEXIS.

that the whole incident should be characterized as an ongoing huge violation of international law where the Security Council, under undue political pressure from the United States, has overstepped its powers under the United Nations Charter. This position certainly bites the bullet, and would presumably also deny the legality of the current practice of the Security Council as exemplified by the other cases discussed here. This argument has the merit of avoiding verbal sophistry, but faces instead a formidable challenge: it is not possible to maintain this view and simultaneously adhere to a positivist conception of international law where state and United Nations practice are the yardstick of legitimacy. The noninterventionist making this argument must supply policy and moral reasons why this practice is illegitimate notwithstanding the fact that it seems to satisfy the requirements of right process (to use Professor Franck's words[108]). For example, noninterventionists might argue, along the lines suggested by Michael Walzer,[109] that the Security Council ignored Haiti's communal integrity, that is, the right of Haitians to resolve their political differences among themselves, and that therefore Resolution 940 must be seen as a violation of article 39 of the Charter (interpreted in the light of Walzer's principle[110]), not as an extension of the permissible grounds for collective action. In the first part of the book I have shown why such position is morally incorrect and ought to be rejected.[111] States exist primarily to protect human rights. A government such as the Haitian junta which seizes power by force and turns against its own citizens betrays its very *raison d'être* and therefore cannot be treated as legitimate. The view that describes governmental murder, rape, and torture as "a process of self-determination" is simply grotesque and may be dismissed without regrets.

---

[108] *See* T. M. Franck, "Legitimacy in the International System," 82 *Am. J. Int'l L.* 705, 706 (1988).

[109] *See* M. Walzer, "The Moral Standing of States: A Reply to Four Critics," in *Int. Ethics* 217 (C. Beitz et al. eds., 1985)

[110] Walzer's principle is "always act so as to recognize and uphold communal integrity." M. Walzer, *supra* n. 109, at 165, 181.

[111] *See supra,* Chapters 3 and 4.

5. The Case of Rwanda, 1994

In another striking example of the change of winds in the United Nations, on June 22, 1994, the Security Council approved France's proposal to intervene in Rwanda, by a vote of ten to zero, with five abstentions.[112] The Security Council Resolution authorized France to use military force ("all necessary means") to protect civilians in a very violent civil war that had erupted in Rwanda. The Council also required the French to conduct a "strictly humanitarian . . . impartial and neutral" operation, that is, one divorced from the merits of the dispute between government and RPF (Rwandan Patriotic Front) forces.

The crisis in Rwanda was triggered on April 6, 1994, when the President of Rwanda was killed when his plane was shot down by a shoulder-fired, surface-to-air missile while approaching the Rwandan capital of Kigali. Although the source of the attack has not been pinpointed, extremist Hutus opposed to any power sharing with Tutsis of the Rwandan Patriotic Front are widely suspected of having carried out the attack.[113] The Hutu-dominated Rwandan military blamed the incident, however, on minority Tutsi, who consitute fifteen percent of Rwanda's population.[114] Within hours, young French-trained Hutu militiamen, known as *interhamwe*, began slaughtering innocent Tutsi and moderate Hutu by the thousands. As a result, the RPF quickly restarted its dormant civil war against the Rwandan government.[115]

The 2,700 U.N. observers already stationed in Rwanda as part of the United Nations Assistance Mission for Rwanda (UNAMIR) to monitor a peace agreement between the Rwandan government and the RPF,

---

[112] See *Draft Resolution Concerning the Deployment of a Temporary Multinational Humanitarian Operation in Rwanda*, S. C.Res. 939, U.N. Doc. S/1994/737, June 21, 1994.

[113] R. Bonner, "Shattered Nation: A Special Report: Rwanda Now Faces Painful Ordeal of Rebirth," *N.Y. Times*, Dec. 29, 1994, at A1.

[114] Id.

[115] See S. Kraft, "*France's Big Gamble Pays Off in Rwanda*," *L. A. Times*, July 16, 1994, at A1. The civil war between the French-backed, Hutu-dominated government of Rwanda and the mostly-Tutsi RPF erupted in October 1990. The RPF attacked government forces from Rwandan refugee bases in Uganda. In August 1993, the government and the RPF signed a peace accord in Arusha, Tanzania; however, the accord was never fully implemented. In November 1993, over 2,000 U.N. troops arrived to monitor the accord. Bonner, *supra* n. 113, at A1.

were powerless to stop the killing. When ten U.N. troops from Belgium assigned to guard Rwandan Prime Minister Agathe Uwilingiyimana were brutally hacked to death, and the Prime Minister killed, Belgium recalled its 440 troops and the remainder of the lightly armed observer force stayed in their barracks.[116] By April 18 the International Committee of the Red Cross had reported that "tens of thousands" of Rwandans had already been killed. The U.N. Security Council voted on April 21 to reduce the number of U.N. personnel in Rwanda to 270 to prevent additional U.N. casualties and in the faint hope that the carnage would somehow cease.[117] Soon, hundreds of thousands of refugees began fleeing to neighboring Tanzania and Zaire.

When the Security Council realized that the killing continued unabated it began in early May to discuss sending a U.N. force of 5,500 African troops to Rwanda. The Security Council voted on May 17 to increase the authorized force level of UNAMIR to 5,500 troops but as yet had obtained no commitments from member nations, who would have to provide such forces.[118] On May 31, U.N. Secretary-General Boutros Boutros-Ghali reported to the Security Council that an estimated 250,000 to 500,000 Rwandan men, women, and children had already been killed.[119] In a nation of approximately 7 million persons, the Secretary-General pointed out that this would equate in proportional population terms to the killing of 2–4 million in France and 9–18 million in the United States.[120] The report concluded with a mix of disgust and anger over the inability of the U.N. to respond to the crisis:

> [T]he magnitude of the human calamity that has engulfed Rwanda might be unimaginable but for its having transpired. On the basis of the evidence that has emerged, there can be little doubt that it constitutes genocide, since there have been large-scale killings of communities and families belonging to a

---

[116] T. W. Lippman, "U.S. Troop Withdrawal Ends Frustrating Mission to Save Rwandan Lives," *Wash. Post,* Oct. 3, 1994, at A11.

[117] *See* U.N. Doc S/1994/912, Apr. 21, 1994; P. Constable, "World Response to Rwanda Crisis Questioned: Critics Cite Lack of Plan, Will to Intervene, *Boston Globe,* July 18, 1994, at 18; Bonner, *supra* n. 113, at A1.

[118] *See* U.N. Doc. S/1994/918, May 17, 1994.

[119] U.N. Doc. S/1994/640, May 31, 1994, at 2.

[120] Id.

particular ethnic group. . . . In the meantime, it is unacceptable that, almost two months since this violence exploded, killings still continue.[121]

A U.N. study subsequently confirmed that Hutu militants were guilty of genocide against the Tutsi, but that no evidence was found that the Tutsi-led RPF committed systematic reprisals as the Hutu had alleged.[122] The United States resisted using the term "genocide" to refer to the slaughter in Rwanda, as such a label would have made U.S. inaction unjustifiable.

Death did not cease at the Rwandan borders as refugee camps in Goma, Zaire were swept with outbreaks of cholera taking as many as 20,000 additional lives.[123] Over the next several weeks the Security Council was unable to obtain commitments from member nations for the needed troops, equipment, logistics, and transportation. The United States, still reeling from unexpectedly large military casualties in Somalia, flatly rejected requests for U.S. participation in the U.N. force and generally opposed the idea of deploying any large U.N. peacekeeping force to Rwanda while the fighting continued and without having secured firm commitments from member nations to supply troops and equipment. The cautious U.S. approach was somewhat justified since, as of mid-June, over two months after the genocide in Rwanda had begun, and a month after the Security Council had authorized an expanded UNAMIR mission in Rwanda, only one country had committed a fully-equipped unit—a single battalion of Ethiopian soldiers.[124] The U.S. was also concerned about the potential costs of a large, extended U.N. mission in Rwanda since the U.S. is required to pay over thirty percent of the costs of such missions.[125]

---

[121] Id. at 10.

[122] R. D. Lyons, "U.N. Study Accuses Hutu in Rwanda Killings," *N.Y. Times,* Dec. 3, 1994, at A17. The U.N. Human Rights Commission investigation concluded that "there exists overwhelming evidence to prove that acts of genocide against the Tutsi group were perpetrated by Hutu elements in a concerted, planned, systematic and methodical way." Id.

[123] U.N. Doc. S/1994/924, Aug. 3, 1994, at 3.

[124] Julia Preston, "U.N. Supports France on Force for Rwanda," *Wash. Post,* June 22, 1994, at A24.

[125] U.S. reluctance to support a major U.N. intervention in Rwanda was based in large measure on the policy directive contained in Presidential Decision Directive 25 (PDD–25) signed by President Clinton on May 2, 1994, during the height of the genocide in Rwanda. PDD–25 spelled out strict guidelines to be considered before the U.S.

On June 19 U.N. Secretary-General Boutros Boutros-Ghali wrote to the Security Council indicating that it would take several additional weeks before the expanded UNAMIR troops and equipment would be available for deployment within Rwanda.[126] With evidence of the scale of the atrocities in Rwanda mounting—a U.N. report on the crisis estimated that 3 million Rwandans were displaced internally and more than 2 million fled to neighboring countries[127]—the French government proposed to the Security Council to intervene unilaterally to halt the bloodshed and establish safe havens for the hundreds of thousands of fleeing refugees.[128] By June 22, three days after Security Council approval of the French intervention, 2,500 French troops were in Rwanda and neighboring Zaire, establishing safe havens for refugees near the border. French troops helped distribute relief supplies and patrolled the countryside in tanks and armored vehicles.

While critics of the intervention had expected French forces to assist Rwandan government troops in the fight against the RPF (as France had done during similar fighting in 1990), French troops instead stood aside as the RPF seized control of the capital city of Kigali on July 4. French forces also did nothing to prevent the fall of Butare, Rwanda's second largest city, to RPF forces on July 5, or the fall of Ruhengeri, the Rwandan government stronghold, on July 14. On July 17 retreating government forces were routed by the RPF at Gisenyi and on July 18 the RPF declared a unilateral cease-fire effectively ending the civil war. On July 19 the RPF formed a government of national unity in Kigali.[129] French

---

agrees to participate in any multilateral military operation, including the impact on U.S. interests, the availability of troops and funds, the necessity of U.S. participation, congressional approval, a clear date for U.S. withdrawal, and acceptable command and control arrangements. PDD–25 also directed that the U.S. not approve any new U.N. operation, with or without U.S. troop participation, unless the crisis represents a threat to international peace and security, specifically including starvation among civilians, gross abuses of human rights, or a violent overthrow of a democratically elected government. Any proposed objective must lay out clear objectives, the availability of adequate funding and troops, the consent of the parties to the conflict, and a realistic exit strategy. See T. G. Weiss, "The United Nations and Civil Wars," 17 *Wash. Q.* 137 (1994).

[126] See *Letter dated 19 June 1994 from the Secretary-General addressed to the President of the Security Council.* U.N. Doc. S/1994/728.

[127] U.N. Doc. S/1994/924, Aug. 3, 1994, at 3.

[128] See *Letter Dated 20 June 1994 From the Permanent Representative of France to the United Nations Addressed to the Secretary-General.* U.N. Doc. S/1994/734.

[129] U.N. Doc. S/1994/924, Aug. 3, 1994, at 1.

forces withdrew from Rwanda after two months, urging the U.N. to send replacements as soon as possible.[130] By August, 1994, several thousand blue-helmeted U.N. troops from Ethiopia, Ghana, and Zimbabwe had replaced the French troops.

There is little doubt that the U.N.-authorized French mission is best described as a case of legitimate humanitarian intervention. Many of the arguments presented in the previous sections apply here as well. The U.N. resolution authorized the use of force, and while there were references to "threat of international peace and security," it is quite obvious that the purpose of the mission was to stop the atrocities that were taking place in the Rwandan civil war. It is also worth noting the relative disinterestedness on the part of the French government, as shown by its prompt withdrawal. The situation in Rwanda has not, unfortunately, been completely alleviated. But the fact that the operation was not entirely successful does not impair its legitimacy: final success is not a requirement of right action.

6. A Note on the Intervention of NATO Into Bosnia, 1994

The complicated conflict in the former Yugoslavia (1991–1995) created one of the toughest dilemmas for the Western alliance at the end of the Cold War. Much has been written about this tragic war, which fortunately seems, at the time of this writing, to have come to a close.[131] Here I will focus on but one aspect of it: the legitimacy of the NATO air operations against Bosnian-Serbian positions. I believe that this is another instance of collective humanitarian intervention, notwithstanding the fact that the operations were motivated also by the aim of forcing the Bosnian Serbs to negotiate peace.

---

[130] P. Lewis, "France Calls Rwanda Mission a Success: Asks for U.N. Force," *N.Y. Times,* July 11, 1994, at A8.

[131] For a general history of the region, *see* V. Dedifer et al., *History of Yugoslavia* (1974). The literature on the war in Bosnia is voluminous. *See, inter alia,* E. O'Ballance, *Civil War in Bosnia* 1992–1994 (1995); A. M. Weisburd, "The Emptiness of the Concept of Ius Cogens, as Illustrated by the War in Bosnia," 17 *Mich. J. Int'l L.* (1995); A. D'Amato, "Peace v. Accountability in Bosnia," 88 *Am. J. Int'l L.* 500 (1994); J. Fink, "From Peacekeeping to Peace Enforcement: The Blurring of the Mandate for the Use of Force in Maintaining International Peace and Security," 19 *Md. J. Int'l L. & Trade* 1 (1995); G. Moor, *The Republic of Bosnia-Herzegovina and Article 51: Inherent Rights and Unmet Responsibilities* (1995); "Symposium on War Crimes: Bosnia and Beyond," 34 *Va. J. Int'l L.*(1994).

Yugoslavia was formed around a Serbian core during a series of wars in the 19th and 20th centuries as the Ottoman Empire gradually lost control of the Balkan territories.[132] After the fall of the Communist government, the republics that made up Yugoslavia started the path toward secession. Croatia and Slovenia proclaimed their independence on June 25, 1991.[133] In Bosnia-Herzegovina, a referendum was held on January 26, 1992, in which sixty-two percent of the voters favored independence.[134] Almost immediately after the government declared independence rebel Bosnian Serb forces began violent efforts to overthrow the government, and with it, the infamous practice of "ethnic cleansing" began.[135] The atrocities that were reported were of such gravity and magnitude as to be compared with those committed by the Nazis in World War II.[136]

The first time that the United Nations Security Council contemplated authorizing coercive measures in the conflict was in the summer of 1992. In its Resolution 770, the Security Council, acting under Chapter VII, called upon states "to take nationally or through regional agencies or arrangements *all measures necessary* to facilitate in coordination with the United Nations the delivery . . . of humanitarian assistance . . . in . . . Bosnia-Herzegovina."[137] While recognizing that the situation in Bosnia

---

[132] For an account of the conflict I rely on "Chronology of Conflict in Former Yugoslavia." *Reuters World Services,* Oct. 12, 1995, BC Cycle, available on LEXIS-NEXIS.

[133] Croatia and Slovenia proclaimed their independence on June 25, 1991. *See* Chronology of Conflict in Former Yugoslavia, *supra* n. 132.

[134] *See* "Bosnian Leader Warns Serbs to Respect Vote Verdict," *The Times (London),* Mar. 4, 1992, at 8.

[135] *See* R. Watson, "Ethnic Cleansing," *Newsweek,* Aug. 17, 1992 , at 16. On "ethnic cleansing" generally, *see* N. Cigar, *Genocide in Bosnia: The Policy of "Ethnic Cleansing"* (1995); on the horrendous crimes against women, *see* The War Against Women in Bosnia-Herzegovina (A. Stiglmayer ed. 1994).

[136] They included: A massacre of 200 Muslim men and boys by Serb police in Central Bosnia, *see N.Y. Times,* Dec. 17, 1995, at A1; murder of 2,000 to 3,000 Muslims by Serb irregulars; summary executions, see Lander, "New Reports on Atrocities," *Newsday,* Nov. 7, 1992, at 4; widespread rape as an instrument to fulfill the goal of ethnic cleansing, *see* L. Morrow, "Unspeakable," *Time,* Feb, 22, 1993, at 48. A moderate estimation places the number of raped women at 20,000, *see* Sciolino, "In Bosnia, Peace at Any Price is Getting More Expensive," *N.Y. Times,* Jan. 10, 1993, at D4.

[137] S/Res/770 (1992). The resolution was adopted by twelve votes in favor and three abstentions (China, India, and Zimbabwe).

amounted to a "threat to international peace and security," the Council was likewise "deeply concerned" by the reports of abuses against civilians. An examination of the debates surrounding the adoption of this resolution brings out two points: First, there was no doubt that the resolution properly authorized the use of force; second, the commission of atrocities was foremost in the minds of the delegates and was thus a powerful motivation for their vote. It is thus abundantly clear from the debates that the Council members endorsed the doctrine of humanitarian intervention.[138]

The following year, the Security Council was faced with the failure of several efforts directed at protecting Bosnian Muslim populations. On October 9, 1993, the Council imposed a "no-fly" zone over Bosnia in order to prevent Serbian assaults from obstructing transfer of humanitarian aid supplies.[139] When this proved difficult to enforce, the Security Council went one step further and authorized member states to take "all necessary measures in the airspace of the Republic of Bosnia and Herzegovina in the event of further violations to ensure compliance with the ban on flights."[140] Here the Council made reference to Resolution 770, and here again, there was wide agreement on the need to put an end, by force if necessary, to the victimization that (for the most part) Bosnian Serbs were inflicting on civilian populations.[141] In pursuance of both these resolutions, NATO air forces conducted a series of bombings and other forms of military action against Bosnian Serb positions. Partly

---

[138] See, inter alia, the statements by representatives of Ecuador (Security Council authorizes states to use force to ensure delivery of humanitarian assistance), U.N. S.C.O.R. (provisional), S/PV.3106, at 9; and India (desperate plight of the population demands urgent response which cannot exclude use of force), id., at 11–15. Even delegates who were skeptical about authorizing individual states to act (as opposed to undertaking a collective United Nations effort) conceded that the situation warranted the use of force. See, e.g., the statement by the delegate of Zimbabwe, id., at 14–17.

[139] S.C. Res. 781, U.N. Doc. S/Res/781. See generally T. McIlmail, "No-Zones: The Imposition and Enforcement of Air Exclusion Regimes Over Bosnia and Iraq," 17 Loy. L.A. Int'l & Comp. L.J. 35 (1994).

[140] S.C. Res 816, U.N. Doc. S/Res/816, at 4. This resolution was adopted by fourteen votes in favor and one abstention (China).

[141] See, inter alia, the statements by delegates from the U.S. (international community resolved to enforce S.C. resolutions against those who commit unspeakable violations of human rights) U.N. S.C.O.R. (provisional), S/PV.3191 (Mar. 31, 1993), at 19–21; France (use of force authorized to enforce flight bans), id., at 3–5; Cape Verde (S.C. must use its authority to put an end to the tragedy of the Bosnian people), id., at 13–15; and Pakistan (citing abhorrent campaign of "ethnic cleansing").

as a result of the NATO demonstrations, the warring parties initiated peace negotiations which concluded in the accord signed in Paris in December 1995.

The intervention by NATO can be explained in part as a humanitarian effort, that is, as an action undertaken by the military alliance and authorized by the United Nations with the purpose of putting an end to the intolerable human rights violations that were taking place in that war. While the initial U.N. authorization to use air power seemed to be limited to securing the delivery of humanitarian assistance and the enforcement of the "no-fly" zone, the intervention by NATO far exceeded those limited purposes. Indeed, the strongest action by NATO took place as a response to the Bosnian Serb shelling of a Sarajevo market that killed 37 people.[142] A few days before that, the U.N. Rapid Reaction Force on Mount Igman outside Sarajevo had turned its heavy 155mm guns on the Serbs.[143]

The incident illustrates the difficulties of insisting upon the neutrality or impartiality of humanitarian actions. This concept, as used by relevant actors and observers, is highly ambiguous in contexts such as Bosnia. For there (as in most cases) the prospective intervenor faces two types of problems. One is what we could call the *territorial* issue, that is, the merits of the dispute. What is the relevant merit of the claims put forth by the different groups? Who has the right to what part of the territory? Is secession justified? These are difficult questions and it is certainly the case that anyone contemplating intervention must be neutral or impartial as to them. The second kind of problem is the one posed by human rights violations, including the violations of humanitarian law and the practice of "ethnic cleansing." As to this issue, there is no such thing as neutral or impartial humanitarian intervention, nor should there be. The intervention must target the culprits, whoever they are, and force them to desist. If there are culprits on both sides, then both must

---

[142] The market shelling occurred on August 28, 1995, followed by more than sixty NATO planes, along with U.N. Rapid Reaction Force artillery, attacking Serb targets on August 30th and 31st. *See* "Chronology of Conflict in Former Yugoslavia," *supra* n. 132.

[143] Id. This operation by the U.N. forces was expressly authorized by the U.N. Secretary-General. *See* "U.N. Orders Its Troops to Act," *N.Y. Times,* Aug. 29, 1995, at A10.

be stopped. Thus supporters of neutrality and impartiality cannot legitimately mean that torturers and their victims count the same as to that
issue, the issue of torture. Maybe they both must be heard on the territorial question, yet the flaw in the traditional United Nations "peacekeeping" approach (and the reason why it has been relatively ineffective) is
the insistence upon neutrality and impartiality between the abusers and
their victims. The logic of the situation in Bosnia forced the intervenors
to ignore directives on impartiality and to take sides, decisively and in
my view correctly, in defense of the victims. Such an action need not
prejudge the merits of the dispute (although in some cases, it can be
argued that perpetrators of crimes against humanity should lose their
normal right to participate in the process of self-determination). Like
other similar events, the intervention in Bosnia was *overdetermined*,
because it could be easily justified as an action both to restore peace
and to stop the atrocities that had been so well documented. The human
rights situation in Bosnia was a chief rationale for the intervention; it
also greatly increased the *urgency* for collective action.

CHAPTER 10

HUMAN RIGHTS AND HUMANITARIAN INTERVENTION IN THE WORLD COURT: THE *NICARAGUA* DECISION

I. INTRODUCTION

Until recently, no international court had dealt extensively with a case involving the principles of nonintervention, nonuse of force, and human rights.[1] On June 27, 1986, the International Court of Justice decided the case of *Military and Paramilitary Activities in and against Nicaragua (Merits)*.[2] We have already examined the status of humanitarian intervention under the United Nations Charter and post–1945 state practice, in the light of the moral-political theory developed in the first chapters of the book. The legal analysis would not be complete without an assessment of the impact of the *Nicaragua* judgment on the doctrine of humanitarian intervention. The Court dealt only incidentally with humanitarian intervention. However, the Court's pronouncement on controversial and largely unresolved issues of international law have

---

[1] The only previous occasion in which the International Court of Justice addressed human rights issues is the justly famous *Namibia* advisory opinion. *See* 1971 *I.C.J. Rep.* 6, 57. As to use of force, in the *Corfu Channel* case, 1949 *I.C.J. Rep.* 5, discussed it only incidentally. The often-quoted passage against intervention refers to the narrow issue of armed intervention to gather evidence for judicial proceedings. Id. at 35. *See* the discussion *supra,* Chapter 7.

[2] Case of Military and Paramilitary Activities in and Against Nicaragua (*Nicaragua v. United States of America*), Merits, Judgment of June 27, 1986, 1986 *I.C.J. Rep.* 14 (*hereinafter Judgment*).

undoubtedly had an impact in the development of the law of use of force, including humanitarian intervention. That impact (whether a result of acceptance or rejection of the Court's reasoning) is magnified by the far-reaching political and philosophical implications of the ruling.

The judgment and the dissents[3] deal for the most part with the main claim put forth by the United States—that the United States, in helping Nicaraguan rebels, was acting in collective self-defense to counter the help provided by the Sandinista regime to the Salvadoran rebels.[4] The controversial argument of the Court rejecting the United States claim of self-defense has stirred heated controversy among commentators and governments.[5] Here, however, I only examine the Court's views on the lawfulness of intervention to protect human rights. The Court held specifically with regard to humanitarian intervention:

---

[3] Judges Schwebel, Oda, and Jennings filed dissenting opinions. Voting majorities were different for each issue. Both the *dispositifs* regarding the U.S. violations of the principles of nonintervention and nonuse of force, however, were adopted by twelve votes to three (the judges mentioned above dissenting). Judgment, *supra* n. 2, at 146–150.

[4] The U.S. withdrew from the proceedings after the Court rendered its judgment on jurisdiction. *See* Military and Paramilitary Activities in and Against Nicaragua (*Nicaragua v. U.S.*), Jurisdiction of the Court and Admissibility of the Application, 1984 *I.C.J. Rep.* 392 . . . *See* Statement on the U.S. Withdrawal from the Proceedings Initiated by Nicaragua in the International Court of Justice, reprinted in 26 *I.L.M.* 246 (1985). Article 53 of the Court's Statute provides that the Court has to satisfy itself that the claim of the party appearing is well-founded in fact and law. In the present judgment, the Court had to be apprised of the U.S. views in ways not provided by the rules of the Court. *See* Judgment, *supra* n. 2, at 23–26.

[5] The Court held, *inter alia*, that the United States could not justify its forcible actions by invoking the customary right of self-defense because:

(i) The acts that Nicaragua had allegedly committed against El Salvador did not amount to "armed attack," which is a requirement to trigger the right of self-defense also in customary law, *i.e.*, besides art. 51 of the Charter;

(ii) Customary law does not recognize a right of a third state to adopt proportionate countermeasures in aid of the state who is victim of indirect aggression (i.e. short of armed attack) by another state. Thus the United States could not rely on a right of "collective countermeasures" analogous to the right of collective self-defense.

See Judgment, *supra* n. 2, at 98–106, 118–123. Judge Schwebel vigorously criticized the Court's confinement of the customary right of self-defense to reaction against a very narrowly defined "armed attack." *See* Judgment (Schwebel, S., dissenting), *supra* n. 2, at 331–381.

See also the scholarly contributions collected in Maier (ed.), *Appraisals of the I.C.J.'s Decision: Nicaragua v. United States (Merits),* 81 *Am. J. Int'l L.* 77 (1987).

[T]he use of force could not be the appropriate method to monitor or ensure . . . respect [for human rights]. With regard to the steps actually taken, the protection of human rights, a strictly humanitarian objective, cannot be compatible with the mining of ports, the destruction of oil installations, or again with the training, arming, and equipping of the *contras*. The Court concludes that the argument derived from the preservation of human rights in Nicaragua cannot afford a legal justification for the conduct of the United States, and cannot in any event be reconciled with the legal strategy of the respondent State, which is based on the right of collective self-defense.[6]

More generally, the Court held that the United States, by *all* the acts in support of the Nicaraguan rebels, ranging from training and arming to mere encouragement, breached its customary obligation not to intervene in the affairs of another state. The Court also held that by those acts of intervention that amount to use of force, the United States breached the customary principle of nonuse of force.[7] The Court discussed and rejected the United States' possible argument, mainly

---

[6] Judgment, *supra* at 134–135.

[7] The relevant *dispositifs* read as follows:

". . . . THE COURT . . .

(3)   By twelve votes to three,

Decides that the United States of America, by training, arming, equipping, financing and supplying the *contra* forces or otherwise encouraging, supporting and aiding military and paramilitary activities in and against Nicaragua, has acted, against the Republic of Nicaragua, in breach of its obligation under customary international law not to intervene in the affairs of another State. . . .

(4)   By twelve votes to three,

Decides that the United States of America, by certain attacks on Nicaraguan territory in 1983–1984 . . . and further by those acts of intervention referred to in subparagraph (3) hereof which involve the use of force, has acted, against the Republic of Nicaragua, in breach of its obligation under customary international law not to use force against another State. . . .

(6)   By twelve votes to three,

Decides that, by laying mines in the internal or territorial waters of the Republic of Nicaragua during the first months of 1984, the United States of America has acted, against the Republic of Nicaragua, in breach of its obligations under customary law not to use force against another State, not to intervene in its affairs, not to violate its sovereignty and not to interrupt peaceful maritime commerce. . . ."

Judgment, *supra* n. 2, at 146–150.

grounded in formal findings by the United States Congress,[8] that its actions were justified as steps to protect democracy and human rights in Nicaragua.[9]

In accordance with the conclusions of preceding chapters, I argue that the Court's *holding* on the question of humanitarian intervention, inasmuch as it has precedential value, must be read narrowly. The holding should be interpreted as declaring only the illegality of *disproportionate forcible intervention to restore democracy*. While the Court's language is broad, the opinion should be read in close connection to the particular facts of the case, and therefore as addressing neither the issue of the legality of intervention in cases of more serious and widespread human rights violations, nor that of non-forcible proportionate countermeasures to enforce human rights.[10] I also suggest that part of the Court's *reasoning* and some of its *findings* should be rejected as being out of touch with contemporary international law. I first examine the Court's definition of unlawful intervention. I conclude that while that definition is generally adequate, it suffers from some inherent ambiguities. Section II addresses the problem of the ends of intervention. I argue that the Court's views on the scope of domestic jurisdiction and the legal force of Nicaragua's commitments to democracy are deeply mistaken. In Section III I discuss the Court's views on humanitarian intervention.

---

[8] *See* H.R. Rep. No. 99–237, 99th Cong., 1st. Sess, at 63–73 (1985).

[9] Judgment, *supra* n. 2, at 130–135. Since the U.S. did not put forth a humanitarian intervention argument during the jurisdictional proceedings, there was an issue whether the Court should consider it *ex officio*. In its discussion of the legal effect of the U.S. withdrawal, the Court correctly observed that it was not "solely dependent on the argument of the parties before it with respect to the applicable law." Id. at 24–25. Later, however, it contradicted itself by citing as a reason for dismissing the humanitarian intervention argument the fact that "it was not part of the legal strategy of respondent." Id. at 134–135.

[10] As far as I know, prior to the ruling on the merits, Professor D'Amato was the only scholar to suggest that U.S. policy toward Nicaragua could only be justified on human rights considerations. *See* D'Amato, "*Nicaragua* and International Law: The "Academic" and the Real," 79 *Am. J. Int'l L.* 657, 659–61 (1985). There, he wrote:

> How enlightened it would have been for the International Court of Justice to hear arguments addressed to this question [human rights in Nicaragua], rather than to the spurious ones that filled the voluminous documents presented to the Court by both parties!

Now finally the Court has addressed such issues. Unfortunately, we cannot say that the Court was enlightened.

A preliminary matter needs attention here. There have been sugges-tions about the Court's possible political bias against the United States.[11] Judge Schwebel seemed to harbor doubts in that regard.[12] Judges Nagen-dra Singh and Lachs unprecedentedly attempted to reassure the readers about the absence of any bias.[13] The Court's arguments, however, should be examined on their merits. The positivist and state-centered philosophy espoused by the Court enjoys considerable popularity among governments and commentators. This seems to suggest that the decision was not prompted by political aversion toward the United States, but rather by a true belief in the arguments the Court marshals. In other words, *it is the Court's legal theory that is questionable.* Conse-quently, the targets of any critique should be the Court's myopic views on human rights and on the value of democratic commitments in the Americas, views that are the natural consequence of the Court's unfet-tered deference to state sovereignty and to the alleged "rights" of dicta-tors. Absent some clear indication of impropriety (for example, that the judges are receiving instructions from governments), the conspiracy method of second-guessing the judges on their supposedly undisclosed political purposes should be avoided.[14]

In order to fully understand what the Court said about forcible hu-manitarian intervention, several intermediate steps in the Court's rea-soning need to be examined. I will first discuss the Court's general definition of unlawful intervention. The Court's view of the scope of Nicaragua's human rights commitments will be subsequently discussed, followed by a review of the Court's scheme of degrees of coercion in international law.

---

[11] The problem of bias was discussed before the Court handed down its decision on the merits. Cf. Franck, "Icy Day at the ICJ," 79 *Am. J. Int'l L.* 379, 382 (1984) (arguing that the Court's finding of jurisdiction, while supported by weak arguments, cannot be regarded as biased) with Reisman, "Has the International Court Exceeded Its Jurisdiction?," 80 *Am. J. Int'l L.* 128, 134 (1985) (Court's image of probity seri-ously injured).

[12] *See* Judgment (Schwebel, S., dissenting) *supra* n. 2, at 133–134 (Court's accep-tance of Nicaraguan false testimony); and at 320–321 (title of the case biased).

[13] *See Judgment, supra* n. 2, at 156–157 (Nagendra Singh, sep. opinion) (judgment of the Court rendered "with utmost sincerity"); and id. at 158–161 (Lachs M., sep. opinion) (deploring, with abundant quotations from U.S. Supreme Court Justices, U.S. withdrawal because of reluctance to present sensitive materials to Communist judges).

[14] On conspiracy theories in international law, *see* Tesón, "International Human Rights and Cultural Relativism," 25 *Va. J. Int'l L.* 869, 896–97 (1985).

II. THE DEFINITION OF UNLAWFUL INTERVENTION

As I pointed out in Chapter 7, defining the notion of intervention in international law has proved quite difficult.[15] The main reason for that difficulty is the fundamental ambiguity of the term "intervention." The word is used first in a descriptive sense, to denote vaguely certain events—a state interfering in the affairs of another. But "intervention" is also used normatively with the implication that the facts referred to possess some negative legal or moral quality.[16] "Intervention," like other words such as "democracy" or "science," is thus an emotionally loaded word. Unlike the other two, however, it carries an unfavorable connotation. Thus when a writer tries to persuade the reader that such and such conduct is "really" intervention, he is not just trying to convince the reader that the necessary empirical conditions for the use of the word are present. In addition, the writer is condemning that conduct and inviting the reader to do the same. In short, he is formulating what the philosopher Charles Stevenson called a *persuasive* definition.[17] As

---

[15] The literature on intervention is voluminous. *See generally*, in addition to references in Chapter 7, A. Thomas & A. J. Thomas, *Nonintervention* (1956); R. J. Vincent, *Nonintervention and International Order* (1974); *Intervention in World Politics* (H. Bull ed., 1984); H. Lauterpacht, *International Law and Human Rights* 167–170 (1950); Moore, "Toward an Applied Theory for the Regulation of Intervention," in *Law and Civil War in the Modern World* 3 (J. N. Moore ed., 1974) and references therein; id., "Legal Standards for Intervention in Internal Conflict," 13 *Ga. J. Int'l & Comp. L.* 191 (1983); Rosenau, "The Concept of Intervention," 22 *J. Int'l Aff.* 165 (1968); Bos, "Intervention and International Law," 25 *Int'l Spectator* 69 (1971); Briggs, "Intervention and the Inter-American Rule of Law," 53 *Am. J. Int'l L.* 873 (1959); Constantopoulos, " 'Droit d'intervention' des Etats membres des Nations Unies," 1965 *Annuario di Diritto Internazionale* 27; Falk, "The United States and the Doctrine of Nonintervention in the Internal Affairs of Independent States," 5 *How. L. J.* 163 (1959); Farer, "The Regulation of Foreign Intervention in Civil Armed Conflict," 142 *R.C.A.D.I.* 291 (1974); id., "Harnessing Rogue Elephants-A Short Discourse on Foreign Intervention in Civil Strife," 82 *Harv. L. Rev.* 511 (1969); Friedmann, "Intervention in International Law," 25 *Int'l Spectator* 40 (1971); Komarnicki, "L'intervention en droit international moderne," 60 *Revue générale de droit international public* 521 (1956); Paust, "Conflicting Norms of Intervention: More Variables for the Equation," 13 *Ga. J. Int'l & Comp. L.* 305 (1985); Schwenninger, "The 1980s: New Doctrines of Intervention or New Norms of Non-Intervention," 33 *Rutgers L. Rev.* 423 (1981); and Wright, "The Legality of Intervention Under the U.N. Charter," 51 *A.S.I.L. Proc.* 79 (1957). The classic pre-1945 monograph is E. Stowell, Intervention in International Law (1923).

[16] *See* W. O'Brien, *U.S. Military Intervention: Law and Morality* 15 (1979)

[17] *See* C. Stevenson, *Ethics and Language* ch. 9 (1944); and R. Hare, *The Language of Morals* 119 (1952).

a result, the debate is obscured by the uncertainty about when the word is used in its descriptive sense or when it is instead implying a normative disapproval. A second source of confusion is that even if there is agreement that the word is being used descriptively, controversy persists about the events to which we intend to apply the word "intervention." Especially arduous has been the debate on whether the use or threat of force is inherent in intervention.[18] A further uncertainty surrounds the question of what matters are the ones targeted by acts of unlawful intervention.[19] The word "intervention" thus suffers from both *connotative* and *denotative* uncertainty.

Once these linguistic confusions have been exposed, it is clear that the final objective should be to reach a normative definition of intervention. Our purpose is not to determine what conducts "essentially" amount to intervention but rather what kinds of conduct, from a legal standpoint, constitute *unlawful* intervention. Yet in doing this it is important to put forth some descriptive definition of "intervention" and proceed from there to define those subsets which ought to be considered as inconsistent with international law.[20] One can say that all intervention is prohibited and then proceed to list instances of intervention

---

[18] The U.N. work in this area has contributed to the confusion. *See,* e.g., The Declaration on the Inadmissibility of Intervention in the Domestic Affairs of States and the Protection of Their Independence and Sovereignty, G.A. Res. 2131, 20 U.N. G.A.O.R. Supp. No. 14 at 12, U.N. Doc. A/6220 (1965) (including economic, political "or any other type of measures" to coerce states as part of the definition of intervention). Cf. Lillich, "Forcible Self-Help by States to Protect Human Rights," 53 *Iowa L. Rev.* 325, 330 (1967) (hereinafter "Forcible Self-Help") (excluding from intervention "permissible techniques of coercion short of use of force"); Stowell, "La théorie et la pratique de l'intervention," 40 *R.C.A.D.I. 91,* 92 (1932–II) (lawful intervention defined as the legal use of force to enforce international law) and Joyner & Grimaldi, "The United States and Nicaragua: Reflections on the Lawfulness of Contemporary Intervention," 25 *Va. J. Int'l L.* 621, 625–26 and n. 18 (1985) (asserting that while the U.N. organs seem to have included economic and diplomatic coercion as part of "intervention," the use of force is inherent in the nonintervention rule). For Oppenheim's classical definition, *see infra,* text accompanying nn. 33–39.

[19] *See infra,* text accompanying nn. 25–32.

[20] Professor Rosalyn Higgins has recently suggested that trying to find a definition of intervention is not a profitable task. She correctly observes that we are dealing with a spectrum which ranges from very mild forms of interference to military intervention, and that not every maximalist intervention is unlawful and not every minimalist interference is lawful. Higgins, "Intervention in International Law," in *Intervention in World Politics* 29, 30 (H. Bull ed., 1984). From this it does not follow, however, that we lawyers should give up the search for principled appraisal of that spectrum, even if we cannot "indicate a particular point in the spectrum and assert that everything from there onwards is unlawful."

(which by definition are unlawful). Or one can stipulate instead that the word "intervention" descriptively *denotes* certain kinds of conduct, and then characterize a subset as unlawful. The second method merely subdivides the denotation of the word "intervention" into permitted and prohibited conduct. Of course, which method one follows depends on a verbal choice.[21]

In a descriptive, presystematic sense, intervention may be defined as pressure exerted by a state over another in order to coerce the latter to do or to abstain from doing something.[22] Thus the element that distinguishes intervention from ordinary diplomatic action is the presence of coercion. The definition says nothing about the nature of the means used to coerce, nor about the conduct upon which the intervenor seeks to exercise influence.[23] More importantly, the definition says nothing about instances of *lawful* coercive action. There are situations where a state or a group of states may lawfully put coercive pressure on another state.[24] Accordingly, we must define the subset of *unlawful* interventions—we must pass from the descriptive to the normative stage. The aim is to identify what conduct encompassed by the general descriptive definition must be normatively characterized as prohibited.

The Court attempted this difficult task by suggesting two variables to define the content of unlawful intervention. I explored those two

---

[21] As Professor Lillich observes, the choice depends only on one's "conceptual preference." Lillich, "Forcible Self-Help," *supra* n. 18, at 330–31.

[22] This presystematic notion is still broader than the definition found in the dictionary:

> *Intervene:* . . . to interfere usually by force or threat of force in another nation's internal affairs, especially to compel or prevent action or to maintain or alter a condition.

Webster Seventh Collegiate Dictionary, at 443. This definition already incorporates forceful means and presupposes that the affairs are "internal."

[23] Professor Lillich, for example, limits the use of the word "intervention" as a term of art to designate "forceful coercive measures designed to maintain or alter the political situation in another state." Lillich, "Forcible Self-Help," *supra* n. 18, at 330. Yet an examination of U.N. materials shows that intervention also includes coercion in respect to the external affairs of states. See the U.N. Declaration on Intervention, supra n. 18.

[24] For example, under Articles 41 and 42 of the U.N. Charter the Security Council can call for a number of coercive measures (both forcible and non-forcible) against delinquent states. Many other examples may be found in customary and treaty law. *See generally* Farer, "Political and Economic Coercion in Contemporary International Law," 79 *Am. J. Int'l L.* 405 (1985).

variables in Chapter 7, and I briefly summarize them here. The first variable refers to the *choices* of the target state that foreign pressure seeks to influence. The second refers to the *means* used by the intervenor to influence those choices. Intervention is unlawful, says the Court, when the two following conditions are met. First, the choices that are under pressure are those that under international law states are *free* to make, such as the choice of their cultural, political, or economic system. Second, the means used by the intervenor are coercive, such as, but not limited to, the use of military force. It is important to emphasize that under the Court's theory *both* elements have to be present:

> A prohibited intervention must . . . be one bearing on matters in which each State is permitted, by the principle of State sovereignty, to decide freely. One of these is the choice of a political, economic, social and cultural system, and the formulation of foreign policy. Intervention is wrongful when it uses methods of coercion in regard to such choices, which must remain free ones. The element of coercion, which defines, and indeed forms the very essence of, prohibited intervention, is particularly obvious in the case of an intervention which uses force, either in the direct form of military action, or in the indirect form of support for subversive or terrorist armed activities within another State.[25]

Thus, if the choices under pressure do not fall within the category of free choices then the pressure will not amount to unlawful intervention.[26] Conversely, if the means used to exert pressure are not coercive, then again there will be no unlawful intervention.[27] However, there are

---

[25] Judgment, *supra* n. 2, at 107–108.

[26] Analogously, Verdross defined unlawful intervention "as taking place when a State threatens another with an evil if the latter refuses to yield on a matter which international law leaves to its exclusive jurisdiction." A. Verdross, *Völkerrecht* 203 (1937), cited by Lauterpacht, *supra* n. 15, at 168.

[27] Governments sometimes use the word "intervention" to complain against "violations" of the first requirement, *i.e.*, that the matter intervened with falls within their exclusive domestic jurisdiction. For example, the Soviet Government denies the right of human rights critics to "intervene" in what it regards as Soviet domestic affairs, although obviously those critics are not using any coercive means. *See* Schreman, "Gorbachev Meets the Press: A Bantering Style and an Echo of Khrushchev," *N.Y. Times,* Oct. 5, 1985, at 4. Article 2(7) of the Charter seems to use the word in this non-technical sense. *See generally* Gilmour, "The Meaning of 'Intervene' Within Article 2(7) of the United Nations Charter—An Historical Perspective," 16 *Int'l & Comp. L.Q.* 330 (1967).

two key concepts whose ambiguity carries over to the Court's definition. The first is "free choice"; the second, "coercive means."[28] In ordinary language, "free choice" may mean a choice that states are *permitted* to make under international law (normative "freedom") or a choice that states can *in fact* make (factual "freedom"). The crucial meaning is the normative one. The Court is concerned, not about what choices are in fact available to states, but what choices instead legally *ought* to be available to them. Yet the factual meaning of "freedom" bears upon the second ambiguous expression—"coercive means." The Court says that coercive means include not only the use of force, but *all other forms of pressure which turn an originally free choice into an unfree one*. This derives from the Court's phrasing ("The element of coercion . . . *is particularly obvious* in the case of an intervention that uses force"[29]). This suggests that pressure may be coercive even in cases where force is not used. In the view of the Court, then, the criterion to label a particular conduct as coercive is its aptitude to thwart the factual "freedom" of the target state. And the intervention will be unlawful if that factual "freedom" corresponds also to *normative* "freedom," that is, if international law grants discretion to the state with regard to that conduct. In addition to the direct and indirect use of force, the Court held that "coercion" included non-forcible acts such as funding and encouraging rebels,[30] although, surprisingly, not economic sanctions.[31]

What remains unclear is the point at which the means used by the intervenor cease to be coercive—when intervention becomes ordinary diplomacy.[32] The Court's refusal to equate "coercive" with "forcible" is crucial to its argument. It entails the conclusion that a state may

---

[28] I attempt here a purely terminological clarification. For a full philosophical critique of the notion of "free" choice, *see infra,* Chapter 3.

[29] *See supra,* text accompanying n. 25.

[30] *See infra,* nn. 119–121.

[31] Judgment, *supra* n. 2, at 125–126. *See infra,* nn. 115–118.

[32] The Court cautiously warned that it would "define only those aspects of the principle [of nonintervention] that appear relevant to the resolution of the dispute." Judgment, *supra* n. 2, at 107–108. As we will see, this apears to be inconsistent with the Court ruling that the United States' mere "encouragement" of the Nicaraguan rebels was in violation of the principle of nonintervention. The only possible, albeit unlikely, interpretation is that because rebels are committed to overthrow the government by violence (a coercive course of action) *any* support for rebels, even moral support, is coercive. *See infra,* text accompanying nn. 112–113.

violate the principle of nonintervention even if it does not violate the principle of nonuse of force. Conversely, a conduct may violate the latter and yet not violate the nonintervention principle. As we shall see, the Court defended the controversial proposition that non-forcible aid to the *contras* was contrary to international law even if did not, and could not, violate the prohibition of use of force.

It might be useful to compare the Court's definition with the classical definition formulated by Oppenheim and adopted by most scholars. According to this standard view, intervention is "dictatorial interference by a State in the affairs of another State for the purpose of maintaining or altering the actual condition of things."[33] This is not yet a definition of *unlawful* intervention, but just a descriptive definition. This is shown by the immediately following passage:

> Such intervention can take place by right or without a right. . . .
> That intervention is, as a rule, forbidden by International Law . . . , there is no doubt. On the other hand, there is just as little doubt that this rule has exceptions, for there are interventions which take place by right, and there are others which, although they do not take place by right, are nevertheless permitted by International Law.[34]

Oppenheim thus defines "intervention" as coercive interference in another state's affairs. For him too, coercive means are not limited to forceful means. Along the same lines, Lauterpacht explains that intervention "implies a peremptory . . . . demand which, if not complied with, involves a threat or recourse to compulsion, though not necessarily physical compulsion, in some form."[35] When the means are noncoercive, Oppenheim refers to "interference pure and simple."[36] He

---

[33] 1 L. Oppenheim, International Law 305 (H. Lauterpacht ed., 1955). *See also* R. Monaco, Manuale di Diritto Internazionale Publico 419 (1960); C. Arellano Garcia, Derecho Internaçional Publico 465–66 (1983). Cf. the discussion of the meaning of "intervention" in art. 2(7) of the U.N. Charter in H. Lauterpacht, *supra* n. 15, at 166–73, and Gilmour, *supra* n. 27.

[34] Oppenheim, *supra* n. 33, at 305.

[35] Lauterpacht, *supra* n. 15, at 167. In the same sense, *see* Reisman, "Humanitarian Intervention to Protect the Ibos," in *Humanitarian Intervention and the United Nations* 167, 169, n. 42 (R. Lillich ed., 1973); Arellano Garcia, *supra* n. 33, at 466; and M. Ganji, *International Protection of Human Rights* 14–15 (1962).

[36] *See* Oppenheim, *supra* n. 33, at n. 1.

acknowledges that intervention, i.e., coercive interference, while illegal as a rule, may on occasion be undertaken "by right" or be otherwise permitted by international law.[37] Thus Oppenheim shares the Court's requirement that the means must be coercive for the intervention to be unlawful. But Oppenheim's definition does not expressly replicate the Court's requirement that the choices interfered with must be those that international law reserves to the states' domestic jurisdiction. It refers only to "altering or maintaining the actual condition of things." Oppenheim's definition is descriptive, as shown by the immediately following discussion of intervention "by right" and "permitted by international law." There he stresses that the intervention will *not* be unlawful if the matter interfered with does not fall within the state's *domaine reserve.*[38] For Oppenheim the word "intervention" descriptively denotes a certain state of affairs (coercive interference in other state's conduct); it does not yet address its legal status. Oppenheim's terminological scheme, then, is as follows. The *genus* is "interference," which means any pressure exerted by a state upon another for the purpose of influencing the latter's conduct. The *species* is "intervention," which denotes the subclass of "interferences" characterized by the dictatorial or coercive means of pressure. Where the means are noncoercive, the conduct should be labeled "interference pure and simple." The legal position, in turn, is that intervention may be lawful or unlawful. While the general rule is that intervention (i.e., dictatorial interference) is prohibited, there are a number of exceptions in international law. Most of the exceptions refer to those situations where the matter interfered with is one that no longer falls within the target state's domestic jurisdiction. On the other hand, Oppenheim's definition does not tell us in what cases simple interference would be unlawful. Analogously, the Court cautiously refused to deal with the legal status of simple interference (i.e., pressure through noncoercive means[39]). Yet the Court's definition is in line with scholarly treatment of intervention. Like Oppenheim, the Court identified the two elements of unlawful intervention. A prohibited intervention must be one carried out by coercive means, which include but are

---

[37] Id. Other commentators share Oppenheim's definition while disagreeing with him on the exceptions to the principle. *See,* e.g., R. C. Hingorani, *Modern International Law* 315–29 (1984).

[38] Oppenheim, *supra* n. 33, at 306–320.

[39] *See supra* n. 32.

not limited to, the use of force, and with respect to legally discretionary choices of the target state. It follows that where one of the elements is absent, we are not facing a case of unlawful intervention, even though that conduct may violate some other principle of international law.

What is confusing about the notion of unlawful intervention is that some means are generally prohibited *per se*, that is, without regard in principle for the ends sought. This is the case of the use of military force. Thus, when the Declaration of Principles of International Law Concerning Friendly Relations and Cooperation among States provides, under the heading of intervention, that "armed intervention" is in violation of international law, one is tempted to conclude that this is just a reiteration of the general prohibition of article 2(4) of the Charter.[40] But under Charter and customary law as read by the Court, armed intervention, absent some justification, violates *both* the prohibition of nonuse of force and the principle of nonintervention, for different reasons. In the case of use of armed force to coerce the target state with respect to matters that *do not* fall within the latter's domestic jurisdiction, the correct legal position is that the state that uses force has violated the principle of nonuse of force (absent one of the exceptions), but not the nonintervention principle. This is so because the coerced conduct is not among those that fall within the state's legal discretion.[41] For example, we have seen that some writers have argued that the 1971 Indian intervention in Bangladesh was a violation of article 2(4) of the Charter.[42] Even if this is conceded, under the Court's definition the Indian action to stop the atrocities in East Pakistan can hardly be stigmatized as unlawful *intervention*. The genocide attempted by the Pakistani army against the Bengalis was not a matter in regard to which Pakistan was "free" to act.[43] (That we even speak seriously about a state's "freedom" to commit genocide shows, once more, the ethical ineptness

---

[40] *See Declaration on Principles of International Law Concerning Friendly Relations and Co-operation among States in Accordance with the Charter of the United Nations, Oct. 24, 1970,* G.A. Res. 2625 (XXV), 25 U.N. G.A.O.R., Supp. No. 28 at 121, U.N. Doc. A/8028 (1971), *reprinted* in 9 *I.L.M* 1292 (1970).

[41] Cf. Judgment, *supra* n. 2, at 383 (Schwebel, dissenting) (independently of whether the U.S. has breached the prohibition of use of force, whatever the U.S. may have done, it has not illegally intervened in Nicaragua's affairs). *See infra,* text accompanying n. 49–102.

[42] *Supra,* Chapter 8.

[43] It is for this reason that humanitarian intervention should be discussed as a possible exception to the principle of nonuse of force, rather than as an exception to the

of conventional international legal discourse.[44]) Conversely, a nation's conduct may amount to unlawful intervention and yet not be a violation of the principle of nonuse of force. For example, Soviet pressure upon Poland to dissolve free trade unions may have been unlawful not because the Soviet Union used forcible means—it did not—but because the Soviet pressure was exerted, probably in a coercive manner, with regard to matters that fell exclusively within Poland's *domaine reserv.* The Soviet Union arguably had no *locus standi* with respect to that matter.[45]

To recapitulate this section: there is a *descriptive* definition of "intervention"—coercive pressure exerted by a state in order to force another to make some choices. While intervention thus defined is generally prohibited in international law, there are instances of legitimate intervention. According to the Court, intervention is *unlawful* when the two following conditions are met:

(1) The choices on which pressure is exerted are among those that under international law fall exclusively within the target state's legal discretion—i.e., choices that the state is "free" to make. This makes the *ends* of the intervention illegal.

(2) The *means* used to influence those choices are *coercive* ("coercion . . . forms the very essence of . . . prohibited intervention"[46]). Coercive acts are those that impair the factual freedom of the target state to make choices. They are not limited to the use of force.

---

principle of nonintervention. *See infra,* text accompanying nn. 139–141. *See also* N. Ronzitti, *Rescuing Nationals Abroad and Intervention on Grounds of Humanity* 89–111 (1985). Slightly more merit has the view that India's action in bringing about the independence of Bangladesh (as opposed to just stopping the atrocities) amounted to unlawful intervention.

[44] *See* the discussion *supra,* Chapter 3.

[45] For an articulation of the Soviet reasons for exerting pressure, *see* L. I. Brezhnev, *Report of the Central Committee of the CPSU to the XXVII Congress of the Communist Party of the Soviet Union and the Immediate Tasks of the Party at Home and Foreign Policy* 7–8 (Moscow, Novosti Press Agency, 1981). *See generally* Simes, "Clash over Poland," 46 *Foreign Pol'y* 49, 51 (1982)

[46] *Supra,* text accompanying n. 25.

Stated in these formal terms, the Court's definition is useful, notwithstanding the ambiguities and gaps already described.[47] The Court's initial approach to the notion of intervention helps dissolve the confusion surrounding careless use of the term. It also highlights the importance of distinguishing between the legality of means and the legality of ends in international law. The irksome task is to identify in concrete cases what "choices" fall within the states' domestic jurisdiction and what means of pressure are coercive in relation to those choices. In the following sections I will examine what the Court had to say first about the *ends*, and then about the *means* of intervention.

III. THE COURT'S VIEWS ON HUMAN RIGHTS AND DOMESTIC JURISDICTION

The Court discussed the United States' contention that the Government of Nicaragua had breached commitments to the Nicaraguan people, to the Organization of American States, and to the United States with regard to Nicaraguan domestic policies.[48] These included "questions such as the composition of the government, its political ideology and alignment, totalitarianism, [and] human rights."[49] The Court then made the following general statement:

[These] questions . . . are questions of domestic policy. The Court would not therefore normally consider it appropriate to

---

[47] The gray areas include the legal status of milder, i.e., noncoercive, forms of action that seek nevertheless to influence legally free choices of the target state. Consider the United States' reaction to the appointment of communist cabinet ministers in France in 1981. *See* Goshko, Bush Voices "Concern" about French Cabinet. Administration Statement Expresses Dissapproval, Washington Post, June 25, 1981, at A1. 1. One would think that the United States did not have a right to complain about that, even if the complaint was put forth in the peaceful form of diplomatic notes and official statements. Yet under the Court's theory it seems that this would not amount to prohibited intervention because, unless it contains some ultimatum, a note of protest is the noncoercive means *par excellence.* Thus we are left in the dark, both by Oppenheim and the Court, about the lawfulness of noncoercive "interference," that is, action that seeks to influence (short of coercing) conduct that nevertheless falls exclusively within the target state's domestic jurisdiction. For hypotheses of "minor" intervention, *see* Higgins, *supra* n. 20, at 30–34.

[48] Judgment, *supra* n. 2, at 130–135. For Congress' formal findings that Nicaragua had breached its human rights obligations, *see* H. R. Rep. No. 99–237, *supra* n. 2; the pertinent part of those findings is reproduced in the Court's judgment, at 90–92.

[49] Judgment, *supra* n. 2, at 130.

engage in a verification of the truth of the assertions of this kind. . . . A State's domestic policy falls within its exclusive jurisdiction, provided of course that it does not violate any obligation of international law. Every State possesses a fundamental right to choose and implement its own political, economic, and social systems. Consequently, there would normally be no need to make any inquiries . . . to ascertain in what sense and along what lines has Nicaragua exercised its right.[50]

This paragraph could be read as merely reaffirming the innocuous tautology that a state is free to do what it is free to do. However, the Court goes further. The opinion establishes the *presumption* that human rights and totalitarianism, *inter alia*, are exclusive domestic matters and as such, are shielded in principle from judicial inquiry. The crucial issue becomes whether human rights (and "totalitarianism," insofar as it has human rights implications) fall within Nicaragua's exclusive jurisdiction in the absence of any formal commitments. Addressing itself to the human rights issue, the Court wrote:

Nicaragua is accused by the 1985 finding of the United States Congress of violating human rights. This particular point needs to be studied separately of the question of the existence of a "legal commitment" by Nicaragua toward the Organization of American States to respect these rights; the absence of such a commitment would not mean that Nicaragua could with impunity violate human rights. However, where human rights are protected by international conventions, that protection takes the form of such arrangements for monitoring or ensuring respect for human rights as are provided for in the conventions themselves.[51]

These two portions of the opinion are quite ambiguous. The Court may mean two different things here. On one reading, the Court may be saying that there are no human rights obligations apart from treaty or other formal commitment. This interpretation is suggested by three factors. First, the Court held that human rights fall within the states' domestic jurisdiction unless there is some "obligation of international law"

---

[50] Id. at 130–131.
[51] Id. at 134.

to the contrary.[52] Second, the Court placed strong emphasis on the inexistence of a human rights commitment by Nicaragua, which seems to suggest that where there is no commitment or treaty there are no human rights duties.[53] And finally, the Court held that human rights may only be monitored through treaty mechanisms. Under this interpretation, the reason why the Court thought that Nicaragua could not "with impunity violate human rights" is *not* that there is a customary law of human rights *en dehors* formal commitments, but rather that Nicaragua is bound by the human rights conventions, in particular by the American Convention on Human Rights.[54] Nicaragua thus must observe human rights solely as a matter of treaty obligation.

This position is stunning, at least for those of us who thought that the law of human rights was already part of the *corpus* of international law. It must be emphasized that the Court was not inquiring here about what matters may or may not legally be coerced by foreign *intervention*, armed or otherwise. Rather, the Court denied, as a matter of principle, *its own power* to discuss human rights and totalitarianism because, absent some commitment, they "essentially" fell within the domestic jurisdiction of Nicaragua. If this is what the Court meant, the Court brushed aside one of the most cherished modern conquests of mankind: the notion that governments are *not* free to treat their citizens as they please, even if they are not parties to specific human rights conventions. That view ignores precedent,[55] U.N. practice,[56] regional practice,[57] state

---

[52] *Supra,* text accompanying n. 51.

[53] *See infra,* text accompanying nn. 75–95.

[54] American Convention on Human Rights, Signed Nov. 22, 1969, entered into force July 18, 1978, O.A.S. Treaty Series No. 36, at 1, O.A.S. Off. Rec. OEA/Ser. L/V/II.23 doc. rev. 2.

[55] As Judge Schwebel reminded the Court, the "essentialist" meaning of art. 2(7) was long ago rejected by the Court's own precedent. *See* Nationality Decrees Issued in Tunis and Morocco, *P.C.I.* Series B, No. 4, at 7, 24. *See also* the Namibia opinion, *supra* n. 1, at 16, 57. The Namibia opinion refers only to the binding force of the Charter provisions. The Court is applying instead customary law because the Charter is excluded by the U.S. multilateral treaty reservation. Yet, as indicated in the text, those provisions should be regarded as having created customary obligations.

[56] It has been long recognized, both by the U.N. organs and by an overwhelming majority of scholars, that human rights are not included in the domestic jurisdiction reservation of art. 2(7). *See* M. Rajan, *The Expanding Jurisdiction of the United Nations* 98–123 (1982); R. Higgins, The Development of the International Law Through the Political Organs of the United Nations (1963); and G. J. Jones, *The United Nations and the Domestic Jurisdiction of States* 33–65 (1979).

[57] Regional human rights law has developed now in Europe, Africa, and the Americas. *See* American Convention on Human Rights, *supra* note 54; European Convention

practice,[58] scholarly writing,[59] and world opinion.[60] At the very least, it must be recognized that the human rights provisions of the U.N. Charter,[61] in conjunction with post-1945 state practice, had the effect of generating a *customary* obligation for governments to respect human rights. When seen under the light of the impressive subsequent development of human rights law, the human rights articles of the U.N. Charter constitute a paradigm of the kind of treaty rule defined by the Court in its leading case on custom as a

> norm-creating provision which has constituted the foundation of, or has generated a rule which, while only conventional or contractual in its origin has since passed into the general *corpus* of international law . . . so as to become binding even for countries which have never become parties to the [treaty]. . . . There is no doubt that this process is a perfectly possible one and does from time to time occur.[62]

on Human Rights and Fundamental Freedoms, 213 *U.N.T.S.* 221, 1950 *Gr. Brit. T.S.* No. 71 (Cmd. 8969) (1950); and African Charter on Human Rights and Peoples' Rights, O.A.U. Doc. CAB/LEG/67/3 Rev. 5 (Jan. 1981), reprinted in 31 *I.L.M.* 58 (1982). When one adds the impact of these conventions to the widespread acceptance of the Universal Declaration of Human Rights, there is little doubt about their contribution to the development of customary law on the subject.

[58] States that are bound by specific human rights conventions do not confine their human rights claims to the parties to those conventions. The Helsinki process is a good example. *See generally Human Rights, International Law and the Helsinki Accord* (T. Buergenthal ed., 1977); and Ghebali, "La question des droits de l'homme a la réunion de Madrid sur les suites de la conférence sur la sécurité et la coopération en Europe," 29 *Annuaire Français de Droit International* 59 (1983). *See also* the Carter Administration's offensive on the Soviet human rights' situation in M. McDougal, H. Lasswell & B. Chen, *Human Rights and World Public Order* 186, n. 66 (1980).

[59] *See* the wealth of scholarship accumulated in Center for the Study of Human Rights, *Human Rights: A Topical Bibliography* (1983); Vincent-Daviss, "Human Rights Law: A Research Guide to the Literature-Part I: International Law and The United Nations," 14 *N.Y.U. J. Int'l L. & Pol.* 209 (1981); id., "Part II: International Protection of Refugees," 14 *N.Y.U. J. Int'l L. & Pol.* 487 (1982); id., "Part III: The International Labor Organization and Human Rights," 15 *N.Y.U. J. Int'l L. & Pol.* 211 (1982). For works in languages other then English, *see* the articles listed in *Public International Law* published periodically by the Max Planck Institute.

[60] The successful work and the growth of non-governmental human rights organizations attest to the importance given human rights in world opinion. *See generally* J. Power, *Against Oblivion, Amnesty International's Fight for Human Rights* (1981); and "Rodley, Monitoring Human Rights in the 1980s," in *Enhancing Global Human Rights* (J. Dominguez, N. Rodley, B. Wood & R. Falk eds. 1979)

[61] Arts. 1(3) and 55)

[62] North Sea Continental Shelf *(F.R.G. v. Denmark and the Netherlands)*, Judgment, 1969 *I.C.J. Rep.* 3, 424.

It is hard to think of better examples of norm-creating provisions than articles 1(3) and 55 of the U.N. Charter.[63] Which human rights obligations are imposed upon states by customary law and which are instead only a matter of treaty or other formal commitment is, of course, open to question.[64] Yet the Court's broad assertion is unwarranted and does not represent international law as it stands at present.[65]

The other possible interpretation of these two excerpts is that regardless of the source of human rights obligations, where there is a convention the *protection* of those rights takes the *form* of those arrangements provided for in the convention. This milder interpretation is supported by the encouraging *dicta* that the human rights issue needed to be studied separately from the existence of a legal commitment, and that Nicaragua "could not with impunity violate human rights." Taken together, they may mean that Nicaragua is bound after all by a law of human rights apart from formal commitments. However, the Court concluded that the United States may not demand human rights observance of the Nicaraguan government because the United States is not a party to the human rights conventions.[66] The Court specifically held that with

---

[63] *See generally* Sohn, "The New International Law; Protection of the Rights of Individuals Rather than States," 32 *Am. U. L. Rev.* 1 (1982) (surveying the evolution of human rights law). Cf. the original view set forth in D'Amato, "The Concept of Human Rights in International Law," 82 *Colum. L. Rev.* 1110 (1982) (arguing *inter alia* that because of the generalization of provisions in human rights conventions nations are now customarily entitled to request human rights observance).

[64] In the justly famous *Filartiga* case the U.S. Court of Appeals for the Second Circuit held, *inter alia,* that official torture was prohibited by *customary* international law. *Filartiga v. Pena-Irala,* 630 F.2d 876 (1980). It does not follow, however, that *only* torture is prohibited by customary law, nor that the International Court of Justice, whose function is to decide controversies by applying international law, should be as restrictive when dealing with human rights issues as a domestic court. The latter is subject to varying degrees of constitutional constraints in the interpretation and application of customary international law. *See generally* Lillich, "Invoking International Human Rights Law in Domestic Courts," 54 *U. Cin. L. Rev.* 367 (1985).

[65] The Court should have perhaps first distinguished among the different matters it mentioned (composition of the government, ideology, alignment, and human rights) in order to determine separately which of those fell within Nicaragua's exclusive domestic jurisdiction, instead of preceding the analysis with this unnecessarily broad and unfortunate *dictum.*

[66] The United States has signed, but not yet ratified, a number of human rights conventions, including the American Convention. *See* Message from the President Transmitting Four Treaties Pertaining to Human Rights, S. Exec. Doc. C, D, E & F, 95th Cong., 2d Sess. (1978); and International Human Rights Treaties, Hearings Before the Senate Commission on Foreign Relations, 96th Cong., 1st Sess. (1979).

regard to Nicaragua's political pledge regarding its domestic policies, including human rights, only the O.A.S. organs were entitled to monitor its observance. The Court observed that the mechanisms provided for in the American Convention "have functioned" and that the O.A.S. could have taken action, if it so wished, on the basis of these reports.[67] The human rights conventions to which Nicaragua is a party contain their own mechanisms to monitor human rights compliance; therefore, only the organs established by those mechanisms following the treaty procedures have legal standing to demand observance of human rights by the Nicaraguan government.

This interpretation, while more favorable to the human rights cause than the first one, is still indefensible. It leads to the absurd result that when a state becomes a party to a human rights convention that state is thereafter sheltered from the monitoring mechanisms provided by general international law.[68] Under this backward-looking theory, if a dictatorial government ratifies a human rights treaty, non-parties automatically lose their *locus standi* to request that government to stop ongoing human rights deprivations. Even the parties to the conventions themselves can only request such compliance through the procedures established by the convention, no matter how weak and ineffective. This reasoning was rejected by the U.N. Third Committee and the General

---

[67] Judgment, *supra* n. 2 at 134. The formalism of the Court is evident once more when it asserts that the inter-American mechanisms "have functioned" in the case of Nicaragua, by which obviously the Court means only that the Commission visited Nicaragua and compiled its reports, not that the human rights situation in Nicaragua was improved. For the human rights situation in Nicaragua, *see infra* n. 162 and accompanying text.

[68] Leaving aside for the moment the use of force, these accepted general mechanisms of human rights enforcement include diplomatic pressure (for example, the efforts of Western European democracies and the United States under the Carter Administration to expose the human rights violations of the Argentine military *junta* between 1976 and 1983, *see Nunca Mas: Informe de la Comision Nacional Sobre la Desaparicion de las Personas* (1984) 429–443; for an overview of the Carter initiatives, *see* R. Lillich & F. Newman, *International Human Rights: Problems of Law and Policy* 824–871 (1979); moral and political support for the pro-human rights opposition (recent events in the Philippines and Haiti illustrate both the legitimacy and the effectiveness of support for the pro-human rights forces against dictators. For an attempt to explain the U.S. position, *see* Jacoby, "The Reagan Turnaround on Human Rights," 64 *Foreign Aff.* 1066 (1986); economic sanctions (*see,* e.g., the sanctions adopted against South Africa by Canada, the European Community, and the United States, compiled in 24 *I.L.M.* 1464–1499 (1985); and generally all kinds of proportionate non-armed countermeasures (*see generally* E. Zoller, *Peacetime Unilateral Countermeasures* (1984).

Assembly in the Chilean case. The Chilean representative sought to block U.N. condemnation on the grounds that the only valid mechanisms to monitor human rights in Chile were those provided for by the International Covenant on Civil and Political Rights, to which Chile was a party.[69] The weakness of the Chilean argument resides in the fact that the undisputed object of any human rights convention is to *strengthen* the human rights obligations of the parties. Any interpretation of the conventions that would diminish the obligation of the parties to respect those rights and freedoms or restrict the competence of other organs dealing with human rights would be contrary to their object.[70] Therefore, the United States does not lose its standing to demand compliance from Nicaragua just because Nicaragua is a party to the American Convention on Human Rights.

Another source of concern for those committed to human dignity is the Court's hasty dismissal of the United States' claim that Nicaragua may be *en route* to establishing a totalitarian dictatorship.[71] Yet if the political system described as "totalitarian dictatorship" results in a consistent pattern of gross violations of internationally recognized human

---

[69] Shortly after the Chilean *junta* overthrew and murdered President Allende, the U.N. Commission on Human Rights established an *Ad-Hoc* Working Group to inquire into the Chilean situation. *See* Bossuyt, "The United Nations and Civil and Political Rights in Chile," 27 *I.C.L.Q.* 462, 463 (1978); Schreiber, "La pratique récente des Nations Unies dans le domaine de la protection des droits de l'homme," 1975 *R.C.A.D.I.* 371–76 (1975, II). The representative of Chile challenged the competence of the Working Group, insisting that it was not a state and not a party to the International Covenant on Civil and Political Rights, which Chile had ratified, and that Chile could not accept that bodies extraneous to it should claim to exercise powers not vested in them by the Covenant. *See* U.N. Docs. A/C.3/31/6 of Oct. 27, 1976, and A/C.3/31/ SR.46, at para. 19. That position was rejected in the Third Committee (Bossuyt, *supra,* at 463–66.) and ignored by the General Assembly which routinely acknowledges or commends the group's report in its resolutions condemning the human rights situation in Chile. *See, e.g.,* G.A. Res. 38/102, 38 U.N. G.A.O.R. Supp. No. 47), at 205, 206, U.N. Doc.A/38/47 (1983).

[70] *See* Bossuyt, *supra* n. 69, at 465.

[71] The Court wrote:

[A]dherence by a State to any particular doctrine does not constitute a violation of customary international law; to hold otherwise would make nonsense of the fundamental principle of State sovereignty, on which the whole of international law rests, and the freedom of choice of the political, social, economic and cultural system of a State. Consequently, Nicaragua's domestic policy options, *even assuming that they correspond to the description given of them by the Congress finding* [i.e., totalitarian dictatorship] cannot justify

rights,[72] then that system cannot validly be "chosen" by a state.[73] A state cannot legally "choose" to violate human rights. Most grave is the fact that the Court is not deciding here a legal issue that may be narrowly dependent on the complex Nicaraguan reality. Ignoring its own well-established guidelines of judicial prudence,[74] the Court instead laid down the principle that establishing a "totalitarian dictatorship" is within a state's "free choices," independently of whether or not a particular "totalitarianism" could withstand the human rights test.

IV. NICARAGUA'S COMMITMENT TO DEMOCRACY AND HUMAN RIGHTS

The Court then paused to examine whether Nicaragua may have bound itself by agreement to implement certain domestic policies, including commitments to democracy and human rights.[75] As a matter of

---

on the legal plane the various actions the Respondent complained of.
Judgment, *supra* n. 2, at 133 *(emphasis added)*.

[72] The requirement of a "consistent pattern of gross and reliably attested violations of human rights" as a necessary condition for raising international concern was developed by U.N. practice, starting with the resolution 1503 adopted in 1970 by the U.N. Economic and Social, 48 U.N. ESCOR, Supp. No. 1A, at 8, U.N. Doc. E/4832/Add. 1 (1970).

[73] One could perhaps agree in principle with the Court's assertion if by "totalitarianism" the Court means just a value-charged label for a particular political system or religion, for example, for socialism or the African one-party system or Moslem fundamentalism, and not a system where the government violates internationally recognized human rights. Thus, the U.S.S.R. having a socialist system is of course not unlawful, but the Soviet Government's internment of political dissidents, or the Soviet prohibition of Jewish emigration, are in breach of the U.S.S.R.'s international duties. *See generally* Dinstein, "The International Obligations of the U.S.S.R. in the Field of Human Rights," 15 *Soviet Jewish Aff.* 165 (1985).

[74] The examples of the Court avoiding the formulations of broad principles unnecessary to the disposition of the case at hand are numerous. *See,* e.g., Nuclear Tests *(Australia v. France),* 1974 *I.C.J. Rep.* 253, 263 (avoiding declaratory judgment on lawfulness of nuclear explosions). The Court's frequent use of ellipsis, once criticized by Judge Lauterpacht, was perhaps called for in the *Nicaragua* case. On the Court's use of ellipsis, *see* S. Rosenne, *The Law and Practice of the International Court* 617–18 (1985).

[75] There is no difference, for the purposes of this critique of the judgment, between the obligation to respect human rights and a commitment to install a liberal democracy: the latter is *also* a human rights commitment. Yet whether a government violates just that commitment or engages in more substantial human rights deprivations has crucial consequences in terms of the lawfulness of countermeasures. I address these matters *infra,* text accompanying nn. 134–164.

principle, the Court found no obstacle in international law to prevent a state from making a commitment of this kind.[76] However, the Court regarded Article 3(d) of the O.A.S. Charter as a political rather than a legal undertaking.[77] As a preliminary matter, the presumption should be that provisions inserted in treaties in force must produce some legal effect, and any conclusion to the contrary must be supported by detailed argument, including a review of the *travaux préparatoires* of the O.A.S. Charter and an assessment of the interplay between that provision and the *corpus* of inter-American human rights law.[78] But even conceding that under proper treaty analysis the O.A.S. Charter has not established a definite legal obligation for each American state to have a democratic system, the Court's approach still reveals an alarming insensitivity toward the general purposes and underlying philosophy of the O.A.S. system. Representative democracy has always been a basic purpose of the inter-American system, even before the San José Pact came into existence.[79] The region may be moving toward the creation of a *requirement* of democracy as a condition for full membership, as is the case

---

[76] Judgment, *supra* n. 2, at 131. This concession is of course completely fictitious; to hold otherwise would have been nothing short of extravagant. *See* the Joint Declaration on Fundamental Rights by the EEC Council, Parliament and Commission about democracy and human rights, April 5, 1977, where the Heads of State of the Members of the EEC declared that the respect and preservation of representative Democracy and Human Rights in each of the member states was an essential element of membership in the EEC. 1978 Bull. of the European Community, No. 3, at 5. For a similar requirement in the projected Argentine-Brazilian common market, *see infra* n. 80 and accompanying text. Judge Schwebel recalled that under the Statute of the Council of Europe every Member of the Council "must accept the principle of the rule of law and of the enjoyment by all persons within its jurisdiction of human rights and fundamental freedoms." Judgment (Schwebel, S., dissenting), *supra* n. 2, at 383.

[77] Judgment, *supra* n. 2, at 126. Article 3(d) reads: "The solidarity of the American States and the high aims which are sought through it require the political organization of those States on the basis of representative democracy."

[78] *See* arts. 31 and 32, Vienna Convention on the Law of Treaties, opened for signature, May 23, 1969, entered into force Jan. 27, 1980, U.N. Conf. on the Law of Treaties, First and Second Sess., U.N. Doc. A/Conf. 39/27, at 289 (1969), *reprinted in* 8 *I.L.M.* 679 (1969).

[79] *See* "American Declaration on the Rights and Duties of Man, Res. XXX of the Ninth International Conference of American States" (1953), reprinted in 1 *Human Rights: The Interamerican System* (T. Buergenthal & R. Norris eds. 1984), part 1, ch. 4, at 1; and the impressive list of human rights-related declarations, resolutions, and recommendations of inter-American conferences and meetings of consultation in id., part 1, Chapter 5, at 1–195, spanning an 80–year period. *See generally* Cabranes, "The Protection of Human Rights by the Organization of American States," 62 *Am. J. Int'l L.* 889 (1968).

today in Western Europe. For example, in a recent unprecedented step, the Presidents of Argentina and Brazil declared that the projected common market will be open only to democratic nations.[80] Treaties provide further evidence that liberal democracy is presupposed in the scheme of human rights protection in the Americas.[81] Liberal democracy is not just one possible system of government among many toward which inter-American institutions are neutral, as would perhaps be the case in other regions of the world.[82] The Court completely failed to account for that general purpose of the inter-American system. The Court retrenched itself behind the formalistic twin distinctions, political intentions *versus* legal undertakings, and binding *versus* non-binding treaty provisions, thus ignoring well-established rules of treaty interpretation.[83] Interestingly enough, Nicaragua only identified *nonintervention* as the basic purpose of the O.A.S. system.[84] Human rights are not mentioned even once.

The decision is also deficient in the treatment of the *specific* acts that might have created an obligation upon the Nicaraguan Government

---

[80] *See* "Latin America's Bold New Partners," *N.Y. Times,* Aug. 12, 1986, at 20. For the liberal tradition in Latin America, *see* Belande, "Human Rights in the Cultural Tradition of Spanish America," 1946 *Annals of the Am. Academy Pol. & Soc. Science* 82. For an overview *see* Sepulveda, "El panorama de los derechos humanos en América Latina. Actualidad y perspectiva," 15 *Boletin Mexicano de Derecho Comparado* 1053 (1982); and T. Buergenthal and D. Shelton, *Protecting Human Rights in the Americas, Selected Problems* (1982).

[81] In addition to article 23 of the American Convention (right to participate in government), there is the requirement that restriction to some rights must be those that are acceptable "in a democratic society." *See,* e.g., arts. 15, 16 and 22, American Convention, *supra* n. 54.

[82] Thus, for example, the American Convention in its Preamble mentions the "framework of democratic institutions" as the necessary background for protecting human rights. Article 23 clearly mandates a Western-type representative democracy. *Supra* n. 54. Cf. the African Charter, where the requirement of democracy is not mentioned in the Preamble. Also, article 13 of the African Charter (right to participate in the government), is much less mandatory and detailed than its inter-American counterpart. *Supra* n. 57.

[83] *See* art. 31 (1), Vienna Convention on the Law of Treaties, *supra* n. 78 (treaties must be interpreted in the light of their object and purpose). The Court, however, did not hesitate to use broad interpretive guidelines in deciding that the U.S. had deprived the Treaty of Friendship, Commerce and Navigation between Nicaragua and the U.S. of its object and purpose. Judgment, *supra* n. 2, at 135–138. *See* the criticism of the Court's misuse of the "object and purpose" rule by Judge Oda, Judgment (Oda, S., dissenting), id. at 249–251.

[84] Nicaraguan memorial (unpublished), at 168–172.

to establish a democratic system based on the respect for human rights.[85] It is well established in the Court's jurisprudence that declarations made by states "by way of unilateral acts . . . may have the effect of creating legal obligations."[86] Nevertheless, the Court concluded that it was "unable to find anything in these documents [the OAS resolution or the Nicaraguan communication] from which it can be inferred that any legal undertaking was intended to exist."[87] The Court's disposition of this issue needs to be quoted *in extenso*:

> Moreover, the Junta made it plain that its invitation to the OAS to supervise Nicaragua's political life should not be allowed to obscure the fact that it was the Nicaraguans themselves who were to decide upon and conduct the country's domestic policy. The resolution of 23 June 1979 also declared that the solution of their problems is a matter "exclusively" for the Nicaraguan people, while stating that the solution was to be based (in Spanish, *debera inspirarse*) on certain foundations which were put forward merely as recommendations to the future government. This . . . is a mere statement which does not comprise any formal offer which if accepted would constitute a promise in law, and hence a legal obligation. Nor can the Court take the view that Nicaragua actually undertook a commitment to organize free elections, and that this commitment was of a legal nature. The . . . Junta . . . planned the holding of free elections . . . , following the . . . [OAS] recommendations . . . [but] . . . [t]his was essentially a political pledge, made not only to the Organization, but to the people of Nicaragua, intended to be its first beneficiaries. But the Court cannot find an instrument with legal force, whether unilateral or synalagmatic, whereby Nicaragua

---

[85] These include the resolution of the XVII Meeting of Consultation of Ministers for Foreign Affairs of the O.A.S., *See Report on the Situation of Human Rights in the Republic of Nicaragua*, OEA/Ser.L/V/II.53, doc. 25 (1981) (hereinafter *O.A.S. Human Rights Rep.)* at 1–3 and the communication of July 12, 1979, sent by the Nicaraguan junta in the aftermath of the victory over the Somoza forces to the O.A.S. Secretary-General. Id. *supra,* n. 2, at 3–7; Judgment, at 88–90. This communication attached a "Plan to Secure Peace" which, among other things, stated the intention of the Nicaraguan Government to respect human rights and govern the country democratically. *O.A.S. Human Rights Rep., supra,* at 5–7; Judgment, *supra* n. 2, at 131.

[86] Nuclear Tests Case, *supra* n. 74, at 267.

[87] Judgment, *supra* n. 2, at 132.

has committed itself in respect of the principle or methods of holding elections.[88]

The Court's formalism here reaches unsurpassed proportions. International commitments, especially in areas so sensitive as those linked to the form of government and domestic policies, rarely take the form of a "formal offer which if accepted would constitute a promise of law." As Judge Ago observed in his concurring opinion (dissenting on this particular point):

> Je ne comprendrais pas en effet que les gouvernements runis a l'O.E.A. aient accept d'adopter une mesure aussi exceptionnelle que le retrait de la rconnaissance d'un gouvernement . . ."lgitime," (i.e., the Somoza Government) sans avoir une solide garantie qu'il serait remplacé par un gouvernement répondant précisément aux caractéristiques définies dans le plan de paix. . . .[89]

Certainly the promises that the Court considered binding in the *Nuclear Tests* case were made in considerable less formal terms than the undertaking of the Nicaraguan Junta.[90] The Court's view that Nicaragua's express consent to O.A.S. recommendations was invalid because it did not comply with imaginary formalities required for synalagmatic compacts or unilateral promises is inconsistent with the Court's liberal approach to consent in other portions of the judgment. Particularly disturbing is the fact that the Court elsewhere in the judgment considered United States or Nicaraguan acquiescence or express consent as

---

[88] Id. (emphasis in the original).

[89] Judgment (Ago, R., sep. opinion), *supra* n. 2, at 18.

[90] The statement by the French President considered binding by the Court read as follows:

> . . . on this question of nuclear tests, you know that the Prime Minister had publicly expressed himself in the National Assembly in his speech introducing the Government's programme. He had indicated that French nuclear testing would continue. I had myself made it clear that this round of atmospheric tests would be the last. . . .

Nuclear Tests, *supra* n. 74, at 266. As Judge Schwebel points out, an international obligation need not be made in a particular form. Judgment (S. Schwebel, dissenting), *supra* n 2., at 384. Thus there is considerable merit to his claim that the successful revolutionaries, by their conduct, assumed an international obligation which the Nicaraguan government later failed to honor. Id.

producing legal effect.[91] The Court's formalistic approach also reveals a serious misunderstanding of the nature and structure of international law.

The Court then assumed *arguendo* that Nicaragua had made a legal and not a political commitment to democracy and free elections. Even then, said the Court, the United States would not have been justified in demanding the fulfillment of that obligation, because the Nicaraguan commitment was made not to the United States but to the Organization of American States, which was alone empowered to demand that fulfillment.[92] This position is simply an unexpected revival of the principle laid down in the Court's infamous 1966 decision on the *South West Africa* cases. Said the Court then:

> [Liberia and Ethiopia's] argument amounts to a plea that the Court should allow the equivalent of an *actio popularis*, or right resident in any member of a community to take legal action in vindication of a public interest. But although a right of this kind may be known to certain municipal systems of law, it is not known to international law as it stands at present.[93]

If the doctrine of that case is rejected, and subsequent developments strongly indicate it should be,[94] and Nicaragua has indeed made a legal commitment to establish a democratic system and observe human rights, then the individual members of the Organization of American States are perfectly entitled to request compliance.[95]

---

[91] *See* Judgment, *supra* n. 2, at 100 (consent of the U.S. to Resolution of Inter-American organizations); and especially at id., 107–108 (consent of U.S. to G.A. resolutions). The Court was even undeterred by the express rejection of the United States of the binding nature of the Resolution on Intervention. Id., at 107. In the jurisdictional phase the Court attached great weight to Nicaragua's "constant acquiescence" as a factor for asserting its own jurisdiction, thus dismissing the rather strong arguments of the United States that Nicaragua had never consented to the jurisdiction of the Court. *See* Nicaragua (jurisdiction), *supra* n. 4, at para. 47. For a sharp critique, *see* Reisman, "Has the International Court Exceeded Its Jurisdiction?," 80 *A.J.I.L.* 128 (1985).

[92] Judgment, *supra* n. 2, at 132–133.

[93] *South West Africa* case (*Liberia & Ethiopia v. S. Africa*), 1966 *I.C.J. Rep.* 6, 47.

[94] *See,* e.g., the Namibia opinion, *supra* n. 1, at 57–58 (apartheid flagrant violation of human rights provisions of U.N. Charter, an illegality which states have the duty to recognize).

[95] *See* Judgment (Schwebel, S., dissenting) *supra* n. 2, at 383. The thrust of the Contadora process clearly confirms this view. *See* the Joint Communique of the Seventh Joint Meeting of the Ministers for Foreign Affairs of the Contadora Group and of the Central American Countries ("there is general recognition that commitments to encour-

The Court's discussion of the human rights issue and the principle of nonintervention reveals a complete adherence by the Court to the Hegelian Myth, that is, the notion that governments deserve protection independently of how they treat their citizens.[96] The Court emphatically asserted that "[e]very State possesses a fundamental right to choose and implement its own political, economic and social systems."[97] When discussing the claim that the Sandinistas were attempting to install a totalitarian dictatorship, the Court said that even if the claim was true, "adherence by a State to any particular doctrine" does not violate international law, and that "to hold otherwise *would make nonsense of the . . . freedom of choice of the political, social, economic and cultural system of a State.*"[98] It is for this reason that intervention is banned. The state has exercised a choice that only the state could exercise, and foreigners do not have a right to interfere with that choice. In fairness to the Court, this type of discourse is fairly common in international law.[99] Yet, as I have tried to show, this idea is indefensible: no meaning can be given to the notion of the state's *freedom* to do something, and especially *to choose* a political system.[100]

A vivid illustration of the Court's endorsement of the Hegelian Myth is shown in its discussion of the meaning of the Sandinistas' pledge to democracy. The Court read the Junta's clarification that "it was the Nicaraguans themselves who were to decide upon . . . the country's domestic policy" as *weakening* the Sandinista pledge to democracy, the implication being that the whole matter fell under Nicaraguan domestic

---

aging democratic institutions are essential factors for peace in the region") and the Contadora Act on Peace and Co-Operation in Central America (Revised Version) (projected commitments on democracy and human rights), 24 *I.L.M.* 187, 188, 191, 195–196 (1985).

[96] *See supra,* Chapter 3.

[97] Judgment, *supra* n. 2, at 130–131. This principle was even exalted by President Nagendra Singh as a "sanctified absolute rule of law." Id. (Nagendra Singh, sep. op.), at 156.

[98] Id., at 133.

[99] *See,* e.g., Declaration of Principles of International Law Concerning Friendly Relations and Cooperation Among States in Accordance with the Charter of the United Nations, G.A. Res. 2625 (XXV), 25 U.N. G.A.O.R., Supp. No. 28, at 121, U.N. Doc. A/8028, (1970). The Court relied exaggeratedly on this non-binding instrument. *See,* e.g., Judgment, *supra* n. 2, at 99–100.

[100] *Supra,* Chapter 3.

jurisdiction.[101] But *that is precisely the content of the undertaking that the United States Congress considered the junta to have violated: that the Nicaraguans themselves must decide upon their domestic policies,* that is, that the government must hold free elections! The declaration by the junta quoted by the Court thus *reinforces* rather than weakens the pledge to democracy and free elections. Denying free elections amounts precisely to denying individuals their right to control their domestic policies. The Court would have been right if the junta had reserved to *itself*, to the government, and not to the *Nicaraguans*, the right to decide upon the country's domestic policies. Here the Court simply confuses government and people—le peuple, c'est moi!

V. THE MEANS OF INTERVENTION: THE POLITICAL SUPPORT FOR REBELS

Before addressing humanitarian intervention proper, we must analyze the Court's general discussion of degrees of coercion in international law—the *means* of intervention. The Court examined and discussed the legality of a whole range of acts performed by the United States to put pressure on the Nicaraguan government. Those acts stretched from mere encouragement of rebels to the use of military force. It will be convenient to examine the Court's views on the legal status of different forms of international pressure in order to place the use of force for human rights purposes in its proper perspective.

To understand the reasoning of the Court, it is crucial to distinguish between three levels of international pressure.[102] First, a state may employ noncoercive means, such as diplomatic notes, to exert pressure on another state. Second, a state may employ coercive yet nonforcible means, such as economic sanctions or funding of rebels. And finally, a state may employ forcible means (which of course are also coercive). In the first case (noncoercive measures), the state will not violate any rule of general international law (apart from specific treaties). In the second case (coercive yet nonforcible measures), the state will violate international law if, and only if, the targeted conduct is one in respect

---

[101] *Supra,* text accompanying n. 88.
[102] *Supra,* text accompanying nn. 15–47.

of which the state is legally free to act. This is a breach of the nonintervention principle.[103] In the last case (use of force) the state will *prima facie* violate the prohibition against the use of force, unless its action falls under one of the recognized exceptions to that prohibition. That state will also violate the principle of nonintervention (in addition to the prohibition against the use of force) if the influenced conduct falls within the scope of legal discretion of the target state.[104]

The mildest means of action is political and moral support for pro-human rights forces. It will be recalled that the Court ruled that all acts by the United States that amounted to "encouraging, supporting and aiding" the rebels in Nicaragua violated the principle of nonintervention.[105] These acts included, but were not limited to, "training, arming, equipping, financing and supplying" the *contra* forces.[106] Thus, the notions of "encouragement, support and aid" are broad and include also moral and political, and not just military, support. We saw that the Court found (mistakenly in my view) that the United States did not have a right to request human rights compliance of Nicaragua.[107] One prong of unlawful intervention, in the eyes of the Court, is thus met. It is therefore crucial for the Court's reasoning to establish that moral and political support is coercive action. If it is found not to be coercive action, then the other prong of the definition of unlawful intervention would not be met.[108]

The Court's hostility toward the moral-political support for rebels can only be explained in conjunction with its ruling on the legal standing of the United States to request human rights compliance.[109] Under the Court's own definition of unlawful intervention, once it has been established that human rights do not fall within the state's domestic jurisdiction, mere demands for human rights compliance do not amount to unlawful intervention. Of course, political support for rebels is not unlawful use of force, because it is not use of force at all. Indeed, as

---

[103] See *supra,* text accompanying nn. 25–32.

[104] See *supra,* text accompanying n. 25.

[105] Judgment, *supra* n. 2, at 146–150.

[106] Id.

[107] See *supra,* text accompanying nn. 48–101.

[108] See *supra,* text accompanying nn. 24–32.

[109] See *supra,* text accompanying nn. 48–101.

we shall see, the Court held that funding of rebels does not amount *per se* to a breach of the principle of nonuse of force.[110] A fortiori, moral and political support for rebels cannot violate that principle either.

The Court, however, held that *general* support for rebels violated the principle of nonintervention. The Court concluded that even if it was not proved that the intention of the United States was to overthrow the Sandinista governnment, it was established that that was the intention of the *contras* themselves. Consequently,

> In international law, if one State, with the view of the coercion of another State, supports and assists armed bands in that State whose purpose is to overthrow the government of that State, that amounts to an intervention by the one State in the internal affairs of the other, whether or not the political objective of the State giving such support and assistance is equally far-reaching.[111]

The Court then went on to find that the support given by the United States to the *contras* "by financial support, training, supply of weapons, intelligence and logistic support" violated the principle of nonintervention.[112] The Court did not mention moral and political support in this passage. Yet the *holding* includes "encouragement" among the unlawful acts of intervention. The Court's holding on this particular point (mere encouragement of rebels) is thus not directly entailed by the arguments marshaled in its support. A possible explanation of this apparent inconsistency is that support, even moral and political support, for rebels is always coercive, because the rebels are fighting; they are using force against the government. The Court's view would then be that *any* support for rebels whose aim is to overthrow an established government is, in the nature of things, coercive. In this view, moral and political support for rebels is coercive action and meets one requirement of the definition of unlawful intervention. Yet it is doubtful that mere political encouragement for the opposition in another state should be considered as carrying a higher level of coercion than what one would expect in

---

[110] See *infra* nn. 119–133, *infra.*

[111] Judgment, *supra* n. 2, at 124.

[112] Judgment, *supra* n. 2, at 124–125.

the normal incidents of diplomacy.[113] Be that as it may, here the Court held that the United States did not have a right to demand democratization of Nicaragua. Therefore, the second prong of the definition of intervention, that the targeted choices must be ones in regard to which the state is legally free, is met as well. But the Court's theory stands or falls along with its view on exclusive jurisdiction. I showed above that the Court erred in denying the United States the right to demand human rights compliance. If that critique holds, then the Court's entire argument on nonintervention must collapse. Nonforcible measures for human rights purposes are legally acceptable, provided that the state that adopts the measures has a right to demand compliance.[114] Even if moral and political support for rebels is considered coercive (a dubious proposition), a judgment of illegality on the moral and political support for rebels depends entirely upon the view that the "intervening" state lacks standing to request human rights compliance.

VI. THE MEANS OF INTERVENTION: ECONOMIC SANCTIONS AND FUNDING OF REBELS

The next category of means of pressure are those that can be defined as clearly *coercive*, yet falling short of the use of force. Unlike mere moral and political support for the opposition, economic sanctions and funding of rebels are instead more serious means of pressure. They must be considered in principle nonforcible means of coercion.

The first question to be considered is the legal status of the adoption of economic sanctions by the United States against Nicaragua. The Court said that it was "unable to regard such action on the economic plane . . . as a breach of the customary-law principle of nonintervention."[115] Yet, again under the Court's own definition, economic sanctions whose purpose and effect is to coerce another government to yield to the demands of the state adopting the measures seems to be a paradigm of unlawful intervention. That conclusion should be particularly commanded by the Court's holding that the United States did not have

---

[113] For an interesting analysis of "minor" coercion, *see* Higgins, *supra* n. 20.

[114] For examples, *see supra* n. 58, 66, and references therein.

[115] Judgment, *supra* n. 2, at 126.

a right to make demands for democratization and human rights observance—much less, one may assume, for nonhumanitarian purposes. If
economic sanctions do not amount to unlawful intervention it must be
either because they are not coercive or because they are not aimed
at influencing discretionary choices. The Court had already held that
Nicaragua had a right to "choose" its own, political, social, and economic system.[116] Therefore, the only reason why the Court may say that
economic sanctions do not amount to unlawful intervention is that they
are not coercive.[117] The Court's holding can be perhaps explained by
the fact that economic sanctions are not directly related to the support
for rebels. They are not strictly linked to the United States' participation
in Nicaragua's civil war. Therefore, it seems, they do not exhibit the
degree of coercion entailed by such participation. But this, of course,
is an empirical matter, and although the Court gave no clues about its
views on how the United States' economic actions may or may not
have exerted pressure on Nicaragua, the presumption should be that
the most powerful nation in the world has coercive economic power
over a country like Nicaragua. In short, if the economic sanctions were
coercive and that coercion was exerted on matters on which Nicaragua
was legally free to act, those sanctions, under the Court's definition,
ought to violate the principle of nonintervention. Of course, I have
argued that the second premise (that human rights and democracy are
matters in regard to which Nicaragua was legally "free") is wrong. I
would therefore concur with the Court that economic sanctions aimed
at coercing Nicaragua to comply with its human rights commitments
are justified under international law. The point here is that this finding
is incongruous with the Court's general analysis of unlawful intervention. Be that as it may, under both the Court's theory and the one
defended here economic sanctions for human rights purposes are perfectly lawful.[118]

The next form of pressure, the funding of the *contras*, was held by
the Court to be a violation of the principle of nonintervention but not
of the prohibition of the nonuse of force. The explanation of this finding

---

[116] *See supra,* text accompanying nn. 96–101.

[117] *See generally* Farer, *supra* n. 24.

[118] *See,* e.g., the economic sanctions imposed by Canada, the EEC and the United
States on South Africa, *supra* n. 68.

seems to be, once again, that coercion is not coextensive with use of force. The Court wrote:

> [W]hile the arming and training of the *contras* can certainly be said to involve the threat or use of force against Nicaragua, *this is not so in respect of all the assistance given by the United States Government. In particular, the Court considers that the mere supply of funds to the contras, while undoubtedly an act of intervention in the internal affairs of Nicaragua . . . does not in itself amount to a use of force.*[119]

This holding also depends entirely on the proposition that the matter upon which the United States exerted pressure fell within the domestic jurisdiction of Nicaragua. Funding of rebels does not violate an independent legal principle, that is, besides nonintervention. Therefore, if it is acknowleged that human rights are a matter of international concern, the funding of pro-human rights rebels cannot be labeled as unlawful intervention. Now it is apparent why the Court had to defend the improbable proposition that Nicaragua had not assumed any human rights obligation beyond the human rights conventions. The *means* used, funding of anti-government forces, considered by itself, is not prohibited by international law, as current international support ("material help") for the non-white majority in South Africa proves.[120] Where the means used in response to a violation of an international obligation are not independently prohibited by international law, the aggrieved state may employ all nonforcible proportionate countermeasures to redress the wrong.[121] Under the Court's definition of unlawful intervention, the reason why the funding of rebels violates the nonintervention principle is that the United States does not have a right to demand human rights observance in Nicaragua. If one adopts instead the contrary view that I have attempted to defend here, nonforcible measures to promote human rights in Nicaragua do not violate the nonintervention principle.

None of the nonforcible acts undertaken by the United States against Nicaragua directed toward the restoration of democracy and human

---

[119] Judgment, *supra* n. 2, at 119 (emphasis added).

[120] See the discussion *supra,* Chapter 7.

[121] *See* D'Amato, "The Concept of Human Rights in International Law," 82 *Colum. L. Rev.* 1110, 1117–1122 (1982), and references therein. *See generally* Zoller, *supra* n. 68.

rights in that country violated international law. States may use nonforcible means, such as diplomatic action, economic sanctions, or even funding rebels (to use the Court's own example of a coercive action short of use of force) to put pressure on non-democratic governments and human rights violators in the hope of liberalizing those regimes.[122] The United States was providing different types of help short of armed force to the Nicaraguan rebels.[123] The Court, as indicated, held that mere financial and political support of rebels, while it may have violated the nonintervention principle, did not amount to prohibited use of force.[124] It follows that *if* Nicaragua has a legal commitment to democracy in which American states have a legal interest, and *if* the *contras* are truly the democratic opposition forces fighting against oppression, and *if* the Sandinista Government has indeed failed to observe human rights, then the United States had a right to support those forces, provided that the measures were proportionate. As a matter of principle, the use of proportionate measures short of force, ranging from moral and political support,[125] diplomatic pressure,[126] economic sanctions,[127] and contrary to what the Court says, encouraging and even financing pro-human rights opposition forces, can hardly be said to run afoul of international law. It is hard to see how states could otherwise discharge their obligations jointly and separately to promote human rights under articles 55 and 56 of the U.N. Charter.[128] Should we accept the Court's theory in the case of help (short of armed force) provided to the oppressed majority in South Africa? Or to the people of the Philippines in their drive against dictator Marcos? Or to the pro-democratic and pro-human rights forces in Chile? If the Court is willing to hesitate in any

---

[122] While the ultimate credit always goes to the people who overthrow their dictators, external pressure plays a very important role, as shown by recent events in the Philippines.

[123] *See* Judgment, *supra* n. 2, at 38–92.

[124] *See supra,* text accompanying n. 120.

[125] *See* examples *supra* nn. 57–59, 68.

[126] *Supra* nn. 57–59, 68.

[127] *Supra* nn. 116–119.

[128] Article 56 of the U.N. Charter provides: "All members pledge themselves to take joint and separate action in cooperation with the Organization for the achievements of the purposes set forth in article 55." Article 55, of course, includes the promotion of human rights among its objectives. I am not making here the argument that articles 55 and 56, standing alone, necessarily support a right of *forcible* humanitarian intervention. The text discusses nonforcible pro-human rights measures.

of these cases it must be because it does not believe either that the Sandinistas are really violating human rights or that the rebels are really pro-human rights forces. If this is the case, then the Court should have said so, instead of laying down an all-embracing noninterventionist rule. Of course, that would have meant an evidentiary inquiry into the human rights situation in Nicaragua, something that the Court, invoking anti-quated notions of domestic jurisdiction, refused to do.[129]

At a key point, the Court rejected the existence of a right of interven-tion in support of internal opposition "whose cause appeared particu-larly worthy by reason of the political and moral values with which it was identified."[130] At first blush, this seems to include pro-human rights opposition. Nonetheless, I have argued that this *dictum* should be inter-preted as denying a *general* right of intervention in favor of rebels whose cause is just politically or morally approved by the intervenor.[131] It should not apply to cases where the rebels, in the light of objectively ascertainable human rights principles, are the pro-human rights and pro-democratic forces struggling against a government that has ignored its international human rights obligations.

In conclusion, nonforcible yet coercive measures to promote human rights violate no rule or principle. In particular, nonmilitary assistance to pro-democratic and pro-human rights opposition cannot be consid-ered as a breach of international law. However, because it is doubtful that the *contras* in Nicaragua can be unequivocally characterized as pro-human rights and pro-democratic rebels, maybe the Court reached, for the wrong reasons, the correct result in this particular case.[132] On these facts, then, the United States' nonforcible action is perhaps not

---

[129] *See* supra nn. 49–51.

[130] Judgment, *supra* n. 2, at 108.

[131] *See supra,* Chapter 7.

[132] *See* Amnesty International, *Nicaragua: The Human Rights Record* (1986), at 32–36 (human rights abuses by rebels); Kinzer, "Nicaraguan Villagers Tell of Brutal Contra Raids," *N.Y. Times,* Mar. 10, 1987, at 1. It would be equally wrong, however, to deny that an important segment of the opposition to the Sandinistas is pro-human rights. *See,* e.g., V. B. de Chamorro, "A Letter to Ortega, *N.Y. Times,* July 29, 1986, at 27. LeMoyne, "Top Contra Quits," Citing Disillusion, *N.Y. Times,* Mar. 10, 1987, at 1. At the time of this writing, there were even reports that the U.S. was providing intelligence to the rebels about civil targets. *See* Brinkley, "C.I.A. Gives Contras Detailed Profiles of Civil Targets," *N.Y. Times,* Mar. 19, 1987, at 1. If that information is correct, there are even more serious doubts about the validity of the whole U.S. enterprise.

accurately described as an effort to promote human rights.[133] Yet one should be concerned about the Court's insensitivity to human rights matters. The way the Court addressed questions of principle is perhaps more important in the long run than reaching a judgment dictated by the particular Nicaraguan situation. It would have been more inspired for the Court to recognize the right of states to adopt nonforcible measures to promote human rights, while at the same time hold that U.S. support for these particular rebels could not be characterized as a pro-human rights measure.

The remaining issue is the legality of pro-democratic and humanitarian use of force. It must be apparent that if nonforcible aid cannot be justified on these facts (because, say, the rebels are not pro-human rights forces,) *a fortiori* the legality of the use of force in the specific case of Nicaragua cannot be upheld. Yet once again the Court's theoretical approach to humanitarian intervention merits close scrutiny, if only to ascertain the scope of the decision and its precedential value. I shall examine first the Court's approach to the question of the legality of pro-democratic use of force, and then its views on the legality of using force to remedy serious human rights deprivations.

VII.   THE COURT'S VIEWS ON PRO-DEMOCRATIC AND HUMANITARIAN FORCIBLE INTERVENTION

The Court examined in detail the most serious form of international coercion: the use of force. Following Resolution 2625 (XXV),[134] the Court distinguished between "the most grave forms of the use of force," i.e., those that are tantamount to an armed attack, and "other less grave forms."[135] Among these less grave forms, the Court listed armed reprisals, force used to deprive peoples of self-determination, the organization and encouragement of irregular forces or armed bands for incursion into the territory of another state, and the organization, instigation, assistance, and participation in acts of civil strife in another state, when the

---

[133] I do not discuss here whether the U.S. action, forcible or not, may be justified on other principles, such as the right of self-defense or to adopt countermeasures. The Court rejected this justification. Judgment, *supra* n. 2, at 118–126.

[134] *Supra* n. 99.

[135] Judgment, *supra* n. 2, at 101.

acts in question involve a threat or use of force.[136] Applying this scheme, the Court found that the United States had violated the principle of nonuse of force, in the terms of Resolution 2625, by "organizing or encouraging the organization of irregular forces or armed bands . . . for incursion into the territory of another State," and "participating in acts of civil strife."[137] This was so because the participation in civil strife amounts to violation of the principle when the acts of civil strife referred to involve a use of force. This was true, thought the Court, of arming and training but not, as indicated above, of other forms of assistance.[138]

As a preliminary matter, *we are not concerned here with a violation of the principle of nonintervention,* as defined by the Court. By the Court's own two-pronged definition, when a matter does not fall within the target state's exclusive jurisdiction the discourse falls outside the domain of unlawful intervention. If an action is still unlawful it cannot be because it violates the principle of nonintervention, but for other reasons. Thus in this book the inquiry has focused on whether there is an exception to *the principle of nonuse of force* allowing for forcible action to protect human rights.[139] "Humanitarian intervention" is therefore a shorthand for such exception. Legally, humanitarian intervention cannot be unlawful *intervention* at all, because human rights do not fall within any state's domestic jurisdiction. The word "intervention" in the term "humanitarian intervention" is therefore used descriptively, to signify pressure exerted by a state upon another to force the latter to do or abstain from doing something.[140] Nor is it appropriate to inquire whether governments have a "right" to oppress their citizens. In view of the fact that human rights no longer pertain to the states' exclusive domestic jurisdiction, governments hold no such right. The question is whether force may be used to put an end to serious human rights violations.

---

[136] *Id.* at 101. On the notion of indirect aggression, *see* Rifaat, *International Aggression* 217–221 (1984) and references therein.

[137] Judgment, *supra* n. 2, at 118–119. The Court also found that laying mines and certain direct attacks violated the principle of nonuse of force. Id. at 118.

[138] Judgment, *supra* n. 2, at 118–119.

[139] *See supra,* Chapter 7.

[140] *See supra* nn. 15–24.

The Court discussed separately the issues of use of force to restore democracy and to enforce human rights. As to the former, the Court was unmistakably hostile:

[E]ven supposing that the United States were entitled to act in lieu of the Organization, it . . . could not be authorized to use force in that event. *Of its nature, a commitment like this* [i.e., the establishment of a democratic system] *is one of a category which, if violated, cannot justify the use of force against a sovereign state.*[141]

In the light of the discussion in Chapter 6, I suggest that if *Nicaragua* is to have any precedential value, this holding means that *unless the undemocratic government plans to remain in power and there are no alternative nonforcible means to effect democratization, the use of force to restore democracy is disproportionate because the mere denial of political rights cannot be characterized as a deprivation of human rights of sufficient gravity, and is therefore unlawful.* This conclusion may raise questions about the 1983 intervention in Grenada, the legality of which I have defended, even though it was ostensibly aimed at restoring democracy.[142] If I am allowed to use a common law analogy, the Grenada case can be decisively distinguished from the situation in Nicaragua. This suggestion requires elaboration.

In the previous chapter I examined Professor Reisman's argument in favor of humanitarian intervention. At that stage I left open the question whether forcible intervention is permissible to restore democracy, and not just to remedy more egregious deprivations.[143] I have indeed argued that notions of rights and political consent should underlie proper international legal analysis. But it does not automatically follow that the use of force is always justified to overthrow unrepresentative governments. Such forcible action may be disproportionate even if the target government is illegitimate under the theory of international law suggested here. The problem with Professor Reisman's argument is that the use of force for democratic purposes will in many cases be disproportionate to the

---

[141] Judgment, *supra* n. 2, at 132–133 (emphasis supplied).

[142] *Supra,* Chapter 8.

[143] *See supra,* Chapter 7.

evil that it is designed to suppress. Indeed, denying political participation is less serious, and therefore less disrespectful in the Kantian sense,[144] than the violation of more basic civil and political rights. Alternative, nonforcible means of diplomatic pressure should therefore be attempted.

The 1983 United States intervention in Grenada crucially differs from the Nicaraguan case in this regard. First, in Grenada the new rulers had unmistakably established the incipient foundations of a totalitarian dictatorship. The individuals in power had showed a disposition for serious and disrespectful (though still potential) disregard for basic human rights.[145] Such is not the case in Nicaragua, notwithstanding the serious reservations, discussed below, about the human rights situation there.[146] The Nicaraguan revolution was born out of concern for restoring human rights thwarted during the Somoza rule. While the Sandinistas seem to have partly betrayed that initial purpose, the contrast with the Grenada rulers who, in the words of Professor D'Amato, had "just machine-gunned their way into power" with the promise of further and irreversible oppression, is vivid.[147] Second, the cost of restoring human rights in Grenada is enormously less than what it would be in Nicaragua. Of course, I have argued that cost alone cannot be a factor.[148] But where human rights violations are not egregious, the cost of intervention becomes crucial; the intervention must always be proportionate to the targeted evil. In Nicaragua, there is even indication that the United States' actions are hindering, rather than promoting, human rights (although there is some suspicion that the Sandinistas use that argument as an excuse for adopting authoritarian measures[149]). Third, the pro-human rights invasion of Grenada was overwhelmingly welcomed by the Grenadians, who saw it as a liberating act.[150] It is unlikely that a significant segment of the Nicaraguan people would welcome a United

---

[144] See supra, Chapter 6.

[145] See supra, Chapter 8.

[146] See infra, n. 162.

[147] See D'Amato, supra n. 10, at 660.

[148] See supra, Chapter 6.

[149] On the declaration of state of emergency, see The Economist, World Human Rights Guide 197 (1986).

[150] Supra, Chapter 8.

States invasion, even if undertaken for democratic purposes.[151] Fourth, there was in Grenada an important support of, and participation in, the invasion from nations from the region.[152] In Nicaragua instead, while neighboring nations are rightly concerned about Nicaragua's armamentism and authoritarian methods, they seem to be increasingly hostile to using military force.[153] And finally, it is at the very least doubtful that the *contras* are true pro-human rights forces ("freedom fighters").[154] Those differences are decisive in a rights-based appraisal of the legality of the use of force in both cases. Grenada should be seen as a case where the use of force was justified on humanitarian grounds because there was an identifiable potential for *extensive, serious, and disrespectful* violations of human rights, not just for denial of the right of the people to elect the government.

I sympathize with Professor Reisman's argument, and believe that it retains validity to demonstrate the lawfulness of using force to remedy more serious human rights deprivations.[155] Yet it falls short of demonstrating the lawfulness of using force *just* to install a liberal democracy. As in any legal analysis where there are competing principles, the balance has to be struck somewhere. Professor Reisman is right that blind obedience to a flat prohibition of forcible intervention does not do justice to the philosophical strength of the right of individuals to determine their own political destiny. The prohibition can and should be ignored where oppression reaches a more substantial level. The problem with Professor Reisman's argument is that even if self-determination ought to be interpreted in this pro-democratic manner,[156] the use of force for the purpose of just compelling democratic reforms seems disproportionate in most cases. While I would agree with his assumption that denying democratic rights should be seen as a violation of international law, such a denial does not seem to amount to a gross violation

---

[151] *See World Human Rights Guide, supra* n. 149 (Sandinistas seem to enjoy support from population).

[152] *See supra,* Chapter 8.

[153] *See,* e.g., Kinzer, "Costa Rica Gets Tougher on Contras," *N.Y. Times,* Sept. 3, 1986, at 3.

[154] *See supra* n. 132 and accompanying text.

[155] *See supra,* Chapter 7.

[156] I have argued for such an interpretation in my article, "International Human Rights and Cultural Relativism," 25 *Va. J. Int'l L.* 869, 879–884 (1985).

of fundamental human rights. This is not to say that force can only be used to prevent genocide. Yet in view of the legal and moral importance of preserving peace, the threshold for allowing the exception should be higher than mere denial of political rights.

So while one should deplore once again the Court's failure to qualify its dictum, it must be conceded that, for the reasons outlined above, the Court seems to be describing correctly the state of the law when it asserts that the direct or indirect use of force cannot be accepted just for the purpose of requiring governments to establish democracy and hold free elections.[157] This is true even if the positivistic arguments are rejected and Professor Reisman's principle of political legitimacy as the moral basis of state sovereignty holds, as I believe it does.[158] The Grenada case, in turn, should be characterized as a more egregious situation warranting forcible intervention and one which, in view of the cost of the intervention and the benefits in terms of maximization of human rights enjoyment, should be distinguished on the facts from Nicaragua. The use of force is an extraordinary remedy that ought to be reserved for more serious human rights violations than just the denial of political rights.

The Court ends its treatment of human rights with the following assertion:

> [T]he use of force could not be the appropriate method to monitor or ensure . . . respect [for human rights]. With regard to the steps actually taken, the protection of human rights, a strictly humanitarian objective, cannot be compatible with the mining of ports, the destruction of oil installations, or again with the training, arming and equipping of the *contras*. The Court concludes that the argument derived from the preservation of human rights in Nicaragua cannot afford a legal justification for the conduct of the United States, and cannot in any event be reconciled with the legal strategy of the respondent State, which is based on the right of collective self-defense.[159]

---

[157] Cf. the Court's rejection of "ideological" intervention, Judgment, *supra* n. 2, at 133. However, the Haiti case, discussed in Chapter 9, seems to point in the opposite direction.

[158] For a critique of the New Haven school of thought, *see supra*, Chapter 1.

[159] Judgment, *supra* n. 2, at 134–135.

Apparently the Court is examining here the case of possible violations of human rights *beyond* the mere failure to establish a democratic system and hold free elections. The Court makes an interesting argument here, one that is rarely encountered in the voluminous literature on humanitarian intervention. According to the Court, use of force for humanitarian purposes is almost a contradiction in terms, because the intervenor is using the same methods and creating the same horrors that it is supposed to remedy with the intervention. The Court believes that the methods used by the United States are incompatible with humanitarian objectives.[160] This analysis is persuasive insofar as the mining of harbors and the bombing of oil installations are concerned. Indeed, no humanitarian objectives can justify such actions. Genuine humanitarian intervention must be aimed at stopping human rights deprivations, and it is hard to see how mining of harbors and bombing of oil facilities could conceivably be related to that aim.[161] Yet the "arming, training and equipment" of pro-human rights forces fighting against dictators, whatever we can say about its consistency with the principle of nonuse of force, is not *incompatible* with a human rights objective. Far from that, one would say that such active support, assuming that the rebels really are pro-human rights forces, is often the only means by which human rights can be restored in dictatorial societies. So although the Court's observation contains an important truth—that means are not always justified by the ends—it is only a partial one.

The Court's holding on humanitarian intervention must be construed in the light of the Nicaraguan reality. Indeed, although at the time of this writing the human rights situation in Nicaragua is a matter of serious concern, it has not reached the grave proportions that would authorize other states to seek forcible remedies.[162] Above all, the United States

---

[160] Cf. D'Amato, *supra* n. 10 (arguing that U.S. action can best be explained by humanitarian intervention doctrine), with Neier, "The Misuse of 'Human Rights'," *N.Y. Times,* Aug. 4, at 17 (arguing that humanitarian intervention argument is flawed because U.S. does not advocate overthrow of other tyrannical governments).

[161] Judge Schwebel, however, thought that these direct actions were justified under self-defense principles. *See* Judgment (Scwebel, S., dissenting) *supra* n. 2, at 378–381.

[162] According to the most reliable and impartial reports available, the human rights violations by the Government of Nicaragua are a matter of serious concern. *See* Amnesty Report, *supra* n. 132. *See also* Dep't of State, *Broken Promises: Sandinista Repression of Human Rights in Nicaragua* (1984). Yet deprivations, while serious, do not seem to have reached egregious proportions. More difficult is the issue whether the rebels,

has failed to use nonforcible means to pressure the Sandinistas to enact liberal reforms. The United States' forcible intervention, to meet the test of legality suggested in this book, must be genuinely aimed at effectively restoring human rights (even if it entertains additional objectives). The intervention must also be necessary, proportionate, and welcomed by the victims themselves.[163]

Those acts of the United States in support of the *contras* that involve the *direct* use of force do not seem to withstand scrutiny under those standards. As I suggested above, the Court erred in denying the United States a legitimate interest to request Nicaragua to observe human rights, including the establishment of democracy. Yet, as the Court correctly points out, acts like the mining of harbors are incompatible with a humanitarian objective. Such an action sheds doubt on the presence of the first requirement, that the intervention has to have chiefly humanitarian objectives.

The *indirect* use of force, that is, what the Court describes as "arming, training" of the Nicaraguan rebels does not fare very well under the humanitarian intervention test either. To be sure, the Court's assertion that arming and training rebels is *incompatible* with humanitarian objectives is mistaken. Again, if the *contras* were the pro-human rights forces fighting against an oppressive regime, one that would extensively and gravely violate human rights, foreign support for them would amount to humanitarian intervention *par excellence.* While acts like the mining of harbors are in most cases incompatible with humanitarian aims, the training and arming of the rebels, that is, the *indirect* use of force in appropriate cases, is not. Still, it is not possible to say that the United States has met the first requirement of humanitarian intervention—that the intervention must be genuinely aimed at restoring human rights—in its support for the Nicaraguan rebels. The reason is that the United States government reportedly undertook actions that are plainly

---

or at least a part of them, can be described as pro-human rights forces. Cf. Amnesty Report, *supra* n. 132, at 32–36 (reporting human rights abuses by opposition forces) with separate opinion of Judge Ago, Judgment (Ago, sep. opinion), *supra* n. 2, at 18 (the rebellion in Nicaragua has its origin in a true disagreement of democratic forces with Sandinistas). *See also* V. B. de Chamorro, "A Letter to Ortega," *N.Y. Times,* July 29, 1986, at 27 (accusing Sandinistas of having created a "great concentration camp" in Nicaragua).

[163] *Supra,* Chapters 6 and 7.

inconsistent with a humanitarian purpose, such as threatening to desta-
bilize the democratic regime in Argentina and other Latin American
nations if they did not support the United States policy in Central
America.[164] And the United States' efforts in Nicaragua do not seem
to meet the other requirements either: necessity, proportionality, and
welcome by the local population.[165] As to necessity, the United States
should have used less intrusive means first. For example, the United
States could have appeared before the Court and perhaps could have
even countersued Nicaragua for human rights violations. Or the United
States could have ratified the human rights conventions and resorted to
those mechanisms to force the Sandinistas to keep their human rights
promises. Nor do the United States actions in Nicaragua (unlike the
Grenada episode) seem to meet the proportionality test. While the violations of human rights in Nicaragua are a reality, it is doubtful that they
have reached proportions that would justify the forcible actions that the
United States was accused of performing. The human rights situation
in Nicaragua does not seem so grave, in terms of what I have called
disrespectful human rights violations, as to justify departure from the
prohibition against the use of force. The final requirement, that the
oppressed population must welcome the intervention, does not seem
to have been met either. Most of the population, while not enthusiasti-
cally pro-Sandinista, would most probably oppose United States intervention. Because humanitarian intervention is defined as support for
victims of oppression, the whole enterprise fails even if the United States
envisions democracy and respect for human rights as a legitimate objective.

To conclude, the *Nicaragua* ruling must be read narrowly, as bearing
only on these particular facts. Because the rebels are not clearly pro-
human rights forces, and because the human rights violations do not
seem grave enough, forcible methods to protect those rights are not
justified *in this specific case*. The Court's ruling should not affect:

(1) The right of states to use proportionate nonforcible means, such

---

[164] *See* Chardy, "White House Reportedly Threatened 5 Latin Nations to Support
Contras," *Arizona Republic,* May 10, 1987, at 1.

[165] The Court mentioned necessity and proportionality only in connection with the
self-defense exception. *See* Judgment, *supra* n. 2, at 122–123.

as diplomatic pressure, economic sanctions, and nonmilitary help to pro-human rights opposition in dictatorial states. In Central America, this entails the right of American states to hold Nicaragua to its commitment to democracy and human rights and thus prevent the Sandinistas from imposing a totalitarian dictatorship on the Nicaraguan people.

(2) The right of coercive intervention, including direct and indirect military action, to stop actual or potentially serious and widespread violations of human rights, whenever such action may be undertaken with reasonable chances of success and with the support of the population.

The Court's discussion of human rights and humanitarian intervention is unsatisfactory. Its reasoning is overly pro-governmental and insufficiently concerned with human dignity. One cannot avoid the impression that the Court has missed a unique opportunity to develop the law in the sense of reinforcement of human rights. The main effect of the Court's endorsement of the sacredness of national borders will be to reassure tyrants from the right and the left against legitimate demands for freedom and human rights. Yet I fear that the Court did no more than reflect the moral impotence of international law as conventionally understood. If so, it is time to abandon the Hegelian Myth and start rethinking the law of nations in a fundamentally different way. International law must be wed to notions of legitimacy associated with human rights and political consent.

SUMMARY AND CONCLUDING THOUGHTS

I have attempted in this book to defend three interrelated propositions. I argued, first, for a *jurisprudence* of international law—that international law and moral philosophy are essentially linked. Second, I
defended a *substantive moral philosophy* of international relations—that the rights of states derive from human rights and consequently wars in defense of human rights are just. And third, I argued for
a specific *legal proposition*—that the right of individual and collective
humanitarian intervention is consistent with the United Nations Charter
and positively supported by state practice, when both are examined in
the light of the normative theory mentioned above.

Drawing upon Ronald Dworkin's thought, I claimed that there is an
essential connection in international legal discourse between propositions of law and moral-political philosophy. I tried to show that even
current positivist analysis cannot escape value choices. The need to
identify values in international legal discourse reveals itself with particular transparency in the case of customary law analysis. I showed that
the proposition that a particular norm is customary law necessitates a
normative moral assumption. The value choice in turn determined
whether the precedents in question are to be characterized either as
creating law, or as violating prior law. My suggestion is that moral
philosophy cannot be absent from international legal analysis. This jurisprudential thesis is conceptual rather than normative. The jurisprudential proposition standing alone, that is, independent of any
substantive component, attempts to challenge current international legal thought. The dominant view in the discipline is still, by and large,
that one should look only at the legal materials, and that moral-philosophical analysis is irrelevant or inappropriate. Thus, state practice (in
the form of diplomatic papers) and treaties are commonly identified as

the two sources of international law, beyond which, it is thought, we are not allowed to inquire. A cursory examination of leading international legal scholarship evidences the dry, flat style that pervades most of that work. Positivism reigns in international law in a way in which it does not in other legal disciplines. My hope is that this book will contribute to efforts directed at rediscovering the moral-philosophical underpinnings of our accepted cluster of international law doctrines and concepts.

The second, normative, thesis defended here is that the rights of states recognized by international law are derived from human rights, and that as a consequence war on behalf of human rights (humanitarian intervention) is morally justified in appropriate cases. After rejecting moral relativism, I argued for the proposition that the rights of states are properly understood as derivative from human rights, that is, from the rights of the individuals that populate the state. The preeminence of human rights was shown not to be causally dependent on pure processes of self-determination, as John Stuart Mill thought. I discussed and rejected theories that defend the autonomous moral standing of states and governments—the Hegelian Myth. I tried to show that social theory can explain both the domestic and the international legitimacy of governments. These institutions exist because individuals have consented, or would rationally consent, to transfer some of their rights in order to make social cooperation possible. But the endurance of the legitimacy of that trust depends on the continuing observance by those in power of the rights of everybody. I discussed in detail John Rawls's theory of international law and showed, contrary to his claim, that an absolute rule of nonintervention cannot be justified under his own social contract theory.

Governments do not necessarily represent the people in international relations. Only governments that are truly representative should be deemed representative by international law. Theories of recognition that rely on Hobbesian notions of effective political power were shown to be morally inadequate. Nor do utilitarian arguments, such as the arguments from the danger of abuse, provide a sufficient basis for rejecting the correctness of humanitarian intervention in appropriate cases. Quite apart from the general inadequacies of utilitarian theory, an exception allowing for humanitarian intervention is not likely to increase the number of human rights deprivations, including here the violations of the rights of innocent victims of war.

The consequences of this substantive moral theory of international law are far-reaching. The most important corollary is that a war is just if, and only if, it is a war in defense of human rights. Humanitarian intervention, is therefore morally justified in appropriate cases. But the theory defended here goes further. A just war is always defensive of rights. A war in self-defense, the legality and morality of which few would challenge, protects the rights of individuals against deprivation by foreigners. Humanitarian intervention protects those same rights against deprivations by their own government. Both types of war are thus covered by the same rationale.

Yet the general assertion that just wars are wars in defense of human rights needs to be fleshed out in order to provide guidance in particular cases. I therefore attempted to sketch the conditions for the correctness of intervention. I suggested that a justified intervention must be genuinely aimed at restoring human rights, necessary, proportionate to the evil that it is designed to suppress, and welcomed by the victims of oppression. This last requirement is crucial. It underscores the nature of humanitarian intervention as help to victims of human rights deprivations, rather than as the result of unilateral decisions by foreigners. It also highlights the moral parallelism between justified revolution and justified intervention. The notion of proportionality must be properly qualified so as to avoid the pitfalls of utilitarianism. The basic idea, suggested by the elucidation of the justification of the Allied effort in World War II, is that, when judging the correctness of an intervention, the nature of the evil against which the intervention is directed counts as much as the cost in terms of human lives and suffering.

The third, legal, thesis defended here is that humanitarian intervention is a recognized exception to the general prohibition against the use of force in international relations. As a natural corollary from the first two steps in the argument, I analyzed state practice, the text of the United Nations Charter, the practice of the United Nations Security Council, and the *Nicaragua* decision in the light of the substantive conclusions reached. I argued that traditional methods of treaty interpretation are unhelpful to determine the content of article 2(4) of the United Nations Charter. That norm is instead properly construed in the light of values, or purposes, of the international legal system. Because the best moral-political theory is one that recognizes the pre-eminence of human rights, article 2(4) should not be read as outlawing humanitarian intervention, which is a use of force to effect one of the main purposes of the United Nations, the promotion of human rights. A detailed study of post-1945 state practice shows that the use of force to stop ongoing or potential serious human rights deprivations is lawful. I analyzed nine cases: the Tanzanian intervention in Uganda, the Indian intervention in Bangladesh, the French intervention in Central Africa, and the United States intervention in Grenada and the United Nation's-authorized interventions in Iraq, Somalia, Haiti, Rwanda, and Bosnia. Each of these illustrates different aspects of the doctrine of humanitarian intervention. Taken together, they unequivocally support the enduring vitality of the doctrine. I also concluded that the *Nicaragua* decision rendered by the International Court of Justice in 1986 must be read narrowly. While the decision's discussion of human rights is gravely flawed, the Court's refusal to accept the humanitarian intervention argument is justified in view of the specific facts in Nicaragua, where the situation, as far as we can grasp it, is not one that warrants forcible intervention. The *Nicaragua* decision thus does not affect the relevance of the genuine precedents of humanitarian intervention discussed above.

Turning Walzer's program upside down, I would describe the argument in this book as an attempt to defend philosophy against the political scientists' and international lawyers' traditional dislike for philosophy.[1] Or, perhaps, as an attempt to defend morality against the traditional impotence of state sovereignty. Ultimately, however, this is a defense of the value of the individual against the alleged sanctity of the state. The thrust of the argument is that governments and states exist only to protect us, to protect our rights against internal and external deprivations. When governments fail to do that, they are no longer morally or legally justified.

The hope I entertained when this book was first published, that international law would be seen in a different light, has been partially realized with the end of the Cold War and the growing triumph of democracy and freedom all around the globe. International law at the

---

[1] See *supra* Chapters 2–5.

end of the millenium is no longer a law of states. Grotius, Vattel and others initially conceived international law as being in harmony with the law of nature. As such, the law of nations was seen as part of a broader system of political morality. International legal thought was but a branch of normative philosophy. The joint rise of nationalism and positivism changed both the cosmopolitan universalism and the unity between law and morals embodied in the Grotian tradition. If the victory in 1945 is still meaningful today, if we are going to remember the teachings of Nuremberg, and if the human rights movements is to maintain and strengthen its momentum, then it is time to go back to that earlier tradition. It is time, in sum, to recognize that law, including international law, governs the conduct of individuals, and that as such it has moral limits. Those moral limits do not differ from the limits imposed upon domestic legal systems by notions of rights and political consent. International law is thus derivative. It does not rest upon an independent moral foundation, be it the rights of states, "communal integrity," the "common will," or the "Volkgeist."

The prohibition of Article 2(4) of the United Nations Charter has a powerful and fundamental meaning. Wars should never be initiated for reasons such as desire for national glory or political domination. Aggressive wars are criminal. Further, there is a strong presumption against war. Wars should be avoided, even sometimes at considerable cost. But some wars are just. The United Nations itself is the child of a victory in a just war. Just wars are those that are waged in defense of the only currency we all have: our basic rights and the individual autonomy from which they derive.

SELECTED BIBLIOGRAPHY

I. BOOKS AND COLLECTIONS OF ESSAYS

A. International Law and Relations

1. Humanitarian Intervention

Harris, J., ed. *The Politics of Humanitarian Intervention.* 1995.

Lillich, Richard B., ed. *Humanitarian Intervention and the United Nations.* Charlottesville: University Press of Virginia, 1973.

Malanczuck, P. *Humanitarian Intervention and the Legitimacy of the Use of Force.* 1993.

Rodley, N., ed. *To Loose the Bands of Wickedness: International Intervention in Defense of Human Rights.* 1992.

Ronzitti, Natalino. *Rescuing Nationals Abroad through Military Coercion and Intervention on Grounds of Humanity.* Dordrecht, The Netherlands; Boston: M. Nijhoff Publishers, 1985.

Thapa, Dhruba Bar Singh. *Humanitarian Intervention: A Study of the Problems and Practices of Collective Intervention in Contemporary International Law for the Protection of Humanity and Human Rights.* Thesis. Montreal, Canada: Institute of Comparative and Foreign Law, McGill University, 1968.

2. Use of Force and Intervention Generally

Bowett, Derek W. *Self-Defence in International Law.* New York: Praeger, 1958.

Brownlie, Ian. *International Law and the Use of Force by States.* Oxford: Clarendon Press, 1963. Revision of thesis. Oxford University.

Bull, Hedley, ed. *Intervention in World Politics.* Oxford (Oxfordshire): Clarendon Press; New York: Oxford University Press, 1984.

Cassesse, Antonio, ed. *The Current Legal Regulation of the Use of Force.* Dordrecht, The Netherlands: M. Nijhoff, 1986.

Chakrabarti, Rhadanaman. *Intervention and the Problem of its Control in the Twentieth Century.* New York: Sterling Publishers, 1974.

Council on Foreign Relations. *Right v. Might: International Law and the Use of Force.* 2d ed., 1991.

D'Amato, Anthony A. *International Law: Process and Prospect.* Dobbs Ferry, NY: Transnational Publishers, 1987.

Damrosch, L., & S. Scheffer, eds. *Law and Force in the International Order.* 1991.

Edwards, Charles S. *Hugo Grotius, the Miracle of Holland: A Study in Political and Legal Thought.* Chicago: Nelson-Hall, 1981.

Grotius, Hugo. *De Jure Belli ac Pacis Libri Tres* [1646] (Francis W. Kelsey, transl.) Indianapolis, IN: Bobbs-Merrill, 1925.

Hodges, Henry G. *The Doctrine of Intervention.* Chicago, IL: The Banner Press, 1915.

Lauterpacht, Hersch. *International Law and Human Rights.* London: Stevens, 1950.

Moore, John N., ed. *Law and Civil War in the Modern World.* Baltimore: Johns Hopkins Press, 1974.

Noel, Jacques. *Le principe de non-intervention: théorie et pratique dans les relations inter-américaines.* Brussels, Belgium: Editions de l'Université de Bruxelles, 1981.

Rifaat, Ahmed M. *International Aggression.* Stockholm: Almqvist & Wiksell International, 1979.

Ronzitti, Natalino. *Le Guerre di Liberazione Nazionale e il Diritto Internazionale.* Pisa, Italy: Pubblicazioni della Facolta di Scienze Politiche della Universita di Pisa, 1974.

Schwarz, Urs. *Confrontation and Intervention in the Modern World.* Dobbs Ferry, NY: Oceana Publications, 1970.

Stone, Julius. *Aggression and World Order; A Critique of United Nations Theories of Aggression.* London: Stevens, 1958.

Stowell, Ellery C. *Intervention in International Law.* Washington, DC: J. Byrne & Co., 1921.

Tanca, A. *Foreign Armed Intervention in Internal Conflict.* 1993.

Thomas, Ann and Aaron J. Thomas. *Non-Intervention: the Law and its Import in the Americas.* Dallas, TX: Southern Methodist University Press, 1956.

de Vattel, Emmerich. *The Law of Nations or the Principles of Natural Law, Applied to the Conduct and to the Affairs of Nations and of Sovereigns* [1758] (Charles Fenwick transl.) Dobbs Ferry, NY: Oceana Publications, 1964.

Vincent, R. J. *Nonintervention and International Order.* Princeton, NJ: Princeton University Press, 1974.

Zourek, Jaroslav. *L'interdiction de l'emploi de la force en droit international.* Leiden: A. W. Sijthoff, 1974.

3. State Practice

D'Amato, Anthony. *The Concept of Custom in International Law.* Ithaca, NY: Cornell University Press, 1971.

Gilmore, William C. *The Grenada Intervention: Analysis and Documentation.* London; New York: Mansell Pub., 1984.

International Commission of Jurists. *The Events in East Pakistan; A Legal Study.* Geneva, International Commission of Jurists, 1972.

Misra, Kashi Prasad. *The Role of the United Nations in the Indo-Pakistani Conflict.* Delhi: Vikas Pub. House, 1973.

O'Halloran, P. *Humanitarian Intervention and the Genocide in Rwanda.* 1995.

Richardson, Michael. *After Amin, the Bloody Pearl.* Atlanta, GA: Majestic Books, 1980.

Rizvi, Hasan Askari. *Internal Strife and External Intervention: India's Role in the Civil War in East Pakistan* (Bangladesh). Lahore: Progressive Publishers, 1981.

B. Philosophy

Beitz, Charles. *Political Theory and International Relations.* Princeton, NJ: Princeton University Press, 1979.

Brilmayer, Lea. *Justifying International Acts,* 1989.

Brilmayer, Lea. *American Hegemony,* 1994.

Buchanan, Allen. *Secession,* 1991.

Bull, Hedley. *The Anarchical Society: A Study of Order in World Politics.* New York: Columbia University Press, 1977.

D'Amato, Anthony. *Jurisprudence: A Descriptive and Normative Analysis of Law.* Dordrecht, The Netherlands; Boston: M. Nijhoff, 1984.

Dworkin, Ronald. *Taking Rights Seriously.* Cambridge, MA: Harvard University Press, 1978.

Dworkin, Ronald. *A Matter of Principle.* Cambridge, MA: Harvard University Press, 1985.

Dworkin, Ronald. *Law's Empire.* Cambridge, MA: Belknap Press, 1986.

Elfstrom, G. *Ethics for a Shrinking World.* 1990.

Forbes,I., & M. Hoffman, eds. *Political Theory, International Relations, and the Ethics of Intervention.* 1993.

Frost, Mervyn. *Towards a Normative Theory of International Relations: A Critical Analysis of the Philosophical and Methodological Assumptions in the Discipline with Proposals toward a Substantive Normative Theory.* Cambridge, (Cambridgeshire); New York: Cambridge University Press, 1986.

Hoffmann, Stanley. *Duties beyond Borders: On the Limits and Possibilities of Ethical International Politics.* Syracuse, NY: Syracuse University Press, 1981.

Holmes, R. *War and Morality.* 1990.

Joynt, Carey & John E. Hare. *Ethics and International Affairs.* New York: St. Martin's Press, 1982.

Kant, Immanuel. *Eternal Peace* (1795) in The Philosophy of Kant: Immanuel Kant's Moral and Political Writings 430 (Carl Friedrich ed. 1949) New York: Modern Library, 1949.

Nardin, Terry. *Law, Morality and the Relations of States.* Princeton, NJ: Princeton University Press, 1983.

Nardin, T., & D. Mapel, eds. *Traditions of International Ethics.* 1992.

O'Brien, William. *The Conduct of Just and Limited War.* New York: Praeger, 1981.

Peltman, Ralph. *Moral Claims in World Affairs.* New York: St. Martin's Press, 1979.

Rawls, John. *A Theory of Justice.* Cambridge, MA: Belknap Press of Harvard University Press, 1971.

Stankiewicz, Wladyslaw Jozef, ed. *In Defence of Sovereignty.* New York: Oxford University Press, 1969.

Waltz, Kenneth Neal. *Man, the State and War: A Theoretical Analysis.* New York: Columbia University Press, 1959.

Walzer, Michael. *Just and Unjust Wars; A Moral Argument with Historical Illustrations.* New York: Basic Books, 1977.

II. ARTICLES AND COMMENTS

Akehurst, "Humanitarian Intervention," in *Intervention in World Politics* 95 (H. Bull ed. 1984).

Arntz, "Lettre à M. Rolin-Jacquemyns," 8 *Revue de droit international et de législation comparée* 675 (1976).

Aroneau, "La guerre internationale d'intervention pour cause d'humanité," 19 *Revue Internationale de droit pénal* 173 (1948).

Bazyler, "Reexamining the Doctrine of Humanitarian Intervention Reexamined in Light of the Atrocities in Kampuchea and Ethiopia," in the *Stanford J. Int'l L.* 547 (1987).

Behuniak, "The Law of Unilateral Intervention by Armed Force: A Legal Survey," 79 *Military Law Rev.* 157 (1978).

Benjamin, "Unilateral Humanitarian Intervention: Legalizing the Use of Force to Prevent Human Rights Atrocities," 16 *Fordham Int'l L. J.*

Beyerlin, "Humanitarian Intervention," in 3 *Encyclopedia of Public International Law* 213 (1982).

Bogen, "The Law of Humanitarian Intervention: U.S. Policy in Cuba (1898) and in the Dominican Republic (1965)," 7 *Harvard Int'l L. Club J.* 296 (1966).

Brown, "The Protection of Human Rights in Disintegrating States: A New Challenge," 68 *Chi.-Kent L. Rev.* 203 (1992).

Brownlie, "Humanitarian Intervention," in *Law and Civil War in the Modern World* 217 (J. N. Moore ed. 1974).

Brownlie, "Thoughts on Kind-Hearted Gunmen," in *Humanitarian Intervention and the United Nations* 139 (R. Lillich ed. 1973).

Chaterjee, "Some Legal Problems of Support Role in International Law: Tanzania and Uganda," 30 *Int'l & Comp. L. Q.*, 755 (1981).

Chilstrom, "Humanitarian Intervention under Contemporary International Law," 1 *Yale Studies in World Public Order* 93 (1974).

Chimni, "Towards a Third World Approach to Non-Intervention: Through the Labyrinth of Western Doctrine," 20 *Indian J. Int'l L.*243 (1980).

Clark, "Humanitarian Intervention: Help to Your Friends and State Practice," 13 *Ga. J. Int'l & Comp. L.* 211 (1983) (Supp.).

Claydon, "Humanitarian Intervention and International Law," 1 *Queen's Intramures L. J.* 36 (1969).

D'Amato, "Nicaragua and International Law: The 'Academic' and the Real," 79 *A.J.I.L.* 657 (1985).

D'Amato, "The Invasion of Panama Was a Lawful Response to Tyranny," 84 *Am. J. Int'l L.* 516 (1990).

Delbruck, "A Fresh Look at Humanitarian Intervention Under the Authority of the United Nations," 67 *Ind. L. J.* 887 (1992).

De Schutter, "Humanitarian Intervention: A United Nations Task," 3 *Calif. West. Int'l L. J.* 23 (1972).

Donnelly, "Human Rights, Humanitarian Intervention and American Foreign Policy. Law, Morality and Politics," 37 *J. Int'l Aff.* 311 (1984).

Dowald-Beck, "The Legality of the U.S. Intervention in Grenada," 31 *Netherlands Int'l L. Rev.* 355 (1984).

Eisner, "Humanitarian Intervention in the Post-Cold War Era," 11 *B.U. Int'l L. J.* 195 (1993).

Fairley, "State Actors, Humanitarian Intervention and International Law: Reopening Pandora's Box," 10 *Ga. J. Int'l & Comp. L.* 29 (1980).

Farer, "Humanitarian Intervention: The View from Charlottesville," in *Humanitarian Intervention and the United Nations* 149 (R. Lillich ed. 1973).

Farer, "Human Rights in Law's Empire: The Jurisprudence War," 85 *Am. J. Int'l L.* 117 (1991).

Farer, "An Inquiry Into the Legitimacy of Humanitarian Intervention," in *Law and Force in the International Order* 191 (L. Damrosch & David Scheffer eds., 1991).

Farer, "Intervention in Unnatural Humanitarian Emergencies: Lessons of the First Phase," 18 *Hum. Rts. Q.* 1 (1996).

Flinterman, "Humanitarian Intervention," 26 Chitty's L. J. 284 (1978).

Fonteyne, "Forcible Self-Help by States to Protect Human Rights: Recent Views from the United Nations," in *Humanitarian Intervention and the United Nations* 197 (R. Lillich ed. 1973).

Fonteyne, "The Customary International Law Doctrine of Humanitarian Intervention: Its Current Validity under the United Nations Charter," 4 *Calif. West. Int'l L. J.* 203 (1974).

Forsythe, "Human Rights, Humanitarian Intervention and World Politics," 15 *Hum. Rts. Q.* 290 (1993).

Franck & Rodley,"After Bangladesh: The Law of Humanitarian Intervention by Military Force," *A.J.I.L.*275 (1973).

Gallant, "Humanitarian Intervention and Security Council Resolution 688: A Reappraisal in Light of Changing World Order," 7 *Am. U. J. Int'l L. & Pol'y* 881 (1992).

Graham, "Humanitarian Intervention," 22 *Mich. L. Rev.* 327 (1924).

Green, "Humanitarian Intervention—1976 Version," 24 *Chitty's L. J.* 217 (1976).

Grossman, "Some Comments on Humanitarian Intervention" (letter), 38 *J. Int'l Aff.* 119 (1984).

Halberstam, "The Legality of Humanitarian Intervention," 3 *Cardozo J. Int'l & Comp. L.* 1 (1995).

Halberstam, "The Copenhagen Document: Intervention in Support of Democracy," 34 *Harv. Int'l L. J.* 163 (1993).

Harrington, "Operation Provide Comfort: A Perspective in International Law," 8 *Conn. J. Int'l L.* 635 (1993).

Henkin, "Use of Force: Law and U.S. Policy," in *Right v. Might: International Law and the Use of Force* 37 (Council on Foreign Relations, 2nd ed., 1991).

Jhabvala, "Unilateral Humanitarian Intervention and International Law," 21 *Indian J. Int'l L.* 208 (1981).

Jhabvala, "Unilateral Humanitarian Intervention: Some Conceptual Problems," in *New Directions in International Law. Essays in Honor of Wolfgang Abendroth* 459 (1982).

Kahn, "From Nuremberg to The Hague: The United States Position in *Nicaragua v. United States* and the Development of International Law," 12 *Yale J. Int'l L.* 1 (1987).

Kresock, " 'Ethnic Cleansing' in the Balkans: The Legal Foundations of Foreign Intervention," 27 *Cornell Int'l L. J.* 203 (1994).

Krylov, "Humanitarian Intervention: Pros and Cons," 17 *Loy. L.A. Int'l & Comp. L. J.* 365 (1995).

Levitin, "The Law of Force and the Force of Law: Grenada, the Falklands, and Humanitarian Intervention," 27 *Harvard Int'l L. J.* 621 (1986).

Lillich, "Forcible Self-Help by States to Protect Human Rights," 53 *Iowa L. Rev.* 325 (1967).

Lillich, "Intervention to Protect Human Rights," 15 *McGill L. J.* 205 (1969).

Lillich, "Humanitarian Intervention: A Reply to Ian Brownlie and a Plea for Constructive Alternatives," in *Law and Civil War in the Modern World* 229 (J. N. Moore ed. 1974).

Lillich, "A United States Policy of Humanitarian Intervention and Intercession," in *Human Rights and American Foreign Policy* (D. Kommers & G. D. Loescher eds. 1979), at 278.

Lillich, "The Role of the United Nations Security Council in Protecting Human Rights in Crisis Situations: United Nations Humanitarian Intervention in the Post-Cold War World," 3 *Tul. J. Int'l & Comp. L.* (1995).

Lukashuk, "The United Nations and Illegitimate Regimes: When to Intervene to Protect Human Rights," in *Law and Force in the New International Order* 143 (1991).

Marshall, "Comment," 3 *Int'l Law*. 438 (1969).

McDougal & Reisman,"Response," 3 *Int'l L*. 438 (1969).

Moore, "Toward an Applied Theory for the Regulation of Intervention," in *Law and Civil War in the Modern World* 3 (J. N. Moore ed. 1974).

Nafziger, "Self-Determination and Humanitarian Intervention in a Community of Power," 20 *Denv. J. Int'l L. & Pol*. 9 (1991).

Nanda, "Tragedies in Northern Iraq, Liberia, Yugoslavia and Haiti—Revisiting the Validity of Humanitarian Intervention Under International Law," 20 *Denv. J. Int'l L. & Pol*. 305 (1992).

Nawaz, "What Limits on the Use of Force? Can Force Be Used to Depose Oppressive Governments?" 24 *Indian J. Int'l L*. 406 (1984).

Note, "A Proposed Resolution Providing for the Authorization of Intervention by the United Nations, a Regional Organization or a Group of States in a State Committing Gross Violations of Human Rights," 13 *Va. J. Int'l L*. 340 (1973).

Note, "The Grenada Invasion: Expanding the Scope of Humanitarian Intervention," 8 *Boston College Int'l & Comp. L. Rev*. 413 (1985).

Pérez Vera, "La protection d'humanité en droit international," 1969 *Revue belge de droit international* 401.

Pogamy, "Humanitarian Intervention in International Law: The French Intervention in Syria Re-Examined," 35 *Int'l & Comp. L. Q*. 182 (1986).

Reisman, "Humanitarian Intervention to Protect the Ibos," in *Humanitarian Intervention and the United Nations* (R. Lillich ed. 1973).

Reisman, "Coercion and Self-determination: Construing Article 2(4)," 78 *A.J.I.L*. 642 (1984).

Reisman, "Sovereignty and Human Rights in Contemporary International Law," 84 *Am. J. Int'l L*. 866 (1990).

Rodley, "Human Rights and Humanitarian Intervention: The Case of the World Court," 38 *Int'l & Comp. L. Q*. 321 (1989).

Rodley, "Collective Intervention to Protect Human Rights and Civilian Populations: The Legal Framework," in *To Loose the Bands of Wickedness* 14 (Rodley ed., 1991).

Rougier, "La théorie de l'intervention d'humanité," 17 *Revue générale de droit international public* 468 (1910).

Schachter, "The Legality of Pro-Democratic Invasion," 78 *A.J.I.L*. 645 (1984).

Scheffer, "Toward a Modern Doctrine of Humanitarian Intervention," 23 *U. Tol. L. Rev*. 253 (1992).

Schweisfurth, "Operations to Rescue Nationals in Third States Involving the Use of Force in Relation to the Protection of Human Rights," 23 *German Yearbook of Int'l L*. 162 (1980).

Sornarajah, "Internal Colonialism and Humanitarian Intervention," 11 *Georgia J. Int'l & Comp. L*. 45 (1981).

Stowell, "Humanitarian Intervention," 33 *A.J.I.L.* 733 (1939).

Suzuki, "A State's Provisional Competence to Protect Human Rights in a Foreign State," 15 *Texas Int'l L. J.* 231 (1980).

Tesón, "Collective Humanitarian Intervention," 17 *Mich. J. Int'l L.* 323 (1996).

Tyagi, "The Concept of Humanitarian Intervention Revisited," 16 *Mich. J. Int'l L.* 883 (1995).

Umozurike, "Tanzanian Intervention in Uganda," 20 *Archiv des Völkerrecht* 301 (1982).

Verwey, "Humanitarian Intervention under International Law," 33 *Netherlands Int'l L. Rev.* 357 (1985).

Verwey, "Humanitarian Intervention," in *The Current Legal Regulation of the Use of Force* 57 (A. Cassesse ed. 1986).

Wani, "Humanitarian Intervention and the Tanzania-Uganda War," 3 *Horn of Africa* 18 (1980).

Weisberg, "The Congo Crisis 1964: A Case Study in Humanitarian Intervention," 12 *Va. J. Int'l L.* 261 (1972).

Weisberg, "Humanitarian Intervention: Lessons from the Nigerian Civil War," 1974 *Human Rights J.* 61 (1974).

Westerdiek, "Humanitare Intervention und Massnahmen zum Schutz eigener Staatsangehöriger im Ausland," 21 *Archiv des Völkerrecht* 383 (1983).

Wright, "A Contemporary Theory of Humanitarian Intervention," 4 *Fla. J. Int'l L.* 435 (1989).

Zorgbibe, "La protection d'humanité," *Le Monde*, July 7, 1976.

B. Philosophy

Aiken, "Realpolitik, Morality and International Affairs," 5 *Humanities in Society* 95 (1982).

Beitz, "Nonintervention and Communal Integrity," *Phil. & Public Aff.* 354 (1979–80).

Cohen, "Moral Skepticism and International Relations," 13 *Phil. & Public Affairs* 299 (1984).

Coste, "Réflexion philosophique sur le problème d'intervention," 71 *Revue générale de droit international public* 369 (1967).

Doppelt, "Walzer's Theory of Morality in International Relations," 8 *Phil. & Public Aff.* 3 (1978–79).

Doppelt, "Statism without Foundations," 9 *Phil. & Public Aff.* 398 (1980).

Doyle, "Kant, Liberal Legacies, and Foreign Affairs," 12 *Phil. & Public Aff.* 205 (Part I) and 323 (Part II) (1982).

Elfstrom, "On Dilemmas on Intervention," 93 *Ethics* 709 (1982–83).

Halpern, "The Morality and Politics of Intervention," in *The Vietnam War and International Law* 39 (R. Falk ed. 1968).

Laberge, "Humanitarian Intervention: Three Ethical Positions," 9 *Ethics & Int'l Aff.* 15 (1995).

Luban, "Just War and Human Rights," 9 *Phil. & Public Aff.* 160 (1979–80).

Luban, "The Romance of the Nation-State," 9 *Phil. & Public Aff.* 392 (1980).

Mill, "A Few Words on Non-Intervention," in 3 *Dissertations and Discussions,* (London 1983), at 153.

Montaldi, "Toward a Human Rights Based Account of the Just War," 11 *Social Theory and Practice* 123 (1985).

Murphy, "The Killing of the Innocent," 57 *The Monist* 527 (1973).

Pogge, "Globalizing Justice as Fairness" (unpublished manuscript, 1987).

Rawls, "The Basic Liberties and Their Priority," in 3 *The Tanner Lectures for Human Values* 1 (1982).

Rawls, "Justice as Fairness: Political not Metaphysical," 14 *Phil. & Public Aff.* 223 (1985).

Rawls, "The Law of Peoples," in *On Human Rights* 41 (S. Shute & S. Hurley eds., 1993).

Shue, "Book Review," 92 *Ethics* 710 (1982).

Simon, "Global Justice and the Authority of States," 66 *The Monist* 557 (1983).

Skubik, "Two Models for a Rawlsian Theory of International Law and Justice," 14 *Denver J. Int'l L. & Pol.* 231 (1986).

Slater & Nardin, "Nonintervention and Human Rights," 48 *J. Politics* 86 (1986).

Taylor, "The Concept of Justice and the Laws of War," 13 *Colum. J. Transnat'l L.* 189 (1974).

Tesón, "The Kantian Theory of International Law," 92 *Colum. L. R.* 53 (1992).

Tesón, "The Rawlsian Theory of International Law," 9 *Ethics & Int'l Aff.* 79 (1995).

Thomspon, "New Reflections on Ethics and Foreign Policy: The Problem of Human Rights," 4 *J. of Politics* 984 (1978).

Walzer, "The Moral Standing of States," 9 *Phil. & Public Aff.* 209 (1978–79).

Wasserstrom, "Book Review," 92 *Harvard L. Rev.* 544 (1978).

Wicclair, "Rawls and the Principle of Non-Intervention," in *John Rawls' Theory of Social Justice* 289 (1980).

INDEX